An
Irresistible
TEMPTATION

An
Irresistible
TEMPTATION

The true story of Jane New
and a colonial scandal

CAROL BAXTER

ALLEN&UNWIN

First published in 2006

This project has been assisted by the Commonwealth
Government through the Australia Council, its arts
funding and advisory body.

Allen & Unwin
83 Alexander Street
Crows Nest NSW 2065
Australia
Phone: (61 2) 8425 0100
Fax: (61 2) 9906 2218
Email: info@allenandunwin.com
Web: www.allenandunwin.com

National Library of Australia
Cataloguing-in-Publication entry:

Baxter, Carol J.
An irresistible temptation: the true story of Jane New and a colonial scandal.

Bibliography.
Includes index.
ISBN 978 1 74114 924 1.

ISBN 1 74114 924 X.

1. New, Jane. 2. Darling, Ralf, Sir, 1775-1858. 3. Female offenders -
New South Wales - Sydney - Biography. 4. Women prisoners - New South Wales -
Sydney - Biography. 5. Scandals - New South Wales - Sydney. I. Title

364.374099441

Set in 12.5/16 pt Centaur MT by Midland Typesetters, Australia
Printed and bound in Australia by Griffin Press

10 9 8 7 6 5 4 3 2 1

CONTENTS

AUTHOR'S NOTE

In literature as in life there are true stories and there are 'true' stories. A current trend is the style known as 'faction': creating a vivid story by interweaving fictionalised dialogue and description into a story about real people and events. The drawback for the reader is the uncertainty as to where fact ends and fiction begins; depending upon the author this can be anywhere along a wide spectrum.

An Irresistible Temptation is neither fiction nor faction; the characters, events and dialogue are all drawn from the wealth of records relating to the Jane New scandal. To generate a sense of immediacy, a feeling that the characters were living their own story rather than a narrator observing them, I used information from court testimonies, affidavits, letters, reports and newspaper articles to describe events as they happened, and I converted recollections into speech. Conversions were not always straightforward: words, phrases, sentences and even paragraphs sometimes had to be omitted, or words added, or the arrangement tweaked slightly for ease of comprehension. Such changes would generally be denoted by the symbols for ellisions {...} and additions [ ], however these were inappropriate for speech so I omitted them. Consistency then dictated that I omitted these symbols from the entire story as one sentence from a particular document could be reproduced as dialogue and another as a quotation.

For ease of comprehension, I eliminated the excessive capitalisation typical of the period, and converted third person petitions and depositions (e.g. 'the petitioner begs ...') into first person where necessary. I referred to Ralph Darling, the Governor of New South Wales, as Governor Darling or General Darling instead of his more accurate military title, Lieutenant-General Darling (ignoring his knighthood which was bestowed upon him years after the scandal). I called his southern counterpart *Governor Arthur* rather than using his full administrative title, *Lieutenant-Governor Arthur*, and referred to the settlement itself as *Tasmania* instead of *Van Diemen's Land*. I used given names for the protagonists and their family members and surnames for all other characters because of the popularity of certain given names, adding *Mrs* where appropriate to distinguish gender.

The sources for general historical information are included in the Bibliography. The sources for material relating to the scandal itself are documented in a chapter-by-chapter summary in the Sources preceding the Bibliography. The Endnotes serve only as a vehicle for my own elaborations.

ACKNOWLEDGMENTS

My heartfelt thanks: to my wonderful friend Kate Wingrove who has shared the journey with me and offered such wise input, and to Jason Wingrove for the Cinderella pictures. To professional advisers Keith Johnson AM, Professor Bruce Kercher of Macquarie University's Department of Law and his invaluable website of important colonial cases: www.law.mq.edu.au, and historians Babette Smith and Dr Alison Alexander (I take all responsibility for any errors). To the Allen & Unwin team, and in particular publisher, Rebecca Kaiser and editor, Alexandra Nahlous for their inspired advice, and to Selena Hanet-Hutchins for recognising merit in my unsolicited manuscript.

To Chris, Mellony and Pete Batten for making my last-minute research trip to England a delightful experience, and to everyone else who contributed in their own way, in particular: Allison Allen, Debbie Drinkell, Michael Flynn, Caroline Forell, Michelle Grossman, Jane Hamby, Susan Holberton, Dr Carol Liston, Dr Perry McIntyre, Kathy Potts, Malcolm Sainty AM, Irene Schaffer, Christine Schwedhelm, Jacqui Simkins, Monnica Stevens, and the staff at State Records of New South Wales and the Mitchell Library, Sydney. Also to the descendants and connections of the First Fleet Nash family who first alerted me to the Jane New scandal.

Finally, to my long-suffering husband Allan Ashmore, my children, Camillie and Jaiden, and my mother Jill, my deepest love and appreciation for supporting and humouring me, and for trying not to glaze over too much when I talked (incessantly) about Jane and John. And to my late father Roy for instilling in me the fundamentals of writing and his appreciation for words: I hope you can see this achievement.

CAST OF CHARACTERS

Arthur, Sir George	(Tas.)	Lieutenant-Governor
Baker, Elizabeth	(NSW)	Jane New's mother (previously Elizabeth Wilkinson)
Baker, Richard	(NSW)	Jane New's stepfather
Baxter, Alexander M.	(NSW)	Attorney-General 1826–30
Bourke, General Sir Richard	(NSW)	Governor 1831–37
Burnett, John	(Tas.)	Colonial Secretary
Crisp, Amos	(NSW)	Settler at Lower Minto
Darling, General Sir Ralph	(NSW)	Governor 1825–31
Dowling, Sir James	(NSW)	Justice, Supreme Court
Forbes, Sir Francis	(NSW)	First Chief Justice, Supreme Court of NSW
Frazier, Ellen	(NSW)	Female Factory inmate
Goderich, Viscount	(UK)	Secretary of State for the Colonies 1830–33
Gordon, Ann	(NSW)	Matron of Female Factory
Hall, Edward Smith	(NSW)	Editor of the *Sydney Monitor*
Hayes, Atwell Edwin	(NSW)	Editor of the *Australian* 1828–32
Hay, Robert	(UK)	Permanent Under-Secretary at the Colonial Office
Henry/Henrie, Jane	(UK)	Alias used by Jane New
Howick, Lord	(UK)	Parliamentary Under-Secretary, Colonial Office 1830–33
Hume, Joseph	(UK)	British Radical parliamentarian

McLeay, Alexander	(NSW)	Colonial Secretary
Morisset, Colonel James T.	(NSW)	Principal Superintendent of Police 1827–29
Murray, General Sir George	(UK)	Secretary of State for the Colonies 1828–30
New, James	(NSW)	Husband of Jane New
New, Jane	(NSW)	née Maria Wilkinson
Officer, Dr Robert	(Tas.)	Jane's employer in Tasmania 1825–26
Raine, John	(NSW)	Notary Public
Raine, Thomas	(NSW)	Merchant
Ralph, Hannah	(NSW)	Jane's accomplice
Rens, Jeanette	(NSW)	aka Jane Rens, daughter of Madame Josephine Rens
Rens, Madame Josephine	(NSW)	Silk mercer in Sydney
Robison, Captain Robert	(NSW)	Brother-in-law of John Stephen Jnr
Rossi, Captain Francis N.	(NSW)	Superintendent of Police 1829–34
Stephen, Sir Alfred	(Tas.)	Solicitor-General; brother of John Stephen Jnr
Stephen, Francis	(NSW)	Solicitor; brother of John Stephen Jnr
Stephen, James	(UK)	Permanent Counsel to Colonial Office; cousin of John Stephen Jnr
Stephen, John Jnr	(NSW)	Registrar of Supreme Court
Stephen, Judge John	(NSW)	Justice, Supreme Court; father of John Stephen Jnr
Stephen, Sidney	(NSW)	Barrister; brother of John Stephen Jnr
Wardell, Robert	(NSW)	Barrister; editor of the *Australian* 1824–28
Wentworth, William C.	(NSW)	Co-founder of the *Australian*; barrister and political aspirant
Wilkinson, Elizabeth	(UK)	Mother of Jane New
Wilkinson, Maria	(UK)	Birth name for Jane New

PROLOGUE

Sydney, 6 January 1829

A menacing courtroom. A judge donning the dreaded black cap. A prisoner cowed. To all appearances it was just another day in the penal settlement of New South Wales. In truth, it was the beginning of the Jane New affair.

Sydney was a town of 15000 souls squatting on the banks of Port Jackson when the spotlight blazed upon Jane New.[1] In the forty years since the First Fleet ejected its cargo of crime into the pristine bushland lining Sydney Cove, a remarkable transformation had occurred. Sydney was no longer such a feared place that British prisoners facing the noose would choose execution over the offer of transportation to 'Botany Bay'. Indeed, a traveller observed that nearly all of the recent transportees had been volunteers, delighted to be sent there.

While convict transports continued to offload British outcasts, they were outnumbered by trading vessels — barques, brigs, schooners, cutters — carrying luxuries unimagined by the early settlers who, tattered and barefoot, had almost starved to death. Whalers regularly scuttled into Sydney Harbour reeking of savage deaths on the high seas, with sailors so desperate for dry land and convivial company that mutiny threatened. Passenger ships materialised in increasing numbers, ferrying the free immigrants who would soon swamp the colony. British and Russian warships and scientific expeditions swanned into the harbour. By 1829 Sydney was a regular port of call on the international shipping routes.

As the penal settlement opened its arms to the outside world, the population balance shifted and society evolved. Gone were the days when convicts outnumbered free people four to one, when a military autocracy was the appropriate form of governance. Gone were the days when emancipated convicts and small settlers would defer to pastoral king John Macarthur and his fellow 'exclusives', and allow that colonial aristocratic body to monopolise most situations of power, prestige and pecuniary advantage. Yet their British overlords appointed the autocratic General Ralph Darling as Governor and he aligned himself with the exclusives, effectively supporting their aspirations.

Darling found himself at loggerheads with William Charles Wentworth of Vaucluse. Described by his friends as a man of the people and by his foes as a vulgar ill-bred demagogue, Wentworth piloted the opposition 'emancipist' cause. Anxious to claw his way into the political limelight, Wentworth grasped every opportunity to strike at the exclusives and Governor Darling. And into his political sights early in 1829 sashayed Jane New.

Wentworth played a pivotal role in one of Jane New's legal confrontations, however his primary role lay in the supporting cast. John Stephen Jnr precipitated the scandal. The son of a Supreme Court judge, John came from a family of legal distinction and liberal outlook. He exuded charm and respectability. But he had a dark side, one revealed by his willingness to dip his toe into the social and political whirlpool of an 'intimate' association with a convicted felon. He was helping a persecuted damsel in her fight against their cruel Governor, he protested. And the political knife-thrust was a secondary advantage. Yet when the maelstrom eased, Jane New had skipped to freedom leaving John Stephen Jnr enmeshed in the consequences.

Was Jane New merely a pawn in this political game of one-upmanship? Or was she a siren luring men to their destruction?

Part I:
TEMPTATION

Vice is so fascinating,
that she cannot be looked upon
without peril to the beholder.

Chief Justice James Dowling

Chapter 1

THE SIREN AWAKES

*Criminality descends, as surely as physical properties
and individual temperament.*
Chief Justice Alfred Stephen

A fresh ruddy complexion, dark brown hair, black eyes: this bald description jotted down by the colonial authorities is the only surviving portrait of Jane New. Yet it fails to communicate any sense of her charms: her beauty, the seductive nature intimated by her contemporaries, the allure that led men to suspend their intelligence and to act against their better judgement. Nor does it reveal that she carried a scar like the 'King's Evil' branded upon her neck.

'My proper name is Maria Wilkinson,' Jane informed the colonial authorities, although she answered to 'Jane' even during her youth. Claiming Leeds in Yorkshire as her native place, she was one of at least three children born to Isaac and Elizabeth Wilkinson. Was she the baby named Maria Wilkinson baptised on 13 October 1805 at Headingly? At that time, Headingly was a village lying a couple of miles north-west of Leeds although it has long since been swallowed by the expanding metropolis.[2]

Little is known about Jane's father. He was most likely the widowed mason who married Elizabeth Cormack in 1804 at Leeds. Jane probably inherited his height (she was a relatively tall five feet three inches) but her mother's allure. Elizabeth — a tiny four feet nine and a half inches with a pale complexion, hazel-grey eyes and dark brown hair — would later marry a man young enough to be her son.

Families like the Wilkinsons tend to slip through the cracks of history; the wealthy, propertied or politically inclined and the destitute or criminally inclined are more often captured in the archival net. In all probability Jane's family was little different from the thousands of others in the Regency period who struggled to survive and were unable to resist the lure of the city that was mushrooming in their backyard. Leeds was among the many British towns transformed by the recent and ongoing Industrial Revolution. Once known for its sedate cottage woollen industry, Leeds by the early 1800s housed a conglomeration of squat manufactories producing engineering and agricultural equipment and, as a by-product, fetid air, stinking piles of refuse, and sluggish rivers and streams.

Jane's childhood in Leeds was one of work, work, work from a young age. She had minimal schooling — one week was all her parents could manage. The teachers had to be paid: a penny here, a halfpenny there. The cost added up, proving too much for most families. Instead, Jane went into service, possibly in Leeds, almost certainly in Manchester.

A revolution in cotton manufacture had transformed Manchester from the thriving but unremarkable textile centre of the 1770s into the textile trade's commercial centre. Jobs abounded for carters, porters, packers and labourers in addition to the essential factory hands. The Wilkinsons were among the hordes drawn towards this burgeoning metropolis.

Forty miles separated Leeds and Manchester. As the Wilkinsons jolted along in an old cart or plodded wearily down the rutted roads, their journey probably provided Jane with her first view of the little-changed rural landscape: sepulchral woods, eerie moors, and, of course, the palette of crops in the miles of tamed fields. Weed-infested fields often bore testimony to a farmer's absence. Through fair means or foul, some had found themselves drafted into Britain's military and naval forces to fight in the two-decade-long Napoleonic Wars. Britain's battle against France was not just the usual story of preventing French domination; it masked a fear that the masses would catch the radicalism that had spawned the French Revolution in 1789. Yet for families like the Wilkinsons, *the War* probably existed only as a background hum. To a child like Jane, the present was all that mattered.

Dotted along the Wilkinsons' route were stately homes and gentlemen's residences similar to those depicted in Jane Austen's literary tales of manners and morals. Despite the social upheaval of the Industrial Revolution and the political and emotional dramas of the interminable war, these families had the same demands: food, clothing and domestic services. Maids of different ages and abilities were required, even untrained young girls like Jane.

Jane's mother later described herself as a house and laundry maid, and she possibly found work for Jane with her own employers. The young girls slaved at the most menial of household tasks: scrubbing floors, peeling potatoes, mending the unimportant fabrics. Jane showed needlework skills and dressmaking soon became her occupation.

Unmitigated drudgery summarises the life of a dressmaker in Regency England. While textile manufacture had early succumbed to industrialisation, clothing manufacture remained in the hands of single women or small workshop enterprises until the mid-1800s. Although dressmakers and milliners were the elite of this needlework industry, the proliferation of women with needlework skills kept wages low. Seamstresses laboured from dawn till dusk and beyond, 8 am to 11 pm in winter, 6 am to 12 am in summer, all night long if necessary during the fashionable season. Backbreaking, eyestraining, exhausting work. Stitch, stitch, hour after hour, day after day. Those who craved excitement, stimulation or change generally turned to alcohol or sex. Some, like Jane, turned to crime.

Jane's first venture into the criminal world was most likely driven by her family's desperation. In 1815 England's future looked rosy. The Duke of Wellington had triumphed in the Battle of Waterloo, the final victory in the Napoleonic Wars. The French defeat had quelled the fear of contagious revolutionary ideals. All was right with the world. Except that 300 000 unemployed British soldiers and sailors flooded the countryside, attempting to rejoin communities who could provide neither support nor jobs. Mass unemployment dimmed the glow of victory; harvest failures doused it. As domestic consumption, production and trade withered, England spiralled into a depression. As usual the poor were the first to suffer.

With few sources of social welfare available other than the dreaded workhouse, the primordial instinct to survive motivated much of Britain's criminal activity, the Wilkinsons' no doubt included. Perhaps Isaac was unemployed or ill. Presumably the family's expenses surpassed their meagre income. Whatever the circumstances, Elizabeth turned to crime to support her family. Her decision to use her alluring thirteen-year-old daughter as an accomplice was undoubtedly deliberate. Jane would be useful as a decoy, or to actually pull off the theft, and to twist any heartstrings — particularly male — if they were caught.

On 13 November 1818, Jane, her mother and a sixteen-year-old accomplice, Josephine Townley, were indeed caught. They had entered the premises of shopkeeper Ann Mainwaring. Elizabeth and Josephine possibly distracted the woman while Jane snatched two pairs of boots. Whether Jane was spotted committing the crime or discovered with the boots in her possession is not documented. The records merely show that Manchester's corrupt deputy constable, Joseph Nadin, already notorious for arresting innocent people and for accumulating wealth through thief-catching and pay-offs, arrested them. He charged all three of them, committed them to stand trial at the next sessions and trundled them off to the New Bailey prison at Salford on the outskirts of Manchester.

Considering the Dickensian image of nineteenth-century prisons, Salford's New Bailey was better than most. Upon their arrival Jane, Elizabeth and Josephine had to strip and hand over their clothing for disinfection, then bathe, the authorities recognising the importance of cleanliness in reducing outbreaks of prison fever. Wearing the appropriately colour-coded prison garb — a drab-coloured wrapper, woollen petticoat, body linen, and clogs for the pre-trial females — the three were escorted through the courtyard to the female quarters where the felons were lodged and fed separately from those facing minor charges. Children received little special treatment, being thrown in with the hardened adult criminals.

Jane attended the prison's school two days a week, although the students were not taught to write; lessons from the Bible served as the foundation for their education. Did the authorities believe that proverbs like the loaves and fishes would miraculously provide them with the sustenance they needed to survive? On the remaining days, Jane toiled at the mundane repetitive work considered appropriate as punishment: weaving, wool-picking, hair-picking, rope-making, pin-heading, clogging, shoemaking, tailoring and the loathed bobbin-winding.

Two months into their incarceration, the women faced court. Considered more serious than the usual misdemeanours brought before the magistrates, their case was presented at the General Quarter Sessions of the Peace held in the prison's courtroom on 19 January 1819. Much pomp and ceremony accompanied the quarter sessions. Black robes, wigs, Latin phrases tripping off the tongue. The crowds resisted the formality, rustling noisily in the gallery, the volume increasing as loud voices and rattling chains heralded the prisoners' arrival. The ever-present tipstaffs cast a black shadow as they hovered in anticipation, ready to take into custody any offender sentenced to imprisonment, transportation, or worse.

Out of sympathy for the girls' youth, Ann Mainwaring valued the boots at only a penny apiece. This 'pious perjury' — undervaluing the stolen goods below the capital threshold — ensured that a conviction would not propel the girls towards the gallows. Such a thought revolted even the most hardened supporters of capital punishment.

'How will you plead?' enquired the judge.

'Guilty,' Jane piped up, acting upon her mother's instructions. Elizabeth and Josephine followed. 'Not guilty,' both pleaded. Although the case against them was evidently less convincing, the jury expressed their scepticism. As it turned out, Jane gained no benefit from pleading guilty. Both girls received fourteen-day sentences although these were passed for time served. Elizabeth was remanded for twelve months.

With her mother in gaol, her family in trouble — her father died within the following two years — and few readily available jobs, particularly for those with a known criminal conviction, Jane's return to criminality seems inevitable. But at some point desire infiltrated necessity. As later financial independence failed to curb her shoplifting pursuits, she must gradually have become enthralled by the sense of exhilaration it gave her. The delicious feeling of anticipation upon venturing into a store, of crossing into 'their' world. The heightened sense of awareness, of watching out for an opportunity while concealing her intentions. The focusing of attention on a particular object which pulled her in, wanting to be possessed. The sleight of hand required to grasp and hide the object. The ruse allowing her to escape undetected. The satisfaction at achieving a successful violation of the rules both moral and legal that shackled her to a tedious existence.

It was a game with a winner and a loser and, as Jane quickly learnt, shoplifters usually won. Constables were in short supply so criminals were rarely apprehended. Victims had to pursue prosecutions, so many grudgingly accepted their losses because of the expense and trouble involved. Adept thieves could follow their calling for years before facing the consequences.

Jane managed eighteen months. With another accomplice, a widow named Ann Ogden, she shoplifted twice in the one day: three scarves and six yards of silk from one shop, two lengths of cotton cloth from another. Committed to the Salford gaol on 21 August 1820, the two faced the quarter sessions on 23 October. The stolen items were again valued at only a few pennies, and both pleaded guilty, received six-month sentences, and were remanded to the same prison. This time, Jane found herself in the garb of a convicted felon — the blue and yellow clothing that shrieked of a more serious offence.

Meanwhile, Elizabeth Wilkinson pursued her own timetable. Indeed, mother and daughter conceivably spent more time together in gaol than out of it. Released in January 1820, Elizabeth remained outside the clutches of the law for twelve months, until she and an accomplice, Elizabeth Hotchin, stole ten handkerchiefs (five silk) from one shop and six pairs of gloves from another. Although the goods were again undervalued and she pleaded guilty to both crimes, Elizabeth Wilkinson was sentenced to hard labour at Lancaster Castle for two years. Her previous conviction undoubtedly contributed to her harsher sentence.

Three months after Elizabeth's second conviction Jane was discharged, however she managed only a month of freedom. On 26 May 1821, Jane and a 33-year-old widow, Ann Bates, were caught stealing twenty yards of ribbon, undervalued again at one penny. By this time Jane knew that a guilty plea carried few benefits. Convicted on 16 July, she was remanded for twelve months although she apparently spent the duration in Liverpool Gaol. Her accomplice joined Jane's mother at Lancaster Castle for twelve months.[3]

When the guards unbolted the gaol door in July 1822, Jane was only sixteen years of age, had three convictions behind her, and was well-known to the corrupt constable Joseph Nadin. She had little chance of eluding his grasp even if she found secure employment and resisted the compulsion to continue shoplifting. Jane slipped away, heading ten miles south to Macclesfield in East Cheshire where she reportedly found work as a dressmaker.

Macclesfield was awash with silk. These shimmering swathes of beauty competed against the supreme French silks made at Lyons, the centre of France's silk industry. Ironically, Lyons was also home to Jane's future nemesis, a woman named Madame Rens, who would sail for Australia two years later carrying a piece of silk fabric that was to prove Jane's undoing.

Chapter 2
RICHES OR RUIN?

I sentence you, says the Judge, but to what I know not: perhaps to
storm and shipwreck; perhaps to infectious disorders; perhaps to
famine; perhaps to be massacred by savages; perhaps to be devoured
by wild beasts. Away, take your chance; perish or prosper, suffer or
enjoy; I rid myself of the sight of you; the ship that bears you away
saves me from witnessing your sufferings.
Jeremy Bentham, *The Rationale of Punishment*[4]

When Jane awoke on 13 March 1824 she could not have known that she
hovered at a crossroads, that the choices she made as the day progressed
would change her future irrevocably. Was it a spur of the moment decision
to enter David Jackson's premises as she wandered past? Had she a desperate
need for the two pieces of cloth valued at five shillings apiece or the money
they would fetch, or was her decision to snatch them merely a flutter of
opportunism? Whatever Jane's motivation, her adversary was determined
to thwart her. Despite beseeching looks, tears, pleas, Jackson remained
firm. He hailed a constable who imprisoned her, he lodged charges against
her, and he pursued the prosecution despite the time and expense involved
in travelling 33 miles west to Chester Castle to do so.

With three previous convictions, Jane knew she faced a harsh penalty
if again found guilty. She told the authorities her name was Jane Henry,

although they soon discovered the truth. She had plenty of time to bemoan her fate as she was carted from Macclesfield to Chester, ankles chained and chafing, at the mercy of the stares and jeers of those she passed. For six weeks she languished in the gaol at the back of Chester Castle, her fears no doubt escalating when another inmate was gibbeted and his body dissected and anatomised.

Trials were swift and the accused benefitted from legal representation only if they could afford it. Eighteen-year-old Jane was most likely alone as she faced the judge and jury on 27 April 1824. She shuffled to the prisoner's box, heard the charges read, and pleaded not guilty. Her accuser David Jackson testified, describing the robbery and the goods stolen, and pointing to Jane as the thief. He was convincing. Two other witnesses, both female, offered their testimony. The prosecution rested. If Jane was granted permission to speak in her own defence she failed to sway the court.

'Guilty,' declared the jury.

'Seven years' transportation to such parts beyond the seas as His Majesty with the advice of the Privy Council should direct,' pronounced the judge. And with the bang of his gavel, Jane's future was ordained.

A seven-year sentence of transportation — which effectively comprised lifelong banishment as few emancipated convicts could afford the return journey — for the theft of goods worth, in today's terms, considerably less than $50? A harsh punishment indeed. Yet it could have been worse. Under the law, convictions for shoplifting goods worth more than five shillings merited a death sentence. The noose. Perhaps Jane's youth and physical attractions had influenced the judge when he sentenced her.

Punishments for criminal behaviour were particularly harsh at that time. For years social reformers battled the general consensus that criminals belonged to a 'criminal class', one found in British society at a level below that of the working class, the 'honest poor', and populated by irredeemable thieves and abandoned prostitutes. Judges, magistrates and politicians believed that criminals inherited these criminal tendencies, that entire families carried the taint from birth, and that they deserved little sympathy or understanding.

Did Jane carry the taint of inherited criminality? The authorities undoubtedly believed so. Nine months previously, in July 1823, her mother had faced the Manchester quarter sessions for the third time. Elizabeth was apprehended after stealing a piece of sarcenet and ten yards of cloth from one store, and four buckles (two gold) from another. These were expensive items; serious trouble loomed. Elizabeth employed an attorney, the items were revalued at a penny apiece, and she was saved from the gallows. Her seven-year sentence of transportation surely seemed like a holiday in paradise when she considered the alternative.

Such evidence of criminality within families, combined with the need for effective deterrents, had led to the draconian punishments inflicted upon criminals: hang 'em or banish 'em. Deterrence was eventually taken to such absurd and barbaric lengths that, by the early 1820s, 223 crimes were punishable by death.

As the century passed, social reformers gradually discredited the concept of inherited criminality, and society began to accept the nexus between poverty and crime. In hindsight transportees like Jane were recast as poor helpless wretches forced from their homeland because economic circumstances had induced such destitution and desperation that they were forced to steal a loaf of bread.

Later, however, statistical analyses proved that most transportees to Australia were multiple offenders, and that a significantly large proportion came from London and industrial cities like Manchester which housed criminal communities so dangerous the authorities feared to venture into their terrain. Historians gradually realised that the higher incidence of crime in these cities was not just a function of poverty, but relative poverty. As the urban poor rubbed shoulders with the extravagantly wealthy, they were surrounded by the surfeit of goods produced by this first industrial society. But they could rarely benefit; they could only watch and desire. Naturally, the temptation towards criminal activity was compelling, not only for those motivated purely by survival but for those like Jane who lusted after the luxuries. Physically the circumstances were ideal: crowds, busyness, anonymity. They pounced.

So, were criminals like Jane innocent victims of poverty and an unjust society, or were they evildoers? The truth is, they included all types. Social and environmental disadvantages, and sometimes rotten luck, precipitated poverty, crushed families and bred social and emotional maladjustment. Such an environment often fuelled criminal activity and encouraged associations with other similarly deprived or like-minded individuals. Congregations of criminals nested in the poorer sections of England's industrialised cities, spawning the concept of a criminal class and an inherited criminality that influenced political thinking in the transportation era.

For the poor in Regency England, it was the rule of the jungle. Survival of the fittest. The resilient ones like Jane survived, the others died.

Chapter 3
THE WILD ONES

It is a melancholy fact, but not the less true, that the far greater
proportion of the female convicts are utterly irreclaimable, being the
most worthless and abandoned of human beings.

W.H. Breton, *Excursions in NSW*

'And in the meantime to be imprisoned in the gaol of the Castle of Chester,' the judge intoned when pronouncing Jane's sentence. Was she grateful? The alternative was worse: to be consigned to the prison hulks hunkering in the malodorous mudflats edging the Thames and other harbour ports. Conditions on the hulks were shocking: rations both meagre and inedible, backbreaking labour, brutality and worse — rape. By the guards, by the other prisoners, even by outsiders. To supplement their pitiful incomes, the guards often rowed the prettiest girls to nearby ships and threw them to the sailors. Innocence had no chance of surviving the degradations of the British penal system.

Instead, Jane spent over four months locked in Chester Castle Gaol while the authorities awaited instructions for her disposal. Her previous incarcerations had armed her. She was tough, she was troublesome and she knew the right people to curry favour with. 'Notorious character, bad connexions,' denounced the gaolkeeper. The gaolkeeper's report also proved premonitory. Within five years word of Jane's notorious colonial escapades would travel halfway around the world.

As summer turned into autumn, two ships anchored in the Thames and prepared to receive 160 female convicts for transportation to Australia. Both Jane and Elizabeth — who had remained in gaol for over twelve months despite a female transport sailing for Hobart in December 1823 — were ordered to London. Jane and her fellow Cheshire transportee presumably travelled with the larger Lancashire contingent on the 170-mile journey. Looks of astonished delight must have crossed their faces as mother and daughter found themselves together again, until they learned that Jane was sailing for Hobart on the *Henry* while Elizabeth was Sydney-bound on the *Grenada*. They made tentative plans to find each other, having no comprehension of the vast distance that separated the two penal settlements.[5]

Jane and Elizabeth would never know that the decision to transport them at this time had little to do with their crimes or sentences. While their male counterparts were transported as a punishment for their crimes — the recidivists, the troublemakers and those with longer sentences singled out first — the female prisoners of Britain were primarily transported for their sexuality. As women committed considerably fewer crimes than men, the penal settlements of Australia were awash with males. This generated its own set of problems, so the British authorities conceived a simple solution: send more women. 'Let it be remembered,' warned the Transportation Committee in 1812, 'how much misery and vice are likely to prevail in a society in which women bear no proportion to the men.' Accordingly, they scoured the hulks and prisons for any suitable women, rejecting the old and unhealthy and hustling the remainder, like Jane and Elizabeth, onto the transports. Nobody cared that this was a serious injustice. The women were all considered prostitutes anyway.

Yet prostitution was not a transportable offence and only a small proportion of the female transportees supported themselves either casually or professionally in this manner. The same mentality that associated criminality with heredity equated prostitution with female criminality. Consequently these women were not only condemned for their crimes, they were punished for their sexuality. And to add insult to injury, when some fulfilled the agenda intended for them, they were lambasted for their behaviour.

On 18 September 1824, Jane was among the female prisoners rowed out to the *Henry*, a 386-ton six-year-old ship rocking gently at anchor at Woolwich on the Thames River. As she neared the vessel, she must have seen a surprising number of sailors lining the decks. The vessel had carried male convicts once before, but never female. Pushed up the ladder with the unceremonious assistance of the sailors and heaved onto deck, she must have felt assaulted by their lascivious eyes.

The officers and crew of female convict ships frequently expressed delight when informed of their cargo. Female convicts, particularly the pretty ones like Jane, were considered fair game by the men they came into contact with. The authorities had set regulations to prevent a return to the floating brothel environment of the early female transports, however enforcement was ultimately the captain's responsibility. Some crew members claimed that the women enticed them into breaking the rules. 'To see twenty wicked fingers beckoning to him,' wrote the surgeon-superintendent of one female transport, 'and twenty wicked eyes winking at him at one and the same time, no wonder his virtue should sometimes experience a fall!' Others reported that the women were not reluctant to provide such services, a defence that was undoubtedly true to some extent. These women were survivors, and better an officer's bed with a decent meal thrown in than imprisonment for months on end in the hold. However, transports were not crewed by well-disciplined men dressed in starched whites; brutality was an intrinsic part of shipboard life. For some convict women, the voyage would prove a living hell.

One by one the women clambered down the ladder to their quarters in the hold. Jane's new home proved to be damp, dim and dismal. Rats and mice; cockroaches; a strange unpleasant smell, a mingling of odours from previous cargoes. The seventy-nine female prisoners were accompanied by ten children: infants, toddlers and even some older children — male children under six and female children under twelve were permitted to travel with them. Elsewhere on the vessel, twenty-five free women and their twenty-three children settled themselves. Their government-paid passages enabled them to join husbands and relatives — usually convicts — in the colony.

The surgeon, Dr William Bell Carlyle, began treating patients shortly after the women arrived, some with ulcers on their legs from travelling in irons, some with 'intestinal derangement'. The bacteria in London's water was apparently taking its toll. One woman — a twenty-year-old prisoner described by the surgeon as a 'very stout heavy young woman' — had a nasty accident, falling backwards into the main hatchway just as the surgeon walked by. Finding her unconscious with her head bent down, he diagnosed a partially broken neck, however his timely assistance enabled her to walk again a few days later.

And then Dr Carlyle diagnosed a case of variola: cowpox or smallpox brought on board by a convict's son. One of the world's most dreaded plagues, the disease could ravage a confined population. The surgeon immediately vaccinated those at risk, however five caught the disease. Only one, a sixteen-year-old female passenger, died. It was a low toll under the circumstances, although some sufferers were undoubtedly disfigured.

On 5 October 1824 as autumn's chills crept into the hold, the *Henry* slunk out of London, inching along the Thames towards the North Sea. First to the alarmingly named Gravesend, then along the north coast of Kent where the variola victim's body slipped into the depths, then around Margate and through the Downs where they awaited the ideal conditions. Finally on 12 October, the *Henry* sailed through the Strait of Dover into the English Channel and began the long journey to Australia. By the 15th, seasickness exacerbated the misery endured by many of the women.

The *Henry* sailed towards the tropics, towards a world the women could never have imagined. Flying fish, sometimes thousands at a time, soared from the depths, and whales were occasionally seen — 'huge monsters that would be a danger if they struck the ship'. On 30 October they passed Madeira, off the coast of Morocco, and headed towards their first port of call. Many transports were plotting a direct route to the penal settlements by this time, shaving two or three weeks off the journey. Jane was perhaps glad to hear that they were breaking up the trip, a release from the incessant rocking, the stifling hold.

On 8 November, the *Henry* stopped for supplies at St Jago [Santiago] in the Cape Verde Islands off the West African coast near Senegal. Perched on the side of a volcano punched up from the ocean depths, the tropical island just north of the equator was hot and dry, with a minimum temperature higher than that of the average English summer day. Even before Jane climbed up to the deck, the odours must have besieged her: overripe tropical fruit, rotting garbage, an alien humanity, all the more noxious somehow because of the smothering heat. Another smell tainted the air, perhaps not so unfamiliar: terror. St Jago was a Portuguese colonial outpost and served as a collection point for slaves until the American slave trade was finally abolished half a century later.

Fresh fruit and vegetables to fight the dreaded scurvy, water and other supplies were loaded, and on 13 November the *Henry* set off on the remaining leg of its journey to Tasmania. Weeks of stultifying heat continued as they lumbered past the equator, hoping to escape the doldrums and to ride the trade winds south. More equable temperatures followed as they steered east of the Island of Tristan d'Acunha, looped around the tip of Africa and kept north of the Roaring Forties until they passed above the island of St Paul on 17 January. Days of paralysing cold tormented them as the Roaring Forties hurled the *Henry* towards Tasmania; hours of terror as storms lashed the ship. Fear, exhaustion, boredom: the litany of emotions experienced by the women during the seemingly never-ending four-month journey climaxed in relief on the afternoon of 5 February 1824 when a sailor yelled, 'Land ahoy.' The Cape of Van Diemen's Land (Tasmania) was in sight.

A pilot boarded at the mouth of the Derwent River and sailed the transport forty miles upriver. Gradually the barrenness disappeared and the scenery became breathtaking as they neared their destination. In sheltered bays and inlets they could see signs of habitation, with settlers' crops appearing like a chequerboard of colour against the sombre mountain backdrop. 'It brought old England and all its dear recollections home to us,' reported one traveller. Finally on 8 February, the *Henry* reached the penal settlement of Hobart. The same traveller described her first impression of the colonial outpost:

Hobart is picturesque beyond measure with carts and cottages, ships and shops, girls in their pattens, boys playing at marbles, above all rosy countenances, chubby cheeks and English voices. You have probably dreamt of Tasmania as a kind of wilderness, an appropriate insular prison for the vagabonds who are sent yearly from England. You have never supposed that it has a beautiful harbour, a fine metropolis, with towns, streets, shops and pretty shopkeepers, like some of the larger towns of Devonshire or of Sussex. The view from the harbour would make the most beautiful panorama in the world, were a painter to give the deep brown and purple tints to the foliage which clothe these hills.

Female convict transports remained an unusual sight in Hobart. While nearly 5500 of Jane's male counterparts had staggered off 33 transports in the two decades since the Derwent River penal settlement was established, the *Henry* was only the eighth transport to offload female convicts. The previous seven had carried a mere 345 women in total. But not just any women. In comparison to their New South Wales sisters, these were considered the worst of the bad lot: 'artful and deceitful'; 'drunken, dissipated and of a bad disposition'; 'impudent, vicious and sullen'. Intimidated neither by their lowly state nor by the attitudes of their superiors, many of the women were considered incorrigible, more troublesome indeed than the men — swearing, hair-pulling, fighting, screaming abuse at each other and the men around them.[6]

Yet as their ship anchored at Hobart, Jane and her fellow transportees decked themselves in their finery — silks, satins, frills and flounces, if they possessed them — and prepared again to go into battle against whatever fate would throw at them.

Chapter 4
A PRISON WITHOUT BARS

I desired liberty; for liberty I gasped; for liberty I uttered a prayer;
it seemed scattered on the wind . . . 'Then,' I cried, half desperate,
'grant me at least a new servitude.'
Charlotte Bronte, *Jane Eyre*

The arrival of a freight of female fodder was viewed with mixed feelings by the penal settlement. Delight by emancipated convicts and small settlers who hoped to find themselves a wife (no romantic arrangement, of course; just a woman to cook, clean and provide night-time solace). Relief by settlers desperate for domestic servants. Concern by the authorities who had limited opportunities to dispose of the less desirable women. Dread by the wives of some married settlers who feared the invasion of a servant whose lack of skills and moral attributes was overshadowed by a fetching appearance and an audacious flirtatious manner.

Revelations that some masters had views regarding the women's duties that differed markedly from those intended by the authorities had become a topic of concern both in the colony and back in Britain. Yet the general consensus was that, under the circumstances, the resulting abuse was inevitable. 'What can be done?' some shrugged. 'The women are used to selling their bodies,' others rationalised.

Of course, the women's behaviour exacerbated the problem. The street-smart women soon realised that judicious use of their bodies empowered them. It was the only currency they had to assert control over their lives and destinies. For services rendered, they could often entice gaolers, masters or other authority figures to manipulate the system in their favour. Once recognised, once acted upon, it was a lesson never forgotten. Their eyes became bold, their smile teasing, their pose provocative. They exuded sexuality, testing their power on every man within their ambit. And for the comely few like Jane, this raw sexuality proved a particularly potent and alluring mix.

The authorities were at a loss to understand convict women. Why were they not appropriately cowed? 'Their fierce and untameable audacity would not be believed,' one Hobart magistrate exclaimed in disgust. 'Bold Amazonians', 'the shameless ones', lashed the press. Settlers had little choice but to bring such women into their homes. Until free immigration became policy, few other candidates were available for domestic service. As one settler reported: 'Servants are not to be had, prisoners supply all the demands. If the histories of every house were made public you would shudder. Even in our small ménage, our cook has committed murder, our footman burglary and the housemaid bigamy!'

Yet employing such women exposed wives and children on a daily, intimate level to tainted lives and experiences. Could children be raised with the appropriate manners and morals if their care was left to women with open and shameless vices? asked the community. Indeed, the degrading and demoralising impact of transportation not only upon transportees but upon the whole community added strength to the movement for the abolition of transportation. The Americans had reached the same conclusion half a century earlier when they protested against Britain's policy of dumping their gaol refuse on American soil. Such actions, denounced Benjamin Franklin, were even more insulting than if the British had emptied their chamber pots onto American tables!

While Jane exposed her employers to the convict taint, she in turn experienced a more refined life among a family of education and influence. She proved fortunate in her place of assignment, although whether her mistress thought the same is doubtful. Her master, 25-year-old

Dr Robert Officer of New Norfolk, was a gentleman. 'No more respectable or well-conducted young man will be found in the colony,' praised the outgoing Governor, Lieutenant-Colonel Sorell, in 1824. Later biographers paid homage to Dr Officer, observing that he won the respect and esteem of the community by his geniality, private virtues, and unimpeachable probity. He proved to be no simple country practitioner. He was later elected to the Legislative Council, participated in drafting Tasmania's constitution, was elected to the new House of Assembly, became Speaker, and was knighted for his services in 1869. Sir Robert Officer was perhaps the first 'worthy' to be bedazzled by Jane.

Dr Officer's home lay twenty miles north-west of Hobart on the banks of the Derwent River, an area originally populated by Norfolk Islanders who had resettled there some two decades earlier when the island was abandoned. New Norfolk lacked a village proper, its small cottages dotting a scenic valley two miles in width. The area still suffered depredations from Aborigines; houses and crops were sometimes destroyed by fire and on rare occasions settlers were murdered.

Jane was probably employed to assist Dr Officer's heavily pregnant wife, Jamima. The Officers had children every year or two for the two decades following their marriage in 1823: their eldest, Robert, was born five weeks after Jane's arrival and a daughter Eliza followed fourteen months later. Whether Jane was the Officers' only domestic servant or one of a few is uncertain, however her duties would have included the usual household chores, some nannying and, undoubtedly, dressmaking.

Was Jane more help than hindrance? Dr Officer would later suggest so:

> I cannot say that her conduct was faultless, but I can most truly declare that she was the best servant I have ever had, and the only one of her class, whom during seven years observation, I have ever perceived to have any permanent feelings of gratitude for kindness received. Of the real existence of such feelings, I have had ample proof up to a very recent date.

Although no clarification is provided regarding the form in which Jane revealed her 'permanent feelings of gratitude', one can only wonder whether these feelings manifested themselves in a physically demonstrative manner!

Jane behaved well during her Tasmanian servitude, with no transgressions listed on her conduct record. Presumably the lack of retail establishments in New Norfolk helped. She was among a minority: only one-fifth of female transportees were as circumspect. At the other end of the spectrum, a small proportion — one in twenty — behaved badly enough to be convicted before a superior court. Jane was later to achieve that distinction as well.

During her seventeen-month assignment to the Officer family, Jane captured the interest of fellow New Norfolk resident James New. Calling herself 'Maria Wilkinson alias Jane Henry', she married James on 24 July 1826 at New Norfolk.

Romance came low on the scale of motivations to marry among convict women. Freedom and prosperity made their eyes glisten. Knowing that they would be assigned to their husbands upon marriage and allowed similar freedoms to an emancipated convict was a powerful incentive to pursue the married state. Yet for Jane, freedom was not the only driving force. An unwillingness to accept an impoverished condition had impelled her behaviour in the past and a desire for luxuries drove her future. She lusted after a partner who would indulge her. And her man of choice, James New, was to provide not only freedom and prosperity, but adoration.

Chapter 5
A MATCH MADE IN HEAVEN

From distant climes, over wide-spread seas we come,
Though not with much éclat, or beat of drum,
True patriots all, for be it understood,
We left our country for our country's good . . .
And none will doubt but that our emigration
Has proved most useful to the British Nation.

George Barrington, *The History of New South Wales*

'True patriot' James New was the son of William and Jane New and was baptised early in 1800 at Mitcham, a village lying a short distance from Wimbledon near London.[7] A picturesque perfumed delight met strangers who wandered into the straggling village during James' youth. Appropriately named 'great dwelling' in Domesday Book, Mitcham's rich soil made it ideal for the cultivation of roses and lavender, as well as medicinal herbs such as peppermint, camomile and licorice.

James New was employed as a gardener and greenkeeper when indicted in 1820 for stealing from his previous master, James Moore. Mitcham's pre-eminent farmer and grower of medicinal herbs, Moore was a driving force in community affairs and had employed and housed James' family for some years. As members of his family remained under Moore's wing, and as James drifted over to Moore's almost every day, it seems unlikely that acrimony precipitated James' termination a few months before the theft. It more likely resulted from Mitcham's economic stagnation in the post-war years.

While necessity triggered much of England's criminal activity, James New's crime is hard to justify on grounds other than stupidity or greed. Whatever circumstances prompted his discharge from Moore's employ, his family's residence and livelihood depended upon Moore's good graces. Yet on 16 March 1820, James approached Messrs Dixon and Co. in London's Covent Garden with a sample of licorice-root stolen from Moore's Mitcham storehouse, precipitating the chain of events that would lead to his own transportation to Tasmania.

James Dixon later testified: 'On 16 March, about eleven or twelve o'clock in the morning, the prisoner brought a sample of licorice-root, and offered it for sale. He said he had about two hundred weight at 50 shillings a hundred. I asked him where he brought it from. He said from Norwood, near the *Jolly Sailor*, and that his name was John Saunders, or some name very similar to that.'

The epitome of a bungling thief, James New had failed to prepare an adequate cover story. Licorice was not grown at Norwood. Predictably, both James Dixon and Covent Garden herbalist James Butler — who had received a similar patter regarding the root's origin — were suspicious. Butler declined James' offer, while Dixon suggested he return with the produce in two days, surreptitiously arranging for a police presence at that meeting.

James New's incompetence continued. He brought 260 pounds of licorice-root to London in a cart inscribed 'Stone, Mitcham'; the cart belonged to George Stone of Mitcham who testified that James had appealed for its use in order to fetch some things for his wife and some boxes from Clapham. The licorice-root was also readily identifiable as originating from James Moore's Mitcham property due to its age, colouring and binding. And most significantly, the licorice-root was not licorice-root at all, but the runners that propagated the root; it was inedible and rarely sold. James' crime not only smacked of incompetence, it shrieked of farce.

Escorted to the police office, James faced his interrogators. For half an hour he repeated the fiction regarding his name and residence, before recanting and admitting to the Bow Street officer that his name was New and that the licorice-root came from his master's place at Mitcham. But he described his master as a man named Armstrong who had recently absconded, and professed that Armstrong had forced him to provide a fictional background and would substantiate his story. No testimony surfaced from Armstrong nor proof that James was ever in his employ. Instead, James was left to defend himself against an offence potentially punishable by hanging.

Incarcerated in the hellhole known as Newgate prison, James wilted for 45 days until 5 May 1820 when he was propelled, shackled and chained, across to the infamous Old Bailey. The odds were against him: a two-in-three chance of conviction.

Eight and a half minutes was the average duration of an Old Bailey trial. For some, a blink; for others, a lifetime. Calling James' name, the clerk of the arraigns read out the charge and asked how he pleaded. 'Not guilty,' James announced. Covent Garden merchant James Dixon took the stand, describing James New's initial visit and his return with the merchandise. The News had employed a barrister to defend James however he had little to work with. Herbalist James Butler confirmed James New's overtures; George Stone attested to the use of his cart; James Moore and his steward corroborated the ownership of the licorice-root; Bow Street officer Lewis Lewis described James' confession.

And then James offered his own defence. 'When a man is hired, is he not to obey his master's orders?' he beseeched. 'He sent me with the property, and told me to give a false name to the people as he was in distress, and I did so. He told me to say it was grown at Norwood. I took it to Dixon's shop, and after it was weighed two officers came in and said it was stolen. I said, "If you think so take me into custody." I was examined four times, and they would not let me speak once. I do not call this showing a prisoner justice.'

Unable to persuade the court with this inadequate defence, James was sentenced to seven years' transportation. As the licorice runners were valued at £6, depending upon whichever of the ridiculously large number of inconsistent statutes he was indicted under, he could have been sentenced to death. His relatively minor sentence suggests that, for the sake of James' family, his prosecutor pleaded for mercy.

Whether this was James' first crime or one of many is not known. If he had committed previous crimes he had evidently escaped through luck rather than good management as his criminal activity reflected poorly on both his intelligence and morality. Despite working in the industry, he knew little about licorice. Despite planning the crime, he left such an incriminating trail of evidence that the authorities would eventually have knocked upon his door. And despite being beholden to James Moore, if not for himself then for his family's wellbeing, James chose to steal from him anyway.

Herded back to Newgate, James and his fellow offenders were locked in their cells while the prison authorities awaited orders for their disposal. James was forwarded to the *Retribution* hulk at Sheerness on 16 May 1820. Another transportee wrote a few years earlier of the filth and vermin on the hulks, the incessant noise of rattling chains, the brutal guards. Many convicts failed to survive their incarceration; James was fortunate to spend only a short time there.

Batches of male convicts were shunted to the penal settlements more regularly than their female counterparts, and orders for James' transportation were soon processed. He behaved well during his period in gaol and on the hulks, and was applauded with the description 'orderly'. Transferred to the *Maria* on 13 July 1820, he was one of 156 male convicts who would sail directly for Tasmania two weeks later.

James' experience of transportation differed considerably from Jane's. Despite their greater weight and bulk, more convicts were packed into the *Maria*, a vessel only slightly larger than the *Henry*. The days of being fettered throughout the journey had fortunately ended, although the ever-present risk of mutiny forced a tighter rein over the male prisoners. A military guard, a detachment of the 48th Regiment, travelled with the transport, and soldiers regularly patrolled the vessel. James and the other prisoners spent only a short time on deck, the remainder in the hold where cells lined the sides. With little to do during the voyage, many developed a passion for gambling, some betting even their clothes and rations on the roll of a dice or the turn of a card.

After a 126-day voyage, the *Maria* reached Hobart on 1 December 1820. The convict authorities mustered the transportees asking James for personal information including his age and occupation while the clerks recorded a physical description — five feet six inches with brown hair and black eyes. With gardening experience and a good gaol report, James was more desirable as an assigned servant than most. The settlers often grumbled about the uselessness of convict assignees: 'As you may infer, not many are sent here who are fond of work. The convicts are in general pickpockets who understand nothing of agriculture.' The principles of banishment were sound; the practicalities inevitably failed to live up to expectations.

Assigned to Edinburgh printer James Neill, who had arrived in Tasmania with his family only four days previously, James New was sent to Macquarie Plains (later New Norfolk) where the Neills received land grants totalling 700 acres. James probably helped clear and cultivate their land and took responsibility for their livestock. As the years passed, other convict servants joined him, indicating that the Neills were successfully farming their land. Visitors to the area in the early 1820s reported that the district produced excellent crops of wheat and grain while the nearby countryside offered good grazing land.

After four years with the same master, well-behaved convicts serving a seven-year sentence were eligible for a ticket-of-leave. James had only one misdemeanour — 'disobedience of orders' — noted on his conduct report, for which he apparently received no punishment. Permission was duly granted and James received the indulgence most convicts strove for: the freedom to seek his own employment, to marry, and to live an ostensibly free life. But a ticket-of-leave provided only a fragile freedom. James' home could be searched without a warrant and his ticket revoked if he stepped outside his registered district or incurred the wrath of a constable or magistrate.

James remained in the New Norfolk district for at least another year, perhaps continuing to work for the Neill family, perhaps seeking employment with another settler. During this period, he met, wooed and married the woman who would later bestow infamy upon his name not only in Tasmania but also in the penal settlement of New South Wales.

Chapter 6
A BESOTTED HUSBAND

Heavens, what a dire confusion beauty makes!
Peter Pindar, *Epistle to Mrs Clarke*

Criminals like James New often fared well in colonial society as opportunities abounded, both respectable and nefarious. James and Jane settled in Hobart soon after their marriage, and a year later were residing at the Spread Eagle public house in Argyle Street, Hobart.[8] By the time James' sentence expired in May 1827 he had profited well from dealing. The publican/dealer combination generally proved lucrative as customers venturing in to purchase alcohol could be tempted by the items on display: not just essentials, but the luxuries that proclaimed success, like the silk fabrics the News were reportedly selling.

Financial prosperity soon bestowed upon the News a freedom most were unable to achieve. One week after James' sentence expired, he sailed to Sydney on board the *Albion*. James, who was responsible for part of the cargo, travelled alone as Jane, still a serving convict, required special approval from the Governor to leave the settlement. Coincidentally, the vessel also carried a female member of the Stephen family, whose fortunes would soon be intertwined with those of the News.[9]

James' jaunt either motivated or bolstered the couple's desire to relocate to Sydney. He had evidently used the opportunity to find Jane's mother and her presence in Sydney contributed to the couple's decision to move there. On 24 September 1827, James petitioned Colonial Secretary John Burnett for permission to have Jane travel with him on the imminently sailing *Medway*. 'I have respectable friends and relations at Sydney,' he implored, 'who are anxious that I should proceed immediately to join them.'

Memoranda bounced between government departments as they considered James' appeal. Governor Arthur requested character assessments for the couple, remarking: 'As James New is only free by servitude, it would not appear that there is anything particularly meritorious in his conduct.' Qualifying his disparaging assessment, Arthur agreed to issue the necessary approval if their characters proved 'tolerable'. Principal Superintendent of Convicts John Lakeland reported: 'These persons are not known to me' — in itself an encouraging sign — 'and on making enquiry I find that James New had a ticket-of-leave for five years before he became free, and his wife has never been in the Factory and was married from private service.'

James' petition also included a surprising and unorthodox addition. Chief Clerk Emmett of the Colonial Secretary's Office urged: 'May she go? I have long known the man James New and never heard anything against him.' His plea possibly tipped the scales. Governor Arthur approved Jane's relocation to Sydney, and the News embarked on the *Medway* late in September 1827.

After a voyage of less than a week, the *Medway* sailed into Sydney Harbour early in October 1827. Some years later a judicial appointee reminisced about his own arrival in Sydney around that time. Sir Roger Therry described passing through the guardian giants at the entrance to Port Jackson which served as a keyhole to the magnificent harbour in front of him. He marvelled at its deep crystal waters and the broad canal dotted with islets and bounded by sandy inlets which led to the Sydney Cove settlement. He likened the strange accents, languages and other noises of Sydney to Babel. He expressed surprise at Sydney's prosperous appearance: wide, well laid-out, clean streets; houses in the English style, many with large gardens and most having a flower garden in front; well-stocked shops with cages containing parrots and cockatoos hanging from the shop-door — a vivid reminder that England was truly just a distant memory. George

Street was particularly splendid being 'brilliant' with jewellers' shops. (He later realised that the convicts served as receivers for jewellery and other goods stolen in Britain.) 'This first impression of Sydney on a summer's evening,' recalled Sir Roger, 'was full of agreeable promise.'

In the morning, however, the gates of the prison barracks opened and the evening's illusion shattered. Hundreds of convicts trudged along the streets of Sydney, their bowed heads and downcast visages reflecting their misery. As the day wore on, bands of convicts yoked to wagons laden with gravel and stone performed the functions usually carried out by bullocks. And the screams of convicts being flogged in the prison yard pierced the town clamour.

Although this grim reality shocked the uninitiated, for Jane, one penal settlement was conceivably little different to another.

Disembarking from the *Medway*, Jane and James trudged up the hill to Jane's mother's residence in Cumberland Street. Upon her own arrival in January 1825, Elizabeth Wilkinson had mentioned her two children in Yorkshire, her daughter arriving in the *Henry*, and her widowed status. Unmarried or widowed female transportees could escape the assignment system through marriage, and Elizabeth did indeed wed again. On 4 February 1826 she married emancipist Richard Baker in a Catholic ceremony at Parramatta.

Richard Baker was two decades younger than Elizabeth. One of three men who robbed an ironmonger's shop of goods worth 26 shillings, he was convicted on the bitter testimony of one accomplice after Baker and the other cheated and bashed him. Was Baker also responsible for the change in Elizabeth's appearance by 1830 — missing lower front teeth and flat nose?

Arriving in Sydney in 1819 on the first voyage of the *Grenada*, Baker remained in government employ throughout his sentence, and his failure to gain a ticket-of-leave suggests undesirable conduct or an unacceptable attitude. By 1828 he was working as a mariner and the couple were residing in Cumberland Street on 'the Rocks', the craggy slopes lying to the west of George Street and rising up towards Observatory Hill.

A sense of wildness and disorderliness permeated the Rocks. The rugged terrain forced streets to meander haphazardly, while the rough-hewn houses crammed into the hillside teetered precariously over each other. The

prevalence of boozing, boarding and bawdy houses, and of drunken sailors
and rowdy convicts loitering in the streets, led contemporary observers to
condemn the area as a den of vice and profligacy inhabited by prostitutes,
adulterers, drunks and thieves. Yet socially the Rocks differed little from
any other area in Sydney populated by the lower orders, and it was ideally
suited for James New's business.

The News resided in the Rocks for the following eighteen months.
James initially ran the Mermaid in Cumberland Street, before acquiring the
liquor and lodging licences for the Shipwright Arms in Cambridge Street.
The *Sydney Monitor* later applauded him as a man of 'good character and
respectable in his sphere of life', and his business thrived. Jane soon became
well-known to Sydney's males; many reportedly noticed her although few
professed to have known her personally. Local residents claimed that she
contributed to the couple's business success, although whether as a barmaid
or merely as a drawcard was not clarified.

A besotted husband with money to burn: Jane's ideal partner. James
willingly paid for the silks and satins and other expensive knick-knacks Jane
craved. Indeed, her attire when she was later escorted to the Female Factory
suggests a dignitary's wife (or perhaps a bordello's madam) rather than a
convict woman: a black silk dress, a black satin bonnet, black silk stockings
and stuff shoes, a green silk handkerchief and tortoiseshell side-combs.

James' adoration is also reflected in his astonishing decision to commission
a work of art: a miniature of his wife. While such an expenditure would
be understandable from a wealthy convict entrepreneur like the Botany
Bay Rothschild, Samuel Terry, it seems surprising from a man who was
little more than a moderately successful ex-convict publican. It speaks
of pretensions to grandeur, of a silk-bedecked woman who desired ever
more expensive reflections of her husband's love and devotion. It reveals
a husband determined to immortalise his wife's beauty, and willing to
indulge her vanity in a desperate attempt to retain her fickle affections.
Jane would later write to him, 'I am almost out of my mind at not seeing
you', suggesting that theirs was a mutually passionate relationship. But
only on the surface. In truth, the siren was lulling her prey with the tune
he wished to hear.

Although a devoted husband, James was not a redeemed character. He remained an opportunist, willing to break the rules and even breach the law if expediency or desire dictated. A few months after his arrival, James petitioned to have his wife's 'brother', James Palmer, assigned to him:[10]

I have recently arrived with my family from Tasmania for the purpose of settling in this Colony. I have rented a farm at Hunter's River whereon I intend to reside and consequently will require the services of some government servants for whom I will make application in the regular way, but I beg to inform your Excellency that my wife's brother James Palmer, prisoner per *Countess of Harcourt*, is attached to the Dockyard as a messenger and who I understand can be spared from that establishment. I therefore most respectfully solicit your Excellency to be pleased to favour me with Palmer's services.

No such relationship existed, this being a ruse on James New's behalf to have a crony assigned to him. He had also lied about his circumstances and intentions.

The authorities agreed with James' reference to Palmer's usefulness, describing him as 'an indifferent character and not of much use to Government'. Yet they rejected his appeal. Governor Darling refused to assign prisoners to those who requested them by name to prevent undesirable associations re-forming in the colony and a return to criminal behaviour.

Rehabilitation played only a minor role in early nineteenth-century attitudes to criminality, and the deterrent factor of a sentence, even when combined with a narrow escape from the gallows, often failed to discourage old lags and newcomers alike. The easy path to riches remained tempting. James faced such a situation some months later.

In June 1828 James sold his licences for the Shipwright Arms to George Morris who wished to transfer them to his house in George Street. But James had no right to sell or transfer the licences to Morris and continued trading. Morris sued him for £140 for 'craftily and subtly' deceiving him and for his business and financial losses. Initially due to be heard in

November 1828, the case was delayed for a month then deferred until June 1829. If the delays were Morris' doing, he made an unfortunate decision. By June 1829, James New and the money were nowhere to be found.

James was not alone in succumbing to temptation. Jane had already done so.

Chapter 7
A CRIMINAL INTENT

Temptation is so strong, surging desire so powerful, so impervious,
so irresistible, that the act is accomplished before reason has time to
plead its cause; for the moment pleasure is everything.
Madame Dubuisson, nineteenth-century psychologist

Despite having an indulgent husband, Jane was dissatisfied. Criminality beckoned. Two months after the News' arrival in Sydney, Jane committed her first known Sydney-based crime: stealing from the 'dwelling house' of Madame Rens. A French widow, Madame Josephine Rens and her twelve-year-old daughter Jeanette had sailed into Sydney in January 1827, settling soon afterwards in a two-room dwelling in George Street.[11] Despite her poor command of English, Madame Rens established a business as a silk mercer and milliner with the assistance of her English-speaking daughter. Shortly before Christmas, Jane New crossed the threshold and entered their lives.

Madame Rens was unaware of Jane's identity when she first visited the shop on 17 December 1827. Jane asked to see a number of items including a length of distinctive chocolate-coloured silk. 'It was a particular sort of French silk,' recollected Madame Rens. 'I had no other silk of that quality and pattern, and had sold none of it. I brought the silk with me from Lyons and then to Batavia [Indonesia] and then here. The silk was worth seven shillings a yard and there were 28 yards.'

Shortly before lunchtime on the following day, Jane returned with a female companion. She asked to see the same chocolate-coloured silk along with some other fabric lengths, and the women gazed at the fabrics for a short time before leaving the shop. 'They bought nothing,' Madame Rens grumbled. 'After they were gone I immediately missed the silk in question, and I looked after Jane New and in a basket on her arm I saw the silk in it. No other person was in the shop but Jane New and the other woman.'

Yet Madame Rens made no attempt to apprehend Jane. 'I did not wish to follow her,' she explained, 'as I had nobody near me. If I understood English I would have sent somebody after her but labouring under that difficulty I could not.'

Madame Rens also decided against lodging an official complaint at this time. Hampered by her inadequate command of English and her inability to identify the culprits, she hesitated. Her concerns proved realistic as her grievance was treated facetiously when eventually reported. 'When I went to the police, to make my complaint,' she protested, 'I saw three or four persons with the appearance of gentlemen, who seemed to know all the business and they laughed. When I saw that they appeared to make a joke of it, I left the office. I heard the words "French Lady", "silk". I understood that they spoke of me.'

Madame Rens' eventual decision to report the theft was prompted by her glimpse soon afterwards of one of the women talking to affluent merchant George Bunn. With her daughter in tow, she approached Bunn and questioned him about the woman's identity. Bunn later testified: 'I told Madame Rens that she was an honest woman. Madame Rens said she thought the woman robbed her of some silk and I replied, "I don't think she would do any such thing!" '

A prisoner of the Crown described as an honest woman? Perhaps the gentlemen of Sydney were unaware of Jane's status as a serving convict or, like her convict-class associates, believed that her sentence had long expired. Perhaps in the penal settlement 'honesty' and 'honourableness' were more loosely defined terms, particularly when used by a gentleman to describe a personable woman. Would Sydney's female worthies have described Jane as an honest woman? Other images probably came to mind as they tucked away their claws.

So strong was George Bunn's belief in Jane's good reputation that he protected her identity in addition to proclaiming her innocence. Jane's name was later revealed to Madame Rens by the Superintendent of Police, Colonel Morisset, long after she lodged her complaint and a pattern of the silk at the police office. Yet despite the discovery of Jane's identity, the police made no attempt to apprehend her. When the case eventually came to trial, Madame Rens complained: 'I can't explain why she was not taken up when I made my complaint of the robbery.'

Old Bailey trial transcripts reveal that convictions often resulted from considerably weaker cases so the police's failure to take Jane into custody and to search her house seems surprising. Why would they ignore a business-person's charge when it indicted a serving convict? Madame Rens' status as a female, a widow, a native of Britain's recent enemy, and a businesswoman (colonial society was starting to look askance at businesswomen by the late 1820s) undoubtedly contributed to their lack of support. Yet the delay in apprehending Jane possibly had a different cause. Perhaps her allure created a reluctance in the officials — naturally all men — to take action against her. It seems unlikely that they would have ignored Madame Rens' charge if the culprit had been a wizened old crone or a menacing thug. Poet John Keats' famous phrase 'beauty is truth' reflects humanity's unconscious tendency to equate beauty with honesty and integrity, a judgement that favoured Jane New. Indeed, later events reveal that Jane's charms captivated the gentlemen of Sydney, who joined forces to support her despite compelling evidence of her illicit behaviour.

Nothing but trouble and humiliation resulted from her denunciation of Jane New, Madame Rens later complained. 'That woman named New' had stolen from her two or three times, she declared, although no corroborating information regarding additional crimes has been located. It is possible that Madame Rens was embellishing the truth to support her claims of unsympathetic treatment by the constabulary and the judicial system. It is also possible that she was telling the truth, that she had been foiled from laying charges on other occasions by the absence of convincing evidence.

Word of Madame Rens' allegations must have reached Jane through street gossip. Having experienced no repercussions she retained her confidence and audacity. A few months later she had the effrontery to re-enter Madame Rens' shop and request a favour. Madame Rens recollected: 'I think I saw Jane New at my shop again about three or four months after the taking of the silk. She came to exchange a silk gown that had been bought at my shop by a gentleman and had a few spots on it. I refused to change the gown and told her to leave the house. She went outside and abused me very much. Since then Jane New has been in my shop once and I ordered her to walk out immediately.'

Madame Rens' daughter confirmed her mother's statement, adding that her mother did not report Jane as no constable was in the vicinity and as she wanted no trouble. Having lodged her complaint with the police, Madame Rens believed she could do no more. Her anger and frustration, however, continued to simmer.

Jane's accomplice during the theft from Madame Rens' shop has not been identified. Perhaps Hannah Ralph filled this role. When Jane and Hannah met, they must have felt an immediate bond, a meeting of minds and souls. Although physically dissimilar — Hannah was red-haired, fair-skinned and hazel-eyed in contrast to Jane's dark sultry looks — they were around the same age, were long-term residents of Manchester and were both habitual shoplifters. Hannah had arrived in New South Wales early in 1827 on the fourth voyage of the *Grenada* transport, after receiving at least three Manchester convictions. She escaped the assignment system by marrying emancipist baker Richard Ralph in a ceremony performed six weeks prior to the shoplifting at Madame Rens' premises. The couple settled in the Rocks, not far from James and Jane New.[12]

Jane and Hannah were clearly partners-in-crime on 11 August 1828 when they swooped on the shops of Sydney. All three newspapers described their crime-spree in detail, a surprising circumstance in itself as Jane's eventual trial on Madame Rens' more serious charges merited only a one-sentence dismissal in the same newspapers. The *Sydney Monitor* reported:

On Monday last Jane New and Hannah Ralph went to Mrs Reynolds' shop in George-street where they requested to be shown some worked muslin dresses but made only a trifling purchase of some ribbon. The prisoner *New* was observed by Mrs Reynolds to make a snatch at some of the articles which lay on the counter and, not long afterwards, a pair of child's shoes were discovered to be missing. In the meantime the women went to Mrs Rickards' shop in Pitt-street whence they purloined some valuable articles of haberdashery. Their next visit was to Mr Appleton's shop in Pitt-street, and during their stay some articles were also missed which induced Mr Appleton to send after the prisoner *New*, in order to have her searched, but it proved useless. In the course of the Police's enquiries, Constable Skinner ascertained that Hannah Ralph had left a bundle at a house which was found to contain property which both Mrs Rickards and Mrs Reynolds recognised to be their stolen property.

Another court; another conviction. The *Australian* reported:

Against Jane New, there was no evidence to incriminate her in the business of purloining the lace or other valuables stolen beyond that of having been in Hannah Ralph's company. The Bench having ascertained from the records of the Colonial Secretary's Office the prisoners' respective sentences, and being of the opinion that Jane New, though not proved to be the actual thief in any of the cases adduced, was in some way *particeps criminis*, directed the original sentence of Hannah Ralph to be extended for two years of which six months were to be spent in the Female Factory, that of Jane New, as the minor offender, for one year.

Curiously, when Jane's extended sentence later came under discussion, the Bench of Magistrates' books revealed a different description: 'being found at large after hours, her husband being in Tasmania and the woman in whose company she was seen being a bad character'. It seems a surprising distortion of the truth. Although Jane's husband was indeed in Tasmania and her accomplice by then considered a bad character, the crimes had been committed during daylight hours and the witnesses' testimonies had implicated Jane. By reducing Jane's crime to a minor breach of convict regulations, the authorities provided her with a shield of innocence against later claims of criminality. And those who attempted to defend Jane's honour by raising this particular shield also declared that her sentence was passed by only one magistrate and was therefore judged illegal. The authorities were sceptical. 'Was it proved?' they jotted. The records remain silent on the answer; the silence itself is revealing.

The community expressed disgust at Jane's sentence. 'Much too lenient!' opined the *Sydney Monitor*. Ironically, over the following few months the *Monitor*'s editor, Edward Smith Hall, modified his attitude to Jane New and her escapades. He distorted his own account of her August 1828 conviction and fabricated additional information when bemoaning her fate:

> On a very *summary* examination and without further trial, she was sentenced by our Sydney Bench to the Factory and to an extension of her original sentence of transportation. This magisterial conviction was afterwards reversed, there being reason to believe that she was not guilty of shoplifting.

Had the self-righteous evangelical Edward Smith Hall succumbed to the siren's song or had he been influenced by a friend with a hidden agenda?

Magistrate John Stephen Jnr glimpsed Jane New at the Bench of Magistrates on that day or soon afterwards. Bold eyes, a suggestive pout, a flirtatious flick of the hair? He was smitten. As it turned out, their encounter was to prove a pivotal moment in both of their lives and indeed the whole Sydney community.

Part II:
PRETENSION

In appointments to official positions,
New South Wales has been perfectly
deluged with the Stephen family.

William Charles Wentworth

Chapter 8
THE STEPHEN MÉNAGE

We must watch out for the welfare of the many
rather than the advantage of the few.

Sir James Stephen

Scion of a colonial legal family, John Stephen Jnr counted among his relatives men of distinction in the legal and political history of the British Empire. Many of these men also had an involvement — either voluntarily or otherwise — in the Jane New affair.

The Stephen family had long prided themselves on their liberal sympathies which began with John's grandfather, James Stephen (I). Unfortunate financial speculations led to his incarceration in London's overcrowded, typhus-ridden King's Bench prison, where he achieved notoriety by writing pamphlets proclaiming that imprisonment for debt was against the Magna Carta, and by organising a prison uprising. His son James Stephen (II) sailed to the West Indies in 1783 to pursue his legal profession and, shocked at the brutality meted out to black slaves, was thereafter prominent in the abolition movement. The mantle passed to his son, Permanent Under-Secretary of the Colonial Office Sir James Stephen, who was ultimately successful in pushing through legislation abolishing the repugnant trade in human beings. Sir James was also responsible for relocating his Stephen relations to Australia.[13]

John Stephen Jnr's father followed his brother James (II) to St Kitts, one of the Leeward Islands in the West Indies, where he distinguished himself as a barrister. He married Mary Anne Pasmore and fathered ten children;[14] his second son, John Stephen Jnr, was born around the year 1798 in America where Mary Anne had temporarily relocated for health reasons.

Although warm, lush and exotically picturesque, St Kitts was home to deadly tropical diseases. Concerned for her family's wellbeing, Mary Anne and her 'younger children' returned to England in 1804 where a fifth son, Francis, was born. The two older boys, Sidney and John Jnr, possibly remained in St Kitts under the care of their father and, presumably, black servants and a tutor. Financial success allowed John Stephen Snr's triumphant return to England a few years later and he leased a house in London. Soon afterwards, his third son, George, died and a curious reference to John Jnr is found in a sympathy letter written by a relation:

I have no doubt that as far as George's tender mind was led to think of eternal things he was desirous of serving God and that he is now with the angels in heaven. I trust his death may have a good effect upon Sidney and John. The latter I feel particularly interested about — the concern he expressed about the confirmation seemed to me to proceed from real piety, and I hope it will increase with his years.

Was John a genuinely pious child or was this the first evidence of guile, of a personality capable of deliberately presenting the image that would best serve his own interests?

In 1810/11 the elder surviving Stephen boys, Sidney, John and Alfred, spent a year at London's Charterhouse school, one of the barbarous institutions where boys were subjected to the sadism of birch-wielding masters, fed little, and herded together in unsanitary conditions. Alfred was later to reminisce about his father's belief in the importance of hardening boys, 'so to the Charterhouse we went, walking daily in all weathers, ice, fog, and snow notwithstanding.'

The Stephens left London when John invested his wealth in a country estate near Wells in County Somerset. Some years later an ill-advised financial speculation forced the sale of the family's home and John Snr returned to St Kitts in 1815 with his son Alfred. Despite being appointed Solicitor-General, fortune no longer favoured him. Recent British legislation had made the slave trade illegal and emancipation would soon follow, so the plantocracy's heyday was over. Desiring a fresh start, John Snr appealed to his nephew, James Stephen, then the Colonial Office's part-time counsel.

When James Stephen eventually retired from the Colonial Office, his admirable performance led a colleague to remark that for a quarter-century James Stephen virtually governed the British Empire. From this position of increasing importance and influence, James recommended his uncle to Earl Bathurst, Secretary of State for the Colonies, for the newly created position of New South Wales Commissioner of the Court of Requests. The King approved John's appointment and £600 salary early in 1824, and a new era began for the Stephen family.

John and his wife, daughters, and two youngest sons, sailed for Sydney on the convict transport *Prince Regent*, arriving in July 1824. John proved popular and in 1825 he was appointed first puisne judge of the New South Wales Supreme Court with a salary increase to £1500 per annum. In this role, he would later preside over one of the courtroom challenges involving Jane New, and provide his own opinion — albeit perfunctory — in the resulting ruling.

Justice Stephen's liberal outlook soon brought him into conflict with the exclusives and with Governor Darling who took over the colony's reins in December 1825. Darling was later to dismiss Justice Stephen as a 'tool in the hands of the Chief Justice', while John Macarthur was vitriolic in his denigration. In contrast, John's liberal-minded colleague Sir Roger Therry wrote: 'He was a man of a very courteous deportment and of a very independent spirit. His conduct was marked with some imprudence in the assumption of a hostile attitude towards the Governor, but his judicial integrity was undoubted.'

Historians have agreed with Therry's assessment, although noting that Justice Stephen could be blunt to the point of rudeness and very discourteous. His hostile attitude reflected his dislike for Governor Darling and his autocratic ways, an attitude shared by his London-based nephew, James Stephen.

With the vigour of youth, Justice Stephen's offspring and their friends took matters a step further. They loathed the Governor and conspired to undermine his authority in the hope of forcing his early dismissal. Their actions contributed to a tumultuous period in colonial history and laid the groundwork for the Jane New scandal.

Chapter 9
BROTHERS-IN-ARMS

*The mischief is that persons from whom better
things might be expected copy men such as Wentworth, and
permit themselves to be infected by feelings of radicalism
and hostility to the established Government.*

Governor Ralph Darling

The most openly antagonistic member of the Stephen youth in the period
prior to the scandal was Justice Stephen's fifth son, the 'lively young spark'
Francis Stephen. Francis would later become Jane's solicitor and would be
responsible for pursuing her historically significant Supreme Court hearing.

Francis first clashed with Governor Darling in 1827 when evidence
of 'radicalism' followed his involvement in one of the many important
political incidents during Darling's administration: the Turf Club affair.
Francis had only recently returned to New South Wales, after a trip to
England,[15] and brought with him a racing cup sponsored by the late
Governor, Sir Thomas Brisbane, which was to be presented at the Turf Club's
inaugural dinner in November 1827. As the evening progressed, the drink
flowed freely, inhibitions eased and tongues loosened. Governor Darling had
declined to attend, largely because of his determination not to mix with
'such Associations', and during the toast to his health the band slyly played
'Over the Hills and Far Away'.

The *Monitor* used the incident to make political capital, describing the tune as an effective display of the community's feelings about the Governor. Deeply offended, Darling also perceived the incident as disloyalty to the government and as an attempt to undermine his administration and he overreacted, sacking a number of government officials who attended the dinner. The incident served as one of the pivotal moments in the deteriorating relations between the liberals and Governor Darling, and the resulting perception that he responded maliciously to personal attacks would later be manipulated by the press during Governor Darling's clash with John Stephen Jnr over the Jane New affair.

After Darling unleashed his wrath, Francis attempted to act as a mediator between the Governor and the Club's chairpersons, William Charles Wentworth and Robert Wardell. Friction already marked their relationship as Wentworth and Wardell were the founding editors of the *Australian*, a newspaper vociferous in its condemnation of Darling's person and politics. Darling thought favourably of Francis' intentions but not of his actions, claiming that he had no business to interfere.

Francis soon graduated from being a pinprick of annoyance to a thorn in Darling's side. In December 1827, Francis wrote to the garrison's commandant protesting that he had been challenged by a sentry at 11 pm the previous evening, had neglected to respond as it was 'as light as day', and in consequence had been 'illegally arrested and assaulted'. He intended to prosecute the sentry, Francis announced.

Darling was awake to this game, having received a similar letter from William Charles Wentworth ten days previously. Yet Francis' behaviour astonished him. Darling had just offered his requisite approval for Francis' appointment as assistant clerk of the Supreme Court and he considered Francis' behaviour a challenge against the authority of the government preparing to employ him. He attempted to rescind his approval, however Chief Justice Forbes advised that such an act would blemish Francis' reputation and prejudice his future prospects. Darling acquiesced, although with undoubted misgivings.

On the surface all remained quiet for the following year while Francis served at the Supreme Court. Perhaps he showed his appreciation for

Darling's consideration by not openly attacking him or his government, although he remained in cahoots with the *Australian's* editors. Whether Francis contributed articles to the newspaper at this time is uncertain although the newspaper's slant when the scandal erupted — extremely favourable to Jane New to the point of being absurdly inaccurate — combined with Francis' later employment as the *Australian's* editor, suggests an ever-increasing input.

By late 1828, Francis was re-evaluating his career options. As Jane New hovered around the Supreme Court waiting for her case to be heard, he petitioned for admittance to the roll of solicitors. His request would only be accepted, he was informed, if he terminated his employment with the Supreme Court. Soon afterwards Francis received word that Governor Darling was reducing his salary. He responded indignantly that private practice would be more profitable and resigned soon afterwards. When Jane New was again in need of legal representation, and when her case carried the prospect of a challenge against Governor Darling, Francis grabbed it.

Francis Stephen was not alone among the Stephen family in serving as Jane New's legal representative. When fortune again smiled upon him, Justice Stephen sent word to his three eldest sons who had all remained abroad. In the mid-to-late 1820s, Sidney, John Jnr and Alfred swarmed to the colony, where each participated in the Jane New drama.

Sidney Stephen was Jane's first barrister, acting on her behalf when she appeared before the Bench of Magistrates on the August 1828 trio of shoplifting charges. Shortly after Sidney's arrival in New South Wales earlier that year,[16] Governor Darling appointed him Acting Solicitor-General until the King's appointee should arrive — another favour bestowed by Darling on a member of the Stephen family. Replaced by John Sampson in March 1828, Sidney offered his services to the community but found that he faced a legal monopoly in Sydney, one he lambasted as 'exclusive, unjust, ridiculous, anti-progressive and un-English'.

Ironically, similar sentiments were expressed some years later regarding the Stephen family's plethora of appointments to legal and judicial positions, after Wentworth remarked in 1850 that over the previous quarter-century the colony had been deluged with members of the Stephen family. Family members dashed off letters to the editors protesting against such claims, while readers listed dozens of posts held by Stephens and their relatives. In truth, the pinnacle in individual achievement within the colonial Stephen family was not reached until later in the century when John Stephen Jnr's brother Alfred who, having served as the third Chief Justice of the Supreme Court and as a member of the Legislative Council, was appointed Lieutenant-Governor of New South Wales.

Although by sheer weight of numbers the Stephen family's influence might appear greater in later years, in terms of political influence relative to population their power in the New South Wales settlement was probably at its peak during the Jane New affair. A triangle of influence existed at high levels, with James Stephen serving the Colonial Office in London, Justice John Stephen serving as the second of the three NSW Supreme Court judges, and Alfred Stephen as the Solicitor-General and Crown-Solicitor of Tasmania with the ear of Governor Arthur. In addition, Francis and Sidney had recently held government positions within the judicial system and had become members of the prestigious legal fraternity, while John Stephen Jnr held a civil appointment. Clearly, the Stephen family was a powerful force during Darling's administration.

The Stephens also hobnobbed with other persons of influence in the New South Wales community. These included the *Australian's* William Charles Wentworth and his brilliant barrister partner Robert Wardell, and Edward Smith Hall, the proprietor and editor of the *Monitor* newspaper. All were liberal-minded and strongly opposed to Governor Darling's autocratic administration. All were determined to use the press to broadcast their views and concerns, with Hall so vociferous in his attacks that he was eventually imprisoned for numerous libels. All latched onto any opportunity to score political points against Darling. And when Jane New found herself in the spotlight, these men instantly recognised her suitability for point scoring. Indeed, without their involvement, Jane's situation would not have generated such a significant legal and political impact.

While the Stephens and their anti-Darling cohorts remained within the legal boundaries they were a powerful force, and their constant complaints to the Colonial Office contributed to the eventual decision to recall Governor Darling. However when they crossed the line, the inevitable happened. A neck was exposed. That pivotal moment in August 1828, when John Stephen Jnr faced Jane New from the Bench of Magistrates, ultimately left him vulnerable to the wrath of the Governor and the might of the law. When the axe later fell, it was John's head that was lopped.

Chapter 10
THE BLACK SHEEP

New South Wales affords an excellent asylum for fools and
madmen as well as rogues and vagabonds.
Governor Darling

While the Stephen family later boasted — no doubt justifiably — about
the achievements of Justice John Stephen and his offspring, little fanfare
was accorded his namesake John Stephen Jnr. Either ignored or dismissed
by Stephen eulogists, John was rarely even granted the benefit of being
damned by faint praise. Even his brother Alfred in his jottings merely
noted that 'my next elder brother John lived a more erratic life, filling at
various times responsible offices, both here and in England'. John's fall
from grace in the Stephen family annals was partly precipitated by his
involvement in the Jane New scandal.

Mystery enshrouds John's early years of employment. Governor Darling
later mentioned having heard of John's admission to Lincoln's Inn, where
barristers learn their craft, although in autobiographical information, John
made no mention of early legal training and was not called to the bar.
Instead, John himself remarked, 'On 2 May 1816 at the recommendation
of my uncle Mr James Stephen, later Master in Chancery, I was appointed a
clerk in the East India House where I was employed in the correspondence
department, principally as Under-Secretary to Mr Charles Grant.' Yet,

curiously, the East India Company's extensive employment records fail to reveal John's presence.

In 1820/21, John married Mary Matthews Hamilton. Twice.[17] Mary had an unusual background. An illegitimate child born around 1803 in the American town of Norfolk, Virginia, she was unofficially adopted by the childless Colonel John Hamilton, Britain's Consul to Virginia, and his wife Claudia Cattel Mullryne Tattnall, and later brought to England.

Could the prospect of potential wealth have influenced John's decision to marry the young girl? Her father had walked away from £200000 in American assets when he chose loyalty to Britain over signing the Oath Of Allegiance during the American Revolution (1775–83). Additional American assets acquired during Hamilton's post-Revolution years as Norfolk's British Consul had been relinquished when the family relocated to London after the outbreak of war in 1812. Claudia also had her own American assets including twenty slaves bequeathed to her by her father, part proceeds from the sale of another fifty slaves, and her father's shares in the British three-per-cent funds.

Mary's status as an underage illegal adoptee created problems when the couple attempted to marry. The ceremony had to be terminated. An application to the Court of Chancery placed her under the guardianship of her mother who approved her marriage, and divulged the information that Mary had no personal estate. John would later claim otherwise.

A couple of years later, John sought new employment. 'Having resigned my situation at East India House,' he later wrote, 'I was appointed on 24 January 1823 Clerk of the Cheque to the Band of Gentlemen Pensioners and Silver Stick to His Majesty George IV, and subsequently Private Secretary to the Captain the Earl of Courtown.' Official records confirm John's appointment to the Gentlemen Pensioners (today the Gentlemen-at-Arms), one of the prestigious units in the King's Household. John's commission cost over one thousand guineas — funded no doubt by his mother-in-law — and entitled him to a resplendent uniform and responsibility for preparing the paymaster's role. Yet although John did serve as Clerk of the Cheque, his other claims were lies. John's willingness to knowingly and blatantly misrepresent the truth would prove one of his many fundamental character flaws.

Sometime after joining the Gentlemen Pensioners, John's thoughts were directed towards New South Wales as a place of settlement:

> About this time I presented a petition to the Prime Minister, Lord Liverpool, for the continuation of a pension of £800 a year or a portion of it to my mother-in-law. Having had several conversations with His Lordship upon the subject, I was prevailed upon, as I had an increasing family and my emoluments in the King's Household were precarious, arising chiefly from fees, to turn my views to New South Wales where my Father had just then obtained an appointment. Lord Liverpool promised me his patronage.

Yet colonial sources include no references to a recommendation from Lord Liverpool. Indeed, when John later flooded the British and New South Wales authorities with verbal and written character testimonies, none surfaced for the period pre-dating his arrival in New South Wales.

John acted on the Prime Minister's advice, or so he reported, and sought the appropriate patrons:

> At the Colonial Office I was subsequently introduced to General Darling, who had lately been appointed Governor of New South Wales, whom I had reason to believe from what then took place, had received some communication upon the subject, and he promised me on my arrival to extend to me his patronage.

Governor Darling later responded with bewilderment: 'I have no recollection of this, nor did I receive any communication respecting him. Mr Stephen arrived in the colony with his wife and family as a private individual, not holding any office or employment under the colonial government.' Darling added caustically that it was only through his own good grace that John succeeded in obtaining employment.

With his patronage assured, or so John claimed, he made plans to relocate his family to New South Wales:

I therefore resigned my office at court and prepared for my departure for the colony, being assisted by funds from my wife's estate amounting to about £5000, two thousand of which I settled in the English Funds for the benefit of my family which still remains. I was engaged at that period in litigation and an appeal to the Privy Council was pending but I saw no probability of this being brought to an early conclusion, and I therefore quitted this country.

Yet in his autobiographical information, John failed to mention a pertinent detail: he had resigned from the Band of Gentlemen Pensioners in May 1824, three years before his arrival in New South Wales. In fact, he had served as Clerk of the Cheque for the second-shortest period in the history of the Gentlemen Pensioners.

So what happened in the period John conveniently bypassed? The colonial authorities received a tantalising glimpse some years later. Governor Darling reported: 'Some time after Mr Stephen's arrival in this Colony, I received a communication from the Lieutenant-Governor of Jersey where it appears he had formerly resided. The object was that proceedings might be instituted against him in consequence of some transactions during his residence at Jersey, but I was not informed of the particulars.'

It was during these years that John's rising star crested and began to fall.

John's problems began when he had the misfortune to make a financial transaction with Gentlemen Pensioner Henry Gompertz. A merchant and wheeler-dealer, Gompertz had numerous bankruptcies and criminal indictments to his name, and continued to leave a trail of creditors and victims behind him in ensuing years. In January 1824, reportedly in return for a valuable reversionary property, John agreed to sign a bill of exchange for £220 made out to Gompertz and payable three months later.[18] Soon afterwards, John discovered that Gompertz had no title to the property. Whether John was an innocent duped or the party to a dubious transaction is uncertain.

Henry Gompertz was a canny conman and he knew that John could refuse to pay the bill when it became due. He passed it to Attorneys

Henry Wright and John Cole who probably accepted it because of the Stephen family name. John did indeed refuse to honour the bill. The attorneys immediately sued him. Surprisingly, John failed to defend his case. Predictably, the verdict went against him and 40 per cent of the plaintiffs' costs as well. The final judgement on 25 June 1824 ordered him to pay £262. But John had no intention of meeting his obligations. He had already resigned from the Gentlemen Pensioners — voluntarily? Involuntarily? — and slipped out of the country.

John's reaction at this time exposed another of his many character flaws: his belief that in running away he could escape the consequences of his own actions.

The Channel Island of Jersey, 100 miles south of England, became John's new residence. Although nestled in the horseshoe-shaped Gulf of St Malo and lying only 20 miles from the French coastline, Jersey and the other Channel Islands were a British possession. John probably believed that employment opportunities would arise in such an environment.

As it turned out, John had not travelled far enough to escape his plaintiffs' reaches. Wright and Cole employed Jersey barrister Matthieu Poingdestre to pursue the debt and he commenced proceedings against John in Jersey's Royal Court early in September 1824. The court ordered John's arrest and compelled him to find bail to cover the £262 claim. When John's case was heard six weeks later, the court upheld the previous verdict and charged costs and interest against him. Yet instead of accepting the court's decision, John appealed in December and again in June 1825 when the court affirmed the former judgements and again condemned John to pay costs. By this time, the combined costs for both parties far outweighed the original £220 bill.

A third character flaw had surfaced, one that would appear repeatedly in his dealings with the authorities. John was unable to recognise when a battle had been fought and lost, to admit that it was time to accept his losses and move on.

John sought leave to appeal to the King's Privy Council, the executive arm of the royal prerogative, which was closely involved in colonial matters. John's Privy Council appeal passed ponderously through the system, with the Council a year later ordering him to submit his printed case. John failed to respond. One source raises the possibility that he had slipped out of the country again, to the Cape of Good Hope, a British possession on the southern tip of Africa.[19] Six months later the Privy Council issued a peremptory order for his printed case. John had evidently employed legal assistance by this time and the Privy Council eventually ruled on his appeal in June 1828, three years after the initial judgement. John lost. The Privy Council upheld the previous rulings and ordered him to pay all costs which were taxed at a hefty £132. John later claimed that the costs from the case alone amounted to over £800.

But John was not around to pay his debts. By this time he had travelled about as far from the bailiffs as it was possible to travel while remaining within the British Empire — to the penal settlement of New South Wales.

The *Admiral Cockburn* sailed from London on 29 August 1826, although it is unclear whether the Stephen family were on board or whether they embarked from one of its ports of call: Falmouth in Cornwall, Tenerife or the Cape of Good Hope. John travelled in style and at huge expense: cabin accommodation, an entourage — his wife, four children, servants, and a relative, Miss Sally Hamilton.[20] He had evidently learnt the wisdom of a dazzling first impression. Presumably the funds came from John's mother-in-law, Claudia, who also appears to have transferred her inherited shares in the British three-per-cent funds to the Stephen family. Claudia, however, had determined John's mettle. She apparently stipulated that they should have no access to the capital, and sent them off with her blessing, a comfortable passage and an annuity.

The Stephens spent some weeks at Hobart during their final port of call early in 1827, where John made a particularly favourable impression. The editor of the liberal *Tasmanian and Asiatic Review* extolled his virtues for a considerable period thereafter. Sailing again late in March, John and his family arrived in Sydney Harbour on 2 April 1827.

Soon after finding accommodation, John donned the uniform of the King's Household and presented himself to the Governor. He offered

Darling a certificate signed by the Pensioners' Captain, the Earl of Courtown, approving his leave of absence for two or three years. But John had resigned from the Gentlemen Pensioners some years earlier, not taken leave. He had no entitlement to wear the uniform of the King's Household although this detail was never communicated to the colonists. So why would the Pensioner's Captain write that John had been granted leave?

Perhaps the hand that penned the letter was not the Earl's. This was to prove another of John's flaws: a 'facility', wrote Governor Darling some years later, 'for writing in the names of others'.

Impressed by John's person and presumably by his employment record as well, Governor Darling kept him in mind. John later reported:

> On my arrival in Sydney, I received every attention from General Darling. He permitted me to select 5000 acres of land as a reserve grant for purchase and subsequently gave me a free grant of 2560 acres. I was nominated a Magistrate and Police Superintendent at Campbelltown, but I did not act in this situation. The Governor had desired me to communicate to him regarding any vacancy in another office, and when one of the Commissioners of Land died I wrote to him and I was immediately nominated to that office.

In October 1827, John succeeded to Crown Land Commissioner John Campbell's £365 position. John proved an able and efficient worker and Governor Darling rewarded him in January 1828 with an appointment to the magistracy, and in February 1828 with the position of Supreme Court Registrar. The Registrar's appointment required Royal approval and paid £800 per annum, although appointees only received half-pay until such approval was granted.

The previous Registrar had voluntarily vacated the position on 14 February: suicide. George Galway Mills' appointment had served as a reward for past services, as so many Royal appointments were, however he proved inexperienced, unsuited and incompetent, and, according to Darling, 'profligate and dissolute'. Darling acted quickly in replacing him. 'In less than two hours,' John reported proudly (or before Mills was in his

coffin let alone his grave, as one historian described the untimely haste),
'I was appointed his successor.'

The tension simmering between the two most powerful men in New
South Wales erupted. Upon the establishment in 1823 of the New South
Wales Supreme Court, William Charles Wentworth had predicted that the
power vested in the Chief Justice would create conflict with the Governor
unless both men were of singular prudence and moderation. While Chief
Justice Forbes admirably reflected these attributes, Governor Darling proved
quick-tempered and suspicious. When Forbes vetoed any of Darling's
proposed legislation upon valid legal grounds, Darling interpreted his
actions as a personal slight and as an attack upon his supreme authority.
So when Governor Darling seized the opportunity to appoint John to this
Supreme Court position, he effectively threw down the gauntlet.

Ironically, while Chief Justice Forbes had a month previously pushed
through Francis Stephen's appointment against Governor Darling's
resistance, the opposite occurred with John's appointment. Forbes considered
the hasty nomination unnecessary, particularly as a reorganisation of the
Supreme Court's ministerial offices had been mooted. He saw Darling's
failure to seek his approval as discourteous. And although he had no
personal complaint about Darling's appointee, he queried John's suitability,
claiming that the position required legal skills and that Mills' inexperience
and unsuitability had proved onerous for himself and the chief clerk.

Undeterred, Governor Darling had John's Letters Patent drawn up,
allowing him to exhibit them in the Supreme Court. Unimpressed, Chief
Justice Forbes informed John that the Letters Patent had not been prepared
in accordance with the Charter of Justice and that the court needed time
to determine their legality. Bitter sniping followed. Darling complained
to the Colonial Office that Forbes was expressing contempt for the
government and should be removed from office. Forbes remonstrated that
he was bound by the Law, although he eventually capitulated in order to
minimise friction with the Governor. Darling was later rebuked by the
Colonial Office.

Curiously, Governor Darling never clarified why he acted so hastily in
replacing the Registrar, or why he chose John for the position. He claimed

that the vacancy needed to be filled promptly as the Supreme Court was in session, that the Registrar did not need to be a lawyer, and that he had 'heard' that John had received some legal training. Yet Chief Justice Forbes' response reveals that Darling's claims were specious.

Perhaps Governor Darling wanted control over the appointment as so many of the King's appointees were incompetent, and wished to replace Mills with a man who had proved himself efficient and capable. Yet this does not explain Darling's want of common courtesy in failing to seek the Chief Justice's approval. Petty power-mongering and obstinacy probably partly account for his actions, nevertheless considering the political environment and his choice of appointee, it seems likely that Darling had an underlying political agenda.

Although John had only recently arrived in the colony, he belonged to a liberal-minded family who were colluding with Darling's enemies. To Darling these men included the Chief Justice himself. Indeed, Darling remarked snidely that Forbes was unlikely to have a personal objection to John's appointment considering his intimacy with the Stephen family. So why would Governor Darling go to such lengths for a member of the opposition? The only logical answer is that Darling saw John as a friend rather than a foe, and believed his actions would induce feelings of obligation and support. As a military strategist, Governor Darling possibly also saw John as his means of penetrating the enemy camp or, in classic military style, of dividing and conquering.

Yet considering John's family background, it seems surprising that Governor Darling would believe him to be a friend. No doubt the answer lay in John's ability to present the image that best suited his own purposes. But as Darling would soon learn to his peril, instead of nurturing an ally, he had embraced a viper.

Chapter 11
AN UNWILLING ADVERSARY

The evil that men do lives after them;
The good is oft interred with their bones.
William Shakespeare, *Julius Caesar*

Tempestuous weather greeted General Ralph Darling as he sailed into Sydney Harbour on the evening of 17 December 1825, a portent, many later claimed, of the political turbulence that would transpire. Was there an inevitability to it all? Did the combination of Governor Darling's personality and the colony's political circumstances mean that disharmony and, eventually, outright hostility would inexorably follow his appointment?

Flaws within Darling's personality and characteristics of his upbringing undoubtedly underpinned some of the political savagery that served as the backdrop to the Jane New affair. Born in 1772 into a middle-ranking military family, Darling travelled with his father's 45th Regiment to the West Indies in the mid-1780s where he remained for seventeen years, initially joining the regiment as a private and later as a commissioned officer. He possibly encountered members of the Stephen family during this period, as military officers socialised with the landed gentry and upper classes in these colonial outposts.

Rising swiftly through the ranks of commissioned officers, Darling served for some years in the office of the Army's Commander-in-Chief, the Duke of York, an able and efficient administrator from whom Darling learnt many useful skills. In the 1830s, when political turmoil degenerated into character assassination driven largely by members of the Stephen family, Darling faced unjust insinuations that his promotion had been pushed through by the notorious Mary Anne Clarke. A manipulative little minx, Mrs Clarke used her attractions to ensnare the Duke of York and her position as his confidante to assist those who wished to purchase military commissions or promotions, in return, naturally, for a nice little financial incentive.

With the Duke of York as his mentor, Darling in 1818 secured the position of Acting Governor of Mauritius. A small British possession strategically situated in the Indian Ocean off the east coast of Africa, Mauritius was similar in many ways to the West Indies with its white domination and black slavery. It was also to become John's temporary residence after the Jane New affair imploded.

During his years in Mauritius, Darling exhibited many of the personality traits and administrative attitudes that would later influence his relations with the New South Wales settlers and in particular the Stephen family. He proved efficient and hardworking as an administrator, and a man of honesty, integrity and loyalty. Yet these admirable characteristics were undermined by his intolerance of criticism and his malicious overreaction when perceiving himself slighted or his administration undermined, responses evident in his behaviour after the Turf Club affair. Darling also revealed innocence in his reactions to duplicitous behaviour and character tendencies, which left him vulnerable in his future dealings with John Stephen Jnr.

Despite these failings, Darling's administration was generally considered successful, placing him in line for a new appointment. With the Duke of York's assistance he succeeded to the governorship of New South Wales, a role he considered himself duly qualified to tackle.

After fifteen years of liberal administration under the 'prince of men', Major-General Lachlan Macquarie, and the sensible but somewhat absent Sir Thomas Brisbane, word had leaked to the criminals of Britain that transportation to 'Botany Bay' was a desirable career move. To reintroduce the concept of the New South Wales penal settlement as a place of horrific punishment, Lord Liverpool's government decided that a strict disciplinarian like General Ralph Darling should take over the reins. A conservative man steeped in the military traditions of duty and obedience, Darling also seemed capable of restraining the free spirits who yearned for liberty from the yoke of British rule. Yet those like the then Secretary of State for the Colonies who were more attuned to colonial nuances had their doubts. With great prescience, Earl Bathurst remarked that the new Governor would prove a 'troublesome man'.

While the principles underlying the administration of slave and convict colonies appeared similar, New South Wales in reality bore little resemblance to the two colonial outposts most familiar to Darling: the West Indies and Mauritius. Underlying many of the differences was one simple factor: colour. The social divide between black slaves and their white masters, and between free-born or freed slaves and their white equals was insurmountable at that time. Even black children born to white fathers were unable to cross the divide. The rigidity of these social classes produced, in simplistic terms, a social structure resembling that of a contemporary military hierarchy. Administering such a settlement called upon skills familiar to General Darling.

Although New South Wales also resembled a military hierarchy in the early days of European settlement, there was no such colour divide or its social equivalent. The Aboriginal population remained largely on the economic periphery, with the role of black slaves being filled by convict servants.

Over the years, however, the status quo quietly but insistently changed as more people became 'civilians'. Convicts served out their sentences or were pardoned. Free settlers arrived in increasing numbers. Military men completed their terms or cashed in their commissions, while civil officers retired or resigned. And, confirming Fibonacci's theory of the procreating rabbits, convicts, free people and unions between the two produced free children who produced more free children who were starting to produce a third generation of free-born Australians. By 1825, those who came comfortably within the purview of Governor Darling's pseudo-military hierarchy — that is, officials, members of the military, and serving convicts — had dropped to less than half of the total population.

In an ideal world, the social hierarchy of the civilian population should have fitted neatly under Darling's umbrella; however this motley bunch of individuals comprised different groups who were developing their own voices and agendas. With no inherited aristocracy, the niche at the top of the colonial social ladder was open to the aspiring middle class. Known as the 'exclusives', this section of the social strata included men like pastoral king John Macarthur, although his star was fading by the late 1820s. Similarly to Macarthur, many sprang from ordinary backgrounds but through good timing and an entrepreneurial spirit had scrabbled their way to the top. Naturally, they were unwilling to let emancipated convicts infiltrate their ranks, even though men like Sir Henry Browne Hayes, the first owner of Sydney's famous Vaucluse House, were their social superiors back in Britain. Some of the exclusives had been the architects of the Rum Rebellion of 1808, those who arrested the much-maligned Governor Bligh for attempting to thwart their wealth-creation and empire-building schemes. In so doing they had, of course, committed what was arguably a treasonable act although they did not consider their own behaviour corresponded to that of the 'common' criminals.

The exclusives had been subdued by Governor Macquarie, a man before his time in his welcoming attitude to emancipated convicts. Macquarie's opinion of the social elite was exemplified in his caustic remark that colonial society consisted of two classes: those who had been sent out here and those who ought to have been! The exclusives bided their time with the easygoing, cautiously liberal Governor Brisbane. And they found acceptance with the conservative Governor Darling, who had also dragged himself up the social ladder. Yet in aligning himself with the exclusives, Governor Darling unwittingly stoked the fire of political tension within the community, one largely dormant since the pre-Rum Rebellion days.

The exclusives' opposition were the 'emancipists', represented most ably and outspokenly by William Charles Wentworth. Despite having an affluent upbringing, Wentworth was doubly cursed by the convict stain: a convict mother and an almost-convicted self-banished adopted father, surgeon D'Arcy Wentworth. Barred by the exclusives from being considered a social equal, Wentworth decided to pursue a legal career in order to push for a free constitution for his country. After being called to the British bar, he returned to New South Wales in 1824, bringing with him fellow barrister and journalist Robert Wardell. The two men intended to agitate for political change — self-government, trial by jury, a free press — through the legal system and their newspaper, the *Australian*.

Wentworth and Wardell excelled in their chosen fields, with one biographer writing that Wentworth 'touched both journalism and the Bar with the fire of his brilliance'. While fire can illuminate the truth, it is also capable of obliterating anything that stands in its path. And it was not long before these two civil libertarians had assessed Darling's style of administration, had exposed his conservative, autocratic and inflexible ways, and had determined to destroy him by whatever means possible.

Darling soon incurred the unmitigated wrath of the liberal-minded community through his involvement in the tragic Sudds and Thompson affair. Convinced that a convict's lot was superior to that of a soldier, Privates Joseph Sudds and Patrick Thompson openly stole a bale of cloth from a Sydney shop, believing that they would be dismissed from the Army and sentenced to a short period of imprisonment before being released to live life as civilians. Instead they received the unexpectedly severe punishment of transportation to a penal settlement for seven years. Determined to make an even more public example of them, Governor Darling 'commuted' their sentence to working in chains on the public roads and adorned them with a particularly harsh set of irons. Five days later, on 27 November 1826, Joseph Sudds died.

In his haste to set an example, the autocratic Governor Darling had failed to take into consideration the simple matter of the law. In addition to being poorly served by his legal advisers, Darling's own legal knowledge was deficient. Indeed, Chief Justice Forbes once remarked that Darling had 'less knowledge of the laws of his country than any gentleman filling his high official station whom it was ever my fortune to meet'. Presumably Darling's nature, combined with his years of exposure to the military justice system, meant that he failed to comprehend the importance of following due process within the civil legal system.

Darling's intervention provided Wardell (reported by this time to be the sole editor of the *Australian*) with the ammunition he needed. A few days after Sudds' death, the *Australian* exposed the illegality of Sudds' and Thompson's original sentence — as first offenders the soldiers should not have been sentenced to transportation — and the inequity of commuting a lighter sentence to a more severe punishment. Over the following few months, the *Australian* and the *Monitor* attacked Governor Darling with increasing vehemence, accusing him of torture and murder, and criticising him for interceding in judicial matters. Darling dismissed their claims as mere legal niceties; however Wardell, a particularly skilled interpreter of the law, knew otherwise. When the Crown Law Officers learnt of Governor Darling's actions, they rebuked him and ordered him to free Patrick Thompson and return him to his regiment.

The Sudds and Thompson affair haunted Governor Darling for the following decade. The source of Darling's torment proved to be Captain Robert Robison of the Royal Veterans, who claimed, and continued to claim for a further nine years, that the irons used on Sudds and Thompson were considerably heavier than those exhibited at the hearing; that the Governor had instigated a cover-up. Captain Robison was the husband of Sibella Stephen, John Stephen Jnr's sister.

The high-profile nature of the Sudds and Thompson case divided Sydney into two political camps along the exclusive/emancipist line. From the initial bickering and sniping at each other, and the bucking at Darling's autocratic rule, the political environment quickly degenerated. Darling faced a situation he had no experience to handle. He was confronted by an insubordinate military. He was undermined by a dissenting judiciary and administrative officers. He was challenged by rebellious civilians who attacked him both politically and personally. And these civilians were the voices of the press so the community was immersed in the torrent of their opinions.

As the Governor, Darling saw himself as the King's defender. As a military man he saw life as a battlefield with the winner taking all. He had no wise counsel to suggest that he suspend his automatic response to such a difficult situation, the type of response that had backfired in Mauritius; no friend to advise a calm approach from a new angle. Lady Forbes, the wife of the Chief Justice, later wrote that Darling's most prudent course would have been one of dignified silence, trusting time to wipe out the memory of his unfortunate mistakes in his administration's early days:

> But such a course of conciliation never seemed to suggest itself to General Darling. Sooner than abate one jot of his authority in an attempt to propitiate public opinion, he seemed rather determined to crush any who dared oppose him, and to ruin all who ventured to question his authority. The newspapers were to be suppressed, and all government officials, who could not agree with his Excellency's high-handed and arbitrary actions, were to be at once dismissed.

As the worthies of Sydney showed their colours, the political tension increased to an unprecedented level. The Governor bitterly chafed at the judiciary, the liberals and conservatives snarled at each other, and the liberals declared war on the Governor. One participant in the Jane New scandal, Notary Public John Raine, later reported that by 1829, 'Party prejudice was so strong that even my own brother and myself were obliged to separate in the public streets, he being considered as attached to General Darling's policy, and myself inimical to it.'

Some of those opposed to Darling and his administration were drawn towards Wentworth, and intentionally or unwittingly became part of his political agenda. Sucked into the maelstrom was the soon-to-be notorious Jane New.

Part III:
INFATUATION

*From this point Jane New's case
became sensational, extraordinary
and potentially 'momentous'.*

Historical Records of Australia

Chapter 12
A MASTERFUL MANIPULATOR

The bee may be likened to deceit for it has honey
in its mouth and poison behind.
Leonardo da Vinci

The two protagonists in the Jane New affair first encountered each other
six months after John Stephen Jnr's contentious appointment, during a
quiet period when Governor Darling probably thought his troubles had
eased. John's version of their encounter was documented in a letter written
some months later:

In August 1828, I was performing the duties of the Superintendent of
Police, who was absent at Port Macquarie, when Mrs New was brought
before me on a charge of shoplifting. She had a few days before been
charged with a similar offence before a Bench of Magistrates and
discharged for want of the slightest evidence. Whilst the investigation
was proceeding, a party specially employed were parading the streets to
obtain other charges, and they contrived to procure two others to be
preferred, which were equally without foundation, from which Mrs New
was accordingly acquitted. The case, which was submitted before me and
two other Magistrates, was a felony said to have been done in December
preceding. The evidence adduced was so extraordinary and contradictory

that had the woman not pressed her committal for trial upon us, being conscious of her own innocence, I doubt not she would have been set at liberty by the Bench. The depositions were submitted to the Crown Officers, who immediately bailed her (although a prisoner) before a Judge of the Supreme Court.

Eloquent; emotive; but erroneous. In a letter to the Secretary of State, Governor Darling later observed with great diplomacy that John's zeal in Jane New's cause had led him into a series of 'misrepresentations'. Darling drew attention to John's many fabrications, including the Bench's decision to extend Jane's sentence after they found her guilty of the charges John had mentioned. Darling also disclosed that John had never performed the duties of Superintendent of Police.

Like James New, John lied to serve his own ends. Indeed, so pervasive would John's lies prove — they were even evident in situations where they served little purpose and where the truth would have proved more beneficial — that it raises serious questions about his fundamental values. He was undoubtedly the black sheep of his illustrious family.

John's involvement in Jane's affairs began shortly after her conviction on the three shoplifting charges. Although the court extended Jane's original seven-year sentence by a year, she was not despatched to the Female Factory at Parramatta, the usual place of incarceration for females found guilty of committing minor infringements. Instead she was allowed to return to her indulgent husband. Jane's sentence generated no hardship whatsoever and she continued to live the life of a free woman with a besotted husband pandering to her every whim.

Madame Rens was outraged by the leniency afforded to Jane. Intending to add her charges to the three counts Jane already faced, she found herself thwarted. In a letter written in her native language, Madame Rens protested to the Superintendent of Police, Lieutenant-Colonel Morisset:

I would not wish to quarrel with the Police of Sydney, but I wish to be permitted to complain of this sentence. The respectable woman named New had robbed three shops in one evening but three robberies being too much for the safety of so interesting a thief, she was obliged to be taken to the Police. I was told to be there at 10 o'clock, to identify the person who had robbed me at three different times — but as I had strong complaints to make against her a man came at the moment I was preparing to go to the Police Office to desire me not to appear there until the next day. Thus have I been deceived and the partiality with which this woman has been judged is most scandalous; she is left at liberty to follow her old trade. This woman is at the head of several men and women; she enters a shop, asks you for some article, at the same time another comes in and asks for something else and it is thus the woman New carries on her trade.

Madame Rens' sarcastic reference to Jane's respectability and her assertion that Jane was involved with a gang of shoplifters serves as an interesting counterpoint to John's avowals of her innocence. Madame Rens' allusion to Jane's special treatment, and her reference to the ploy that prevented her from laying her own charges, is also the first documented evidence that a conspiracy to protect Jane was in operation, and a scandal brewing.

At long last the authorities took action. Madame Rens later credited Colonel Morisset as the man responsible for pursuing her claims, although he was perhaps a reluctant supporter. Having failed to lay charges against Jane despite strong evidence linking her to the crime, and later choosing to ignore an express command from the Governor to apprehend and incarcerate her, Morisset appears to have been one of the men conspiring to protect her from the consequences of her crimes.

Madame Rens later described the evidence linking Jane New to the theft:

I saw a lady passing my shop with a silk dress upon her. I later found out she was Mrs Tomkins. I asked her where she got the silk her gown was made of, as it was stolen from me. She answered she bought it in barter off a man named McCann and sent him to me. The man McCann told me when I saw him that Jane New had sold the silk to him.

On 23 August 1828 Jane appeared before John Stephen Jnr and the other two members of the Bench of Magistrates on Madame Rens' shoplifting charge. Madame Rens provided her evidence and the Bench concluded that there were reasonable grounds for a conviction. They bound her over to the Criminal Court for trial and in the meantime incarcerated her in Sydney Gaol. Yet Jane remained in prison only a short time, being approved for release on bail five days later. An irate Madame Rens complained to 'The Magistrate':

> I have been to the Police for four days. On the fourth my case was pleaded. I say pleaded because it pleased the lawyer to treat this case as a sniggering affair, this being a humiliating application to see me judged with this woman. The lawyer was more driven by money than glory and he pardoned her. He wanted me to ask that my plea be withdrawn to avoid the consequence that this woman would be hanged. I found this step on his part to be uncalled for and I decided that if this were the case there would not be enough order in Sydney. I gave the oath; I gave evidence that theft be known. To the men present I asked what else could I do. She used the excuse that her husband was not there. God be pleased that he turn up but she is separated from him for some time. This woman is now free.

Under the law, the theft from a dwelling house of goods worth more than £5 was a capital offence so Jane could face the gallows if found guilty of stealing Madame Rens' fabric. No wonder Jane's supporters, who, Madame Rens indignantly reported, included her own counsel, were endeavouring to deflect the prosecution.

Not only did Madame Rens activate the justice system at this time, her letter sparked the Governor's interest. His request for further information elicited from Attorney-General Baxter the news that Sidney Stephen had petitioned for bail upon the grounds that Jane New's husband, a material witness for the defence, was in Tasmania and that Justice Dowling had approved the petition. Baxter added:

> I am not aware that Mr Justice Dowling was apprised of the fact that Jane New was suffering under another sentence passed by an inferior tribunal. At any rate his Honour could not have taken judicial notice of it and he

merely availed himself of the discretionary power vested in him *virtute officie* to admit to bail.

Baxter's opinion, that the law would have prevented Justice Dowling from taking Jane's previous conviction into consideration when granting bail, was inaccurate. In fact, Baxter was renowned for his poor legal skills. Two months after he commenced his duties as Attorney-General, Governor Darling complained that Baxter 'had never before had a brief in his life, was totally inexperienced as a lawyer and was incapable of addressing either court or jury'. Baxter's skills failed to improve and within the following few years alcoholism joined incompetence Yet in typical bureaucratic fashion the promotions continued. Early in 1831 Governor Arthur took a stand, declaring that Baxter was 'such an habitual sot that it would have been a violation of all public decency to have suffered him to take his recently appointed seat on the Tasmanian Bench'.

Not only was Attorney-General Baxter's opinion in this matter inaccurate, his incompetence was later seen in the charges he laid against Jane. As it transpired, Baxter's ineptitude contributed to the ensuing drama.

Meanwhile, Governor Darling found it both surprising and unacceptable that Judge Dowling had not been informed of Jane's recent colonial conviction, allowing her to be granted bail. He overrode Jane's bail approval, decreeing that she was a prisoner of the Crown at large and that Police Superintendent Morisset must apprehend her and send her to the Factory. Both the Governor and Colonial Secretary McLeay believed that the order was implemented at this time, and reacted with astonishment and concern upon later hearing of Jane's continued freedom and the delays in bringing her to justice. They despatched further requests for enlightenment:

Although the Prosecutrix Madame Rens used every exertion in her power to have the matter brought forward, these were defeated seemingly by some secret intervention and an extraordinary delay took place in bringing Jane New to trial. His Excellency however trusts that satisfactory proof will be furnished that no branch of the Government has been wanting in giving effect to the executions of the Prosecutrix.

Attorney-General Baxter responded by explaining that Jane's case had been moved to the next Criminal Sessions because of her husband's absence and because he regularly disposed of country cases at the commencement of each criminal session to reduce the inconvenience and expense to country witnesses. Postponing Sydney cases to the end of the session caused little inconvenience to those out on bail, he claimed, and although Jane New was reportedly in constant attendance for three weeks, the pressure of business meant that he could not comply with her request to bring on her trial. He added:

> During the proceedings no application was ever made to me or to the Court on the part of Madame Rens, nor had I the slightest idea that the delay which I have narrated, could have been conceived by any one to be the result of any 'secret intervention'; of the existence of such, I am entirely ignorant.

Baxter's letter omitted any reference to the eight-month delay between crime and committal.

While Baxter's response was both courteous and detailed, Police Superintendent Morisset's response was curt and brief. Although mentioning that Jane had been committed for trial in August 1828, Morisset refrained from revealing that she had been granted bail a few days later, that Governor Darling had revoked her bail and ordered him to send her to the Female Factory, and that he had not acted upon his orders. It is possible that Morisset's failure to follow orders was the result of an unfortunate mix-up, and his inadequate explanation an attempted cover-up. Yet such an astonishing degree of leniency had been granted Jane New throughout this criminal process that McLeay's reference to a secret intervention would appear to have merit.

Governor Darling evidently continued to doubt the proffered explanations as he later reported to the British authorities: 'From some extraordinary interposition, whenever an attempt was made to bring on the trial, it was defeated, and did not take place until twelve months after the robbery. Jane New had been bailed and was at large during the whole of this period.'

Although Jane was bound over to the Criminal Court in August 1828, another four and a half months passed before her case came to trial. Madame Rens was incensed. 'I don't know the reason why the prisoner has not been brought to trial before,' she fumed to the court. 'I am astonished myself and I think I have been used very ill.'

John Stephen Jnr as Registrar of the Supreme Court was probably able to influence case scheduling. He would have been well aware that a simple strategy for improving a defendant's odds was delay! delay! delay! In a society where life spans were short and deadly diseases rife, an accident or an infection could extinguish a witness' testimony forever. Jane's case was delayed to the very last minute: the last case tried at the seven-week long Criminal Sessions.

On 3 January 1829, Attorney-General Baxter signed the 'information', or formal accusation, in *The King vs Jane New*. It announced that:

> Jane the wife of James New of Sydney, Victualler, on the 18th December 1827 with force and arms at Sydney, then and there feloniously did steal, take and carry away twenty-eight yards of silk at the value of £5 of the goods and chattels of Josephine Rens, Widow, in the dwelling house of the said Josephine Rens, against the form of the statute in such case — made and provided against the peace of our Lord the King, his Crown and dignity.

With 'force and arms'? A curious incongruity. Shoplifting by its very essence could never involve force and arms. Shoplifters and pickpockets were magicians, masters in the art of the sleight-of-hand. There was a simple explanation: a legal formality on a pre-printed form, the terminology having its origin some centuries earlier.

On the evening before Baxter signed Jane's formal accusation, a curious incident occurred. Jane was standing at her door when a man approached her. 'Would you step over to the opposite side of the street?' he asked. 'I have something most material to mention on the subject of your trial which is to be brought on tomorrow.'

Jane complied and he whispered to her: 'In the event of your being found guilty you will be transported to Moreton Bay. I have a great many notes which might be useful to you there as you might sell them to persons who would be returning by the same vessel that will take you there. As your husband has plenty of money, you might request him to give you what you please. I am determined I will do the damned Bank and make them pay their notes which they could not refuse when brought from Moreton Bay. In the event of your being convicted you will hear more. I will see you in gaol or going down, and put you up to receiving as many notes as you choose to buy.'

Jane had just received a visit from one of the infamous Bank of Australia robbers. On Sunday 14 September 1828, these men stole over £13 000 in coins and notes from the Bank of Australia, having, over the previous few weekends, tunnelled into the premises. A newspaper article a century later described it as a singularly audacious enterprise, adding that criminal exploits had to be uncommonly daring to excite much astonishment in a community populated by convicts, and that although a huge sum had been stolen, the robbery became memorable more because of the thieves' amazingly bold plan.

To foil the robbers, the Bank's directors had organised to recall and exchange their notes, however those who wished to take advantage of this programme, and possessed more than the odd note, had to describe how and when each note came into their possession. There was a catch: the Bank directors had numbers for some of the stolen notes and also knew when their notes were printed and circulated, making it easier to trip up those who were lying. As the robbers would be unable to adequately account for their possession, they had no means of readily disposing of their booty.

Jane's visitor had just offered her a money-laundering proposition. He wished her to purchase notes at a discounted price and, when she arrived at Moreton Bay, to sell them to time-expired convicts who were waiting to board the vessel on its return journey to Sydney. It was a clever strategy.

The authorities would recognise — or so the robbers believed — that these convicts could not have participated in the robbery or acted as receivers, and would exchange the prisoners' notes without going through the rigmarole of making them account for their possession.

To have chosen Jane as an accomplice indicates that the criminal fraternity considered her one of their own and not a redeemed character, that they believed she would look favourably on such a business opportunity and would not inform on them, and that her husband was wealthy enough to purchase a considerable number of notes at a discounted price.

But they had picked the wrong woman. Or was it merely the wrong moment?

On the morning of 3 January 1829, Jane approached John Stephen Jnr. 'I have something particular to communicate to you as a magistrate,' she informed him. 'I have been anxious to speak to my counsel, Mr Sidney Stephen, about the matter but not being able to find him I thought it best to mention the matter at once.' And she recounted the events of the previous evening, adding a description of the man who accosted her.

'As nothing can come of this information except in case of a conviction,' John counselled, 'I advise you to be silent to everyone on the subject.' Jane followed his advice and they waited to see what would transpire.

Chapter 13
THE TRIAL

*If I have been bad, your Honour, what has been
done to make me better?*

Convict's defence

Jane's case eventually came to trial at Sydney's Supreme Court on 5 January
1829, in a courtroom heavy with expectation. Court proceedings were the
ultimate public theatre for the masses in colonial Sydney, full of drama,
intrigue and heartache. Crowding in to view the spectacle, the audience
would ogle the participants, listen with mouths agape to the testimonies,
rock with mirth at the melodrama, and nod or shudder as the verdict was
handed down.

Madame Rens employed Thomas Deane Rowe, one of the colourful
performers of Sydney's early courtroom stage, as her barrister. Although
Rowe had arrived some years earlier bearing testimonies to a respectable
character and connections, his rascally behaviour thereafter suggests that
he was one of those rogues and vagabonds regularly shunted towards
the colonies. He was frequently reported for professional misconduct,
eventually being struck off the rolls some years after the Jane New hearing.
Rowe mainly practised criminal law and his clients were primarily from the
lower orders. As a courtroom practitioner, he was fearless, grandiloquent,
and had a mischievous and sometimes malicious sense of humour. He

worked hard for his clients and, according to Attorney-General Baxter, conducted Madame Rens' case with great zeal and ability.

After Judge James Dowling banged his gavel and called the court to order, the clerk read the charges against Jane New. Madame Rens was the first to take the stand. Facing a sea of British faces and surrounded by a cacophony of gibberish, she must have felt intimidated. But she was a strong woman. While the town was awash with convict women who had been propelled to the colony, convict wives ushered out by the government, and the wives and daughters of officials, military men and settlers who had travelled under or towards the umbrella of male-protection, Madame Rens was in a category of her own. She had resolved to leave her homeland and travel halfway around the world without male protection or the expectation of receiving any. She was solely responsible for the safety of her young daughter during the long and dangerous voyage. She had exchanged her homeland for one governed by her native country's enemy and populated by speakers of their alien language, one she did not herself understand. And she had done so with the intention of establishing her own business. Madame Rens was not a woman to be beaten by some young whippersnapper, particularly one who was fawned over by the males of Sydney. She was angry and she wanted justice.

As Madame Rens prepared to testify, an interpreter attended her. She had rejected the court's interpreter and chosen to use a friend, emancipated convict and publican Francis Jean Girard. 'I was a housekeeper in the latter end of December 1827 . . .' And Madame Rens proceeded to provide her account of Jane's theft of the silk fabric from her shop.[21]

After describing the crime, Madame Rens detailed her efforts to have Jane New charged and brought to trial. She described her unsuccessful and humiliating visit to the police office, her attempt to elicit Jane's identity from George Bunn, her recognition of the stolen fabric in passer-by Emma Tomkins' dress, Jane's return to her shop to exchange the damaged gown, and her abusive language when Madame Rens refused to oblige her.

After completing her testimony, Madame Rens examined the silk from Emma Tomkins' gown and the pattern of the fabric she had left with the police. 'This is part of the piece of silk taken by the prisoner,' she declared.

Finally, she responded to questions posed by Jane New's counsel as well as those from the judge and jury in their attempts to clarify her statement. Eventually she was allowed to step down.

The testimonies of Constable Francis Fieudard and office-keeper William Cooke followed. Cooke testified to the chain of evidence, namely that the silk exhibited to the court was that owned by Emma Tomkins and held at the police office. Mrs Tomkins was then called and called, however she failed to respond. John alluded to her non-appearance in later correspondence:

> In January 1829, Mrs New pressed on with her trial, notwithstanding the absence of a most important witness. The prosecutrix employed her own counsel to conduct the case, and at his earnest request the cause was suspended for nearly two hours to enable fresh evidence to be adduced after all the witnesses for the prosecution, whose names were endorsed in the information, had been examined.

It was another mendacious statement. Jane New did not press on with her trial; it was forced upon her. The missing witness was not a defence witness, as John's letter implied, but played a key role for the prosecution and had been subpoenaed to appear. The case was not suspended so that the prosecutors could find fresh evidence after the appearance of all the witnesses. Indeed, Emma Tomkins' non-appearance threatened the prosecution's case and the adjournment was presumably granted to allow the prosecutors to locate her. When their attempts failed, the prosecution called Madame Rens' daughter Jeanette who had not been listed as a witness in the original information.

Prior to Jeanette Rens' appearance, however, John McCann testified. 'I know the prisoner Jane New,' he declared. 'I sell goods in the market. I purchased ten yards of silk from the prisoner who lives on the Rocks. She kept a public shop and public house there. I bought it openly in the shop. A man named Lincoln was present and bought some other articles. I believe it is six or seven months ago. It was a kind of a plum-coloured brownish-figured silk. I sold it to Mrs Tomkins, and it was on her the silk was challenged. This is exactly similar to what I sold to Mrs Tomkins. I believe it to be the same silk from its being the same colour and pattern. It is like French silk.'

McCann added that he had purchased the fabric from Jane New for around three shillings and six pence a yard and sold it the following day at a loss due to its damaged condition. Under cross-examination he admitted that he had asked five shillings per yard for the fabric, a considerable sum for supposedly damaged goods.

Jeanette Rens served as the final witness for the prosecution. She confirmed her mother's testimony by describing her own memory of the shoplifting, the discovery of Jane New's identity, and Jane's reappearance in the shop a few months later. However, her importance lay in her recollection of the day Emma Tomkins passed the shop.

'I never saw any such silk in the colony,' Jeanette Rens began, 'either before or since except what I saw on the person of a lady passing the shop about six months after the robbery. I sent a little boy after the lady. She came back. I knew her to be Mrs Tomkins, having seen her before at the shop. I stopped her to ask where she got the silk from which her gown was made. I took hold of the gown. This is the gown I saw on Mrs Tomkins. I will swear to it being the same.'

Jeanette Rens could readily identify the fabric having previously owned a dress of the same material, according to her testimony, although her dress had reportedly been stolen in a burglary. Although no longer possessing a fabric sample, both mother and daughter testified that the stolen silk was French and was unusual in pattern and colour. Indeed Madame Rens claimed that the fabric's distinctive qualities had motivated her to lodge her complaint with the police.

The prosecution rested after Jeanette Rens left the stand, and the defence's case began. Jane had again employed John's brother, Sidney Stephen, as her barrister. Sidney called Cambridge Street resident John Wilson, a watchmaker by trade and a former Tasmanian inhabitant. Some fifteen or sixteen months previously — that is, prior to the date of the shoplifting — Wilson reported having seen Jane selling silk in Hobart, at the Spread Eagle in Argyle Street where the News were residing as tenants.

'I saw the prisoner there,' John Wilson testified. 'I saw a great many different kinds of silk in her possession. I don't know whether the prisoner was in the habit of selling silk. I saw some chocolate-coloured silk Mrs Hobsole bought from Mrs New and made up into a gown. I saw her wear the gown. She bought only eight yards from Mrs New. There were about twenty yards. I did not then examine it; but I did afterwards. It had a kind of a sprig or a flower on it. It is a kind of sprig — not a rose. There was a bit of a leaf beside the flower. I can't say whether it was a shamrock, rose or lily. I could swear to the same pattern if I could see it.'

Under cross-examination, Wilson disclosed that he was an emancipated convict currently working as a house servant. This was a pertinent revelation as by virtue of his background he could not be considered a witness of unimpeachable integrity. In truth, doubts about his honesty must have soon arisen. After initially informing the prosecutor that he 'never spoke to Mrs New or her husband', Wilson revealed, 'Mrs New told me she wanted me to swear to the silk that Mrs Hobsole bought.' When reminded that he had never spoken to the News, he attempted to downplay his admission. 'She never spoke about the colour,' he protested slyly. 'I was never told by anybody the colour of the silk Mrs Rens swore to.'

Wilson was adamant that he would recognise the fabric if he saw it, so the court handed it to him to examine. 'This is just the same pattern,' he exulted. But what about the leaf pattern, the court asked? 'There is no leaf on it,' he admitted. Evidently considering his own contradiction unimportant, he continued, 'This is just the same pattern upon my oath.' His duty done, John Wilson proudly exited the stand. He had needed little assistance in demolishing his own credibility.

The defence called Merchant George Bunn as their next witness, his role to provide expert testimony. 'I am a merchant of Sydney and have had very large quantities of silk consigned to me,' he boasted to the court. 'I have imported for Ingleby Jones & Co. London, silks made up in pelisses and dresses to the amount of £2000 in three years.' Asked to examine the silk, he responded dismissively, 'It is a flimsy silk with nothing uncommon in the pattern.'

But Bunn proved to be an unobservant expert witness. Under cross-examination he admitted: 'I have never examined the silks so as to know the patterns. I can't say whether the patterns of silk I have spoken of, or those of the ladies passing were the same as those now produced. I do not know the difference between English and French silk.'

Not only did George Bunn fail to provide a convincing testimony for the defence, he proved useful for the prosecution. During cross-examination Bunn revealed that he was the man Madame Rens had appealed to for assistance in identifying Jane New, thereby corroborating her testimony. His final response — 'I have always considered Jane New an honest woman' — proved a pitiful end to a weak testimony.

Two more expert witnesses were called, both merchants and silk importers who claimed impartiality. George Thomas Savage testified, 'I never spoke to the prisoner before today.' Edward Aspinall announced, 'I heard of the case at the police office.' Both attested to their familiarity with silk although under cross-examination Savage admitted, 'I think I would know French from English,' while Aspinall confessed, 'I don't know the difference.'

Savage's testimony was intended to reveal that in May 1827 he had imported silk from Mauritius of the same quality and colour as the fabric in question. Being slightly damaged through spotting, some of Savage's fabric had been used for furniture-making and the rest sold to a customer. Yet the value of Savage's testimony was diminished by his admission on three separate occasions, 'I can't swear as to the pattern.'

Aspinall testified to the popularity of the silk in question. 'I am acquainted with silks and have imported large quantities. I have seen silks of the same description as this. I call it a very common pattern. It is a sort of sprig which is a very common pattern. I saw some silk at the police office but I can't swear this is the same. There is nothing uncommon in the colour, quality, and pattern.' Yet Aspinall then admitted, 'I don't think I ever saw any other silk of this kind in the colony.'

Not only were these men sorry excuses for expert witnesses, they were — unbeknown to the court — not at all impartial. Two days later, the men were among a group of Sydney worthies who eagerly added their names to Jane's plea to Governor Darling for assistance.

Aspinall was followed by attorney Frederick Dawes, who served as a character witness. 'I have been residing at the Derwent [Hobart district] for some few years,' he testified. 'I know the prisoner perfectly well. I knew her first about two or three years ago at the Derwent. She worked for my wife. She has borne the character of an honest woman as I have been told.'

Dawes' words intimated that Jane had worked for his wife as a servant. Later, however, he admitted that his wife had merely employed her as a dressmaker: 'She brought back the remnants of goods delivered to her to make by my wife.' In all likelihood, the full extent of Dawes' involvement with Jane New was minimal. He had presumably heard about her from his wife and other acquaintances and had afterwards seen or spoken to her when she returned the goods to his wife. To be willing to serve as a character witness under these circumstances seems surprising.

The sixth and final witness for the defence was Lydia Farley who testified that Jane and her husband had lodged with her in Cumberland Street for nearly a week after their arrival in Sydney fifteen months previously. 'I saw some silks of different patterns in Mrs New's trunk,' Mrs Farley recollected. 'I can't say whether I should know any of them. There were some of different patterns. A handsome peach blossom, black silk. There were so many I can't speak positively to any particular one. I saw some silk something like this but I can't swear to it. It was just like that but it seems to be faded. It had just the same sprig as near as I can guess. It was new silk. She offered it to me for sale. It is brighter when new than when worn.'

Obvious disparities are evident in Mrs Farley's testimony. Although the defence counsel's questions were not noted in the transcript, her responses suggest that she was being led towards a more positive identification. Yet the probability that Mrs Farley would be able to positively identify a fabric seen so long ago and under such circumstances is slight indeed.

With the completion of Mrs Farley's testimony, the defence rested their case. Although Mrs Tomkins' absence meant that the prosecution was unable to introduce her testimony, the case against Jane remained damning. In contrast, the defence's argument was pitiful.

The jury took little time to reach a verdict. Guilty.

Chapter 14
GUILTY OR INNOCENT?

An infamous perjury convicted this most unfortunate female.
John Stephen Jnr

Was Jane New guilty? Her counsel, Sidney Stephen, initially thought so. A week after her conviction, he wrote to Judge Dowling:

> I feel no hesitation in admitting that I considered at the time of the trial that Jane New had been justly convicted of the act charged upon her though there were some few incongruities which I noticed in Madame Rens' evidence. At the time I was also impressed with the same idea that I saw impressed Your Honour's mind, that Mrs Tomkins had been kept away by Jane New's means.

Yet since the trial, Sidney explained, he had learnt that Mrs Tomkins was a respectable woman and that her failure to attend court was not by anyone's contrivance but through ill health and confusion. She had attended court on the scheduled day, had taken ill as a result of the inclement weather, and had thought she would receive due notice when the hearing was rescheduled. Sidney believed that her evidence would have favoured Jane and asked if he could submit details for Judge Dowling to transmit to the Governor. He concluded virtuously:

In all cases of professional duty I cannot but admit that I feel anxious to succeed in the cause I undertake yet I submit to a failure with resignation in the consciousness that I have done my duty. But where I ultimately discover that I am defeated by a case made at the trial which I was not prepared to meet, I then feel myself imperatively called upon to adopt measures that may benefit my client.

Having received Dowling's permission, Sidney prepared a nine-page letter summarising eighteen documents supporting his claim that Jane was innocent of Madame Rens' crime. Some of these documents refuted evidence presented at the trial; the remainder provided the groundwork for a new theory accounting for Jane's possession of the fabric. Was Sidney attempting to obstruct the course of justice, as some of his contemporaries smirked, or had he discovered the truth?

Sidney began by expressing concerns about Madame Rens' testimony at the trial: the obvious incongruities in time-frame estimates, the doubtful translations and the evidence of perjury. French-speaking barrister, William Henry Kerr, served as the source for his claim that Madame Rens' friend Francis Jean Girard had misled the court by misinterpreting the questions posed to her and the answers she provided. 'Girard seldom gave the whole meaning to the answers of Madame Rens,' Kerr reported, 'and whenever the prosecutrix's answer appeared favourable to Jane New he would argue the point with Madame Rens and elicit a different reply.' Yet Kerr said nothing at the time. 'Supposing the judge, counsel and jury to be equally well versed as myself in the French language,' Kerr said in explanation for his reticence, 'I did not presume to intrude myself on the Court.' It seems an extraordinarily ignorant and indifferent response. If the judge, counsel and jury had indeed understood French, why would an interpreter be required?

Sidney also reported that Madame Rens had stated at the committal hearing that her daughter was absent at the time of the robbery. Yet at the trial both mother and daughter swore that Jeanette was present, even though some of Madame Rens' testimony intimated that she was alone. If Jeanette Rens was not present, her testimony could not have come from personal knowledge and should not have carried so much weight in the trial, Sidney argued.

He continued by questioning whether Madame Rens had truly seen the stolen silk in the basket on Jane New's arm, that from such a distance — 130 paces according to one affidavit — it was impossible to distinguish colour. In truth, it does seem unlikely that such a seasoned shoplifter would have left the fabric visible in her basket, yet a 28-yard piece of fabric would have been bulky, creating problems purloining and secreting it.[22]

Sidney Stephen's greatest concern, however, was the accuracy of Madame Rens' testimony regarding the time frame between her report of the crime and her identification of Jane New as the thief. Madame Rens stated that she discovered Jane's identity soon after the crime and before Emma Tomkins passed her shop. Yet Sidney believed that Madame Rens decided to finger Jane as the culprit long after the fabric had been traced back to her.

To support his claim, Sidney offered three affidavits. First, Emma Tomkins' affidavit, in which she mentioned purchasing the considerably mildew-damaged fabric from John McCann for four shillings per yard around the 20th of December 1827, being accosted by Madame Rens when she passed her shop in February 1828, and sending McCann to her around the 24th. Mrs Tomkins concluded her affidavit by stating:

> From the manner of Madame Rens on perceiving the silk dress, I thought she might have suspected me of having taken it. But Madame Rens certainly did not seem to know on whom to cast suspicion and requested me to send McCann to tell her from whom he obtained the silk.

Second, Sidney presented John Stephen Jnr's affidavit in which John stated that, at the committal hearing, Madame Rens said that she first saw the silk again on 1 August 1828, six months after Emma Tomkins claimed that Madame Rens approached her. And Madame Rens reportedly said that she became acquainted with all the particulars two weeks later, enabling her to trace the fabric into Jane New's hands. Third, Sidney referred to George Bunn's affidavit which confirmed Madame Rens' conversation with George Bunn regarding Jane's identity, but revealed that the conversation itself could not have occurred until the middle of the year as Bunn had broken his leg and was unable to walk prior to the end of April.

These three affidavits, Sidney declared, clearly revealed that Jane had not committed the crime, that Madame Rens had not identified her as the thief at the time, and that she had only done so after the fabric was traced back to Jane. Madame Rens' motivation in charging Jane had nothing to do with the crime itself, Sidney concluded. It had a different origin: malice.

This led to Sidney's new explanation for the altercation between the two women. Madame Rens did not order Jane to leave her shop because she was a thief, but because Jane had abused her for unfairly refusing to change the dress — 'a bad article passed off to a gentleman who knew nothing of silks'. 'Animus,' proclaimed Sidney, had influenced the prosecution. Or in John Stephen Jnr's surprisingly milder words: 'From what I have been able to collect since the trial, I have little doubt but there has been a little jealousy and bad feeling on the part of the prosecution and that as Madame Rens was repeatedly in the habit of talking with her customers about the business in the presence of her daughter, the girl imagined the whole transaction.'

While powerful, Sidney's argument contained some serious flaws. He presented Bunn's broken leg as a critical link in refuting Madame Rens' claim that she discovered Jane New's identity shortly after the theft. Yet as it turned out, the reference to Bunn's injury had been added to Bunn's affidavit after he had signed and John had witnessed it. The affidavit was recorded in John's handwriting and had John's initials attached. Bunn — literate and himself a Justice of the Peace — would have known to sign or initial any additional information. It seems unlikely that he knew of John's little contribution.

And John's reference to Madame Rens' statement at the committal hearing that Mrs Tomkins passed her shop dressed in the silk gown on I August? If this was true, why did the other committing magistrate ignore the subject in his own affidavit? As John was responsible for gathering these affidavits, it seems astonishing that he would allow the magistrate to omit such an important piece of information.

After demolishing Madame Rens' claim that Jane stole the silk fabric, Sidney presented affidavits to support his trial argument, that Jane's possession of the silk was by honest means. Ellen Gravestocks swore to buying a chocolate-coloured and water-spotted 'Christmas' dress from Jane New in November 1827. She attached a fabric remnant to her deposition, and John noted on her affidavit that the silk matched Madame Rens' pattern. Another deponent, Mary Mackay, reported having frequently seen Ellen Gravestocks in that particular silk dress in November and December 1827.

These compelling affidavits were dated 9 January 1829. Why didn't Sidney call these witnesses at Jane's trial a mere four days previously? Mrs Gravestocks would have proved a more convincing witness than John Wilson and Lydia Farley who could only testify to having seen the fabric in passing fifteen months earlier.

To account for Jane's honest acquisition of the fabric, Sidney Stephen presented a new defence. French silk was universally made in 56-yard lengths, he reported, and Madame Rens had mentioned having either lost or disposed of the other 28 yards. In truth, he claimed, the remaining length had been stolen by Madame Rens' servant, a man named Kelly, who sent the fabric to a relative in Hobart, another Kelly, who sold it to the News prior to their departure in September 1827.

To support his claim, Sidney referred to James New's deposition and attached subpoena. Dated a couple of days after James' return from Tasmania in September 1828, the subpoena ordered 'Kelly' of Liverpool Street, Hobart, to appear at the Supreme Court on 17 November 1828 to testify in Jane's defence. But 'Kelly' could not be found and the letter and subpoena arrived back in Sydney eleven days after Jane's trial.

Sidney then flourished the affidavit of Bank of Australia manager, Thomas Macvitie:

Madame Rens one day waited on me for the purpose of giving some information respecting the robbery at the Bank [on 14 September 1828]. In the conversation she stated that having lost some silk from her shop, she suspected a man living on the Rocks named Kelly (I think she stated Kelly had been her servant) of having stolen the same by means of false keys. She had seen soon after the robbery a female pass the door with some of the property so stolen on her person but Madame Rens did not say that she thought Mrs New the person who had actually stolen the property. Kelly was by her suspected of the Bank robbery and the badness of his character left no doubt of his guilt in her mind.

Yet Macvitie's statement seems surprising. After Madame Rens had managed to indict Jane New, why would she suggest a few weeks later to so upright a gentleman as the Bank of Australia manager that someone else was guilty of the crime? Perhaps in his recollection of a conversation carried out some months earlier in a different language, Macvitie had confused Madame Rens' remarks. A man named Kelly had indeed been convicted in October 1828 of receiving property — some 'trifling articles of wearing apparel' — stolen from Madame Rens' premises in September. Perhaps Madame Rens was muttering about the numerous thefts from her premises and Macvitie mixed up the incidents.

Finally, Sidney referred to Emma Tomkins' claim that Madame Rens had not known who to blame for the theft and had actually thought that Mrs Tomkins might have been the thief.

Sidney summarised his new defence:

The trial was postponed in September 1828 to enable the husband to procure a witness named Kelly. It was known therefore to Jane New whence this silk was obtained and a subpoena immediately issued to procure Kelly's attendance. The subpoena's date and details show when it was obtained. The letter returned has the postmark on it. This could not have been fabricated to meet Mr Macvitie's affidavit. His station in society will not allow the imputation that he has sworn other than the truth, that Madame Rens suspects Kelly of stealing the silk and that this Kelly has a brother at the Derwent who sold the silk to Jane New's husband at the Derwent.

So why didn't Sidney call James New and Thomas Macvitie as defence witnesses?

Sidney attempted to pre-empt such an argument by claiming that he had only learnt of the Kelly defence and Macvitie's information after the trial. Yet the evidence suggests that Sidney was lying. He had been Jane's counsel in August 1828 when James New was in Tasmania. He had presented the affidavit asking for Jane to be admitted to bail on the grounds that her absent husband was a material witness for the defence. He was claiming in his letter that James' importance for the defence lay in his ability to identify Kelly as the source of the fabric purchase. And, as Jane's counsel in August 1828, he therefore must have been involved in the decision to subpoena Kelly and the preparation of the subpoena.

Sidney attempted to justify his ignorance by stating: 'Jane always seemed careless about the trial and never entered into any particulars, always laughing at the idea of being tried for this charge.' Such a statement seems ludicrous. As if an innocent woman charged with a hanging offence would not have vehemently and indignantly justified her innocence when discussing the case with her barrister.

They were all lying: Jane and James New, Madame Rens and her daughter, the defence witnesses, John Stephen Jnr and even Sidney Stephen.

So was Jane guilty? At her trial, the case presented by the prosecution was so persuasive and the defence's case so unconvincing that her conviction was justified. But was she the thief? Perhaps the Stephen brothers were not attempting to obstruct the course of justice. Perhaps Madame Rens had accused Jane of this particular crime because the distinctive fabric had been traced back to Jane and because this charge could serve as retribution for other thefts she was unable to indict Jane for. Perhaps Madame Rens was capable of such vindictiveness that she could send Jane to a date with death for a crime she did not actually commit.

Yet Occam's Razor, which essentially argues that one must give preference to the theory covering all the known facts with the simplest explanation,[23] suggests that Jane was indeed Madame Rens' thief. She had previously received five convictions for theft, her method of operation and the type of goods stolen were the same, and she had been identified as the culprit. Could she have acquired the fabric honestly? Paradoxically, even if Jane had purchased the fabric from Kelly, it seems unlikely to have been an honest transaction. The Hobart member of the Kelly family, if such a person truly existed, was evidently a receiver, and strong argument could be made that in purchasing the fabric Jane too was guilty of knowingly receiving stolen goods. Perhaps Jane's legal team had been afraid to pursue the Kelly defence during her trial for fear that they might unleash a new set of charges.

Sidney Stephen was adamant that Jane was innocent. He completed his letter to Judge Dowling by enveloping his own motivations in a shroud of honesty, sincerity and responsibility:

> In conclusion, I have only to observe that those who knew the above facts were bound to disclose them. As a principle of justice is to consign the guilty to punishment, so the dictates of humanity and mercy are imperative on us to defend the innocent. Whilst the former cannot be censured, the latter who exercises this godlike quality should not be branded nor accused as striving to obstruct the due course of justice. I have heard that this has been insinuated against me and others. These observations are too contemptible to deserve my noticing.

Yet, two years later, Sidney wrote: 'Jane New was found guilty as I conceive very properly and as I stated at the time to Mr Henry Shadforth who was one of the jury.' He admitted that he saw some affidavits shortly after her trial that made him think she 'might' have been innocent, although he did not mention procuring or forwarding them to the Governor. Instead he claimed that his letter to Judge Dowling at that time — the letter and bundle of documents protesting the injustice of Jane's conviction — communicated his concerns regarding the legality of her conviction. It was an important distinction and the legality of her conviction would indeed become an issue in the future. But Sidney's claim was fallacious. In truth, his letter to Judge Dowling said nothing of the kind.

So, did Sidney truly believe Jane was innocent? Perhaps he had been deliberately misled.

Chapter 15
THE VALUE OF A LIFE

The death sentence was then called for in crimes that now
shock the conscience for having been so trifling.
J.R. Bennett, *Lives of the Australian Justices: Sir James Dowling*

At the Supreme Court building in King Street, Sydney, a breathless hush
descended on the courtroom as Justice James Dowling ascended the
podium. It was sentencing day for those convicted at the recent Criminal
Sessions. Focusing his attention on 23-year-old Jane New, he seized the
dreaded black cap and raised it to his head. She must have gasped at
the sight, and quailed at his judgement.

Perhaps Dowling borrowed words used to berate another prisoner: 'You
had not the plea of distress, no large family perishing for food or necessaries.
You were actuated by a lawless disposition without any possible inducement
but from indulgence in a course of predatory habits. Justice has at length
overtaken you.' However, only the words of her sentence have lingered: 'For
the prisoner Jane New, I order sentence of death to be recorded.'

Typical of the barbarity of Britain's criminal laws, Jane's life was
considered to be worth less than a piece of silk.

A sense of horror must have engulfed Jane as she heard her fate ringing
out in the courtroom. Was she aware that Judge Dowling had granted her
a glimmer of hope?

Described by contemporaries and biographers as a man of tact, geniality and innate kindness, Judge Dowling, like most of his contemporaries, was unconcerned about the savagery of the criminal laws he upheld or their failure to provide punishments that suited the crimes. Indeed, just a few months previously he had declared that for wise reasons the law made stealing a cow a hanging offence and that such a severe sentence operated as an example to the community and to those who took advantage of others. In Jane's case, however, he extended her some leniency. By ordering that 'death be recorded', he had followed the sentencing guidelines but indicated his willingness that she be reprieved.

John would have been thankful. As Registrar of the Supreme Court his duties included recording Jane's sentencing details on the cover sheet of her trial papers. If Judge Dowling had sentenced her 'to death', John would have been signing her death warrant.

Jane immediately appealed for mercy:

> I beg leave most humbly to state to this Honourable Court at this very particular crisis of my life, that before God I solemnly protest my innocence of the crime of which I have been found Guilty. It has been my earnest endeavour to support myself in a creditable manner and to avoid every approach to incorrect conduct. Again most solemnly protesting my innocence, I most humbly throw myself on the merciful consideration of the Court.

Curiously, Jane then declared that '*my prosecutor* has promised to offer a petition on my behalf but has not yet had time'. As the irate Madame Rens and her counsel were Jane's prosecutors, this seems a surprising remark. Yet perhaps Jane's reference was accurate, that her prosecutor's counsel, Thomas Deane Rowe, was indeed concerned about her sentence. If so, it reflects the groundswell of support from the gentlemen of Sydney that would soon bring Jane's case to the attention of the widespread community.

A day later, Jane addressed a lengthy petition to the Governor's advisory body, the Executive Council, appealing for a remission of her sentence. While maintaining that she had no desire to impugn the judge's impartiality or the conscientiousness and integrity of the jurors, Jane announced that she felt it a 'duty to my own Character, and Conscience, and to the Sacred Cause of Truth, in the presence of the Judge of all hearts, and in the Face of the World' to proclaim her innocence. She had frequently visited Madame Rens' premises in the ten months since the crime had allegedly taken place, she claimed, and had purchased many items. Yet Madame Rens had never made any insinuations about her integrity nor preferred criminal charges against her. It was not until much later, after the altercation between them over the damaged gown, that Madame Rens laid charges. 'This was a measure stimulated by revenge, and supported by the most malicious falsehood,' Jane seethed.

Such a charge failed to alarm the authorities. They reported that Madame Rens had used every exertion but found it impossible to have Jane brought to trial.

Jane's petition continued:

When my hearing took place in August 1828 their Worships, from insufficiency of evidence, were disposed to dismiss the case; when I, bold in conscious innocence and anxious to establish that innocence to the world, earnestly requested that it might be sent to a jury, to which their Worships consented. However, as a consequence of 'their strong doubts upon the case', they recommended I should be admitted to bail until called upon for trial which indulgence was accordingly conceded.

In making these claims, Jane hoped to gain official sympathy — 'to shake the credibility of my actual commission of so heinous a crime without temptation, without even the miserable plea of necessity'. Yet Jane's petition suggested behaviour so illogical and unbelievable as to be quite absurd.

Indeed, the absurdities continued. Reporting that Madame Rens had made repeated overtures for an 'accommodation', Jane declared that these had been uniformly rejected. 'I disdain any compromise that might leave my entire innocence in any degree equivocal,' she announced imperiously. The tone of this statement suggests that Jane was taking Madame Rens to court for slander, rather than Madame Rens prosecuting Jane for theft.

And having expected a far different result, Jane continued, she had insisted that her counsel expedite the hearing. Yet when her case came to trial, Mrs Tomkins was absent — 'a respectable witness for the prosecution whose testimony I am confident would have tended to establish my innocence' — and her place taken by Madame Rens' daughter — 'a female who from private feelings is personally inimical to me and palpably under the influence of her mother'. Such a substitution operated against her, Jane protested.

Jane continued to proclaim her innocence: 'My integrity and the correctness of my previous life and conduct may be taken as the best criterion for judging the probability of my present criminality or innocence.' Had Jane forgotten about her four pre-transportation and two colonial convictions? Her brazenness continued: 'I have through life uniformly sustained a fair reputation, and lived in circumstances of, at least, decent mediocrity.' With hindsight Jane's claim is truly ironic, as notoriety would replace mediocrity a short time later.

Jane humbly submitted her petition to the Executive Council for their decision regarding her fate — 'that dread fiat from which there is no appeal' — and concluded:

> I will only add, with feelings which would be insupportable save under that inward consciousness which has sustained me through this agonising conflict, my humble prayer, that should that fiat be favourable I may be restored to my beloved husband and my domestic comforts; but that should your decision prove adverse to my hopes, you will in mercy be pleased to recommend the immediate execution of my sentence as I faithfully declare my decided preference of instant death to the misery and horror of a prolonged existence deprived of all that can render life desirable, branded with unjust infamy, and depressed by unmerited sufferings.

So plaintive. So eloquent. So unlikely to have reflected Jane's own words.

Fourteen signatories earnestly recommended the Executive Council to have mercy. John Stephen Jnr's name headed the list. He would prove Jane's most vigorous protector and was undoubtedly the petition's author. Tellingly, the attitudes and actions revealed in the petition presaged John's own behaviour when later accused of an involvement in the Jane New scandal. And the petition's many falsehoods also reflected John's stamp, his penchant for deviating from the truth. Evidently, the secret to a good lie — that it contains as much truth as inherently possible — was lost upon him.

The thirteen other signatories were from the higher echelons of colonial society and included merchants, a bank manager, the Colonial Treasurer and a solicitor.[24] Clearly Jane was well-known around town. However, many of these men were also Bank of Australia directors and were expressing their appreciation for Jane's revelations regarding the money-laundering scheme. Bank of Australia Managing Director Thomas Macvitie appended a qualifying remark to his signature: 'Although I do not approve of the reflections made on Madame Rens and her daughter, I nevertheless on account of former good conduct recommend the applicant to mercy.'

John Stephen Jnr later explained Jane's good conduct, recounting the events that followed her disclosure of the robber's proposition:

On Monday morning, 5 January 1829, previous to Mrs New being arraigned, I communicated the particulars to Mr E Aspinall, the Bank of Australia's Director. At the request of the Managing Director, I visited Mrs New in gaol after she had received the promised intelligence and learnt the particulars from her. In consequence of which, I recovered some few of the notes. Mr Wollstonecraft has informed me that the information given by her has been of the most material benefit to the Directors.

Meanwhile, John's exertions in Jane's defence soon came to the Governor's attention, leading Colonial Secretary McLeay to question whether the attempts to save her from punishment despite the clearest proof of her guilt were intended to defeat the ends of justice. One such attempt comprised a written appeal to Jane's trial judge, James Dowling. Although John's letter has not survived,[25] Dowling's reply proves enlightening:

I can answer your very creditable and Gentlemanly letter, this moment received, only by saying that your application on behalf of the unfortunate

woman alluded to needs no sort of apology, proceeding, as I am sensible
it did, from that goodness of heart to which I shall always bear testimony
you possess in the highest degree. With unaffected esteem and regard, I
am, My Dear Sir, very faithfully yours, James Dowling.

Despite his kind response, Dowling ignored John's request, suggesting that
it was inappropriate. In his zeal and determination to champion Jane New,
John was beginning to breach socially acceptable boundaries.

Chapter 16
A SECOND OPINION

I have never yet had an Attorney-General whose judgement I could
depend upon, or whose advice I could look to with confidence.
Governor Ralph Darling

The wheels of justice continued to turn in *Rex versus Jane New*. On
8 January, Governor Darling convened the Executive Council (nicknamed
the 'Execution Council' by Chief Justice Forbes, who remarked acerbically
that it never met except to consider the cases of condemned felons).
Comprising the Governor and Chief Justice, as well as Archdeacon Thomas
Hobbes Scott and Colonial Secretary Alexander McLeay, the Council
had a number of responsibilities associated with colonial administration
including a review of all death sentences to determine whether they should
be upheld or commuted.

Judge Dowling appeared before the Council and reported on Jane's
case. Her petition was presented, meeting with some success: the Council
commuted her death sentence. Nevertheless, instead of returning Jane to
her husband and domestic comforts as she had beseeched, the Council
ordered her transportation to Moreton Bay for fourteen years.

Governor Darling had frequently expressed his determination to punish
with the full weight of the law those convicted of colonial offences. 'Every
one, by an honest and decorous course of life may avoid being sent to

a penal settlement,' he proclaimed. 'If a man voluntarily and wantonly plunges into vice and indulges in evil propensities, he relinquishes every claim to indulgence and must submit to the punishment due to his crimes.' Although the Council members decreed that Jane's crime did not warrant the noose, they ruled that she should suffer appropriately.

To be sentenced to the Moreton Bay penal settlement was considered a harsh punishment by Darling's liberal-minded contemporaries. Lady Forbes later claimed that under Governor Darling the cruel discipline of the newly established penal settlement at Moreton Bay recalled the worst days of Norfolk Island and Tasmania's Macquarie Harbour. The Executive Council's indulgence in commuting Jane's death sentence condemned her to fourteen years of hard labour under the sadistic Captain Patrick Logan, unrelieved by visits from family or friends. Many convicts preferred to die. Yet, as it turned out, the horrors of transportation to a penal settlement did not await Jane. An unexpected piece of good fortune saved her from this particular fate.

When the Executive Council examined Jane's case, Chief Justice Forbes expressed doubts about the legality of her conviction. The Council directed the Supreme Court justices to examine the statutes, Jane's commuted sentence being subject to their opinion. Forbes' concerns proved valid. The incompetent Attorney-General had struck again.

Baxter had charged Jane with 'stealing in a dwelling house' even though the fabric came from Madame Rens' shop. The charge was valid as the shop was also the Rens' sleeping quarters. But unbeknown to both prosecution and defence, Baxter had charged Jane under a repealed statute.

It seems astounding that the Attorney-General, of all people, would not know the laws of the land. The problem arose from an anomaly in the system. Sir Robert Peel — whose police reforms resulted in the moniker 'bobbies' for members of the British constabulary — had been aghast at the number and nature of the crimes eliciting a death sentence. He had convinced Parliament to replace the death penalty with transportation for numerous crimes including larceny in a shop. Stealing from a dwelling house was only to be a capital offence if the stolen goods exceeded £5 in value, an increase from the previous £2 ceiling. The laws were duly repealed in 1827 and new statutes passed, however their operation in New South Wales required colonial legislation.

Receiving a copy of the new Acts in December 1827, Chief Justice Forbes advised Governor Darling to extend them to the colony immediately, suggesting that the adoption of a short Act should suffice. But Darling shelved the matter for three months, the period during which Madame Rens' silk was stolen. This inexplicable delay occurred in the post-Turf Club period when Darling was also battling Chief Justice Forbes over Francis Stephen and John Stephen Jnr's appointments. Clearly Darling was preoccupied, however his unwillingness to follow Forbes' advice provided a loophole in the system, one that proved a boon for a number of convicted criminals including Jane New.

If Jane had been indicted under either of the old statutes, the mandatory sentence was death. By choosing to indict her under the new 'dwelling house' statute rather than the more logical shoplifting statute, and by valuing the stolen goods at over £5, Baxter was directing Jane towards a death sentence. Instead, he unwittingly allowed her conviction to be overturned.

The three Supreme Court justices officially met to discuss the validity of Jane's conviction a month after the Executive Council meeting. Jane was not the only prisoner convicted under these repealed statutes. A year previously the judiciary's attention was drawn to a number of cases tried during the problematic three-month window. The justices had agreed then, and continued to do so in Jane's case, that such convictions could not be upheld nor the resulting judgements executed.[26]

Jane's conviction had been quashed on a technicality. Yet, ironically, if Attorney-General Baxter had indicted Jane under the 'stealing from a shop' statute, she would not have received a capital conviction, her sentence would not have merited the Executive Council's attention and concerns regarding its validity might never have surfaced.

Jane's trial judge appears to have reassessed his position soon after leaving the meeting, claiming a possible distinction between Jane's case and those used as precedents, although his argument proved flawed. Had Dowling continued to ponder the matter because he believed that justice would be served only if her conviction was upheld? Perhaps Sidney Stephen's bundle of documents proclaiming Jane's innocence had influenced his ruminations. In Sidney's letter, dated the day previously, he asked Judge Dowling to peruse the recently obtained documents, fawning: 'I am sure I shall not appeal in vain to your highly honourable mind to allow me to submit these for your consideration particularly where so heavy a penalty is attached to her conviction.'

Natural curiosity must have motivated Dowling to glance through the documents before transmitting them to the Governor, particularly as he had presided over the case. Would he have pushed to uphold her conviction if he thought the claims convincing? If he had indeed been influenced favourably, Darling's response undoubtedly discouraged him. Returning the packet of enclosures a week later, Darling remarked:

> I must presume that the Gentlemen who have interested themselves in the fate of this woman and signed her petition, could not have been aware that independent of the robbery which she committed in the house of Madame Rens in December 1827, she was also convicted of another robbery in the month of August last, and appears to be a shoplifter of notorious character.

The message was clear: Dowling should not consider joining their ranks.

When the news reached Jane of her overturned conviction, she must have been amazed at her continued good fortune, euphoric at her reprieve, and eager to be released. To have escaped from punishment a second time was an astonishing achievement and would have excited jealousy and awe.

During the previous month, while Jane's future remained in doubt, those convicted at the same Criminal Sessions were forwarded to their respective situations. On 6 February the *Australian* remarked upon her continued detention: 'Jane New has in consequence of a new presumption of her innocence been detained in the Sydney Gaol to await the decision of Council.'

A legal technicality was no presumption of innocence. The slant unmasks the source. John Stephen Jnr had evidently used the official blanket cloaking the news of Jane's likely invalid conviction to initiate a new game: manipulating public opinion via the press. And the liberal *Australian* was happy to oblige — anything to goad the establishment.

John's imprint is also evident in the report published two weeks later by the conservative *Sydney Gazette*:

> Jane New, who was convicted of stealing in the dwelling house of Madame Rens, and ordered to have sentence of death recorded against her, has been liberated, in consequence of a variety of depositions laid before the Executive Council, strongly presumptive of her innocence. One of the circumstances which operated in her favour was Madame Rens having stated to the Magistrates that 28 yards of the same piece of silk which Mrs New was convicted of stealing had been some time previously stolen from her shop, as she supposed by a male servant in her employ.

A detailed description of the Kelly defence followed.

Two days later the *Sydney Gazette* retracted the reference to Jane's innocence and provided an accurate account, before remonstrating: 'We are always concerned when we learn that our journal has been made the medium of propagating statements of any description that are not based on truth.' The editor would certainly be wary of accepting information from the same source again.

Although John's intention in broadcasting Jane's situation was to ignite interest in his damsel-in-distress, his strategy hiccuped. The *Sydney Gazette*'s description of the circumstances behind Jane's discharge caused concern among the intelligentsia of Sydney. A letter to the editor bemoaning convictions under repealed statutes protested against the recent repeal of sixty Acts including the old statutes relating to murder and violent assault. 'Are we now without law on this important class of criminal judicature?' he fretted. 'It is a question of great moment, for the greatest criminal, the most atrocious murderer, may escape if indicted on the repealed laws as we have already witnessed in the two notorious recent cases!' One was Jane New's.

It was a serious concern. Nonetheless Governor Darling had a remedy, one that would solve the problem of criminally inclined serving convicts who came under his jurisdiction. He would ignore due process and invoke his powers.

Evidently Governor Darling had not learnt from the debacle of the Sudds and Thompson affair.

Twenty-five recently convicted criminals were freed in 1828 after the judiciary recognised that they had been convicted under Peel's repealed statutes. And it was about to happen again. The Supreme Court justices had opined that Jane New's conviction was invalid, and Governor Darling was obliged to act upon their opinion. He had no choice but to remit Jane's sentence and release her.

Darling loathed releasing criminals, particularly when compelled to do so on a legal technicality. His official instructions had been to instil a sense of fear into the community through harsh punishments for criminal behaviour, not to let convicted criminals loose. He must have cringed at receiving such advice from the despised judiciary, those who well knew — but refrained from mentioning — that the root of the problem lay in the Governor's failure to follow Forbes' advice and speedily legislate Peel's Acts.

Wishing to circumvent the problem, Darling hesitated. Surely, as the Governor of a penal settlement, he could contrive to punish such a notorious shoplifter and prevent her from preying again on the merchants of Sydney.

Surviving records reveal an absence of correspondence, memoranda and newspaper reports in the middle of February 1829. An air of portent hovered — Jane and her cohorts eagerly listening for news of her release from Sydney Gaol, Governor Darling hoping to solve his dilemma. It was the calm before the storm.

By 19 February some bright spark — the Governor? The Colonial Secretary? A minion? — had conceived a solution: revoke Jane New's assignment to her husband and incarcerate her in the Female Factory.

Official correspondence fails to disclose the Governor's full intentions regarding Jane's disposal at this time. The only surviving documentation is a letter from the Colonial Secretary to Sheriff Thomas Macquoid containing the politely phrased order:

> His Excellency the Governor having been pleased to remit the sentence of transportation passed on Jane New and now in your custody, I am directed to desire that you will forward her to the Factory at Parramatta by the earliest opportunity.

Having initially believed the reports of Jane's innocence, the *Sydney Gazette* expressed surprise at this decision:

> The direct and presumptive proof of her innocence, as we have been informed, is very strong; but still, we hear, it has been thought advisable to transmit her to the Factory. If she be deemed innocent, why should this be? But doubtless there has been sufficient reason.

An explanation soon followed:

> The Governor never entertained the least doubt of her guilt, but her conviction was considered not to be valid and she was in consequence discharged. A short time previous to her trial before the Supreme Court, this woman was convicted before the Magistrates of a similar offence and sentenced to have her original sentence extended. Upon the subsequent occasion, as she was considered to be fully though not legally convicted of robbery, she was deemed to have forfeited all claim to indulgence and sent to the Female Factory.

Had Jane been informed of this reversal in her fortunes prior to the arrival of the Sheriff's deputy? Her husband certainly had not. Having received word of Jane's imminent discharge, James New presented himself at Sydney Gaol only to be told of her impending transfer to the Female Factory. Concerned, perplexed and no doubt angry at this turn of events,

James scurried off to report Governor Darling's coup to Jane's advocate, John Stephen Jnr, and her counsel.

Governor Darling probably felt satisfaction at having solved his dilemma. Little did he realise that this decision would serve as a pretext for William Charles Wentworth to continue his outcry against autocratic government. And that it would unleash upon the government a legal suit that would question and ultimately undermine the power held by the governors of penal settlements over their subjects, both convict and free.

Jane's euphoria must have turned to despair. Instead of freedom, she was facing a new servitude. Prison clothes, bad food, hard work and too many women.

Released from Sydney Gaol on 20 February, Jane was ferried 14 miles west to the Female Factory at Parramatta. The weather probably added to her misery. Was it a typical February day in Sydney? Searing heat; smothering humidity. Her black silk gown and petticoat must have been sodden by the time she arrived at her new home.[27]

Perched across the river from the town of Parramatta, architect Francis Greenway's splendid edifice of white squared stone was a sight to behold. The Factory's inhabitants, however, failed to grace the building. 'Between four and five hundred of the most abandoned women of the empire,' lashed one contemporary. A 'sanctuary of virgins', quipped the *Monitor*. In truth, the outrageous behaviour of a proportion of the women condemned them all in the eyes of the Sydney community. Most of the inmates hated being damned and lampooned in this way. The ringleader of a Factory riot a couple of years later advocated taking revenge on the *Monitor's* editor — the man who reviled them most publicly — by destroying his press. Governor Darling, she added with surprising insight, would pardon them all for muzzling his enemy. Ironically, the *Monitor's* editor would end up publicly pitying and supporting one particular Factory inmate despite well-justified grounds for doing otherwise — Jane New.

Matron Ann Gordon took charge of Jane upon her arrival at the Female Factory. She ordered a physical search and relieved Jane of her money, then told her to strip and bathe. Taking charge of Jane's possessions, Matron Gordon logged and locked them away. In place of her silks and satins, Jane had to suffer the indignity of a prison uniform: a long shapeless dress, an apron, a straw bonnet, clunky shoes, thick stockings and a jacket. At least her uniform lacked the final indignity, the large garishly coloured 'C' adorning the jackets of some of the other inmates.

During Darling's administration, the Factory fulfilled multiple functions for the female convicts of New South Wales: a home for the unassigned and the 'deserving poor', a maternity home for the unmarried, a place of punishment and, in order that these women serve a useful function, a cloth manufactory. Darling had introduced a three-part class system to ensure that the women were treated appropriately, yet McLeay failed to provide instructions regarding Jane's disposal.

Matron Gordon deposited Jane in the first class while a committee member wrote to the Colonial Secretary begging to know if Jane should be received into the first or third class. If placed in the first class, he asked, should she be considered eligible for assigned service? The first class housed the recently arrived convicts who were suitable for assignment. These women received the most lenient treatment: a privileged diet, a superior style of dress, visitors once a week, supervised visits to church and the right to earn money. But on 25 February, McLeay replied that Jane was to be kept in the second class until further orders were received, and Jane was accordingly transferred.

The second class housed the old, weak, infirm and pregnant as well as the convicts returned from assignment, and it also served as a transit zone for those demoted from the first class or promoted from the third. These women were allowed some concessions after they had behaved well for three months. Classified as a convict returned from assignment, Jane's placement was appropriate. Nonetheless, she railed against her confinement. 'The second class is a place of severe punishment,' she complained petulantly, 'and I have been deprived of my shoes and stockings, and habited in a coarse cloth petticoat, and kept at labour.'

Jane had been indulged for too long. Had she forgotten that Moreton Bay's shadow hovered over her?

Jane exaggerated when complaining of harsh treatment. Although the second-class women experienced tighter controls and inferior allowances than their first-class sisters, their treatment was mild in comparison to those in the third class, the penitentiary and place of punishment where the women lacked all but the essentials for health and cleanliness.

Admittedly the regime for all Factory inmates was strict: obligatory attendance at morning and evening prayers and Sunday services; regular employment. To keep the women from becoming useless encumbrances, they worked during daylight hours, from 6 am to 8 am, 9 am to 1 pm and 2 pm to 6 pm during Jane's period of incarceration. The first-class women produced clothes for the inmates and male convicts, while the second- and third-class women prepared flax and wool for weaving. Cash incentives motivated first-class and well-behaved second-class women to exceed their quotas, although an insufficient supply of wool and flax meant that the women's services were often under-utilised.

In fact, insufficiency was the hallmark of the Factory. Built to accommodate 300 women, the Factory housed 600 women and children in Jane's time. Beds were in short supply and the women regularly tussled, scratched and hair-pulled as they fought for a share of the inadequate bedding. Regulations ordered that the women bathe weekly and they faced daily inspections for cleanliness and tidiness, yet no provisions were made for towels, combs or brushes. The lack of such essentials was bad enough. Even worse, for Jane, was the male-free existence: no one she could entice to manipulate the system in her favour.

Locked within this imposing stone prison and separated from the outside world by a nine-foot wall and a moat, the inmates should have had no contact with the townspeople. However they quickly learnt to manipulate their environment, to toss messages and illicit goods over the wall. And those desperate enough to risk life and limb could clamber up the wall, teeter precariously at the top, and drop down the other side. Only a few were willing to try.

Chapter 17
AN ILLEGAL IMPRISONMENT

The writ of Habeas Corpus *is the great constitutional
process by which every subject of His Majesty being in a state of
confinement, may upon sufficient grounds bring his case before
the Court and demand his liberation as a matter of right if his
confinement be contrary to Law.*
Chief Justice Francis Forbes

When Governor Darling outmanoeuvred the legal system by transferring
Jane New to the Female Factory, he momentarily floored her supporters.
John's voice was undoubtedly among those squawking about the injustice.
He probably suggested that James New consult his brother Francis Stephen,
the recently admitted attorney. Francis was perhaps the first to broach the
subject of illegal imprisonment, to suggest that a writ of *habeas corpus* might
be the solution. He pursued the idea, offering his brother Sidney a brief
with a ten-guinea fee. Sidney refused the brief: 'I was of opinion that
the Governor held the power to revoke assignments, an opinion which I
expressed to several persons at the time.' Francis then offered the brief and
fee to William Charles Wentworth.

One of the courtroom kings had been summoned. Barristers William
Charles Wentworth and Robert Wardell were the elite of the colonial legal
profession and regularly outsmarted Darling's legal officers. With immense

frustration tinged with admiration, even the Governor acknowledged that 'Wentworth and Wardell kept the Court and the Bar equally in subjection by their effrontery and talent'. More astute than Sidney Stephen, Wentworth could discern the appropriate legal arguments and the potentially serious ramifications of the case.

Francis Stephen initiated the process on 6 March 1829. Appearing before the three Supreme Court justices, he presented James New's affidavit which explained the situation regarding Jane's confinement and concluded:

> My wife has not been legally convicted of any crime during her residence in this colony and her imprisonment is not warranted by any order of the Bench of Magistrates. She was assigned to me as my servant and the loss of her services has had ruinous consequences to my business. My wife resided upwards of four years at Tasmania without any offence laid to her charge and has ever proved herself an affectionate and faithful wife.

Francis then moved that Jane be brought to court to clarify the question of her continued imprisonment. Although the Crown law officers objected, Chief Justice Forbes agreed, reminding the law officers that Jane's conviction had been declared invalid and that she had a right to know why she was still detained. He decreed that the court would examine the case on Saturday 14 March.

Jane had struck it lucky again.

The newspapers described the writ and its background, each adding their own slant. The conservative *Sydney Gazette* provided a brief but accurate report. The liberal newspapers tried not to let the truth intrude. The *Monitor*'s editor bemoaned the false accusation against Jane, her punishment without trial, the convicting magistrates' belief in her innocence, the Governor's sentence of unlimited imprisonment in the Female Factory, the lack of any written evidence attesting to her status as a prisoner of the Crown. The *Australian*'s description was similarly creative.

Despite being snowed under by the blizzard of lies, some members of the wider community glimpsed the truth. Under the pseudonym 'Mentor' one reader castigated the *Monitor*'s editor for concealing the true facts. He questioned whether Jane could be retried given that jeopardy should not apply. 'Has she been tried at all,' he challenged, 'if she has not been tried according to law!' Of course, as no law was in operation at the time of the theft, legally Jane had committed no crime.

As Jane remained locked in the Parramatta Female Factory, the bureaucractic engine had to be cranked before the *habeas corpus* hearing could take place. Orders were sent, requisitions submitted, and on Friday 13 March 1829 a constable appeared at the Factory's gates ready to take Jane to Sydney.

But there was a slip-up. Neither Matron Gordon nor Parramatta Police Superintendent, Major Archibald Innes, gave instructions for Jane's disposal in the hours between her arrival in Sydney and her appearance at the Supreme Court the following morning. Each had probably expected the other to inform the constable, while the constable himself failed to seek the necessary directions.

Jane and her escort — Constable Bernard Crummy, a 46-year-old ticket-of-leave holder with a wife and family — departed in a coach early on the 13th. They travelled swiftly, arriving in Sydney by 11 am. Constable Crummy delivered Jane to the Supreme Court, informed the staff of their arrival and awaited instructions. Naturally the news filtered through to the Registrar — John Stephen Jnr himself.

John sent word to Constable Crummy to remain with Jane at the courthouse, that instructions would be furnished as the day progressed. Some time later, John ordered the constable to accompany Jane to her husband's place, to remain there overnight, and to deliver her to the courthouse by 10 the following morning. Crummy understandably followed these instructions — they came from a court officer after all. Little did Crummy realise that he would become one of the first dupes in the Jane New scandal, that during the night at the News' residence, plans were being hatched.

Constable Crummy escorted Jane to the courthouse the following morning where he delivered her to the Keeper of the Gaol. 'Where have you been?' the keeper must have asked. Consternation followed Crummy's response. The hearing was delayed.

Colonial Secretary McLeay immediately despatched a peremptory letter to Major Innes at Parramatta demanding that Constable Crummy account for his actions. Why had he permitted Jane to be out of his charge? Why hadn't he lodged her in the gaol? Why hadn't he asked at the Colonial Secretary's Office for instructions regarding her disposal if none had been provided?

No doubt startled to be called to task in this way, Crummy explained to Major Innes that he had acted upon John Stephen Jnr's instructions. Innes communicated this information to the Colonial Secretary.

McLeay dashed off another letter to Major Innes. Why had they transmitted Jane New to Sydney on the 13th? What instructions had Matron Gordon given Constable Crummy for Jane's disposal upon their arrival in Sydney? Why had Crummy sought instructions from the Registrar of the Supreme Court who had nothing whatsoever to do with the custody of the prisoner until she was due in court? Innes responded with great civility that it was customary to send prisoners on the preceding day to ensure that they arrived at the courthouse on time, that the constable had received no instructions from Matron Gordon, and that he had sought instructions at the courthouse because he had been ordered to deliver her there.

This unfortunate communication breakdown largely resulted from Major Innes' failure to issue adequate instructions. Under the circumstances, the Governor and Colonial Secretary no doubt realised that Constable Crummy was not at fault. Yet John's behaviour must have appeared both irregular and inappropriate. This was a situation in which a woman detained in the Female Factory under the Governor's orders had been brought to the Supreme Court to determine if her detention was illegal. Why would a civil officer of the Supreme Court, a man employed by the government, order the constable to escort the woman to her home for the night?

The Governor and Colonial Secretary's initial bewilderment must have led inexorably to the conclusion that mischief was afoot.

Chapter 18
THE *HABEAS CORPUS* HEARING

So singular in its character and so important in its
bearings do the learned Judges of our Supreme Court consider
the case of the woman Jane New.
Australian

Monday, 16 March 1829

The Supreme Court's courtroom was alive with excited twittering. Jane New's story had already piqued the community's interest. A beautiful woman well-known about town. A cruel Governor who had imprisoned her. What damsel-in-distress story ever failed to appeal to the hearts of the community, particularly after the press' cleverly crafted stories had manipulated their emotions?

The fiasco following Jane's arrival at the court had delayed the hearing for two days, giving both sides additional time to prepare their cases. Yet the ineffectual Attorney-General remained inadequately prepared. Asked for the documentation associated with Jane's detention, he handed over a Return to the Writ stating that Jane had been sent to the Factory by virtue of an order signed by the Deputy Sheriff.

Francis Stephen pounced. 'I move that Jane New be discharged from custody on the grounds that the Deputy Sheriff had no power to commit her and that the charge is not set out.' He quoted the regulations described in Chitty's *Criminal Law*.

All eyes turned to Attorney-General Baxter, who evidently had not recently read Chitty's *Criminal Law* or any other useful legal tome. 'I would like time to amend the return,' he implored, 'and request that Jane New in the meantime be remanded into custody.'

Wentworth entered the fray, declaring that Baxter's document was the most extraordinary Return to the Writ he had ever seen and that the Factory had no 'legal' existence although the judges might personally know of its existence as a place for the disposal of unassigned prisoners. 'But Jane New has already been assigned,' he argued. 'The question for the court is whether Jane New is in a legal state of restraint. Has she committed some offence or has she not? If she has, there are proper places provided by law in which she could be confined; but the Factory is nothing in the eye of the law.'

Baxter countered: 'The Factory is the common asylum for female prisoners in the same way as the Prisoners' Barracks is for the male. Jane New has not been sent there for punishment, and is subject only to the same measure of restraint as the other prisoners who are employed there.'

Chief Justice Forbes waded in. 'The Return laid before the Court is defective — it shows nothing,' he rebuked the Attorney-General. Forbes was exasperated. He had previously expressed his awareness of the embarrassing situation Darling faced for want of competent legal advisers. He had even admitted extending more leniency to the Crown Officers than legal requirements dictated. And he chose to do so again. He allowed the Attorney-General to amend the writ and, as Baxter did so, he urged the gentlemen on both sides to confine themselves to the matter at hand: 'We request it as a matter of personal favour to ourselves, that you will argue the case on its merits, temperately and calmly, divested of all ill-feeling and personal allusions.'

After Wentworth examined the amended writ he recognised further problems. As he began to clarify their nature, Chief Justice Forbes interrupted. 'The Court is anxious that this case should receive the fullest investigation. As it appears that a claim of property right in the prisoner is to be made and as Tasmania has been mentioned as the place to which she was originally transported, the Court does not think that all the circumstances of the case are sufficiently before it to enable the Court to pronounce a decision.'

An astute judge, Chief Justice Forbes had recognised that two critical issues relating to the administration of the penal settlements had surfaced, and that superficial treatment would be unwise. He adjourned the hearing for another two days while further affidavits were prepared, and remanded Jane 'merely for safekeeping' until the hearing reconvened.

Day two had ended without resolution. Instead the case had ballooned to envelop broader issues of significance to the entire settlement.

Wednesday, 18 March 1829

'This strange case was again mooted before the three Judges on Wednesday and was again postponed!' the *Australian* exclaimed. For the News, the hearing was proving prolonged, nerve-racking and expensive.

The Supreme Court's clerk began by reading the affidavits prepared by both sides. Some were crucial to the case; others were legal niceties, neither interesting nor important. James New's affidavit was read first. It concentrated on Governor Arthur's reassignment to him of Jane's services after their marriage, the illegality of Jane's conviction, her consequent discharge from gaol, and his right to her services which he claimed had not been legally divested from him or forfeited.

James' affidavit painted a picture of a convict illegally detained, a husband deprived of his wife, a settler robbed of his servant. Yet as his words echoed around the courtroom, the wider implications bounced back. What were a settler's rights regarding the services of an assigned convict? As the assignment system underpinned the colony's economic foundation, this issue bridged the gap dividing the personal from the political. Jane New's *habeas corpus* hearing was about to become historic in its implications for the whole community.

Governor Darling and Chief Justice Forbes had two years previously bickered over the other side of this question: what were the Governor's rights over an assigned convict? Darling believed that the Governor retained all rights, and implemented regulations accordingly. The sagacious Chief Justice, however, construed the New South Wales Act to mean that the Governor only retained the King's prerogative of mercy (he could grant the prisoner a pardon), and that a settler could not be divested of his rights except by law or reassignment. The Crown Law officers in Downing Street upheld Forbes' interpretation, and added a new section to the Act to invest the Governor with the authority he required. Forwarding a copy to Governor Darling, Sir George Murray observed that the Legislature's intention must be determined exclusively from the language employed. But he then added that the clause relating to the Governor's right to issue tickets-of-leave or revoke assignments had been accidentally inserted in the wrong place. He had evidently failed to realise that this error made the language ambiguous.

As Wednesday 18 March dawned, the community knew that the vital question of a settler's rights to an assigned convict had not been tested through the courts. The barristers were eager, the law officers wary, the journalists poised.

Through James New's affidavit, Wentworth exposed the central issues in Jane's case. For the edification of its readers, the *Australian* (under its new editor, Attwell Edwin Hayes) explained the problem. After mentioning Jane's invalid conviction and the Colonial Secretary's letter ordering her discharge from gaol, the report continued:

> But what follows this? O strange, O unaccountable fatality — Jane New obtains her discharge from the gaol, and by sort of a writ under the hand of the Sheriff's Deputy — not the Sheriff but 'the Sheriff's Deputy' is — is — despatched and confined to — the female factory!
>
> This, it appears, is done by the order of the Governor. Now having been illegally, and it would appear by affidavits wrongfully convicted, was the woman entitled to her discharge? Or was she not? If she were, then her subsequent confinement in the Factory could not be deemed lawful. If she were not, still the mode of her transfer from one prison to another was informal and unconstitutional. Jane New also was an assigned servant to her husband and *de facto* a sort of property was vested in her assignee.

Could the Governor rightly deprive this assignee of such property when his assigned servant had been illegally convicted? Could he commute a punishment when the conviction itself was null and void? If the Governor could do all we have inferred, he should do so on the authority of some extant Act of Parliament. If he did so *au discretion*, then His Excellency has left the propriety of doing so open to investigation, and to dispute.

The arguments began. Wentworth offered his multifaceted case. Articulately presented, cogently argued, he claimed, in essence, that the Supreme Court was responsible for Jane New's invalid conviction and could bypass the Governor's authority and quash her conviction if it chose. That being the case, the issue in question was the Governor's right to revoke her assignment. On the one hand, he argued, Governor Darling had no right to interfere in the assignment of a Tasmanian transportee. On the other, Governor Darling only had the right to interfere in an assignment in order to 'remit' or improve the situation of the prisoner.[28]

It was a powerful argument.

Attorney-General Baxter stood up to respond. Reading from the same piece of legislation, he claimed that the power of assigning prisoners transported from England or convicted in the colony, and the power of revoking and reassigning them, lay with the Governor. He could do so at his will. Jane New, he contended, had been legally detained.

But Baxter stumbled as Justice Stephen challenged him — a query here, a rebuke there — over assumptions made and conclusions reached during his argument. As he returned to his seat was he aware that his presentation had been but a squeak to Wentworth's roar?

Solicitor-General John Sampson followed. He maintained that Jane's conviction was still good under the common law, and that the Governor had the absolute right to cancel assignments whatever the circumstances. He also suggested that Jane was perhaps a prisoner of the Crown illegally at large.

The Supreme Court intended to pass judgement that afternoon, however Attorney-General Baxter made a curious demand. He asked for the court's opinion on the Governor's right to revoke a convict's assignment, 'not so much for this particular case,' he explained, 'but so as to guide the discretion of the executive government in other cases now under consideration.'

Chief Justice Forbes hesitated. 'May not this case be disposed of on another point?' he urged. 'It is a question of considerable delicacy, and we wish to avoid its discussion unless in a case where no other question arises.'

Baxter insisted and Forbes reluctantly agreed, explaining that he was doing so only to assist the government. 'The Court will reserve its judgement until Saturday morning,' he announced.

One final matter needed to be addressed, that of Jane's disposal. Justice Stephen asked Solicitor-General Sampson if he would agree to bail. Sampson objected. Justice Stephen persisted, asserting his conviction that Jane had been illegally detained and declaring that she should be admitted to bail pending the court's decision.

Unhappy with Justice Stephen's intercession, the Chief Justice quietly remonstrated with him, a conversation the *Australian* correspondent overheard:

> The learned Judge spoke in a low voice; but we heard sufficient to collect that his opinion was meant to be delivered with a delicate sense of deference towards his learned brethren, and with a feeling of justice towards the party whose case was the object of discussion. Upon the order of the other two learned Judges, the prisoner was remanded into custody.

By Saturday, Justice Stephen had reconsidered his opinion.

Saturday, 21 March 1829

'This important case drew together a very crowded auditory on Saturday,' reported the *Australian*, 'with an unusually full attendance of the professional gentlemen within the bar.' Word had spread that on the final day of the Jane New *habeas corpus* hearing, legal history could be in the making.

As the protagonists filed into the Supreme Court, they probably radiated their expectations: Wentworth cocksure, Baxter ambivalent, Jane New hopeful, reassured by Justice Stephen's stance in appealing for her bail. As the three Supreme Court justices filed into the courtroom, they must have known that their decision would again incur the wrath of the Governor.

Chief Justice Forbes was the first to deliver his opinion. 'This is an application to the Court to enlarge the Prisoner Jane New upon the ground that she is unlawfully detained in the Factory at Parramatta,' he began, and continued for half an hour covering the arguments presented by both sides. He believed that two questions had been raised for the court's determination: whether Jane New's conviction on Madame Rens' charges was valid (placing her at the Governor's disposal), and whether the Governor could revoke her assignment to her husband and either reassign her or retain her in the service of the Crown. Regarding Jane's colonial conviction, Forbes declared that the Colonial Secretary's letter discharging Jane New from Sydney Gaol expressly stated that the Governor had remitted her sentence. The court was bound to admit her to bail, he concluded, while she awaited her full pardon.

A sense of elation must have been simmering inside Jane. Wentworth no doubt remained supremely confident. Baxter was probably perturbed.

The second question, however, Forbes considered more important. As Jane New had been transported to Tasmania and assigned by the Tasmanian Governor, he believed that the New South Wales Governor did not have the power to revoke her assignment. But he also believed that neither governor had the power to revoke any assignment at will. As land without labour was useless, as assigned servants were the only secure labour, and as property rights were held inviolable under English law, he believed that Parliament had no intention of allowing settlers' rights to an assigned servant to be taken away without judicial investigation. 'The clause of the Act under consideration is certainly expressed in an ambiguous manner, and is capable of two readings. In my opinion,' announced Forbes, directing his remarks at Attorney-General Baxter who had pressured him into providing such an opinion, 'the Governor has the power of revoking the assignment of a convict servant only for the purpose of remitting his sentence.'

Jane New undoubtedly glowed.

'But I do not think that the decision on this point of law, which has been incidentally raised, is essential to the final disposal of the case,' the

Chief Justice continued. 'Jane New was transported to Tasmania from England and her sentence has neither expired nor been remitted. She is therefore a transported felon found at large in New South Wales. It is true that she has been permitted by the Governor of Tasmania to follow her husband and master to this colony; but I am constrained to hold that such permission was not within the power of that Governor to grant. We feel ourselves bound to remand her to the custody of the Government for the purpose of being sent back to Tasmania, the place of her original and unsatisfied term of transportation.'

The unthinkable had happened. Jane New must have looked shell-shocked.

Chief Justice Forbes settled back to allow Justice Stephen to deliver his opinion. 'I entirely coincide in the view taken of this case by His Honour the Chief Justice,' Justice Stephen announced. 'He has gone so fully into the subject that I think it unnecessary to add anything. I think that the Prisoner Jane New under the circumstances must be remanded.'

Would there be a dissenting opinion?

Justice Dowling followed, another lengthy discourse lasting for at least half an hour. He was kind enough, however, to provide his judgement early in the piece. He concurred with the other justices.

The courtroom must have erupted. Two legal precedents had just been set, both of profound importance to the day-to-day running of the New South Wales and Tasmanian penal settlements. The two governors had been deprived of their right to cancel assignments unless their intention was to improve the prisoner's situation, raising the spectre of legal challenges over past assignment revocations. And the previously accepted practice of approving transfers between the two penal settlements had been disallowed, placing in doubt the status of every serving convict who in the previous six years had been transferred in such a manner or had been ordered to disembark in the 'wrong' penal settlement.

Baxter was no doubt horrified, envisaging another bureaucratic nightmare and the ire of the Governor. Again.

Chapter 19
THE DECISION

*The transaction out of which this decision arose is comparatively
unimportant; we shall proceed at once to the Decision: a clear and
clever production — cool in its temper, ingenious in its reasoning,
and perspicuous in its diction.*

Sydney Gazette

To the editors of Sydney's newspapers, Jane New's difficulties had suddenly diminished into insignificance. They quickly moved on to 'The Decision', as the ruling came to be known. 'This case certainly embraced some of the most important points that ever claimed public attention in this colony, involving points vitally interesting to the colony at large. It is no mean triumph to us to know that we had anticipated their concurrent opinion,' gloated the *Australian*. The *Monitor* trilled: 'This decision is most important as well as most righteous in its effects.' Indeed, so momentous did the liberal newspapers consider the rulings that they established a subscription fund to assist James New in paying his enormous expenses.

Shocked by the ruling, the conservative *Sydney Gazette* reported:

Of so much importance, and so utterly at variance with our pre-conceived opinions are some of the doctrines and inferences which that decision involves, that we are anxious to review it in the calmest temper and with

the clearest views and firmest convictions. By Thursday morning we hope
we shall be prepared to look at it without prejudice or partiality. Others
will doubtless make it a theme of vehement declamation — but far be it
for us to imitate their turbulent example.

Issue after issue followed with lengthy discourses on the decision. The
Sydney Gazette followed the government line, expressing astonishment at the
suggestion of ambiguous wording in the legislation. 'This appears to us as
clear as sunshine,' the editor proclaimed. John Stephen Jnr's conservative
brother, Tasmania's Solicitor-General, Alfred Stephen, agreed. Called upon
by Governor Arthur for his assessment, Alfred's lengthy analysis concluded
with the summary: 'There is no ambiguity in the words. The Section appears
to me to authorise, unrestrictedly, the revocation of assignments.' He
admitted, however, that he and the Tasmanian Attorney-General disagreed.

Despite claiming that the wording was clear and incontestable, and
opining that the judges had erred in their ruling, the *Sydney Gazette's* editor
concluded with a surprising observation: 'While we sincerely think the
judges *intellectually wrong*, we with equal sincerity think them *morally right*.'
Evidently the editor agreed that the Governor's right to revoke assignments
should only be used for a prisoner's benefit.

Naturally, Governors Darling and Arthur disagreed. Such a ruling
limited their control not only over the thousands of convicts in the two
penal settlements, but over those they were assigned to. Darling rebuked the
judges, declaring that their views were contrary to Parliament's intentions,
and demanding a report of their opinions to transmit to England.
Forwarding the requested opinions, Chief Justice Forbes suggested that
the colonial legislature pass an Act to ensure that Parliament's assumed
intentions were not compromised. Darling ignored the suggestion and
fretted to the Secretary of State that any curtailment of his absolute power
to revoke assignments would be a serious inconvenience indeed.

Governor Arthur also reacted angrily. On the issue of convict relocations
he grumbled: 'The case unfortunately will involve some hundreds of others,
and how a remedy is to be applied without the interposition of Parliament,
I really do not know.' But Arthur had more immediate concerns.

Important as this case is, it sinks into nothing compared to the momentous
one which was incidentally brought forward on this occasion. It is quite
monstrous of the Supreme Court Judges to have unnecessarily involved
the colony in discussions on a subject of such immense importance, one
affecting the Government as well as a very large class of persons. It certainly
is a little hard upon those who are entrusted with the administration
of prisoners to be making every effort to restore to the punishment of
transportation some of its early terrors, whilst there is another power in
the country acting upon the contrary principle.

Further opinions were demanded, irate letters despatched, and the
Governors waited impatiently for a response from Britain. Meanwhile,
the effects of the ruling rippled across the New South Wales community.

One consequence of the decision was immediate. Before the judges had
time to leave their chairs, the *Australian*'s proprietor, Attwell Edwin Hayes,
lurched up and addressed them.

'My reporter named Ledsham and one of my principals named Monks
have lately been forcibly taken from me by constables,' he complained.
'Ledsham was taken out of the Court, out of the very box allotted by their
Honours for the reporters to take their notes in.'

In his complaint to the court, Hayes had highlighted the latest saga in
the long-running battle between Governor Darling and the press. Since the
Sudds and Thompson affair late in 1826, Governor Darling had been at
the mercy of the liberal press. Publicly lashed for months, he attempted
to curb the press' licentiousness by proposing bills relating to newspaper
registration, stamp duty charges and recognisances to cover fines for libel.
He was foiled by Chief Justice Forbes who argued that parts were invalid
and unconstitutional and that the Governor's true intention was to diminish
newspaper circulation if not destroy the newspapers altogether.

Thwarted, Darling resorted to prosecutions for libel. The *Australian*'s
wily editor, Robert Wardell, managed to escape the net despite publishing
an outrageous letter to the editor regarding their esteemed Governor:

Posterity will be dazzled by the blaze of his glory, and will exclaim in astonishment, what a consummate politician! What a profound legislator! Would to heaven that we knew the length of his * * * *; for surely so much wisdom and magnanimity argue something super-human.

Ultimately, Wardell's successor, Attwell Edwin Hayes, and the *Monitor's* Edward Smith Hall published their newspapers from gaol after being convicted on numerous libel counts.

Meanwhile, Governor Darling devised another strategy to control the press: he withdrew convicts assigned to the editors of the two liberal newspapers. As Darling later explained, his intention was to allow the editors less opportunity to disseminate their poison, to ensure that the colony's tranquillity be better preserved.

On 12 March 1829, nine days before the Supreme Court judges ruled in Jane's case, Edward Smith Hall wrote to the Secretary of State railing against Governor Darling's action in revoking his own convicts' assignment, and claiming that the legislation intended reassignment only for a convict's benefit. All such correspondence passed by the Governor, hence Attorney-General Baxter's appeal for the Supreme Court's opinion when they considered Jane's case.

In the aftermath, Hall persuaded his printer to return to work. The magistrates defied the Supreme Court's ruling and fined him for harbouring a runaway. Hall appealed. The Supreme Court quashed his conviction and censured the magistrates. Suit and countersuit followed. The legal consequences of the Jane New ruling had become a critical factor in Darling's battle with the liberal press and, by extension, the liberal community.

Anxiously awaiting a response from Britain, Governor Darling felt vindicated when the despatches arrived. 'The real intention of the enactment was the very opposite of that which the Sydney judges have construed its words to import,' thundered Under-Secretary Horace Twiss. He censured the judges, suggesting that political intrigue drove their decision.

The Colonial Office and Crown law officers were unjust in their condemnation. Sir George Murray had himself advised that the legislature's intention was to be determined from the language. He had ordered Forbes and Darling to stop bickering and work together or both would be recalled. Forbes had been heeding Sir George's advice when he agreed to provide the ruling for the government's benefit. And Forbes had grounded his opinion on the legislation's language backed up by sound legal reasoning, as it should have been.

Nevertheless, describing the ruling as 'destitute of authority', Sir George Murray advised the judges to alter their opinion if another opportunity arose to do so. If they chose not to, he ordered Governor Darling to disregard any such ruling until the judgement was reviewed or the legislation changed.

A wanton woman had lusted after a piece of cloth; a constitutional crisis hovered. Parliament, the Crown Law officers and the New South Wales Governor had firmly entrenched themselves on one side; the Supreme Court judges were tentatively anchored on the other.

But the judges could be dismissed by the scratch of a pen and their vulnerability weakened their position. They buckled. Dowling with obsequious platitudes, Forbes with dignified restraint. While all were censured by the Colonial Office and Crown Law officers, Forbes received the most scathing denunciation, being informed that the ill-advised ruling had damaged his judicial authority.

Darling crowed when he received word of the Colonial Office's opinion and the justices' castigation. Triumphantly, he again revoked the assignments of the *Australian*'s and *Monitor*'s convicts. However, he made the mistake of reporting his actions to the Secretary of State. 'The single object of Parliament,' Sir George Murray coldly admonished, 'in enabling the Governors of New South Wales and Tasmania to remove assigned servants was to benefit the convicts themselves, or to protect the public against the improper use of a master's authority.'

It was an astounding remark, as this very principle underlay the Supreme Court justices' decision in Jane New's case, the ruling that had brought such resounding censure upon their heads.

'It would be vain to expect from the public at large,' Sir George continued, 'any other construction than that you were endeavouring by this use of your power to harass a political opponent and to cripple his operations.' Sir George ordered that Darling never again use his power to revoke an assignment for such reasons and indicated that the Colonial Office had reflected again on the judges' ruling and was considering amending the statute law. The ruling had come full circle.

The ramifications resulting from the Supreme Court judges' rulings in Jane's case unfolded over the following couple of years. Meanwhile, the dramas of the day continued after the judges exited the courtroom.

Part IV:
GRATIFICATION

I was under the firm impression
that Mr Stephen's interposition at
that time was influenced solely by
motives of disinterested humanity
and compassion.

Justice James Dowling

Chapter 20
A CONFOUNDED CONSTABLE

The bird has flown.

Australian

After the judges ruled that Jane was a convict at large and remanded her to the Female Factory at Parramatta, confusion arose regarding her transfer. Sheriff Macquoid assumed that she would be returned to Sydney Gaol with a court order for her transmission to the Factory — the usual procedure — and called upon Police Constable John Kelly to undertake this responsibility. 'Constable, that woman is to go back to the Gaol,' he ordered. 'Keep a look out on her.'

Finding Jane in the care of Gaol Constable Cleme, Kelly explained that he was to take charge of her. Cleme refused to relinquish responsibility. 'I brought her up and can take her back again,' he retorted obstinately. Accompanying the alluring Jane New was less onerous than his usual duties.

Meanwhile, Sheriff Macquoid explained the transfer arrangements to Under-Sheriff Prout, adding with surprising prescience: 'Make sure that the constables are duly attending to her safe custody.' When Prout found Jane, she was surrounded by seven or eight constables and complaining of harsh treatment. Blood flowed from a wound on her head and had settled on her face and her ear. The constables later reported that the wound

135

resulted from a violent blow from a constable's staff. It was an accident, they claimed.

Curiously, no reference to Jane's injury was included in the constables' reports, only surfacing a year later. The constables had covered up the altercation. Had the lions been tussling over who would be king of this one-woman pride?

As the constables hovered around Jane, John Stephen Jnr appeared, bringing with him an air of authority and decisiveness. 'Surely one man is enough to take care of one woman,' he declared and told her to sit down, her husband joining her on one side and Gaol Constable Cleme on the other. 'Mrs New is to be left in the charge of the Gaol Constable who brought her up this morning!' he ordered.

Cleme queried: 'I brought a paper up with this woman. I ought to have one to take back.'

Under-Sheriff Prout turned to John: 'Is an order necessary for her to be sent to the Gaol?'

'She is not to be sent to the Gaol but to the Factory,' John decreed. 'I will write the order for the judge's signature directly.'

And with these words saga turned to scandal.

While John prepared the court order, Prout communicated the change in plan to Sheriff Macquoid: that Jane was to be sent directly to the Factory. Macquoid asked to see the order, and later reported:

> John Stephen Jnr showed it to me, observing that she could not be sent to the Gaol under it, but ought to be forwarded at once to the Factory which he considered it was his duty to carry into effect. As I looked upon the Registrar as the organ of the Court whose directions he was obeying, it appeared to me that Jane New was removed from my charge and responsibility. I therefore did not interfere any further in the matter but left it to that officer to do what he might deem his duty on the occasion.

After Macquoid departed, John ordered Gaol Constable Cleme to take sole charge. Handing over the court order, he told Cleme to escort Jane to the Colonial Secretary's Office.[29]

Constable Cleme and Jane New left the Supreme Court building and traipsed down Phillip Street towards the harbour. Soon afterwards, Jane turned to the constable and begged: 'Please may I be allowed to get a drink of water?' Cleme consented and followed her into Thomas Evans' house on Phillip Street.[30] Jane discarded her bonnet and shawl and slipped into a bedroom. From motives of delicacy, Cleme later reported, he did not follow her.

After waiting for some time, Cleme realised that Jane had not returned. He turned to James New who had accompanied them and asked, 'Could you seek your wife?'

The woman of the house interceded: 'She's gone out the front door!'

A look of horror must have crossed Cleme's face. 'This is a pretty concern,' he said to James.

'I would not have had this happen for one hundred and fifty pounds,' came James' curious response. Was that the cost of Jane's escape?

Cleme grabbed Jane's bonnet and shawl and hovered uncertainly in the doorway. James was outside leaning on a fence and laughing. He suggested, 'Perhaps she is gone to see Mr Stephen on some business she may have forgotten.' Almost instantly, according to Cleme's statement, Mr Stephen appeared. 'New, where is your wife?' he asked. James continued laughing. 'New, take care of your wife!' Mr Stephen ordered.

'She's gone, Sir, she has made her escape!' The plans hatched during Jane's unexpected visit home a week previously had been executed.

Rumours soon surfaced that John had carried Jane away after her escape from the constable. Jane's friend, Ellen Frazier later revealed that after Jane crept from the Phillip Street property, she stole into another house in Phillip Street where she changed clothes. Gliding past the Court House — probably the last place anyone would expect to look for her — she scurried to Hyde Park Race Course where a person with a horse and gig met her. 'Afterwards,' Frazier recounted, 'they proceeded on, when Mr John Stephen came and accompanied her in the gig to Cunningham's, a house on the Liverpool Road.'

The plan was to sneak Jane from Cunningham's to another house five miles away, however it was foiled. On 28 March, a week after her escape, Chief Constable Jilks and his assistant, Constable Skinner, arrived at Cunningham's and apprehended her.[31]

Of the circumstances surrounding Jane's recapture, official records remain silent. The *Sydney Gazette* and *Australian* provided brief reports. The *Monitor* ignored Jane's escape and recapture, perhaps to prevent any tarnishing of her image as a persecuted innocent, a female David battling the mighty Goliath.

After taking Jane into custody, Constables Jilks and Skinner received instructions to lodge her in Sydney Gaol, however Governor Darling countermanded the instructions, ordering Jane's removal to the Female Factory without delay. She remained in gaol for only half an hour before being despatched to the Factory under the escort of not one but two constables. The authorities had evidently recognised Jane's ability to weasel her way out of the care of a single man.

Incarcerated again in the Factory, Jane probably boasted about her escape and shared a laugh at male ineptitude. She disclosed the full details to Female Factory laundress, Ellen Frazier, who repeated them to the authorities a short time later. Mrs Frazier was another Lancashire transportee. She claimed to have known Jane's mother prior to transportation and to have befriended Jane in the Factory.[32] Darling believed her account of Jane's escape, arguing that she was closely confined to the Factory and must have obtained the details from Jane herself.

When John eventually heard that Ellen Frazier had confirmed rumours of his involvement in Jane's escape, he was furious. 'The accusation of my having conveyed Mrs New to the house where she was discovered rests solely on the assertion of the most abandoned prisoner in the Factory, whose profligacy is notorious over the colony,' he raged. 'Upon no other occasion would this infamous woman's words have been allowed to make the slightest impression.'

Matron Gordon responded similarly when asked some years later if she believed Ellen Frazier to be worthy of credit. 'No,' was the brusque response.

'Would you believe anything she stated?'

'I don't think I should,' Matron Gordon declared.

However, Matron Gordon later admitted that Mrs Frazier was a well-behaved Factory resident, that she had only heard of the woman's bad character after she left the Factory, and that she did not think Mrs Frazier would take a false oath regarding her conversation with Jane New. Matron Gordon's attitude was undoubtedly influenced by the charges Mrs Frazier brought against her regarding her willingness to receive gifts from inmates, charges that elicited a severe reprimand from the Factory's management committee. Matron Gordon could not be considered an impartial witness regarding Ellen Frazier's character or honesty.

John defended himself against these accusations by claiming that Jane was not the source of Ellen Frazier's information, that rumours penetrated the Factory with each inmate's arrival. However the press reports regarding Jane's escape were both brief and inaccurate, and rumours often bear little resemblance to the truth. In contrast, Mrs Frazier's information neatly complemented and supplemented the known information. She was undoubtedly the recipient of inside information and the most likely source, as she herself declared, was Jane New.

Ellen Frazier reported that Jane's escape was planned in advance. She described the strategy Jane used to distract the constable, revealing information omitted, not surprisingly, by the constable himself. After entering the Phillip Street property, Jane asked the constable to take a glass of wine, but instead gave him a tumbler of brandy. She then remarked that she felt unwell and asked the lodger to let her go into the bedroom, leaving her bonnet and shawl on the table. She left the house immediately.

Clearly, Ellen Frazier's testimony exposed Constable Cleme's irresponsibility. Sheriff Macquoid had already recognised the truth, condemning Cleme's conduct as stupid and negligent, and removing him from his position.

Although John was unaware until much later of the incriminating information contained in Mrs Frazier's statement, he contradicted the rumours of his alleged involvement via an affidavit. He subsequently protested that Governor Darling had personally assured him that his affidavit was satisfactory. Governor Darling responded dryly that John was not overscrupulous in the matter of the affidavits he signed.

Some years later, John's brother Sidney indirectly confirmed John's participation and revealed his own involvement in Jane's apprehension:

> Having heard that Jane New was illegally at large, and there being a report that my brother had assisted in her escape, I felt exceedingly anxious that she should be apprehended wherever she was. After some time I heard from a client of mine that there was a female staying at a house of the name of Cunningham on Liverpool Road, and I mentioned to the constable that I imagined it was Jane New. I understood afterwards that she was apprehended there and taken to the Factory.

John saw Sidney's action as the ultimate betrayal. He took his revenge. Referring to the bundle of petitions Sidney had submitted to the authorities early in February 1829, John remarked a few months later:

> These petitions are said to have been withheld from the Governor's perusal, and public rumour has assigned the cause for this arbitrary and most cruel act to a feeling of revenge in the breast of the party whose duty it was to deliver them. Subsequent conduct of that individual seems to confirm this suspicion.

If such a public rumour had indeed whispered its way around Sydney, John was undoubtedly the source. But what led to their initial falling out? A mutual interest in Jane New? Jane had many admirers. The *Australian* reported after her escape from the constable: 'A certain influential personage, we are told, endeavoured once to take improper liberties with Jane New in which the satyr was worsted; and hence, busy rumours say, maybe dated the rancour, which pursued her even beyond conviction.' And which 'old gentleman' was 'very anxious' about her safety a couple of weeks later — perhaps Justice Stephen?

Sidney later exhibited his own unbrotherly reaction towards John. When asked about John's suspected involvement with Jane New and if he had attempted to show that such suspicions were unfounded, he answered: 'I don't believe I felt any greater interest than if I had heard the same charge against a common stranger.'

In revealing Jane's safe haven, Sidney Stephen also incurred James New's wrath:

> The husband afterwards having some intimation from the constables, I believe, that I had given the information, came to me and said that if he could find out the person who informed, he would blow their brains out. He hinted that he had understood it was one of my family — either myself or Mr John Stephen.

As James knew of John's involvement in the escape, he could readily dismiss him as the culprit, so in effect the constable's hint directly accused Sidney Stephen. Under the circumstances, James' aggressive response was understandable although undoubtedly intimidating. Despite Sidney's regular association with felons, he would rarely have found himself on the receiving end of their violent intentions.

After James' unwelcome visit, Sidney appears to have washed his hands of the News and their shenanigans. When John later tried to draw his brother back into their game, he made a serious miscalculation.

Chapter 21
ACCUSATIONS UNLEASHED

'Tis odd, 'tis passing odd, the convenient and
short memories of some people, and with what grace
they can varnish over a doubtful story!
'Miles' — pseudonym used by John Stephen Jnr

In the aftermath of Jane's escape, accusations ricocheted between the various Government departments with the initial feedback implicating Sheriff Macquoid. John claimed that Macquoid had refused to take responsibility for Jane. Macquoid, horrified at the suggestion of his culpability, angrily demanded a retraction. John responded in writing, an ill-judged decision. His description of the day's events contained significant discrepancies when compared with the statements provided by the constables and Under-Sheriff.

John reported that he had ordered the constable to detain Jane New until the court order was delivered to him, that he took the court order to Colonial Secretary McLeay's office to enquire what steps should be taken regarding Jane's transfer, and that upon his return the constables reported Jane's escape. Yet the constables' statements reveal that John returned with the court order and used it to wrest control from Sheriff Macquoid. By taking charge, John contrived to place Jane New in the custody of only one constable, presumably the man he considered the most inept. He then directed them towards the Colonial Secretary's Office and past Evans' house in Phillip Street. As Jane afterwards fled to another house in Phillip Street, her escape plans evidently included at least two safe houses for use as circumstances dictated.

After shooing Jane and the constable towards the safe house, John probably approached Colonial Secretary McLeay regarding Jane's transfer in an attempt to cover himself. Yet the Colonial Secretary realised after receiving Macquoid's packet of correspondence that John was dissembling. John had concluded his letter to Macquoid by declaring, 'I have stated all the facts of the case just as they occurred, and my intercourse with Mr McLeay nearly verbatim.' But McLeay had a different recollection of their conversation. Astonishment and dismay surely crept over the Governor and Colonial Secretary when they realised that John had participated in Jane's escape.

John's culpability and duplicity proved immensely disappointing to the Governor. Having chosen John for the coveted position of Registrar and pushed through his appointment against Chief Justice Forbes' wishes, he naturally expected appreciation and support, not a Judas-like betrayal.

Rumours of John's involvement spread rapidly. Were the co-conspirators the source: a murmured secret endlessly repeated? Perhaps they began with the upper classes, those privy to the authorities' confusion and later enlightenment as the truth dawned. Perhaps speculation initiated the rumours, suggestions alluding to John's prominent role in the previous attempts to legally free Jane New. These 'busy whisperings of those who delight in the disgrace of others' soon came to John's ears.

John attempted to quash the rumours in a letter to Colonial Secretary McLeay five days after Jane's escape. 'I trust that you will consider me sincere in expressing my deep regret to find that you should entertain towards me other than a friendly feeling,' he crawled. 'I should have passed over as idle tales the rumours which are afloat had not you indicated towards me at Mr Balcombe's funeral that there really did exist some cause of displeasure.'[33]

Recognising that his own discrepancies had exposed him, John had the effrontery to challenge the Colonial Secretary. Had his correspondence with Sheriff Macquoid led McLeay to believe that there was a 'misconception' about their conversation? John also expressed concern about the insinuations that he had aided-and-abetted Jane's escape. Yet instead of explicitly denying any involvement, John wriggled around the issue by justifying Jane's need for support and his grounds for helping her:

> My interference on behalf of that female has been designated as an attempt to obstruct the due course of justice. The result has proved how far such a charge was merited. The motive however has been ascribed to unlawful passions, to the misguided exertions of unhallowed lust. My solemn denial before Heaven of such an imputation may I trust be received as satisfactory as I make it sincerely. The interest I took in this unhappy woman's welfare arose from the purest feeling of humanity, and a well-grounded conviction of her innocence, with a knowledge of the undeserved aspersions that were heaped upon her fame. Nothing but this could have averted from its channel that stream of mercy which I attempted with many others to make flow from its fountain — and I would fain here ask whether it were likely that a body of gentlemen such as the Bank of Australia Directors would lend themselves to pander to my sinful appetites!

John's letter backfired. Governor Darling saw through his evasive response and ordered an enquiry. When John later heard that Jane had been questioned about his involvement, he was irate. He dashed off a letter to Dr Mathew Anderson at the General Hospital:

> I feel myself under the unpleasant necessity of calling for an explanation of a circumstance which has just been communicated to me. Your denial or avowal of the grounds on which you acted in this matter, is what I am strictly entitled to demand, and I trust that no delay may take place in your reply. It is stated that you called on a female in the Factory named New to state whether I had assisted in her escape from the custody of the constables on the 21st March last, adding that 'the Government were anxious of ascertaining that fact, and that they would reward her if she

confessed'. This communication has been made to me by my brother, Mr
Sidney Stephen, who received the information from Mr New, his client,
who states that there were witnesses present when you thus addressed
his wife.

The reference to Sidney Stephen is surprising. Francis served as the News'
counsel at the *habeas corpus* hearing, and the News did not require the
services of a barrister — either Sidney or anyone else — in April 1829
when these events occurred. Indeed, Sidney would probably have rejected
any commission from James New after his threatening behaviour a short
time earlier. Significantly, John failed to mention Sidney's name in a later
communication on the subject when he reported that the information had
been 'vaguely' repeated to him.

Dr Anderson responded to John's importunate letter:

Without admitting for a moment your title to demand any explanation
of the kind, I beg to say that your name was never either mentioned or
alluded to in any communication I might have had with the woman in
question.

Dr Anderson had also been present when Ellen Frazier implicated John
in Jane's escape. John was unaware of this investigation until a year later,
and complained that he had been offered no opportunity to reply to this
secret enquiry into matters affecting his reputation. 'Why was I not made
acquainted with this examination before?' he demanded. 'Because the
Governor knew that an investigation into the matter by asking Cunningham
(the man who harboured Jane) about my engagement at that time would
have disproved such a scandalous assertion.'

In truth, John did have an opportunity to reply, albeit indirectly
through his affidavit. But Darling later observed that John's affidavit did
not contradict Ellen Frazier's statement that he had conveyed Jane from
Sydney after she effected her escape from custody.

So why didn't Governor Darling pursue the matter at this time?
Perhaps he granted John the benefit of the doubt. Perhaps he believed that

infatuation had led John momentarily astray. Perhaps he decided that for reasons of political expediency it was not an opportune moment to rock this particular boat.

It would prove a rash decision.

Chapter 22
MANIPULATIONS AND MACHINATIONS

Mr Stephen is busily engaged in getting affidavits to rebut the facts.
Governor Ralph Darling

John Stephen Jnr was playing with the authorities, vehemently and with apparent sincerity protesting his innocence while quietly orchestrating plans to assist Jane in her bid for freedom. Indeed on 26 March, the very day John sent his protestations of innocence to Colonial Secretary McLeay, he was scheming to prove that Jane's sentence was about to expire and thereby justify her flight from forced repatriation to Tasmania.

Through his position as Registrar, John knew of two anomalies in the New South Wales record of Jane's British conviction and transportation. Colonial Secretary Burnett's letter to Colonial Secretary McLeay authorising Jane's relocation to Sydney provided the only New South Wales record of her sentence of transportation. It noted that she arrived on the *Brothers* in 1825, having been convicted at Cheshire in April 1824. As the *Brothers* actually arrived in April 1824, either Jane's ship of arrival or her date of conviction was recorded incorrectly. Upon closer examination, John discovered that Jane's date of conviction revealed evidence of an erasure, that the year '1822' had been overwritten '1824'. He required no further ammunition to attack Jane's problem from a new direction.

Late in March 1829, John prepared a series of affidavits. Jane New herself signed one — ostensibly drawn in Sidney Stephen's office and sworn in open court on the final day of her *habeas corpus* hearing! — alleging that she was tried in April 1822 rather than 1824 and had been detained at Chester for many months because of a severe illness. Alluding to confusion caused by her use of an alias, Jane explained that she was then placed in gaol and confined there until ordered to her Tasmanian transport.

By describing how she was held back from transportation through illness and then confusion, Jane's story attempted to account for the significant delay between her alleged conviction in 1822 and her sailing date, whether by the inaccurately recorded *Brothers* late in 1823 or by the *Henry* late in 1824. The authorities later dismissed Jane's affidavit. No Justice of the Peace would place any value on an affidavit prepared by a convicted felon asserting an earlier conviction date, they observed, particularly when an official document and order of court contradicted such a statement.

Three other men supported Jane's statement through their own affidavits. Seaman James Horton agreed with Jane's Spring 1822 conviction, declaring that he knew her in Chester and attended her trial. He reported being confident that this date was correct as he had left Chester in June of that year and had not since returned.

Horton's affidavit also received short shrift. Jane could have been tried at Chester in 1822 and also in 1824, the authorities observed, without Horton being aware of the latter conviction.

Surgeon Superintendent William Bell Carlyle who travelled with the *Henry* 'verily believed' that Jane had been confined in gaol for a considerable period before her embarkation. From his recollection of the convict indents, he believed that her sentence should have almost expired. And since her ship of arrival had been recorded incorrectly, perhaps her trial date was also incorrect.

Carlyle's affidavit merely corroborated Jane's arrival on the *Henry*. His higher social status should have lent greater credence to his statement, however his assertions were hazy and unconvincing. Governor Darling later remarked that Carlyle's affidavit was neither creditable to him nor to its framer. He could easily identify the hand guiding the pen.

James New provided the final affidavit, declaring that, upon his marriage in 1826, the Tasmanian authorities reported that Jane had only three years left to serve. The Tasmanian authorities later proved that he was lying by transmitting a copy of his 1827 petition in which he mentioned her April 1824 conviction date.

Although John gathered these four affidavits in March 1829, he chose not to file them in the Supreme Court or present them to the authorities at that time. He intended to use them for maximum effect. John knew that once he presented them, a request would be transmitted to Tasmania for verification. The resulting response would invalidate the affidavits and any claim he might make to ignorance of the truth. Their window of effectiveness would only be narrow.

Curiously, when John eventually presented the affidavits they were attached to an affidavit by Frederick Finlay — 'late law clerk in the office of Sidney Stephen' — declaring that he was responsible for their preparation. Why Finlay was no longer in Sidney's employ is unknown. Perhaps his involvement in the affidavits' preparations had led to his dismissal. Perhaps by using Sidney's law clerk, John had risked implicating his brother in the conspiracy. If so, Sidney's role in exposing Jane's hide-out could have served both as retribution and as a means of distancing himself from the scandal, instead of his stated concern for his brother's reputation.

James New signed another affidavit on the day the constables apprehended Jane and returned her to the Female Factory. Referring to the Supreme Court's ruling that his wife had arrived in New South Wales contrary to law and was to be lodged in the Female Factory until her return to Tasmania, he protested its injustice. He had obtained Governor Arthur's sanction to bring her to New South Wales as had many others in similar situations, he complained, and had relied upon Governor Darling's assurances that deserving prisoners might accompany their relatives to Sydney and reside there.

It was a reasonable complaint. No general order had been issued for the immediate incarceration and forced repatriation of any other Tasmanian prisoner residing in New South Wales. Jane was suffering alone. And she was indeed suffering, James continued:

> My wife is treated at the Factory as a Prisoner of the Crown, being deprived of all her own clothing even the combs that are necessary to keep her hair from falling over her eyes and she is dressed in the woollen garments of the Factory and kept at labour which is not only contrary to the order of the Supreme Court but in direct violation of a Government Order from His Excellency dated 27 June 1826 that 'no woman being the wife of a free man or a man holding a ticket-of-leave is to be kept in the Factory except under the immediate sentence of the law'.

James also drafted a petition to the Supreme Court judges, asking that Jane be allowed out on bail so he could remove her to Tasmania as soon as his affairs were settled. Yet he did not sign, date or present it. James' affidavit intimated that Jane had been languishing in the Female Factory since the Supreme Court's ruling. The authorities knew otherwise and would have accorded his complaint and his request for bail little sympathy.

As it transpired, James' appeals were not intended to fulfil their purported aims. John had conspired with James New to produce these documents with other intentions in mind.

Chapter 23

A WHIRLPOOL OF INTRIGUE

Governor Darling was eager to revenge himself upon an individual
who had caused him considerable anxiety by casually having
announced the probability of his recall.

John Stephen Jnr

John Stephen Jnr was in his element. The monotony of juggling just the
one ball — his own life — was long gone. Multiple balls kept his hands
and mind busy and his adrenaline charged: his involvement with Jane New,
his participation in her escape, his strategy to convince the authorities
of his innocence, his quietly orchestrated plans for the future. It was
his own version of a delightful game: full of excitement, danger and the
risk of social suicide.

And it was time for another ball to join the array.

Presumably with the idea of alarming and deflecting Governor Darling
and also diverting the busy whisperers onto a new topic, John spread a
rumour that the Governor and Colonial Secretary were being recalled to
Britain. Early in April, word reached Colonial Secretary McLeay by way of
Commissioner Foster of the Court of Requests that John possessed a letter
containing such information sent by a person of undoubted authority.

Immediately suspecting John's involvement in generating such a rumour,
McLeay wrote to him on 4 April demanding that he explicitly state the

source of his information and his reasons for circulating such a report. The colony's current political climate made such a claim highly injurious, he remonstrated.

John expressed indignation at the suggestion of his culpability and vehemently denied having either raised or circulated the report. The rumour had gained general notoriety before he repeated it, he retorted, although he agreed to 'plainly and candidly' relate how he first mentioned the subject:

> On going to Court on, I think, Wednesday morning April 1st, I was met on the steps of the Court by a gentleman who asked me if I had heard the news, adding that it was such as the season would justify to make April Fools. I remarked that 'it was no April Fool's joke to me', on which we parted.

The 'unnamed gentleman' was never identified and almost certainly never existed, although the reference to an April Fool's joke is enlightening. John probably initiated the rumour to serve his own ends, knowing that 'April Fool's!' could be his refuge if called to task. As proved the case with most of John's chicanery, however, the joke developed its own momentum, spinning quickly out of his control.

That April Fool's day, John had a busy morning. After his alleged conversation with the 'gentleman', he spoke with Sheriff William Carter, remarking that he, his brother and Commissioner Foster had been superseded in their knowledge of the Governor's recall. 'In giving him this intelligence as authentic,' John earnestly reported to McLeay, 'I expressed my fears as to the probability of the truth of the rumour respecting the Governor and yourself.'

A few minutes later the Sheriff and Chief Justice both broached the subject. John recalled: 'I then mentioned that I had certainly received a letter on the subject but there were other letters in the colony from which the rumour had obtained notoriety.'

As his duties prevented him from leaving the court, John asked Commissioner Foster to relay the report to the Colonial Secretary as Governor Darling would want to know the particulars. No doubt John wished to ensure that the rumour reached the Governor's ears as quickly as possible. John later oozed: 'My manner to him, I am sure, must have been demonstrative of the regret I felt, not only as it affected the Governor, but myself; not only in losing my appointment but in the chance of losing my kind patron.'

Although John's responsibility for generating the rumour was not confirmed until months later, clues were evident in the related correspondence. John intimated that Commissioner Foster had independent knowledge of the rumour, however Foster indicated otherwise. John also failed to mention that he had asked Sheriff William Carter to inform the Colonial Secretary. Carter later provided details of their conversation.

'Have you heard the news?' John had asked.

'What news?' Carter said.

'The Governor and the whole of his personal establishment and the Colonial Secretary are recalled and the new Governor might be expected in a few weeks,' John explained. 'He is to sail immediately after Christmas.'

'We have been told the same story so often,' Carter sneered, 'I cannot believe it but upon very good authority.'

'It has been received from a person whose high connections with Government render it impossible that he should be deceived,' John revealed.

Had the layers of John's deception been meticulously planned or had he merely intended to spread an elusive rumour? John's reference to a person with high connections failed to convince Carter who queried whether this was John's cousin, James Stephen. John had probably imagined that those hearing the rumour would focus on its contents and simply assume that his Colonial-Office cousin was the source. Instead, he found himself spinning a more intricate web to convince this particular sceptic.

'It came from the brother of a nobleman connected with the Government,' he disclosed. Probably unable to resist the impulse, he added: 'There are two other letters in town containing the same information.' An unfortunate addition, this claim led to more questions.

'How has it happened that such important information has been kept a secret so long, there being no late shipping arrivals?' Carter scoffed.

Another layer had to be spun. 'A box or bag of letters was mislaid,' John explained, 'and was only found a few days ago.' Again, he could not resist elaborating on his lie, adding the name of the vessel. Fortunately for John, Carter was later unable to recall the details.

Carter concluded his letter to the Colonial Secretary with the wry observation: 'My faith was very weak. I thought there was a particular object in view, which I explained to you. It related to a *New* and an important personage.'

Carter was no fool.

On 4 April, when Governor Darling commanded John to explain himself, he could have backed away and claimed 'April Fool's!'. Instead, John advanced the joke to the next level, to a point beyond retreat. He requested an interview with the Governor and offered a letter purportedly written by his wife, who was then in England, referring to the Governor and Colonial Secretary's recall. In the letter John's wife expressed her regret as she knew both men were John's 'warm friends'.

A few days later John provided a written explanation:

The more positive assertions of the Governor's recall were in a letter to my brother Frank, and as 'Mr Stephen' was referred to generally, I was supposed to be the source or one of the sources of the report. I have shown my letter to no one individual, and except for the members of my family I have not spoken on the subject until after it appeared in the public journals, and then not admitting my 'proofs' as they are called of its probability.

In concluding his letter John milked injured innocence to its fullest, alluding to a conspiracy to condemn him:

I was most surprised to find that your letter to me on this matter was known to be in existence before it reached my hands, and its contents exaggerated and grossly perverted to my injury.

Despite John's denials, the authorities remained unconvinced. Governor Darling wrote a private letter to Sir George Murray containing details of

John's claims including his reference to James Stephen's appointment as a Commissioner of Enquiry in New South Wales. Sir George immediately questioned James Stephen who denied writing the letter to John or any other letter mentioning appointments or recalls. In his response to Darling Sir George dismissed John's claims, and concluded that the letter was a forgery. 'It is not very skilfully contrived,' he added 'since it does not profess to be written by the hand of the person to whom it is ascribed and has no date, signature or post mark.' He added: 'I am unwilling to suppose that Mr John Stephen made use of this letter with any knowledge or belief that it was a forgery.' Yet he admitted to having his suspicions:

I am informed by James Stephen that he has received a letter from Mr John Stephen dated 14th April last, in which no reference is made to the subject, although your letter is dated on the 11th of the same month. Mr John Stephen's silence on a subject of such recent occurrence and of such evident interest to his correspondent and to himself is a circumstance which cannot but provoke some doubt of his own belief in the genuineness of the letter. You will call upon him for such explanations as he may think proper to give.

Sir George requested that Governor Darling forward the original of the letter along with details of ships from Britain arriving in New South Wales between January and April. He sent a request to Governor Arthur to ask Alfred Stephen about his involvement in transmitting the letter from Tasmania to Sydney. And he concluded his letter to Darling by remarking that in justice to those implicated and for Darling's own interest, he had investigated the origins of the rumour although he attached little importance to it. Another rebuke followed:

I fear that in a Society so constituted as is that under your Government, you can never escape that petty hostility which vents itself in the dissemination of false and injurious rumours. Attacks of such nature derive their principal efficacy from the real or supposed sensibility of those against whom they are directed, and are usually better repelled by silence and indifference than by more active measures.

It was a repetition of his many previous rebukes, containing a message Governor Darling seemed incapable of absorbing.

By the time Darling received Sir George's letter, more than a year had passed. As Darling explained in his response, John Stephen Jnr could no longer be questioned, although his own investigation had continued. He reported that Alfred Stephen had denied any knowledge of the letter, that all communication had apparently long ceased between John and James Stephen, and that John had probably only affected to write familiarly to his cousin because his letter passed across the Governor's desk.

Darling concluded: 'I have never doubted that the letters which he stated he had received from his wife and his cousin, Mr James Stephen, were both fabricated by himself, the clumsiness of the latter being necessarily occasioned by his desire to screen himself from the consequences of forgery.' What astonished Darling was John's indefatigable exertions in pursuing his object, and his willingness to advance the game from simple rumour-mongering to the criminal act of forgery.

Chapter 24
DESPERATION

I never hear the word 'escape',
Without a quicker blood,
A sudden expectation.
Emily Dickinson

When the gates of the Female Factory clanged behind Jane New on 28 March 1829, a sense of despair must have engulfed her. Would her next view of the outside world be under escort to a boat bound for Tasmania?

As Matron Gordon ushered her towards the accommodation quarters, Jane was no doubt expecting to be relegated to the third class. Indeed, her escape should have justified an appearance before the magistrates on a 'convict at large' charge, resulting perhaps in an extension of her sentence and almost certainly in an order for her confinement in the penitentiary section. Yet any question of a magisterial hearing had been sidestepped by Governor Darling's order that Jane be immediately returned to the Female Factory. Perhaps he was averse to facing any more Jane New-associated dramas.

Instead, Jane was upgraded to the first class, a move reflecting either another extraordinary oversight or one of the many indulgences that somehow continued to be allowed her. Admittedly, Police Superintendent Innes ordered Matron Gordon to be vigilant in preventing Jane from having any contact with persons outside the Factory. Matron Gordon solved this problem by employing Jane separately from the general body of women in a small room inside an internal building, and making frequent personal visits to ensure that she was still present. Mrs Gordon also examined all of the women admitted to the Factory, suspecting that attempts would be made to smuggle in letters. When Jane bribed a woman to carry a letter to her husband, word quickly reached Matron Gordon. The intercepted letter, dated 3 April 1829 and presumably written by a literate inmate, beseeched James to visit her at the Factory:

Dear Husband,

I hear that you are in Parramatta; I hope and trust that you will get a order to come and see me, for I am almost out of my mind at not seeing you. Please do send me word where you are stopping at, as I wish you to stop in Parramatta a few days; if you cannot come, send me an answer to this.

I remain, loving wife tho unfortunate till death, Jane New.

Despite Mrs Gordon's vigilance, Jane had evidently received word of events outside the Factory's walls. Perhaps by the same route suggestions were communicated for her escape.

Haste was essential. Jane could be escorted to a Tasmania-bound ship at any time. Sunday 5 April was chosen. As the sun set, Jane's plans were implemented. Matron Gordon recollected seeing her around 5.15 pm. Evening worship having just ended, Jane and the other first-class women were strolling to their yard, perhaps chattering and giggling or pretending to reflect soberly upon the preacher's words. Monitress Mary Ann Carroll reported seeing Jane walking up and down the first-class yard shortly before the women went in to tea. She was probably lying.

When the women assembled in the mess room at 6 pm, Jane was missing. Inmate Susan Courtnay was the first to notice. After glancing around the room, she asked, 'Where is Jane New?'

'She would not come in,' Mary Gannon quickly responded. 'We quarrelled this morning and she has gone to another mess.' Mary Gannon reportedly followed this remark with a sly look at another inmate.

Mrs Nairn, the Assistant Matron of the first class, usually mustered the women at mealtimes, however she was 'otherwise engaged' at this time. Had she been deliberately waylaid, perhaps with a bottle of some intoxicating substance? Mary Ann Carroll covered her duties, playing a key role in the plot. She accepted Mary Gannon's excuse and failed to report Jane's absence, earning Jane a critical half-hour reprieve.

Exiting the mess at 6.30 pm, the first-class women traipsed to their bedroom where they were again mustered. Inmate Mary Cox noted Jane's absence and informed overseer Sarah Johnson. Mary Ann Carroll piped up that Jane had also been missing at teatime. Sarah Johnson dashed off to report Jane's absence to Matron Gordon. A diligent search throughout the building failed to locate her. At 7 pm a messenger carried the news to the Chief Constable at Parramatta that Jane New had escaped. Again.

The *Sydney Gazette* was the only newspaper to cover the latest instalment in the Jane New scandal, reporting:

> On the evening of Sunday last it was discovered that Jane New, who has already become so celebrated in our colonial annals, had made her escape by some as yet undiscovered contrivance from the Female Factory at Parramatta, to which she had been committed under the order of the Supreme Court. An investigation was taking place by the Committee of Management as to the means by which her flight was accomplished when the news reached us; but our informant promises to communicate early intelligence of the result.

The Female Factory Management Committee met the day after Jane's escape to investigate the circumstances. Comprising Reverend Samuel Marsden, Parramatta Police Superintendent Major Innes, Darling's aide-de-camp Thomas de la Condamine and Dr Mathew Anderson, the Committee sought information from the Matron, the Assistant Matrons and seven inmates. Mrs Nairn proposed that Jane must have escaped immediately after evening worship by passing into the second-class yard. The Assistant

Matron of the second class, Mrs Pegg, refuted this suggestion. She reported being present in the second-class mess room from 5 pm until 6 pm, remaining there until all of the women left the room, and then locking the door behind her and pocketing the key. 'It was impossible,' she swore, 'for Jane New to have escaped that way.' In the absence of any other suggestions or theories, the Committee failed to reach any conclusions regarding Jane's method of escape from the Factory. She never returned.

Matron Gordon was not blamed for Jane's escape. Instead the Committee concluded that she had been vigilant in discharging her duties. However, they deemed the absent Mrs Nairn neglectful, and deduced that Mary Gannon knew more than she disclosed. Their harshest judgement landed upon monitress Mary Ann Carroll whom they considered both culpable and complicit:

> It appears that Jane New could not have affected her escape from the Factory without the assistance and connivance of some persons of the same class to which she belonged; and the Committee are further of opinion that the monitress Mary Ann Carroll is guilty of great neglect of duty in not immediately reporting the absence of Jane New on her discovering that she was not present with her mess at tea.

Carroll's avid interest in the News' activities, as reported by another inmate who used to work for James New, contributed to the Committee's conclusion regarding her involvement in Jane's escape.

Although the Committee speculated about the identities of Jane's likely accomplices, they offered no suggestions regarding the mechanics of her escape. The Governor and Colonial Secretary's thoughts evidently remained verbal and the press ignored the topic, so clues cannot be gleaned from contemporary sources. When the subject came under discussion some years later, Matron Gordon raised the possibility that Jane had escaped over the back wall. 'I think she could have escaped without assistance from within,' she observed, 'but I don't know from without. They frequently escape without assistance. I have seen women with their ankles cut and their legs broken from dropping from the walls.' When asked if she thought Jane had received outside assistance, Matron Gordon qualified her statement by admitting that women frequently escaped unhurt.

Was Matron Gordon concealing the involvement of a man in Jane's escape? Perhaps Jane had ensnared the one male resident at the Female Factory — Matron Gordon's own husband. Indirect reports later surfaced that Robert Gordon had found the isolated women a temptation too powerful to resist.

Alternatively, Jane might have bribed a staff member. When Ellen Frazier later laid charges against Matrons Gordon and Kingaby, she revealed that Mrs Kingaby (the penitentiary's matron) had given Jane's side-combs to Matron Gordon's daughter. When Jane reportedly enquired about them, Mrs Kingaby informed her that they were broken. Perhaps this was the truth, or perhaps a story concocted to conceal a bribe.

Whatever the nature of Jane's inside assistance, she was apparently on her own after breaching the Factory's walls. 'After Mrs New escaped on the Sunday afternoon,' James New's employee, James Middleton, later disclosed, 'she walked down to Sydney that night.'

Did Jane truly walk in her factory dress from Parramatta to Sydney? A distance of 14 miles, it must have taken her most of the night. Plodding along what was little more than a dark track, guided by no light but the moon or the filtered glow from the widely spaced residences. Startling at every noise, uncertain whether it came from farm animals settling for the night, native animals assessing her status as friend or foe, or the biggest threat of all, the human predators lurking in the dark waiting for their prey. Scuttling into the bushes at the sound of a horse or carriage in case it carried a member of the constabulary despatched to apprehend her. By the time she reached Sydney on Monday morning she must have been cold, tired, footsore and — having missed dinner — very hungry.

Jane presumably slipped into a friend's residence on the outskirts of Sydney and asked for James to be contacted and informed of her escape and current whereabouts. James waited until evening to collect her. Using the darkness and male clothing to conceal her identity, he brought her back to their residence in Cambridge Street. Her factory dress travelled with her, probably concealed in a bundle. Not liking the male disguise, Jane soon retreated to her room and changed into her own clothes.

The following evening a strange incident occurred. Back at the Female Factory at Parramatta, military guard James Pegg was on duty at the main gate, preventing undesirables from entering and inmates from leaving. Around 7.30 pm on Tuesday 7 April, two men materialised out of the gloom and approached him, handing over a letter. One of the men — who later proved to be Jane's stepfather Richard Baker — asked that the letter be delivered to Matron Gordon. He then handed a bundle to the gatekeeper and the two men departed.

Matron Gordon was absent at this time. The gatekeeper quickly called her husband Robert Gordon and reported the surprising incident. Perhaps Gordon read the letter, examined the parcel, and expressed concerns about a criminal conspiracy. More likely he directed the guard to apprehend the two men before being certain there was a reason for doing so. Pegg returned with Baker, reporting that the other man had escaped.

Robert Gordon's prompt action was validated when he examined the items. The bundle contained clothes worn by the first-class women that were the property of the government. The attached letter stated that Jane New had worn these clothes when she escaped from the Factory. Gordon must have been astounded and perplexed at such a delivery.

A messenger hurried off to inform the Parramatta constabulary that assistance was required. No doubt Police Superintendent Innes reacted with suspicion, wondering what game Jane's supporters were now playing. He despatched a constable to the Factory where Richard Baker was questioned regarding his companion's identity. Baker disclosed, without any evident reticence, that his companion was James New. The constables took Baker into custody and escorted him to the police lock-up at Parramatta.

Brought before the Police Superintendent the following day, Richard Baker was asked to account for his actions. 'On yesterday afternoon,' he reported, 'whilst I was at the coach office in Sydney for the purpose of taking a seat on the coach to Parramatta, James New delivered to me a bundle and a letter directed to the Matron of the Factory, and which bundle and letter I accordingly did deliver and was taken into custody for so doing.'

Major Innes ordered Baker to procure bail and to appear before the court when called upon. He summoned James New to appear the following Saturday to explain how Government property came into his possession. He then sent the depositions to Colonial Secretary McLeay with a request for Attorney-General Baxter's opinion on the procedures necessary to convict the parties. Baxter opined that there was insufficient evidence against Richard Baker to warrant his conviction and expressed doubts that charges against James New could be pursued. No doubt Governor Darling experienced a moment of intense frustration when he heard the news, particularly as the accuracy of Baxter's advice was inevitably open to doubt. Whatever Darling's thoughts, however, he conveyed Baxter's opinion to the Parramatta Bench and the matter was dropped.

Yet despite Baxter's opinion, it seems surprising that the authorities failed to question James New. Richard Baker's possession of clothes apparently given to him by James, and apparently worn by Jane when she left the Factory, indicated that James had been in contact with, and was conceivably harbouring, a runaway. To have forsaken the opportunity to at least question James about these circumstances suggests that the authorities made no real attempt to apprehend Jane New at this time.

Richard Baker and James New's decision to put themselves at risk by returning Jane's clothes seems surprising at first glance, however it probably reflected the hand of one versed in the law. In escaping from the Female Factory, Jane was of course a runaway and was open to charges on that account. Having escaped in her Factory gown she could also be accused of having stolen government property, and if apprehended with the clothes, she could face a 'possession' charge. Destroying the clothes would eliminate one potential charge; returning them would eliminate all risk.

Perhaps this danger occurred to Jane or one of her relatives and perhaps they devised the strategy of returning her clothes to the Factory. But, if so, who wrote the letter? The Bakers and News were illiterate as were most of their associates. It seems more likely that James New contacted John Stephen Jnr upon receiving word of Jane's escape, and asked his advice, and that John devised the plan and wrote the letter.

Nevertheless it seems odd that Jane's husband and stepfather — those most likely to be harbouring her — would personally take the incriminating letter and bundle to the Factory, placing themselves at risk. Richard Baker did indeed find himself in this difficult position, and James New was facing a summons. So why did they expose themselves in this way?

Possibly Jane's family decided that it would be more risky to send the parcel by mail or to involve someone else. Possibly someone suggested hand-delivering Jane's clothes to the Factory in order to mock the authorities. Yet since the risk of being apprehended surely outweighed the rewards gained by such behaviour, this seems a luxury that could only have been conceived by John Stephen Jnr, the man who made a habit of playing such games. And if this was indeed John's plan, perhaps there was an underlying sinister intent. If James New was apprehended and convicted, Jane would have no one to support her financially. Naturally, she would seek a new protector.

Chapter 25
A TEMPORARY HAVEN

*All constables and others are hereby required and commanded to
use their utmost exertions in apprehending and lodging absconded
prisoners in safe custody.*
Government notice

The authorities made no attempt to apprehend Jane New after her uniform
was returned to the Female Factory, nor did they take any action in the
ensuing weeks. Had they exerted themselves even slightly, they would have
discovered her easily. She was hiding out in her own home.

Jane remained in the couple's Cambridge Street residence for two or
three weeks after her escape from the Factory. She presumably hid indoors
for most of this period, although her male attire would've allowed her to
venture outdoors on occasion. Gradually, however, rumours of her presence
were spreading through the streets of Sydney and would inevitably reach
the ears of the authorities.

Despite having a successful business, James New had already begun
converting his assets to cash. By late April he had sold his stock and received
part payment. He relinquished his Cambridge Street property and took rooms
at Eliza James Jones' lodging house in Pitt Street, depositing £20 as a bond.

When James rented the Pitt Street apartment he informed Mrs Jones
that the rooms would be occupied by himself and a young man coming

down from the country. He provided his own name but not that of his companion. Mrs Jones only discovered by accident the true identity of James' co-tenant. A couple of days after the News moved in, a gentleman friend asked if she knew who her tenants were. When she expressed ignorance, he disclosed that they were 'New and his wife in men's clothes'.

Mrs Jones immediately stormed up to the News' room and demanded the truth. James confessed that his companion was his wife. Mrs Jones ordered him to take Jane away immediately. Jane whined: 'It is very hard. I have no place to be in.'

Although realising that Jane's friends were unwilling to harbour her, Mrs Jones had no sympathy for her plight. 'You must leave!' she insisted. 'I will have no person I am under any fear of in my house!'

Although James continued to reside at the lodging house for the following couple of weeks, Jane left the next evening. Perhaps she went to her mother's house; perhaps John found her a sanctuary. The records remain silent.

While residing at Mrs Jones', James purchased passages for himself and his wife on the *Mary* which was due to sail early in May for Batavia. Cambridge Street butcher John Jobbins advanced some money to assist with James' downpayment, and accepted a box of Jane's clothes as security. James never reclaimed them and they were ultimately sold at auction. James also brought the *Mary*'s captain and another gentleman to Mrs Jones' house and organised for £5 of his bond money to be advanced to the captain.

And he readied himself to slip out of the country.

Between 7 and 8 pm on Friday 8 May, two days before the *Mary* was due to sail, Constables Edward Fenton and Patrick Naughton were patrolling Goulburn Street. Ex-felons themselves, they were adept at recognising suspicious behaviour. A short distance away they spied two men trudging towards a back street. One had a bundle tied in a blanket on his back. Immediately suspecting that the bundle contained stolen property, the constables approached the men.

'Where are you going,' asked Fenton, 'and what have you got there?'

Both men innocently chorused: 'We're just going home.'

The bundle-free man, recognised by the constables as emancipated convict James Dooley, added: 'It's all right.'

'Well, if it's all right,' quipped Constable Fenton, 'you must come back with me to the watchhouse.'

Fenton beckoned his partner to help surround the men while reassuring them: 'If everything is all right after we've been to the watchhouse, you might go about your business.'

As the constables closed in, the two men looked at each other, tossed the bundle in Fenton's face, and ran. Ordering Naughton to stay with the bundle, Fenton sprinted after them shouting, 'Stop thief!' Upon reaching the George Street intersection, the two men split up. Fenton followed Dooley and eventually grabbed him. Dooley's accomplice, a man the constables believed to be named Cooke, eluded apprehension.

The constables steered Dooley and the bundle to the watchhouse, summoned Chief Constable George Jilks, and unwrapped the blanket. It contained a jacket, coat, shirt, four pairs of trousers, six waistcoats, braces, stockings, towel, brush, pocketbook and papers. While separating and itemising the goods, they found a painting nestled in the clothing. When closely examined, there was no mistaking the face of the woman captured in the miniature: Jane New.

James had not reported the theft of his belongings. Indeed his mother-in-law Elizabeth Baker later claimed that James had not even noticed the disappearance from the foot of his bed of the large sailor's trunk containing the items he planned to take away with him two days hence. He only discovered the theft, she declared, when Constable Jilks arrived at his door. Jilks called upon James New the same evening the items were recovered, and found him in bed. He informed James of the constables' discovery, however, as Jilks later reported, James would not swear to the items.

James' reluctance to identify his belongings was confirmed by his ex-employee, James Middleton, who later reported: 'I met James New a day or two before he left the colony, and he told me that he had been robbed, and asked me if I could identify his clothes. They were then in the police office. I told him that he was the proper person to claim his clothes, but he said he would not stop.' James excused his reluctance by claiming that he had taken a passage for himself and his wife, that the ship was about to sail, and that he would rather lose his clothes than forfeit his passage. Yet he subsequently chose to identify his possessions. He attended the police office on Saturday 9th, identified the items as his property and requested permission to take possession of Jane's miniature as well as his all-important certificate of freedom.

Perhaps James feared drawing the police's attention upon himself, being not only the husband and likely harbourer of an absconded prisoner but one showing every sign of undertaking a lengthy sea voyage. Perhaps startled and disconcerted when the goods were quickly discovered and traced back to him, he overreacted and attempted to distance himself from the items and any associated questions. By morning he was probably castigating himself for his stupidity, having recognised that such a response would seem even more suspicious. He trotted off to the police office to do so.

James had no reason to worry. The police failed to recognise the signs of imminent departure, perhaps deliberately, through incompetence, or because James was able to weave a good story.

Nevertheless, James failed to recover the remainder of his possessions valued at over £11. Retained by the police, they served as evidence at James Dooley's eventual trial upon charges of receiving stolen goods. In his defence, Dooley claimed: 'I was up the country at the time of the robbery; I sent for two witnesses but they would not come.' Since Dooley was well-known to both of the constables, his defence failed to convince the jury and he was sentenced to seven years' transportation. His companion, the man actually carrying the bundle when approached by the constables, remained free.

While James New brushed off the police and busily prepared to flee the country, John tackled Jane's situation from a different angle. Explaining that he was writing under Jane's earnest directions, he appealed on 5 May 1829 to her erstwhile employer, Dr Robert Officer, for assistance in petitioning

Governor Arthur for her emancipation. John's letter also included a detailed description of the 'facts' in case the newspapers had created an unfavourable impression.

As it turned out, the conservative Tasmanian newspapers had largely ignored Jane's story while the liberal *Tasmanian and Asiatic Review* had picked up the innocent-woman-maligned-and-maltreated version promulgated by the liberal Sydney newspapers. Indeed, the editor managed an even more melodramatic tone than his Sydney counterparts. Lamenting that Jane New had been residing with her husband in Sydney 'peaceably and uninterruptedly' until a certain Madame Rens had 'lost' some articles from her shop and was induced 'twelve months later' to charge Jane with robbery, the editor embroidered a truly pathetic scenario. John had no need to worry that Dr Officer might have received an unfavourable impression.

John's letter to Dr Officer comprised a clever intermingling of fact and fiction. In addition to the old stories — that the August 1828 shoplifting charges were discharged for want of evidence, that Madame Rens' case came to trial only because of Jane's determination to prove her innocence — some new stories surfaced. John claimed that the subscription fund was established to pay Jane's passage to England should the Governor grant her an emancipation; in truth, it was intended to reimburse James New for his court costs. John reported that soon after the *habeas corpus* ruling, James appealed for his wife to be forwarded to Tasmania on a vessel about to sail for Hobart but his entreaties were refused. It seems a strangely unnecessary lie. Considering that Jane escaped from custody immediately after the judges' ruling, James' only entreaty at this time was for his accomplices to keep her well hidden. John also explained that Jane had been advised to petition Governor Arthur for her emancipation, hence his appeal to Dr Officer. Naturally he failed to reveal the trivial detail that she was again on the run from the authorities, and that the only people offering such advice were his cronies.

Governor Darling later remarked: 'Out of charity, I would willingly suppose these statements to be the effect of infatuation and not a wilful determination to misrepresent the facts.' It would prove an astonishingly charitable remark.

Accompanying John's letter to Dr Officer was an undated petition from James New to Governor Arthur. Pleading for a remission of Jane's sentence to remedy the problems arising from the Supreme Court ruling, James' petition was supported by the signatures of eighteen Sydney worthies. This included John, five men who had signed Jane's January 1829 petition, and a number of first timers.[34] The wording implied that Jane was languishing in the Factory, yet, in the 45 days between the judges' decision and the composition of John's accompanying letter to Dr Officer, Jane was imprisoned for only eight days. Either this petition was crafted during that short time frame or the eighteen worthies — justices of the peace, magistrates, solicitors — were appending their names to a deceitful document.

Other documents accompanied John's letter: affidavits, statements and petitions, including those transmitted to Governor Darling in February 1829 as part of the Kelly defence, but returned unread. The bundle also included James New's unsigned petition to the Supreme Court justices and his affidavit protesting against Jane's incarceration. These were shipped to Alfred Stephen in Tasmania, and he forwarded them to Dr Officer. On 1 June, Officer addressed a covering note to Governor Arthur describing Jane's case as one which had recently excited the attention and sympathy of the public. He earnestly recommended Jane's petition to the Governor, explaining that he was not only motivated by pity for the unfortunate female and a sense of justice, but that it afforded him much pleasure to do so.

Unfortunately for the News, Governor Arthur had already received details about Jane's case from Governor Darling. Colonial Secretary Burnett pointedly informed Dr Officer that Jane New had escaped from her place of confinement instead of submitting to the Supreme Court's decree, and that Governor Arthur could not consider the petition until she returned to Tasmania as ordered by the court.

Governor Arthur forwarded Dr Officer's letter and some of the attached documents to Governor Darling. In his covering letter he asked if any evidence of Jane's innocence had surfaced, as he presumed she was being sent to Tasmania by the first convenient opportunity and her treatment in

Tasmania would be regulated accordingly. By the time Governor Darling received this letter, significant developments had occurred, although none suggestive of Jane's innocence.

Would Governor Arthur have heeded the pleas if they had not been pre-empted by Darling's letter? It seems unlikely. Arthur would have contacted his New South Wales counterpart for confirmation before taking any action and the truth would soon have emerged.

Instead of helping Jane, John's letters and documents boomeranged back to Sydney, into Governor Darling's hands. The net effect was further confirmation of John's excessive involvement in her case and, as Darling was gradually realising, of his duplicity.

Chapter 26
A SURPRISING TALE

Curiouser and curiouser!
Lewis Carroll, *Alice's Adventures in Wonderland*

A strange incident followed, evidence of John's continued plotting. Shortly after sending the package of pleas to Tasmania, John requested assistance from Bernard Fitzpatrick, a wardsman of the police (a level higher than that of a constable). Fitzpatrick was questioned about the incident some years later at an Executive Council hearing convened to examine John Stephen Jnr's role in the Jane New scandal. Fitzpatrick testified that on 8 May 1829, the day James New was robbed, John notified him of a rumour that the News were about to leave the colony. Handing Fitzpatrick a warrant, John asked that he forestall James' departure if the rumour was true. John explained — or so Fitzpatrick testified — that he had forwarded a petition to Governor Arthur for Jane's emancipation, and that, although he believed her to be free, he was determined to prevent the News from leaving New South Wales until he had received a reply.

The following evening, Fitzpatrick knocked on James New's door. Finding him home, Fitzpatrick showed him the warrant and announced: 'This warrant is to prevent you or any person belonging to you from departing the colony in any clandestine way without further orders from some higher authority.' James appeared intimidated, Fitzpatrick recollected. After extracting James' promise that he would not flee the colony, Fitzpatrick took his leave.

A day later Fitzpatrick heard a rumour that James had slipped out of the colony accompanied by his wife. He lamented to the Executive Council: 'About that time I returned the warrant to Mr Stephen. Hearing by common report that James New had gone, I was chagrined with myself for having returned the warrant as I might have gone on board any ship and brought him on shore.'

If James and his wife had indeed absconded, no warrant was required to institute a search, Assistant Police Magistrate Charles Windeyer later revealed. As a prisoner, Jane could be apprehended at any time. James was free, however, and could leave the colony whenever he chose; no warrant to prevent his departure could be issued unless he was facing criminal or civil charges.

The incident was decidedly odd, realised the Executive Council. Determined to uncover the full story, they asked Windeyer his opinion of Fitzpatrick. He was one of the most intelligent and correct of the whole constabulary, Windeyer praised. Yet when questioned, Fitzpatrick's testimony confused rather than clarified the issue.

'Who gave you the warrant?' asked the Council.

'Mr Stephen,' Fitzpatrick replied.

'Was it a warrant to apprehend?'

'Yes, under the conditions that I found James New attempting to escape.'

'Were those conditions entered in the warrant?'

'No,' Fitzpatrick admitted.

'Did you see New after you got the warrant?'

'I did.'

'Why did you not apprehend him?'

'Because the stipulated reason Magistrate John Stephen Jnr gave me was that I was not to apprehend him unless I perceived him about to quit his residence,' Fitzpatrick explained, 'or if I received any information that he was on board a ship.'

'Did you take the warrant to the Superintendent of Police?'

'No.'

'Did you report having received such a warrant to any officer of the police?'

'No.'

'Did you report to the Superintendent of Police that you had not executed the warrant in the way you describe?'

'I made no report of it at all.'

The Council expressed their surprise. 'Were you not bound by your office to report to a superior officer the acts you do in the execution of your duty?'

'Yes.'

'Then why did you not report this transaction?'

'Sufficient report was made, as I thought, by returning the warrant and reporting to the magistrate who placed it in my hands.'

It was a curiously unprofessional action, the Council realised. They continued to probe. 'Did you send in a report of every other act you did on the day you received the warrant in question?'

'Certainly,' Fitzpatrick said.

'Were you not bound to send in a report once a day of the duties upon which you were employed?'

'Undoubtedly,' Fitzpatrick concurred.

'Then why did you omit to state this transaction?'

'Having done my duty, I reported to the magistrate who authorised me to act.'

'Was that magistrate in the police?' the Council attempted to clarify.

'He was a justice of the peace and often sat in the police court.'

'Was he the magistrate to whom you were bound to make the daily return?'

'Had I acted in a coercive measure according to the warrant I should have reported to the Principal Superintendent of Police,' Fitzpatrick acknowledged.

'But were you not bound to report to the Principal Superintendent of Police all the acts you did in the execution of your duty as a constable?'

'Undoubtedly if I was not guided by a magistrate.'

They were getting nowhere. Attacking from a different angle, the Council asked, 'Was it any part of your instructions that you were not to make a return of any act asked of you by a magistrate who was not in the police?'

'I never received any such instruction and I was fourteen years in the police.'

'Then why did you not report this transaction to the Principal Superintendent of Police in your daily return?'

'I must resort to my former answer — because the Principal Superintendent of Police did not guide me in any part of the matter, nor do I know that he was cognisant of it — I mean of the warrant or of the attempt to escape.'

Recognising the futility of continuing with this line of questioning, the Council moved on, although later seeking clarification from Assistant Police Magistrate Charles Windeyer. He declared that it was most irregular for a magistrate to place in a constable's hands a warrant to arrest a free person without any information under oath, and not to report the circumstance afterwards. He also confirmed that members of the constabulary had to report to a superior officer everything that occurred in the line of their duty.

Attempting to alleviate any suggestion of wrongdoing, John Stephen Jnr asked Windeyer, 'But if a wardsman received a warrant from a private magistrate which he did not execute because it appeared that the information on which the warrant was granted was not correct, would there be any impropriety on the part of the wardsman delivering up the warrant to the magistrate to be cancelled, and taking no further notice of it?'

'I think it would indeed be an impropriety,' Windeyer repeated, 'as the constable would constitute himself a judge of the propriety of the first proceeding.'

'But if the magistrate were satisfied that the wardsman acted from a conscientious belief that the information may have been incorrect, would there be any impropriety?' John persisted.

Windeyer reaffirmed that the situation was both irregular and improper.

The Council took over the questioning. 'As Fitzpatrick was an active intelligent officer, do you think he would have returned the warrant to the magistrate unless suspicions had been altogether removed with regard to the intention of the free person against whom the warrant was directed?'

'The constable executing the warrant has no discretion,' Windeyer explained firmly. 'He must take the man and bring him before the magistrate. His suspicions have nothing to do with the matter.'

'Suppose that such a circumstance did occur within your practice as a magistrate, should you consider it suspicious, and requiring strict investigation?'

'Undoubtedly,' Windeyer declared damningly. 'And punishment also, unless a good reason was given.'

Despite being classified by his superiors as an intelligent and well-respected officer, Bernard Fitzpatrick testified to having acted in a manner that was irregular, improper and highly suspicious. Possibly John Stephen Jnr had some control over him — bribery? Blackmail? — to induce him to act so unprofessionally. Possibly Fitzpatrick's testimony was a sham solicited by John, the warrant having neither been issued nor acted upon.

But what if Fitzpatrick was telling the truth? Perhaps the warrant was part of John's game of smoke and mirrors and was intended to communicate to James New an important message: that John was so omnipotent he could manipulate the constabulary and the legal system, and that James New was an insect who could be squashed in an instant.

Chapter 27
TASMANIA BOUND

Oh, what a tangled web we weave, when first we practise to deceive!
Sir Walter Scott, *Marmion*

As the day dawned on Sunday 10 May 1829, James and Jane New prepared to flee Sydney. Having awoken early, James gathered together the remainder of his belongings and soon after dawn exited the lodging house. Waiting for him at the front gate was a person dressed in a sailor's jacket. Although lodging-housekeeper Mrs Jones could not swear to his companion's identity, she later testified that in view of the person's height and appearance, she had no doubt in her own mind that it was Jane New.

James and his companion walked down to the King's Wharf where Jane's mother farewelled them. Waterman Thomas John Parkes and his son helped them on board their boat and stowed their two bags before rowing them out to the *Mary*, which was anchored below Bradley's Head. Parkes initially believed he was transporting two men, however as his passengers quietly conversed he realised one was a female. They reached the *Mary* around 7 am. Parkes heard the mate say, 'Good morning, Mr New' and 'Good morning, Mrs New' as his passengers clambered onto the deck. The mate shook James' hand then went aft to signal the vessel's readiness to sail. The Parkes remained on board for 30 to 45 minutes before returning to their boat. They rowed against a strong tide on their return journey and did not reach the wharf until between 9 and 10 am.

Although ready to sail, the *Mary* did not weigh anchor. In the meantime, James realised he had forgotten some personal linen and returned to his lodging house. Mrs Jones recollected James' return, partly because he accidentally collected another lodger's linen. As he walked out the door for the second time, James turned to her and smirked: 'All is right.' Mrs Jones concluded that Jane had successfully escaped.

Carrying several bundles, James arrived back at the King's Wharf around 10 am. Waterman James Wood, who knew James and Jane New well, rowed him out to the *Mary*. This second journey to the *Mary* took nearly an hour and they arrived around 11 am. Upon boarding the ship, Wood was astonished to see Jane New dressed in men's apparel; a blue jacket and trousers. After receiving his payment, Wood was preparing to disembark when Jane said to him: 'Goodbye, Jem.'

Predictably, the passenger list for the *Mary* made no mention of Jane's presence. Tide-surveyor Thomas Oliver noted three passengers on board: William Bourke, James New and James Middleton. Bourke and Middleton were friends of the News, and Bourke later declared: 'My name was made use of as a passenger on board the ship *Mary* merely as a blind to effect the safe embarkation of Mrs New.' Middleton reported being unaware until much later that his name had also been used.

The *Mary* sailed soon afterwards. After passing from Sydney Harbour through the Heads and into the Pacific Ocean, they dropped anchor near a Tasmania-bound vessel which was hovering outside the Heads. The crew carefully lowered Jane into a boat, rowed her across to the other vessel, and assisted her on board. The captain had agreed to carry her to Tasmania and then forward her to New Zealand where James would later join her.

For some reason, the plans went awry. Jane disembarked at Launceston on the north coast of Tasmania. John Kettle, who had previously known the News, was keeping a boarding house in Launceston when Jane knocked at his door on 25 or 26 May and asked for lodgings. They immediately recognised each other. Jane remained for four days during which she recounted the story of her departure from Sydney. She told the same story to Sydney butcher George Glew who was visiting Launceston on business.

Jane left Launceston around 29 or 30 May and travelled to Hobart where she posted a letter to Sidney Stephen a few days later. As she strolled through her old stomping ground, she came across friends and acquaintances from the past. Law clerk James Dow had never previously met Jane however his two companions, Mills and Dickson, pointed her out to him as the notorious Jane New. During the few hours Dow spent in her company he heard others refer to her by name. Her presence in Hobart could not remain secret for long.

That was the story presented to the New South Wales Executive Council some years later to chronicle Jane's departure from Sydney and to lay a framework around the letter dated 1 June 1829 that Jane purportedly wrote at Hobart. Containing a list of the clothes she was wearing when admitted to the Female Factory, the letter demanded Sidney Stephen's assistance:

> I hope you will excuse the liberty I have taken by writing to you, but it is my wish to let you know that I am now in Hobart Town. I authorise you to get my property from Mrs Gordon the Matron of the Factory; and if she refuses to give them up to you, I give you full authority in my name to bring an action against her. By so doing, you will oblige, your humble and obedient servant, Jane New.

But Jane was not the author: she was illiterate. And no convict genuinely on the run would flaunt their whereabouts. Someone else was clearly involved. The tone of the letter — arrogant and self-righteous — and its obsequious well-crafted phrases alluded to its origin. It smacked of a hoax jointly perpetrated by John Stephen Jnr and Jane New.

Had Jane really sent the letter from Hobart? Although directing Sidney Stephen to take legal action, the letter contained no return address and no retainer to finance his services. And, significantly, no envelope surfaced from Sidney's files to suggest that the letter had arrived by mail. No doubt

Sidney was supposed to forward the letter to the authorities as evidence of Jane's departure from the colony, however he refused to play the game. 'Considering her a Prisoner of the Crown and having no legal right,' he later remarked, 'I did not choose to become the medium of a request to the Matron of the Factory. I did not see how I could act professionally in the case.' Ignoring the unspoken intention behind the letter, Sidney filed Jane's letter under 'N' for 'New' where it remained for the following four years.

So was Jane truly in Hobart early in June 1829? A clerk had mentioned seeing her there in the company of his friends, Dickson, another clerk, and Mills, a saddler. An affidavit from Joseph Dickson demolished the claim:

In 1826 and 1827, I was clerk to the Van Diemen's Land Company in Hobart Town. I went to Circular Head in October 1827 and did not again visit Hobart Town until December 1830. I knew a person named Mills, a saddler who resided in Hobart. I received intelligence at Circular Head in November or December 1827 of Mills having been killed by his horse falling upon him.

The time required to undertake the journey from Launceston to Hobart was the next dubious issue. One hundred and twenty miles of rough roads separated the two towns, roads that could be impassable in winter. Yet when asked how long such a journey would take, Launceston lodging-housekeeper John Kettle prevaricated. A Launceston resident had made the journey in his curricle and pair in one and a half days, he announced, although he expressed ignorance as to the season. He had himself taken three days to travel to Hobart in a cart with two bullocks, he added, although admitting that the journey was not undertaken in winter. 'I am very little acquainted with bullocks,' he demurred when asked to estimate how long such a journey would take in winter. He also avoided answering questions about the time frame of winter caravan journeys.

Master Builder Daniel Egan provided the answer. He had sailed to Hobart late in May 1829 before travelling by horseback from Hobart to Launceston in the first week of June. 'The weather was so bad that it was impossible to travel,' he informed the Council, 'and the journey took six or seven days.' Horseback was the fastest method of travel between the two destinations. If Jane had indeed departed Launceston around 29 May, she could not have reached Hobart until at least 4 June, probably later if she took the longer and safer caravan. Yet her letter was purportedly written in Hobart on 1 June.

And Jane's sojourn in Launceston? The two men, John Kettle and George Glew, who reported seeing Jane there, offered astonishingly detailed recollections of dates and events supposedly mentioned to them in passing some four and a half years previously.

'When did you go from Sydney to Launceston?' the Council asked Glew.

'I sailed out of this harbour on 17 May 1829 in the *Hetty* and reached Launceston on May 25th.'

'Were you at John Kettle's house in Launceston when Jane New arrived?'

'No.'

'When did you first see her?'

'I think it was on May 27th. I had not been on shore two days when I went to Mr Kettle's. I saw her sitting in the room taking some refreshment. Kettle kept a sort of boarding house.'

'What day did Jane New go to Hobart Town?'

'I rather think it was the latter end of May. I think it was the 29th or 30th of May. I am sure it was.'

'Do you know by what conveyance or in what manner she went to Hobart Town?'

'I cannot say. There is a caravan that went backwards and forwards between the two towns.'

Launceston lodging-housekeeper John Kettle confirmed George Glew's arrival on the *Hetty* late in May 1829, described Jane's arrival at his lodging house, and mentioned Glew's visits during the few days she lodged with him.

As it transpired, however, Glew's and Kettle's statements were undermined by a small but significant error. The *Hetty* took twenty days to undertake the journey from Sydney, not eight. Glew could not have been in Launceston late in May 1829 as the *Hetty* did not reach Launceston until 6 June.

So did Jane spend any time in Launceston in May or June 1829? The Police Magistrate at Launceston later declared: 'Depend upon it Jane New never came down here — they allude to another person.'

Did she even travel to Tasmania at this time? Only two vessels sailed from Sydney to Tasmania on 10 May 1829, the *Resolution* and the *Henry*, and both were bound for Launceston. The *Henry* and its five passengers arrived on 24 or 25 May, while the *Resolution* arrived on the 26th; both remained in Launceston for some time before departing. The *Henry*'s supercargo Hugh McLean reported:

I was on board the *Henry* in company with the schooner *Resolution*. I recollect that three ships sailed from the Heads at the same time we sailed. One or two of these vessels were bound for Batavia, one was called the *Guide*, another the *Mary*, I do not recollect the name of the third vessel. We parted company with these vessels outside the Heads. They stood to the northward for Torres Straits, and we kept company with the *Resolution* until the other vessels were out of sight as we were bound for Launceston. No boat came to the schooner *Henry* from any of the ships we were in company with, nor did any female or passenger of any kind come on board. We had only four or five male passengers who embarked at Sydney. I do not think there was any communication between the *Resolution* and the before-mentioned vessels.

Master builder Daniel Egan reported having sailed for Hobart a week after his father sailed for Launceston on the other Tasmania-bound vessel, the *Resolution*. His father, who had known Jane New, had discussed the *Resolution*'s journey with him. If Jane had been on board, his father would have recognised her and spoken of her, Egan declared, particularly in view of the unusual circumstances of her reported embarkation. Egan was also well acquainted with the masters of both the *Resolution* and the *Henry* and had met them frequently while in Launceston at that time. Neither had mentioned an unusual cargo, particularly not a female in disguise.

And finally, the most obvious question of all served as an answer in its own right: why would Jane be so imprudent as to transfer to a vessel bound for Tasmania, to the very place the authorities were intending to send her, where she was well-known and still at the mercy of colonial law, when she had just made a successful escape from Sydney on a ship bound for Batavia, a destination outside the colonial authorities' reach?

Or had she? John Gray piloted the *Mary* out of Sydney Harbour on 10 May 1829, however he could not recollect any passengers embarking on the *Mary* or attending the ship's muster during the hours he spent on board. He had himself embarked around 6 am, weighed anchor between 6 and 7 am, and after piloting the vessel down the harbour and clearing the Heads, disembarked between 9 and 10 am. During that time he saw the crew mustered and also recollected a Mr Wallace spending about twenty minutes on board, but no one else.

'If there had been any passengers on board would you have seen them?' the Executive Council asked at the hearing some years later.

'I certainly should,' John Gray replied, 'for I was in the cabin with the Master before I left the ship.'

'Did you personally know James New who formerly kept a public house in this town?'

'I did not.'

'Did you know his wife?'

'I have seen her, but never spoken to her. I did not know her personally.'

'Do you think that you would have recognised her if you had seen her on board the *Mary*?'

'I certainly should,' he responded adamantly.

Not only was John Gray unaware of any passengers on board the vessel, he saw no boat travelling between the *Mary* and the southward-facing Tasmania-bound schooners standing half a mile away.

To support John Gray's testimony, questions were posed to Captain Samuel Ashmore who had commanded the *Guide* when it sailed for Torres Strait in convoy with the *Mary*.

'Did you go on board the *Mary* during the voyage to Batavia?'

'Yes,' Ashmore acknowledged.

'Did you see any passengers on board the *Mary* at that time?'

'None.'

'Are you sure that she had no passengers at the time you went on board?'

'I neither saw nor heard of any.'

'Shortly after passing the Heads, did you see any boat leave the *Mary* to put a passenger on board any other vessel?'

'No,' came the unequivocal response.

Having dismissed the question of passengers on board the *Mary* and a passenger transhipment, the Executive Council considered the subject of the tide-surveyor's list of the *Mary's* passengers. They asked Controller of Customs, Burman Langa: 'Is that a paper which should officially be in the charge of the tide-surveyor?'

'I never knew the tide-surveyor to have any such list,' Langa admitted. 'Why, it is an irregular thing altogether. I don't know how he could have come by such a list as this, except if he was to compile it for himself or for some other purpose I cannot say.'

Perhaps the ship or the date was inaccurate. Waterman Thomas John Parkes declared that he rowed the News to the *Mary* on the 18th not the 10th, arguing that he recollected the date clearly because it was the anniversary of his first marriage. 'If three or four other witnesses have stated that the vessel quitted the harbour on the 10th of May,' John Stephen Jnr asked him, 'may you not be mistaken as to the actual day that the *Mary* sailed?'

'I am positive because of the 18th of May being my wedding day,' Parkes asserted.

'At all events whether it was the 10th or the 18th, are you sure that the circumstances you have stated with respect to James New and his wife are perfectly true?'

Parkes dug his heels in. 'As I have before stated I am sure on account of its being the 18th.'

Parkes was not alone in disputing the date. Jane's mother Elizabeth

Baker also expressed her conviction that the News sailed on board the *Mary* on the 18th of May.

'Did you see them embark?' asked the Executive Council.

'I did not see them go on board, but I saw them go to embark on the 18th of May, on board the *Mary*.'

'What day of the week was this?'

'I cannot exactly say,' Elizabeth admitted. 'It was right in the middle of the week; it was not a Sunday.'

'What makes you recollect it was the 18th of May?'

'I had a little washing bill to receive on the day before, on the 17th of the month, and she sailed the day after.'

'From whom did you receive it?'

'From the mate of the *Liverpool*. He is drowned since.'

'What makes you remember so particularly that you had to receive this of him on the 17th of May?'

'The little bill I had to receive was from Captain Leveson, and the day of the month was on it.'

In truth, 18 May 1829 was a Monday, Elizabeth was illiterate, and Elizabeth also mentioned that the News sailed two days after the robbery, undermining her reference to a May 18th departure. And the only vessel named *Mary* moored in Sydney Harbour in May 1829 sailed on the 10th — without the News on board.

Yet the News apparently did leave Sydney that day. James reportedly converted notes to dollars the previous evening, explaining that he was leaving the country. He left his lodging-house on the morning of the 10th and, apart from his quick return a few hours later, disappeared. Witnesses subsequently heard that he had left the country.

So what did happen on 10 May? James New's plans to flee the colony with his wife were well-known and understandable. Eliza James Jones reported: 'I heard him say repeatedly that he would quit the colony and take her with him, particularly so when I insisted on her being taken out of the house. I think he would not have quitted the colony leaving her behind, from all I heard him say and from all I heard at the time.'

'Do you know any reason besides that of effecting the secret embarkation of his wife that should have led James New to adopt any concealment of his movements?' the Executive Council asked.

'I know of none.'

'Was he reputed to be a man of tolerably easy circumstances as a tradesman?'

'He was,' Mrs Jones acknowledged. 'I have understood so and I have heard him say that he was doing very well until his wife was taken from him by the Government.'

'Do you mean by that, that the Government's revoking the assignment of Jane New to her husband, was the inducement for his giving up his business?'

'Yes, certainly. He was not able to carry it on after his wife was taken from him,' claimed Mrs Jones.

One witness, waterman James Wood, suggested that James' financial concerns motivated his departure. He insisted that the News were 'enthralled in debt', that James' public house the Shipwright Arms had no custom, and that he was running away from his creditors. There was indeed the matter of the £140 civil action against him.

But did James New leave the colony with his wife or on his own?

James New's employee, James Middleton, later offered a curious observation: 'I know James New was trying to get his wife to go along with him.' Perhaps Jane was reluctant to leave the colony with her husband, aware that James could no longer indulge her, that he had overextended himself in fulfilling her desires and meeting her legal costs. Perhaps her aspirations had been raised by the evidence of so many important gentlemen scrambling to help her.

James Middleton was asked: 'Might not both or either of them have gone up the country, instead of going on board the *Mary*?'

'They might,' he replied, 'but I think they did not, as I heard afterwards that they were gone.'

James New disappears from colonial records thereafter, surfacing two years later in England. He either secretly embarked on another vessel on 10 May 1829 or hid for a few days, embarked at a later date — perhaps the 18th — and sailed soon afterwards. But Jane did not accompany her husband. Instead, on that same day, John Stephen Jnr spirited her away to his country retreat.

Chapter 28

A NEW SANCTUARY

*John Stephen Jnr has possessed himself of general
esteem in New South Wales for his open, frank, liberal,
and gentlemanly conduct in every way.*
Tasmanian & Asiatic Review, 1829

A country retreat or a nook John acquired with illicit intentions in mind? According to John's own testimony, he leased a small room in the house of ticket-of-leave holder Amos Crisp at Lower Minto in January 1829. Yet John had a wife and four children so it seems surprising that he would lease such small premises as a country escape. The timing is undoubtedly significant: Jane's conviction occurred in the early days of January 1829. John evidently acquired his country retreat for his own pursuits, not for the benefit of his family.

Involving himself with Amos Crisp, however, would prove a grave mistake. John had met his match. Unlike the majority of transportees who adopted a relatively law-abiding lifestyle after landing on colonial shores, Crisp was a cunning opportunist whose proclivities became so well-recognised that he spent the following two decades with the law snapping at his heels.

Crisp was a porter and servant at the Tavistock Hotel in London in 1814 when charged with stealing money from his master. The police searched his home and discovered a watch recently purloined from a hotel customer's room. At his Old Bailey trial, it soon became apparent that greed rather than necessity motivated his actions. In addition to his own employment, Crisp's wife kept a chandler's shop.[35]

Sentenced to death but reprieved to life transportation, Crisp arrived in Sydney in 1816 and soon afterwards petitioned for his family to join him. Through good behaviour he convinced the authorities he was worthy of a ticket-of-leave, and he settled down to farm at Liverpool. Small-scale farming, however, was only for the faint-hearted, and with an entrepreneurial spirit Crisp had higher aspirations. He kept an ear out for more profitable business ventures. A cart licence acquired in 1821 and used for either flour or bread deliveries proved ideal, until it led to his first-known colonial confrontation with the law: 'extensive depredations' on the Lachlan and Waterloo Flour Company. Ever the opportunist, Crisp and two others escaped prosecution by serving as the prosecution's witnesses, providing the evidence that convicted the other eight participants.

Returning to farming, Crisp continued to seek more lucrative income streams and soon turned to horse-breeding and horse-breaking. By the mid-1820s, he could afford to employ a schoolmaster for his children and free workers in addition to maintaining half-a-dozen assigned convicts. Requiring larger premises, the family moved to Lower Minto some 25 miles from Sydney, where Crisp accepted mares sent from Sydney to be covered by his two stallions, and horses to be broken. Some owners regularly visited the property to see to their livestock, John Stephen Jnr among them.

Such innocent intentions underlay his decision to lease Crisp's room, John later claimed. 'I rented apartments in the house of Mr Amos Crisp commencing from January 1829 for the purpose of country air and exercise, and also occasionally overlooking some stock, which are under the care of Amos Crisp. I have been in the habit of riding up there on a Friday, and returning to business in Sydney on the Sunday evening or Monday following, and occasionally remaining for a longer period.'

Yet this was the first and only occasion he had rented out a room, Crisp admitted. As his house comprised a mere five rooms and housed his large family, he was not advertising for tenants. So why did he rent a room to John Stephen Jnr?

Despite appearances, Crisp had a reputation for skirting the law. Lower Minto Constable John Burrows revealed that he had searched Crisp's property several times. 'It was reported he harboured bushrangers and stolen property,' he explained, 'but I never found anything there.'

John Stephen Jnr had no need for a law-abiding landlord. He required one who would connive at illicit activities or at the very least disregard the obvious. Perhaps John had heard of Crisp's reputation or recognised the glint in his eye. The two came to a mutually beneficial agreement. Crisp charged John ten shillings a week — that is, around £2 per month — for the privilege of leasing one small broken-windowed room at the back of his house. John paid, week after week, month after month. To the suspicious-minded, such a hefty rental suggested hush money.

Some months later, John felt the need for a female servant to care for his property during his absence. He employed a woman named Frances Dickson to fill this role and asked Thomas Henry Hart to ferry her to the Crisps' residence as Hart passed the property on the way to his own farm.

Involving Hart proved a curious decision considering his recent participation in a titillating sex-scandal. Another entrepreneur of the colonial variety — a twice-convicted felon cum successful businessman — Hart had sued Principal Surgeon of New South Wales, James Bowman, for £2000 in damages for 'criminal conversation' — seducing and impregnating Hart's wife leaving her unable to manage Hart's business affairs while he was under sentence of colonial transportation to Port Macquarie. Many considered Hart's suit little more than a thinly disguised extortion, however opportunistic seems a more apt description, an entrepreneur's willingness to manipulate any situation for financial gain. Clearly the hip pocket served as a powerful motivating force for Thomas Henry Hart and probably drove his willingness to assist John Stephen Jnr.

When Hart deposited Frances Dickson on the Crisp's doorstep, Amos Crisp was not at home although his children later described the circumstances of her arrival. Frances was welcomed into Crisp's home and even into his daughter's bed, Crisp reported, sleeping there when John was using the outside room. Frances' role was neither that of a servant nor of a friend, Crisp admitted, and she and John breakfasted and dined together.

While the Crisps' neighbours probably suspected that Frances was a kept woman, they also believed the story leaked by Hart at John's instigation. Hart claimed previous knowledge of Frances Dickson: that she had escaped from her common-law husband because of ill treatment. Crisp's neighbour, Mary Seymour, thought Frances must have run away from her husband as they had seen her hide from visitors.

For the following few weeks, Frances Dickson joined the Crisps in their daily activities. These included regular visits to the home of John and Frances Lake some three miles away, where Mrs Dickson often read the newspaper to John Lake. As they strolled to and from the Lakes' residence, the Crisp entourage passed the door of District Constable John Burrows. On one occasion, Frances Dickson greeted the constable by remarking, 'Good afternoon, Mr Burrows.'

It was an audacious move. Frances was not just being friendly; she was flirting with danger. As the community would soon learn, Frances was no refugee from an abusive marriage. She was the notorious runaway Jane New.

Word of Frances Dickson's true identity gradually leaked to the community, either through supposition based upon John's involvement with Jane New, or through Crisp's neighbour, Mary Seymour. Mrs Seymour discovered the truth a few weeks after Frances' arrival. Employed by Amos Crisp to manage the washing, Mrs Seymour was alone with Frances one afternoon when some men from Sydney knocked at the door. Frances was tipsy, Mrs Seymour revealed, and horrified to see them. Sneaking out of the house to hide in her room, she implored Mrs Seymour, 'Would you tell the people that the family are not home?'

Mrs Seymour was surprised. 'You are the fittest person to speak to them as you have charge of the house,' she admonished.

And then the secret came out. 'The men might know me. I am a prisoner and have run away from the constables. My name is not Frances Dickson. It is Jane New. Please don't tell anyone,' Jane begged.

Mrs Seymour later claimed that she had never heard of Jane New prior to Frances Dickson's revelation. She offered no statement regarding the nature of Jane's relationship with John Stephen Jnr although alluding to her own suspicions. 'I said several times that it must cost Mr Stephen a great deal of money keeping her at Crisp's,' she reported. 'I have seen cases of gin and brandy, and chests of tea and bags of sugar, and cups and saucers and plates; and Mrs Dickson told me that Mr Stephen had sent them all, and glass for the windows. Mr Stephen glazed the panes himself where they were broken in the windows and the doors.'

Mrs Seymour commented scathingly to her friends on the wisdom of John's actions: 'Mr Stephen must be a damned fool to bring a convict illegally at large to such a notorious place as Crisp's.' Or so John claimed at the second Executive Council hearing. When asked whether she had ever made such a statement, Mrs Seymour vehemently denied the charge. 'I never make use of such words,' she added primly. Yet the words themselves echo the truth. If Mrs Seymour had not uttered such thoughts, someone else undoubtedly had.

Crisp's friend, Frances Lake, also expressed concern about Crisp's involvement in such a risky activity. 'Send her away,' she urged Crisp on a number of occasions, 'or you will get into trouble for harbouring the woman.' Crisp chose not to do so. He had taken the necessary precautions, or so he believed.

Amos Crisp was later to provide multiple statements and testimonies regarding John's tenancy and Frances Dickson's presence in his home, each varying considerably in detail and containing numerous contradictions. The most accurate was undoubtedly Crisp's first testimony, when his memory was fresh and the opportunities for coaching minimal. Crisp reported that around the middle of May, Mr Hart drove Frances to his home, and that she carried a certificate of freedom signed by Magistrate John Stephen Jnr.

Crisp's reference to this certificate proves pivotal in determining the truth regarding Jane New's appearance at the Crisps'. Soon afterwards Crisp repudiated his own estimation of Frances' arrival date, claiming that she had settled at his property in March 1829. Having examined his accounts, he explained, he had realised that she resided with him a lot longer than originally estimated. Thomas Henry Hart and Frances Lake confirmed his statement.

Amos Crisp and his cohorts were deliberately pinpointing Frances' arrival at the Crisps' at a time when Jane New was incarcerated in the Female Factory. Their claim might have succeeded except for one small issue. Mrs Dickson's certificate of freedom was inscribed, most tellingly, '10 May 1829'.

Amos Crisp was a wily operator. For self-protection, he required proof that he was not harbouring a runaway and a certificate of freedom was his insurance. If Frances had indeed presented this certificate to Amos Crisp upon being introduced, as he reported, she must have arrived on 10 May 1829 or soon after. Any earlier, and she would not have carried this important certificate, and John's substantial rental payments would not have compensated Crisp for the serious repercussions he faced if discovered harbouring a runaway.

So did Mrs Dickson bring this certificate of freedom with her? It seems unlikely. John thought he was clever but Amos Crisp proved the master at evading the consequences of his own criminal actions. Upon John's arrival at the Crisp homestead, Amos probably demanded that he produce a certificate of freedom for Mrs Dickson or take her elsewhere. John dashed one off but in his haste made a disastrous error. He automatically inscribed it with the current date.

If this certificate had not been written hastily, if it had been prepared with forethought, the last date John would have deliberately chosen was 10 May 1829. Too many witnesses could attest to the News' departure from Sydney on that date. Clearly, this date was written inadvertently. Clearly, Mrs Dickson arrived at the Crisps' Minto residence on 10 May, the very same day Jane New left Sydney.

Chapter 29
BY A WHISKER

*It was unfortunate for me that even a distant resemblance
existed between Mrs Dickson and Jane New. This probably
led to the mistake on the part of my secret informer who
committed this stab upon my reputation.*

John Stephen Jnr

Jane's halcyon days at the Crisps' ended on 17 June 1829. Although the
authorities had reportedly kept an ear out, two-and-a-half months passed
before news of her likely whereabouts whispered its way to them. 'Her
concealment was so well contrived,' Governor Darling declared, 'that she
eluded the utmost vigilance of the Police until lately.' Was he aware that
his vigilant police officers had not even searched for Jane in her own home,
and had acted only upon information thrust at them?

Having received word that Jane New was harboured at Amos Crisp's
house at Lower Minto, Principal Superintendent of Police Francis Rossi
called upon Assistant Chief Constable John Skinner for assistance.
Skinner knew Jane. He had taken her into custody after her August 1828
shoplifting spree and also after her escape following the *habeas corpus*
hearing, and would easily recognise her. Rossi ordered Skinner to proceed
immediately to Liverpool, to search Crisp's property, to apprehend Jane
and to escort her back to Sydney. No warrant was required. Crisp was

a ticket-of-leave holder so the police could legally search his property whenever they desired.

Arriving at Liverpool on Wednesday 17 June, Skinner called upon the district's Chief Constable, Frederick Meredith, who was happy to provide information about Amos Crisp's situation and reputation. Deciding upon a midnight ambush, Constables Skinner and Meredith, and the latter's brother, Constable William Meredith, set off late in the evening in a gig. Reaching Crisp's property around midnight, they turned into the drive.

'Forewarned is forearmed' was a motto Crisp probably lived by. A pack of dogs served as his sentry. Jumping, barking and snapping, they chased the gig down the drive then surrounded it, preventing the constables from alighting. As the dogs' fury abated, the constables climbed down and knocked on the door. Silence greeted them. Hearing movement inside, Skinner called out that he wished to search the house.

'Who are you?' Crisp retorted.

Skinner lowered his head to the keyhole and answered loudly: 'Skinner the constable from Sydney.'

Although alerted to the danger he and his lodger faced, Crisp had no choice but to allow them in. He warily opened the door. Stationing William Meredith outside to ensure that no one escaped, the other two constables entered the house. They began searching. Entering one bedroom they found two children in bed. In another, Crisp's daughter Elizabeth and a younger child were in bed. But of Jane New there was no sign. They searched the whole house, or what they believed to be the whole house, without finding any trace of her.

Skinner turned to his host who had dogged his footsteps. 'Mr Crisp, don't be offended; it is my duty,' he apologised.

'Not at all,' Crisp responded amiably.

As the constables completed their internal search, they heard a loud noise coming from the stable. 'Let us go. She might be there,' Skinner shouted. Leaving William Meredith searching a room containing a number of beef casks, they raced over to the stables. Under the manger; in the hayloft; they searched everywhere but found nothing. The workers' quarters were next. Ordering the men to get up, they searched again. Nothing.

As they trudged back to the house, the dogs' vociferous barking drew their attention. Skinner turned to Meredith: 'The dogs are barking terribly; perhaps she might be in the garden.'

About to head down the passage towards the garden, Skinner swivelled slightly and saw a room Crisp had not shown them, one with a door ajar.

Turning to Crisp, he demanded, 'Who sleeps there?'

'My daughter,' Crisp answered.

'Why is the door open at such a late hour of the night?'

Quick with an excuse, Amos responded, 'I suppose they must have gone to bed and forgotten to fasten it.'

Calling for a light, Skinner and Meredith entered the room. It contained a bed and clothing, as well as boxes and other items. Glancing at the bed, Skinner noticed that the bedding was half turned down. Reaching out to touch it, he felt warm linen as if a person had recently slept there. Female apparel lying at the head of the bed and slippers underneath suggested that a woman had recently exited the room. He turned to Crisp and asked again, 'Who sleeps here?'

'My daughter,' Crisp repeated.

'How could she sleep in two beds when I saw her in bed in another part of the house?'

Crisp expressed confusion at the question and reiterated, 'It is her bedroom.'

'Who do the clothes belong to?' Skinner demanded.

'The women's apparel belongs to my daughter and the men's apparel to myself.'

Sensing that he was lying, Skinner admonished, 'I am afraid Mr Crisp you are telling me a falsehood. I am partly sure that you know what I want, and you had better give her up.'

Crisp was silent.

Skinner sifted through the clothes and goods stored there. Frederick Meredith perused the paperwork. He asked Crisp's daughter Elizabeth, who claimed the property as her own, for permission to examine the trunks and boxes. As he later explained, 'I thought I might discover some traces that would lead to the person who had been sleeping there.' Opening a small box standing on a table, Meredith found a certificate:

I hereby certify that the Bearer hereof Mrs Dickson is free.
10th May 1829   John Stephen Jnr, J.P.

Continuing the search, Meredith asked Elizabeth to open a trunk. Inside he found a woman's white pocket: a little fabric bag eight or ten inches in length with a slit at the top and tied with two strings.

'Whose is this?' he asked Elizabeth Crisp.

'It is mine,' she said.

Meredith put his hand into the pocket and found a piece of paper and some money.

'That's money,' Elizabeth exclaimed.

'It is not money I am looking for,' Meredith retorted. Discarding the money, he picked up the paper. After a quick perusal, he realised that it was another certificate.

Sydney, 1st May 1829
To certify that the Bearer hereof, Jane New, became free on the 27th ultimo, as appears by Affidavits filed in my office.
John Stephen Jnr, Registrar of the Supreme Court

Turning to Amos Crisp, Constable Meredith triumphantly announced, 'This certificate contains the name of the person Jane New I am searching for and plainly testifies that she was here.'

Both Crisp and his daughter shook their heads, emphatically denying that she had ever been in their house. The constables were sceptical. The trunk containing Jane New's certificate included numerous gowns and petticoats. Some were silk and undoubtedly expensive. Elizabeth Crisp's clothes? Not likely, declared Constable Meredith who knew Elizabeth well. The two constables muttered to each other that many of the items stored in the room were valuable. The advantages of being a kept woman, they probably smirked.

After a brief consultation, Skinner informed Crisp that they were taking him into custody. Crisp immediately expressed concern at leaving his children alone. 'Could we visit my neighbour Mrs Seymour,' he asked, 'to enquire if she will mind my children?' The constables agreed.

Leaving William Meredith in charge of the room, the two constables and Amos Crisp tramped half a mile through the darkness to the Seymour homestead. Little did they realise they were following in Jane's footsteps.

Woken by the angry barking, Jane had climbed out of bed to see what was happening. She recognised the sounds of a vehicle arriving and wondered if it might be Mr Hart's carriage delivering John Stephen Jnr. Opening the door, she waited and listened. She heard Amos Crisp get up and walk out of the house, speak to somebody and then call off the dogs. She heard people entering the house and someone walking through the parlour into Crisp's bedroom. She heard the storeroom door being unlocked, the room situated behind her own bedroom. Something was clearly amiss.

Jane tiptoed out of her room and darted across to Amos Crisp's bedroom window which was situated at the front of the house. Seeing Elizabeth Crisp dressing, Jane crept over to the side of the house, to a low window with broken glass. Catching Elizabeth's attention, she whispered, 'Who are they?'

Elizabeth whispered back, 'Be off! It is Skinner the constable come to take you.'

Dressed only in a nightgown and mob cap but unable to return to her room for fear of being seen, Jane raced through the darkness to the end of the garden. The dogs announced her presence, but the sight of the open doorway into her room distracted the constables. Ironically, their decision to search the house at midnight had cloaked her in darkness, allowing her to slip away unnoticed.

Heart hammering, Jane stood by the side of a tree watching. She saw the constables walk out of Crisp's parlour door and enter her own room carrying a light. Realising that her sanctuary had been discovered, she turned and fled across Captain Brooks' paddock, losing her cap as she brushed through the bushes. Arriving at Mary Seymour's house, she pounded on the door.

'Who's there?' Mrs Seymour hollered.

'Mrs Dickson,' Jane gasped.

'What fetches you here at this time of the night?' Mrs Seymour demanded.

'Constable Skinner has come to take me,' Jane wailed.

Opening the door, Mrs Seymour let her distressed neighbour into the house. Jane plopped down by the fire. Spotting a pair of Mrs Seymour's shoes lying by the sofa she pulled them on and quickly recounted the story of her escape. And then a dog barked. Jane jumped up. 'The constables are coming!' she cried and ran out the back door. As Mrs Seymour watched, she saw Jane on her knees by the garden fence.

From the Seymours', Jane scrambled across the paddocks to a hut on William Cordeaux's farm tenanted by a Scottish woman named Marg and her husband. Pleading with the couple for assistance, Jane explained, 'The constables have come to take me by an order from my husband. I have run away from him.'

Mrs Seymour later reported that Marg had her doubts about Jane's story. 'Marg told me that she thought she was a prisoner, particularly as she dressed in men's apparel to go away.' Yet, despite their scepticism, they offered Jane refuge. After dusk the following evening, they ferried her to another safe haven, to the house of Nathaniel Boon, an emancipated convict who had settled in the district of Airds. There Jane waited until news of her predicament reached John Stephen Jnr in Sydney.

John hurried down to Minto as soon as his working week ended. Mrs Seymour saw him at Crisp's house. 'He desired me to go into his room in company with himself,' Mrs Seymour later recalled, 'and pick out some dark dresses for Mrs Dickson. I picked out the dresses and tied them up for him, and he took them away in the gig.'

Mrs Seymour saw Jane herself soon afterwards. Jane was travelling in a gig with John Stephen Jnr and was dressed in male attire — a coat and a blue cap resembling an officer's cap. The gig stopped and Jane asked Mrs Seymour if she recognised her. Despite the disguise, she did indeed.

John was probably escorting Jane to her next sanctuary at this time, to Vaucluse House, the famous home of William Charles Wentworth. Commenced in 1803 by Irish heiress-napper and convict transportee, Sir Henry Browne Hayes, this genteel dwelling-house and surrounding 105 acres of land was purchased by Wentworth in 1827 for a princely £1500. Considering it a very uncomfortable place, Wentworth immediately employed an architect to design a suite of outbuildings in the Tudor–Gothic style. Jane was possibly housed in one of these buildings. If so, it was a far cry from her recent residences: a ramshackle pub, a shared bed (if she was lucky) with numerous other women, a tiny nook at the back of a ticket-of-leaver's broken-windowed cottage.

As Jane hid in the seclusion of the Vaucluse estate, John considered his options. It was time to leave the colony, he realised. Jane was too well-known and Governor Darling too determined. Wherever he stashed her, word would eventually leak out and the authorities would come knocking.

But any ship's captain who carried a serving convict out of the colony without the Governor's approval faced harsh penalties. Bribery was the only option: a large enough bribe for greed to swing the pendulum from wariness to willingness. The serious consequences of exposure meant that he must not approach the wrong person, although in a settlement populated by convicts and ex-convicts, such a person should not prove difficult to locate. The appropriate name surfaced. The bribe was offered and accepted.

Having agreed a passage — perhaps with the Captain of the *Reliance* which sailed for Calcutta on 28 June 1829 — John and Jane packed their bags and prepared themselves. They must have been nervous, knowing that the ramifications would be dire if they were caught. Yet Jane's nervousness was undoubtedly tinged with excitement. This was the type of adrenaline rush she thrived upon: committing a crime under the nose of those in authority. And John was a master at conveying an air of charming innocence, of talking himself out of trouble. If they could sneak away under the watchful eyes of the authorities it would be a wonderful achievement indeed, one to cap all others.

But they were foiled. As Governor Darling later reported:

Jane New went to Vaucluse, the residence of Mr William Wentworth near the entrance of Port Jackson, for the purpose of embarking from thence with Mr John Stephen. But in consequence of the strict personal inspection of which Mr Stephen later complained, it was found impracticable to embark her, although in boy's clothes. She therefore returned to Vaucluse.

The risk was too high. They would need to separate. Another passage was required; another approachable captain sought; another bribe offered. Captain Kent of the *Emma Kemp* agreed to the arrangement.

Curiously, Captain Kent communicated the offer to his employer, shipowner Francis Mitchell. 'Would you allow a passenger to travel to Tasmania?' he enquired. 'I am not at liberty to mention the person's name.'

Mitchell refused. 'Without knowing the name, I cannot permit it as it might be someone who is indebted in the Colony. It might prevent the vessel from prosecuting the voyage.'

'They are willing to pay £50 or £60,' Kent coaxed.

Well aware that a passage to Tasmania was worth a fraction of that sum, Mitchell knew that an illicit departure was intended. 'No!' he declared with finality.

Captain Kent was probably testing his employer. As Mitchell would not agree to carrying a highly profitable but potentially illegal passenger to Tasmania, he would not ask permission to carry such a passenger to New Zealand where his own vessel was heading. He would quietly accept the cargo. The usual fare for a passage to New Zealand was only £20. It would be a lucrative profit margin indeed.

On 5 July 1829, six months exactly after Jane's trial on Madame Rens' charges, the *Emma Kemp* slipped out of Sydney Cove.[36] Weighing only 38 tons and with an eight-man crew, the cutter had no need for the services or inquisitiveness of a pilot. Gliding along Sydney Harbour towards the Heads, the *Emma Kemp* made an unscheduled stop near Vaucluse. A boat pulled alongside and a boy clambered on board.

Seaman Thomas Franklin later revealed that the boy, Thomas Jones, who was named in the *Emma Kemp*'s crew list, did not exist and that the cutter instead carried an undocumented passenger. 'I was a seaman on board the cutter *Emma Kemp* on 5 July 1829, the day she went to sea,' he reported. 'I was drunk when the cutter left Port Jackson bound for New Zealand, and three days afterwards I first saw on board the cutter a lady passenger who slept in the Captain's cabin. I knew this female when she kept a public house on the Rocks with her husband. Her name was Jane New.'

That the boy who embarked near the Heads was Jane New in disguise was later confirmed by Captain Kent. His involvement in the notorious Jane New's escape from Sydney became his claim to fame among his fellow ship's commanders and probably in the tap rooms of his other ports of call. But as he sailed from port to port, he was unaware that the colonial authorities had heard of his involvement and were readying themselves to pounce when he returned to New South Wales.

Meanwhile rumours of Jane New's escape had probably circulated. Such a delicious piece of gossip must have proved too difficult to contain, bursting to be told. Just one person here; another there. Whether John hugged the secret to himself or gloated is uncertain. He told at least one person of Jane's departure. Mrs Seymour later reported that she bumped into John in Sydney. 'Mrs Dickson has gone out of the country,' he told her. 'She is safe from the constables now.'

Jane New was never to return.

Part V:
INDIGNATION

I have been kept in a state of the most painful nature, subjected to every species of false accusation, and the object of pity, neglect or scorn from the whole community.

John Stephen Jnr

Chapter 30
SMOKE AND MIRRORS

Truth cannot be hoodwinked by such sophistry.

John Stephen Jnr

The death knell tolled for John Stephen Jnr's position as a civil officer of the New South Wales Government in the early hours of Thursday 18 June 1829. And John was not even awake to hear it.

John had been having a difficult two months. Despite his best efforts, he had lost his job. While his appointment as Commissioner of Crown Lands had received Royal approval, he had been rejected for the post of Registrar. Forced to hand over his responsibilities when the new Registrar John Edye Manning arrived in Sydney, John returned to the Commissioner's role. He undoubtedly felt bitter. He was well-suited to the Registrar's role, so much so that the Supreme Court justices and Attorney-General signed a testimonial in his favour praising his diligence, efficient performance, and punctual and regular attendance. His bitterness no doubt escalated at the thought of his salary decrease: from a potential £800 to a mere £365 per year.

Determined to recoup some of his lost pay, John requested £300 in salary arrears. Darling demurred upon solid grounds. John persisted, and eventually Darling agreed on the condition that John legally bind himself to repay the money if the British authorities disallowed the payment. As

Darling breached the regulations, his gesture seems surprisingly considerate. It was a decision he no doubt regretted when he received news of the certificates stashed in Amos Crisp's back room.

Immediate repercussions resulted from the discovery. Amos Crisp was the first to suffer. Informed by the police that he was to be taken into custody, Crisp requested permission to seek Mary Seymour's assistance. They arrived at Mrs Seymour's shortly after Jane dashed out the back. As they banged on the door, Mrs Seymour probably responded slowly, allowing Jane a few moments longer to elude her pursuers.

'We are going to search your house,' the constables informed her as she opened the door. A free woman, Mrs Seymour had a right to be affronted at such an imposition, although she was forced to submit as her husband was a ticket-of-leave holder. The constables had evidently decided to search her house as they plodded across the fields, recognising that if Crisp knew Mrs Seymour well enough to request assistance, her home was a likely haven for Jane New. They would not know until much later how accurately they had read the situation.

Despite having seven children of her own ranging from infancy upwards, Mrs Seymour agreed to take care of the Crisp children and returned with the men to Crisp's cottage. Her support freed Elizabeth Crisp to attend to her father, and she decided to accompany him to Liverpool. She needed to apprise John Stephen Jnr of Jane's escape and of her father's incarceration, and to request assistance.

Climbing into the gig, the constables and the Crisps set off for Liverpool. During the journey, Crisp made Constable Meredith the ultimate offer. Some lessons from his past had been learnt well; ratting on his accomplices was one of them. 'If the magistrates would allow it,' Crisp suggested craftily, 'I'll go back and find the woman.'

Brought to Liverpool Court House on Thursday morning, Crisp appeared before the magistrates. His tempting offer was communicated but, not surprisingly, rejected. Instead, the magistrates decreed that he should be forwarded to the Bench of Magistrates in Sydney. Constables John

Skinner and Frederick Meredith signed depositions and the magistrates included a covering note addressed to Captain Rossi:

> The person Jane New has not yet been found, but from the within testimony, and the articles found in Crisp's house, there can be no doubt that she made her escape on the constables entering the premises. We have placed two constables in charge of the room and property . . . and we have no doubt that Jane New will soon be apprehended as we have ordered a strict search after her. We have sent Amos Crisp to Sydney in the charge of Constable Skinner.

After leaving Liverpool Court House, Constable Skinner escorted Crisp to Sydney and handed him over to Captain Rossi. Yet instead of taking him before the Bench, Rossi locked him in the watchhouse without laying any charges. Rossi reported that he was detaining Crisp until His Excellency's pleasure be known, however John Stephen Jnr later condemned Rossi's action as that of a pliant magistrate who had imprisoned Amos Crisp without any proof of wrongdoing.

Captain Rossi's decision not to charge Crisp is understandable. Leasing a room was no criminal offence, nor was Crisp's failure to reveal that he had done so. When details of his tenancy arrangements came to the authorities' attention, his cleverness in ensuring that Mrs Dickson carried a certificate of freedom allowed him to argue reasonably (and no doubt plausibly) that he was unaware his tenant's servant carried a false passport. Indeed, he could protest that he had no reason to suspect any wrongdoing as his tenant was a magistrate and government official, and even less right to question such an important personage. And as the authorities had no evidence to prove that Crisp knew Mrs Dickson's true identity, his I-know-nothing denial was both simple and in the long run effective. Under the circumstances, imprisoning Amos Crisp in the watchhouse was intended to intimidate him and perhaps even to prevent him from communicating with John Stephen Jnr until the Governor's pleasure regarding both men was determined.

The authorities were unable to keep the news of Jane's escape and Crisp's imprisonment from John. He visited Crisp in the watchhouse and saw him again in the public office the following day. These were evidently brief visits as the men were unable to construct a plausible story covering all the loose ends.

Nevertheless, John did attempt to alleviate Crisp's concerns about his plight. 'Do not be under any apprehension for your children,' he reassured Crisp. 'If you lose your liberty I will send someone to take charge of them.' It was a kind thought, but one made with less than altruistic intentions. If Crisp revealed the truth in return for his freedom, the authorities would have the evidence they required to incriminate John.

The Governor's pleasure was revealed on Saturday 20 June. Darling ordered the cancellation of Crisp's ticket-of-leave and his incarceration in the prison hulk. Yet surprisingly, Rossi ignored the Governor's orders. He confined Crisp in one of the solitary dungeons, where he suffered the misery of a dank cell for nearly 48 hours before being released and brought into the open air. Crisp's reprieve proved short-lived as he was then taken on board the gaol's annexe, the *Phoenix* hulk, as Darling had ordered. Chained in double irons, Crisp endured another 24 hours of imprisonment, or so he claimed in a later statement. Darling expressed his scepticism: 'I doubt the truth of this. But if the landlord, a convict, was found harbouring a runaway convict, the police would of course take such steps as might appear necessary to come at the fact.'

At 11 am on Tuesday 23 June, the Under-Sheriff and two constables arrived at the *Phoenix* to collect Amos Crisp and take him to the Executive Council chambers where he would face an interrogation by the Governor.

Serious trouble loomed for John Stephen Jnr. His accomplice was locked away in gaol and would soon be forced to testify, and the authorities held incriminating documents signed in his own hand. The spinning balls were beginning to tumble around him.

Never one to admit defeat, John devised another plan of action. On the day following Crisp's arrival in Sydney, he sauntered into the courtroom where Captain Rossi was serving on the Bench, and examined the list of prisoners due to make an appearance. Rossi presumed John was there to assist him. Instead, John asked that Amos Crisp's case be held back until Mr Wentworth arrived in court. After loitering for some time, John asked Rossi for a pen and paper, wrote something down, then begged Rossi to allow him to swear an oath, thereby turning the document into an affidavit. After doing so, Rossi appended his signature and handed the paper back to John without reading it.

The paper Captain Rossi signed proved to be an affidavit relating to the search at Crisp's property. John mentioned renting apartments from Amos Crisp and employing Mrs Dickson to care for his property. He reported receiving information that constables had entered his sleeping apartment, ransacked his goods and abstracted some papers. And he declared Mrs Dickson to be a free woman and expressed his willingness to produce her.

When Wentworth entered the courtroom a short time later, John scurried over to speak to him, then the two men fronted up to Captain Rossi.

'I wish to claim the papers belonging to Mr John Stephen,' Wentworth announced.

'I am sorry but I cannot give you the papers,' Rossi said.

'Mr John Stephen is ready to make an affidavit that the papers are his property,' Wentworth argued.

'I do not know what affidavit Mr Stephen wishes to make however he has already made one which I have sworn him to,' Rossi replied patiently. 'Under the circumstances in which the papers came into my possession, I will not give them up on any account and I will send them to His Excellency the Governor.'

'I demand the return of my documents!' John interrupted. 'They are my property, they were taken out of a box belonging to me, and I insist that you give them up. I will make an affidavit that they are my property.'

Wentworth knew they had little chance of success. He turned to John and warned, 'It is no use to make an affidavit. Rossi won't give them up.' The two men walked away.

Unwilling to be so readily thwarted, John returned alone to see Captain Rossi. After expressing his wish to make another affidavit, Rossi took him into his private room. John insisted again that his papers be returned.

'There is a strong suspicion,' Rossi quietly informed him, 'that your servant Mrs Dickson is Mrs New, a prisoner who has escaped from custody.'

'I wish to make an affidavit that the woman who left Amos Crisp's house on the night of the constables' search was a woman named Frances Dickson and not Jane New,' John demanded.

'Don't you think it rather extraordinary,' Rossi interjected, 'that the two certificates, one in the name of "Frances Dickson" and the other "Jane New" and both stating the parties to be free, were found in a woman's pocket which had been left in that room in Crisp's house and which both have your signature?'

John blustered, 'I have not lived with Jane New.'

'It is a matter of notoriety that you have,' Rossi remonstrated.

After a short conversation, Rossi added with finality, 'You have already made an affidavit, the contents of which are unknown to me. You can make another affidavit if you please. But you cannot in my opinion rebut the affidavits made by the constables and you will repent such steps. I make these observations from the respect I bear to your family.' John said nothing further and left the room.

John later recounted a different story. After demanding the return of his papers and tendering the affidavit in which he offered to produce Mrs Dickson, he challenged Captain Rossi to do his duty: if Rossi suspected him of harbouring a prisoner, he should immediately charge him. Instead Rossi announced that he would transmit the associated paperwork to the Governor. 'He refused to allow my affidavit to accompany the paperwork,' John accused.

The issue of John's affidavit and his offer to produce Frances Dickson and thereby refute claims that she was Jane New would be returned to frequently in the ensuing years. Rossi repeatedly denied reading John's affidavit, and swore that he had no knowledge of the offer, a claim largely supported by future events. John continued to proffer the affidavit signed by Captain Rossi as evidence that Rossi knew of John's offer. And he insisted that, by refusing to transmit the affidavit to Governor Darling, Rossi had prevented him from proving that he had not harboured Jane New.

The Colonial Office eventually offered their opinion. 'The affidavit on which you so confidently rely,' Under-Secretary Robert Hay pointedly remarked to John, 'does not invalidate Captain Rossi's statement. On the contrary it leads to a suspicion that you swore the affidavit before him with the disingenuous design of afterwards converting it into the proof of an offer which you never effectively made.'

John never let exposure deter him. 'I appeal to the probability of Captain Rossi's declaration,' he sneered. 'Colonial magistrates invariably read the contents of affidavits prior to signing them. In a matter where he was adopting an unusual line of conduct which he was fully aware would be publicly commented on, would he have neglected to peruse half a sheet of paper on which he was required to administer an oath?'

John considered this defence unbeatable. The Colonial Office could have little knowledge of expedient local practice and would have difficulty rebutting his claims. However he gloated too soon. A witness at the later Executive Council hearing — the chief clerk of the Supreme Court, no less — revealed that he did not customarily read affidavits before swearing deponents to them. Ironically, John had called the witness in his own defence.

Captain Rossi's refusal to lay charges and his decision to transmit the paperwork to Governor Darling was John's second complaint. As Rossi legally had the right if not the obligation to proceed against John, it seems a surprising move. John was later to remark disparagingly: 'Being an alien and a Frenchman, ignorant of the English law, is Rossi's only excuse.'

When later questioned about his decision, Rossi's responses were evasive. He was evidently hiding the truth, that he had decided to insulate himself against the consequences of such a politically difficult situation by immediately forwarding the problem to the Governor.

Chapter 31

THE EXECUTIVE COUNCIL HEARING

How utterly devoid of foundation are Governor Darling's
charges, and how illegally and irregularly have those charges been
investigated and unjustly decided upon.

John Stephen Jnr

When Governor Darling received word of the discoveries at Amos Crisp's property, he found himself in an awkward position. While the evidence implicated John in a breach of duty (at the very least), his father was one of the Supreme Court justices. Out of consideration for Justice Stephen's situation, Darling offered John the opportunity to resign his appointment without facing an enquiry. Altruism was not the Governor's only motive. This course of action would enable him to sidestep another nasty political scene. The Stephens, Wentworth, and their fellow liberals were a source of torment and were collaborating with the press who refused to allow him to forget the debacle of the Sudds and Thompson affair. If John would go quietly into the night, it would be advantageous for them all.

But John was determined to brazen it out.

Colonial Secretary McLeay served as Darling's conduit in making this verbal offer. Upon John's return from Lower Minto, he found a note from the Colonial Secretary asking him to call. 'It is His Excellency's desire that you should immediately withdraw your name from the magistracy and resign your situation as Commissioner of Lands,' McLeay announced when John arrived at the office. 'I advise compliance *instantly* to save yourself from public exposure.'

'I court public enquiry into my conduct and I certainly shall not comply with the Governor's and your wishes with respect to retiring from my office,' John retorted.

Despite roundly dismissing the verbal offer, John wrote to McLeay later that day requesting a written offer. The matter was of serious importance to him, he explained. Wiser minds had perhaps recognised the opportunity for political gain. Understandably, Governor Darling was unwilling to accede to such a request. To put into writing even the suggestion that he might be willing to ignore criminal behaviour for political expediency would be political suicide. The Colonial Secretary did not deign to reply.

Having failed to circumvent the problem, Governor Darling sought the assistance of the Executive Council. The two certificates of freedom, one signed in John's capacity as a magistrate and the other in his role as Registrar, comprised the strongest evidence against him and reflected an abuse of his duties and responsibilities as a civil officer. As a government employee, John was answerable to the Governor, the Crown's representative in New South Wales, and Darling justifiably decided that his own advisory body was the appropriate tribunal for considering the charges. He ordered John to appear before the Council the following day.

The Executive Council convened on 23 June 1829 and the hearing began. After a brief report describing the current situation — Jane's escape from the Factory and probable concealment at Amos Crisp's, the search of his property, the discovery of a warm bed recently vacated by a woman, and the certificates naming Mrs Dickson and Jane New — the Council called John into their chamber.

'Certain matters have been brought under the notice of the Government,' the Council began, 'which appear to implicate your character and conduct as a public officer, and which therefore render it necessary that you should be called upon to explain the circumstances. With this view you are now brought before the Council. Have you been in the habit of granting certificates of the freedom of individuals and under what circumstances?'

And so the examination commenced. The first few questions related to the certificate of freedom John had issued Frances Dickson. John responded that he frequently granted them as passes of protection, as magistrates do, and that he had indeed issued one to his servant, Mrs Dickson, whom he 'imagined' to be a native of the colony. However, as Governor Darling clarified in his report to Britain:

It is *not* the practice for Magistrates to grant such certificates as he gave to Mrs Dickson, to free persons born in the colony. They are granted only to individuals who, having been transported and known as convicts, have become free. These certificates have been invariably signed by the Governor until the end of last month, and since that date by the Colonial Secretary.

When Mrs Dickson's employment situation became the topic of the next question, John's attitude became arrogant and antagonistic.

'How long has Mrs Dickson been in your service?' asked the Council.

'This Board has no authority to enquire into my private affairs,' John retorted.

Persuasion via an appeal to John's civic-mindedness followed: 'I, as Governor, enquire of you as a civil officer of this government.' The attempt was in vain.

'Unprepared, Gentlemen, as I must be to meet any interrogatories from you, and having been informed that there were circumstances which have induced your Excellency to require my resignation as an officer of the Government, I should wish to know what motive there may be for making this enquiry. Will your Excellency prefer any charge against me?' John taunted.

Governor Darling repeated the contents of his opening address, however John considered the answer inadequate. 'Your Excellency must see the difficult situation in which I am placed in being called upon to answer questions in reference to a matter about which I am not yet informed.'

The Governor clearly had no desire to elaborate on the subject of the enquiry and rejoined, 'You will be informed of the matter as the questions are put.' The critical questions followed. 'Did you grant a certificate to a woman named Jane New that she became free on April 27th?'

'I granted a certificate from affidavits lodged by Jane's counsel on March 21st and 26th that such appeared to be the fact on May 1st. This was in preference to giving up these affidavits to her husband, but the certificate was subsequently returned to me.'

'Was it your duty as Registrar of the Supreme Court to grant certificates of the freedom of prisoners based upon affidavits which you state were filed in the Registrar's Office?'

'It is the custom of parties making affidavits in court to hand them over to their counsel and, if required, they are left with the clerk of the Court and marked as filed,' began John, and on and on he droned, evading the question by elaborating on the procedures associated with lodging affidavits. He failed to deflect the Council.

'On what ground did you as an officer of the Government consider yourself justified in granting the certificate to Jane New without apprising the Government of the fact, knowing that the Government considered Jane New a prisoner who had absconded from the Factory at Parramatta?'

The histrionics began. 'I object to that question as assuming my knowledge of Jane New being considered by the Government as a prisoner. And further I consider that any affidavits left with me were under the seal of the secrecy of my office, and that I should not have been justified in making the contents of any affidavits public.' When later reporting to England, Darling described John's answer as a subterfuge. The affidavits were not intended for use in a private matter coming before the courts; rather they were to serve a bureaucratic purpose in clarifying the date of expiry of Jane's sentence.

Although unaware at this time of the affidavits' contents, the Council realised that John in his professional capacity knew of Jane's status as a prisoner. 'As Registrar of the Supreme Court, did you not communicate to the Government that it was ordered by the Supreme Court, "that Jane New be remanded to the Factory at Parramatta for safe custody until His Excellency the Governor shall cause her to be transmitted to Tasmania, from whence she came to this Colony contrary to law"?'

John had a ready answer. 'On March 21st, Jane New appeared by affidavits then before the Court to be a Prisoner of the Crown at Tasmania, but at the same time it was in my knowledge privately, from the affidavits alluded to, that on April 27th her original sentence would expire.'

Naturally, the Council was curious to know the identities of those responsible for the affidavits, and asked accordingly. John withdrew the affidavits from his pocket and glanced at them.

'What are those papers?' Governor Darling enquired.

'The original affidavits,' John replied, and named the signatories: James New, Jane New, Dr Carlyle and James Horton. 'But there are several others,' John continued, 'which I think are in my brother's office, unless they were stolen out of my apartments up the country by the parties who stole the certificate His Excellency has produced.' The taunt was typical of John's diversionary strategies.

Although John failed to hand over the affidavits, their appearance at this particular time clarified one issue. John knew the purpose of the enquiry. His claim to ignorance and unpreparedness was proven a fallacy by his own revelation that he was carrying documents relating to Jane New's situation. The Council let this slide and moved on to another subject.

'Were you aware that Jane New had absconded from the Factory when you granted the certificate of freedom on May 1st, and where did you give her that certificate?'

Not surprisingly, John claimed the colonial equivalent of the fifth amendment. 'As it appears that this question has a tendency to criminate myself if I have done anything illegal, I decline answering it. At the same time, I have to remark that my conduct if illegal is open to the proper tribunals. Having been advised that the whole of these proceedings, like those of the Star Chamber, are contrary to the true spirit of British Law, I must protest against this Council interrogating me further. If I am guilty of any offence cognisable by the law, to its power alone am I liable. I do not mean to be contumacious or disrespectful, but I must decline answering any more questions. Prove me guilty of any offence, and I will subscribe to the punishment prescribed without a murmur.' John prepared to leave the room.

John's denunciation enraged Governor Darling. He later wrote that John's fear of self-incrimination revealed his knowledge of the hearing's intentions, and that his reference to the Star Chamber was an insult of the 'grossest character'. Nevertheless, determined to continue with the hearing, the Council submitted to one of John's earlier requests, asking the clerk to read the documents relating to the search and discoveries at Amos Crisp's. Petulantly, John declined to listen unless furnished with a copy. The Council refused to oblige him. John walked out of the Council Chambers.

For the record, the Council remarked upon the irrelevancy of John's answers, adding that he responded in writing and, despite requests, refused to provide more direct or satisfactory responses. It must have proved a long and drawn-out session.

After John exited the Council chambers, Amos Crisp was ushered in. Did he feel intimidated as he came face to face with the most powerful men in the New South Wales penal settlement, those who could deprive him of his freedom at the snap of their fingers? Crisp initially faced questions regarding his own background before the Council moved on to his involvement with John Stephen Jnr and Frances Dickson.

'Have you been in the habit of letting lodgings?' the Council enquired.

'Never but on one occasion,' Crisp admitted, 'when I let a small room to Mr John Stephen.'

'About what period did you let these lodgings to Mr Stephen?'

'About the month of January and he still hires them.'

'How has the room generally been made use of while it has been so hired?'

'It has been occupied by Mr John Stephen when he occasionally visited the country, and by a Mrs Dickson when he was not there. Mrs Dickson slept with my daughter when Mr Stephen was there,' Crisp disclosed.

'Who is Mrs Dickson?'

'I don't know who she is,' he confessed.

'When did she first come to your house?'

'About five weeks ago to the best of my recollection.'

'Who brought her to your house?'

'I was not at home at the time,' he said, 'but I understand from my children that Mr Hart of Sydney brought her to my house.'

'In what capacity did Mrs Dickson live there?'

'I cannot exactly say,' Crisp prevaricated. 'She did not appear as a servant, nor yet as a friend.'

'Where did Mr Stephen board for the days he resided at your house?'

'He and Mrs Dickson breakfasted and dined together,' he revealed.

'Was Mrs Dickson in the room when the constables came on the night of the 17th instant?'

'I do not know positively that she was as I came home so late,' Crisp admitted, 'but as the bed was warm when the constables examined it, I conclude that she had been, as she always slept in that bed when Mr Stephen was not there.'

'What was the cause of her running away?'

'I don't know, but from the circumstances of her having absconded, I immediately entertained doubts of her being the person she had represented herself to be,' he confided.

'Had Mrs Dickson any certificate to show that she was free?'

'She had.'

'By whom was that certificate signed?'

'By Mr John Stephen, a magistrate, and I thought I did not do wrong to admit a person into my house who held such a certificate,' Crisp added earnestly.

'Did you see any other certificates found by the constables on that occasion?'

'I saw one in the pocket or little bag found by the constables amongst Mrs Dickson's clothes,' he recollected.

'What was the purport of that certificate?'

'It was to certify that Mrs Jane New was free, and it was signed by Mr John Stephen.'

Amos Crisp had just provided the independent evidence they needed to support the constables' claim regarding Jane New's certificate of freedom. The noose had tightened.

Questions about the constables' search and the discovery of the outside room followed, before the Council returned to the subject of the certificates. 'Did Mr Meredith ask your daughter to allow him to examine any of Mrs Dickson's boxes?'

'He did,' confirmed Crisp, 'and my daughter opened the boxes, which were not locked, that they might examine the contents.'

'Did the constables take anything away but the two certificates already alluded to?'

'They did not,' Crisp declared decisively.

Yet two days previously Elizabeth Crisp had written to John Stephen Jnr complaining that some items were missing from her box, including a few pounds in notes and coins as well as 'the paper which you gave me'. Elizabeth's statement was at odds with those of the constables and of her own father, leading the members of the second Executive Council hearing some years later to conclude that her letter had been written at Mr Stephen's behest for the sake of the reference to 'the paper'. Clearly John was hoping to discredit the constables' behaviour and thereby undermine their reports and the value of their evidence.

Crisp's interrogation ended soon afterwards and the Council ordered him to leave the Chambers. Exiting the room, he met Captain Rossi who dismissed him and told him to make his own way home. No offers of transport, food or money were provided. No doubt these were minor inconveniences compared to Crisp's relief at regaining his freedom. Friends could be called upon for assistance or at worst it was merely an extremely long walk home.

Amos Crisp was lucky. The Governor had ordered the cancellation of his ticket-of-leave and his confinement in the prisoners' barracks; from there he faced assignment to a settler or to a road or clearing gang. Instead Captain Rossi ignored the Governor's decree and allowed him to retain his precious ticket-of-leave. Why? Because Rossi knew that the Governor's order breached the law, that the precedent set in Jane New's *habeas corpus* ruling precluded the Governor from revoking Crisp's assignment. Was Governor Darling deliberately flouting the Supreme Court ruling, or had it simply not occurred to him that he was breaking the law? Again.

After Amos Crisp left the Council Chambers, the members conferred and reached their decision: that the evidence satisfactorily proved that 'Frances Dickson' was a pseudonym for Jane New. That John Stephen Jnr had clearly communicated with Jane New, a runaway prisoner, without taking steps for her apprehension as was his duty. That he had exercised an authority he did not possess as a magistrate in granting Frances Dickson's certificate of freedom. That he had usurped the Governor's power in granting Jane New's certificate of freedom. That he had abused his authority as Registrar, as his office held official records showing that Jane's sentence would not expire for a further two years. And that in granting these certificates John had been attempting to defeat the ends of justice. The Council ruled:

> Considering the dangerous example this affords to a colony constituted as this is, the Council are of opinion that Mr John Stephen Junior has been guilty of a most flagrant dereliction of his duty, and therefore recommend that his name be struck out of the Commission of the Peace, and that he be suspended from the office which he now holds as a commissioner for apportioning the territory, until His Majesty's pleasure shall be known.

The axe had fallen.

Yet, a significant omission is evident in the Council's ruling. If 'Frances Dickson' was a fictitious name for Jane New, then John had been harbouring a runaway. This was not just a dereliction of duty, flagrant or otherwise, but an offence against the laws of the land. So why did the Council ignore this obvious conclusion?

Political expediency is the most likely answer: a lack of evidence strong enough to achieve a conviction particularly if Wentworth or Wardell were chosen to carry John's banner; an awareness that the case could easily transmogrify into another political circus; a desire not to expose the government and judiciary to humiliation and ridicule through the revelation that one of their own, the son of a Supreme Court justice no less, had breached such a law. It was the stuff of nightmares and the

Council members must collectively have shuddered at the thought. Under the circumstances, Governor Darling and the Council decided to ignore the evidence that John had harboured a runaway and to forgo the opportunity to bring charges against him. It was a decision Governor Darling would later regret.

Chapter 32
THE REPERCUSSIONS

It is important that the confirmation of Mr John Stephen's
dismissal should be publicly notified in order to show the
determination of His Majesty's Government to support the local
authority in punishing vice and immorality.
Governor Ralph Darling

Before implementing the Executive Council's ruling, Governor Darling questioned the Chief Justice about the affidavits John had mentioned. Forbes revealed that they had not been filed in the Supreme Court. John had lied to the Executive Council.

Governor Darling took immediate action. On 26 June he notified John that his services as a magistrate were no longer required and that he had been suspended from his duties as Commissioner of Crown Lands. John's discharge from the magistracy was published in the *Sydney Gazette* a day later. The worthies of Sydney must have been agape at the news.

But why was John suspended and not sacked? Governor Darling later alluded to the problem, revealing that civil officers could not be removed for misconduct unless the evidence could convict them in a court of law and was used for that purpose. Ironically, historians claim that one of Permanent Under-Secretary James Stephen's greatest contributions to colonial government was in pushing for a new ruling allowing the dismissal of civil officers. No doubt thoughts of his cousin's behaviour and the years of ensuing drama were in James Stephen's mind as he helped implement this ruling.

If Governor Darling had even the slightest doubt about John's guilt, his concerns would have been quashed the following day when a communication arrived from Governor Arthur. It included John's letter to Dr Officer appealing for assistance in petitioning for Jane's emancipation, a letter which carried the date 5 May 1829. Yet John had signed Jane's certificate of freedom on 1 May 1829. These two documents provided conclusive proof of John's duplicity, Darling later reported to the Colonial Office. 'Mr Stephen granted that Certificate knowing that Jane New *was not free*.' This fact alone was enough to justify his dismissal, Darling prompted, and he urged the Secretary of State to replace John's suspension with a termination.

John waited a week before responding to Darling's letter detailing his suspension. He had probably been busy trying to effect his escape from the colony with Jane New. In his response, John continued to affect the ignorance-reveals-innocence defence, demanding to be informed of the grounds for his suspension. 'As I am totally ignorant of any just cause for such a proceeding, I trust that this reasonable and just request may be granted to enable me to meet the question on fair grounds with your Excellency when my case is laid before the Secretary of State.'

John also wrote to the Secretary of State beseeching him to defer judgement until he received John's response:

In making this appeal to your impartial consideration, I can only pledge myself as a man of honour and a gentleman, that I have in no instance done any act derogatory to my character and situation in life, much less have I committed or even been accused of having committed any act of impropriety in any office which I have held under the Government. By the next vessel I shall be fully prepared to verify this assertion.

Yet nine months passed before John continued his defence. Meanwhile, Governor Darling concluded his report to Sir George Murray with the lament:

It is with extreme reluctance that I have brought the case of Mr John Stephen forward. It may be a merit to live on terms with those about you, but this must more or less depend on the character of the individuals. It has been my lot unfortunately to encounter some of the most exceptional.

Governor Darling knew that John would not bow his head and accept his suspension as just retribution for unconscionable behaviour. Nevertheless, he could never have imagined the depths to which John would descend in order to fight his suspension, reclaim his character and take his revenge.

As John collected documentary evidence and affidavits to substantiate his claims and quash the charges against him, he also had another agenda: destroy those responsible for the charges. John's first target was the Colonial Secretary, Alexander McLeay.

McLeay found himself in John's sights as a result of the anomalies on Tasmanian Colonial Secretary Burnett's letter recording Jane's Cheshire trial date and ship of transportation. McLeay had attached the letter to an affidavit clarifying Jane's status as a prisoner of the Crown, and filed the documents in the Supreme Court. John had used the anomalies as the basis for his affidavits claiming that Jane's trial date was 1822 rather than 1824. They were to have another useful purpose as well.

After John alluded to the errors at the Executive Council hearing, the Governor realised that Burnett's letter — the only New South Wales record of Jane's transportation — was still held by the Supreme Court. The Solicitor-General filed a motion for its return to the Colonial Secretary's Office and for a copy to be lodged in its place.

John prepared an affidavit and employed Wentworth to resist the motion. It was to prove an astonishing attack. Wentworth informed the court: 'On 23 June, Mr Stephen was cited before the Executive Council and there alleged that the paper in question was not a genuine document, but had been fabricated in a certain part. He believes that Mr McLeay wishes to relieve himself from the imputation of having fabricated the document, and wishes to have the same taken from the files of the Court.'

In open court, John and his counsel had accused the Colonial Secretary of New South Wales of forgery and perjury!

The Supreme Court justices were left floundering. Chief Justice Forbes eventually responded: 'The Court cannot receive in this way any suggestion of fraud. If an offence has been committed it ought to be brought before the Court in a regular way.' The judges refused to file John's affidavit, remonstrated with John and his counsel for pursuing such a course, and agreed to release the letter to the Colonial Secretary's Office if the Solicitor-General supported his motion with an affidavit.

On the following Monday morning, Sydney's civil officers exclaimed at John's latest assault. The gall of the man. However, work had to be done, and letters went backwards and forwards as the appropriate affidavit was prepared and filed, and Burnett's letter eventually released.

To solve the problem of the anomalies, Colonial Secretary McLeay wrote to Colonial Secretary Burnett for enlightenment. Chief Clerk Henry Emmett accepted responsibility and apologised profusely for the error. Burnett provided the correct details and added: 'I trust the mistake has not occasioned any very material inconvenience.' He probably never learnt the truth.

By the time Burnett's despatch arrived in Sydney, the matter had snowballed. Edward Smith Hall was never afraid to inform the public of any transgression — proven or otherwise — on the part of those in authority, and delightedly published the background to the Solicitor-General's motion. He concluded:

This was resisted by Mr Wentworth who averred that the motion of the Solicitor-General had been made with a view to shield Mr McLeay from the legal responsibility of having placed a document on the files of the Court as a genuine one, which was not genuine.

John's charge against Alexander McLeay had just been broadcast to the world. Sydney's newspapers were not only read by the local literati; they were bundled together and forwarded to Tasmania and to Britain, to the government and to the press in both places. Even if the press chose not to publish the report, such claims became grist for the active rumour mills in both places.

Alexander McLeay accordingly sued Edward Smith Hall for libel. What else could he do, grieved the *Sydney Gazette*:

> Nothing but the award of a Court of Justice could atone for so cruel a stab at Mr McLeay's feelings, so deadly an attempt to ruin his reputation. No man in his senses could suppose him capable of such villainy and even the very persons who have invented the horrid calumny, and taken pains to disseminate it, no more believe McLeay could be guilty of any such conduct, than they believe him able to extinguish sun, moon and stars.

John had attacked Colonial Secretary McLeay under the guise of preventing an injustice but in truth for no other reason than a malicious desire to take revenge, and had left havoc in his wake.

The libel case was eventually heard by Justice Dowling late in December 1829. McLeay's barrister argued that the newspaper account was not a court report but an editorial article fraught with gross insinuations about the Colonial Secretary. 'Where is there an allegation that McLeay had placed a false document on the files of the Court?' he asked. The Supreme Court's refusal to file John's affidavit contributed to Hall's undoing. Justice Dowling summed up that a newspaper editor could publish court proceedings so long as they contained nothing 'defamatory, scandalous, or immoral', which could prejudice a person who had no opportunity of vindicating himself.

Hall's resulting libel conviction created consternation among the press, both liberal and conservative. 'Scarcely is there a single trial in which there is not something brought forward injurious to the character of individuals,' fretted the *Sydney Gazette*. 'Nothing would be more subversive of the purposes of the law than the trammelling of those reports with an intimidating responsibility.'

The repercussions of the Jane New scandal continued to reverberate through the settlement to the detriment of all.

As the days passed, those ensnared in John's net included the willing as well as the unwilling. On the day after Jane New slipped out of the colony on board the *Emma Kemp*, Frances Dickson appeared at the office of Notary Public John Raine. Or so Raine swore in his own affidavit signed the same day:

On 6 July 1829 personally came and appeared Frances Dickson of Sydney who declared that she is a free woman having been born in this colony, and that she never did any act to deprive her of her liberty. That she was living with a man resident in Sydney as his wife but was obliged to separate from him and conceal herself in consequence of ill usage. That she was recommended to John Stephen Jnr. Esq in the month of March last to take care of his wearing apparel and other property in the apartments he had rented of one Amos Crisp on the Campbell Town Road about twenty-five miles from Sydney. That she was taken to the house of Amos Crisp on or about the ninth or tenth day of March last by Mr Hart of Pitt Street, by the direction of Mr Stephen where she remained until Wednesday 17 June when between the hours of twelve and one at night, she was awoke by some persons coming into the house, and imagining that her reputed husband had discovered her, she ran away from the premises and returned to Sydney where she now remains.

Raine described Frances Dickson as having dark brown hair, hazel eyes and a fresh complexion, and that she was a surprisingly tall five feet six or seven inches and about 21 years of age. He claimed to have met Jane New on several occasions, and swore that although a strong resemblance existed between the two women, Frances Dickson was not Jane New.

Yet instead of proving that Frances Dickson was not Jane New, John Raine's affidavit posed a new set of questions. If Frances Dickson truly appeared before John Raine, a notary public who was legally authorised to administer oaths and attest documents, why was no affidavit prepared for her to sign at this time? She appeared at the behest of and presumably accompanied by John Stephen Jnr. He knew that affidavits carried more weight than declarations and had himself been gathering affidavits to that end. And all he had to do to prove his innocence and reclaim his character and position was to organise for 'Frances Dickson' to swear an affidavit attesting to her identity, and to present herself and the affidavit to the Governor. John's unwillingness to pursue this obvious course demolished his own claim regarding her identity, cast suspicion upon Raine's claim that Frances Dickson had appeared at his office, and raised doubts about the honesty and integrity of John Raine himself.

Justice James Dowling had previously expressed concerns about Raine's integrity when he rejected his application for admission as a solicitor:

> Mr Raine was punished by a fine of £20 for a contempt in altering the process of the Court on 12 July 1828 and since then has been indicted with several others for aiding in the escape of a convict named Doran but acquitted.

The circumstances behind James Doran's escape reveal Raine's willingness to defy the law when he perceived injustice. Perhaps he believed Jane had suffered in the same way.

John Raine was not the only signatory to an affidavit of doubtful veracity at this time. Thomas Henry Hart and Amos Crisp also signed affidavits claiming that Mrs Dickson had arrived at the Crisps' around 9 or 10 March. Crisp's affidavit declared:

> On 17th June last, my house was entered by three Constables who stated that they had no warrant or written authority but had received the orders of Monsieur Captain Rossi, Superintendent of Police at Sydney, to search my house. They proceeded closely to examine every part of my premises, even the room and bed of my daughter, a girl of seventeen years of age. The Constables then quitted my own immediate premises and proceeded to the apartment of John Stephen Esq and opened the bedroom door thereof, which had no communication with my part of the dwelling, being built on one side of the house and having only one door which opened

into the garden. The Constables ransacked Mr John Stephen's boxes, carpet bag, etc. They took from thence sundry papers, stating at the same time their knowledge that the room was Mr John Stephen's private apartment and the articles therein his property except the woman's apparel, which I stated to the Constables was partly Mrs Dickson's and partly my daughter's clothes who occupied the room in the temporary absence of Mr Stephen. And upon remonstrating with the Constables upon the impropriety of their conduct, the Constables took me into custody.

Not only were many of these claims absurd, Crisp's affidavit contradicted some of his own responses at the recent Executive Council hearing, including his remark that Mrs Dickson had arrived at his property some five weeks earlier. John had evidently composed Crisp's affidavit to serve as his own mouthpiece.

Governor Darling knew that John was gathering affidavits to rebut the charges against him and reported to Sir George Murray:

But these charges speak for themselves and no affidavit which he can make (and it is on record that he is not over scrupulous in these matters) or Mr Wentworth can procure, can in any degree shake the conclusion which so inevitably results from the chain of circumstances I have laid before you.

Instead of delivering these affidavits to the Governor, however, John pursued a different course, attacking another target on his list. He sued Captain Rossi for illegal conduct. The charges: causing the constables to illegally enter his apartment within Amos Crisp's house, unlawfully taking away money, documents and private papers which were in his safekeeping, and detaining those items contrary to his will. With Crisp's affidavit as his foundation, John intended to prove that the search of his apartment was illegal and therefore that the constables had no right to confiscate any papers. Without these papers the authorities had no evidence against him.

As it transpired, John was forced to abandon the suit although he broached his concerns at the later Executive Council hearing.

'Did you issue a warrant to search my premises?' John asked Captain Rossi.

'I had no idea that you would have gone to live in a ticket-of-leave holder's house. Had I thought so, I would have issued a warrant.'

'How could I possibly know that he was a ticket-of-leave holder?' John demanded.

Rossi's disdain was evident. 'I don't know, but I knew it and I therefore ordered his house to be searched.'

Had John Stephen Jnr, a magistrate and officer of the court, truly failed to question Amos Crisp regarding his status? If so, it had proved a serious miscalculation.

Chapter 33
MALEFACTOR OR MARTYR?

John Stephen Jnr's principles appear to be too manly and
uncompromising to permit him to mix with the Court Persecutors
and Court Intriguers. He seems to be superior to such.
Tasmanian Asiatic Review

As the weeks passed, a grumble of discontent at John's suspension gradually percolated through the liberals' ranks, reflecting their ignorance of the true circumstances underlying the Governor's action. Many saw John's dismissal as part of a larger political picture: William Charles Wentworth's recent attempt to impeach Governor Darling over his treatment of Privates Joseph Sudds and Patrick Thompson.

Wentworth's actions against the Governor had an unintended consequence within the colonial community: he antagonised the conservatives, many of the moderates and even some reformists. Rising up to defend the Governor, these worthies signed addresses condemning the licentious press for inflaming the minds of the lower orders against Darling's administration, and expressing their sincere wish that he would long continue administering the colony. Governor Darling later boasted that the second address was signed by every respectable man residing in this part of the colony with the exception of three persons. One was John Stephen Jnr.

The liberal *Tasmanian and Asiatic Review* latched onto the story. Condemning the signatories as those already in favour and those who sought to curry favour, the newspaper championed John's refusal to sign the address. 'An open, frank and liberal gentleman with uncompromising principles,' the editor gushed, 'John Stephen Jnr had an opinion of his own, and did not think it proper to sign the Secret Address.' John's subsequent dismissal was considered a consequence of his unwillingness to act as a signatory:

> Strange to say that a few days after the receipt of the Address, Mr John Stephen was summarily dismissed from the magistracy and, in another day, also from his office of Land Commissioner, which was bestowed upon a man of more compliant mould, one of the *Address Signers*, a Mr George Innes!!

The *Tasmanian and Asiatic Review* had expressed the consensus of the liberals, those unaware of the simmering Jane New scandal. A Sydney resident some years later confirmed the report: 'Politics at that time ran very high, and Mr Stephen's removal or dismissal was considered in my mind to have arisen from political prejudice. He was extremely popular with all classes of this community, and I believe very few knew the real cause of his removal from office.'

Clearly, the secrecy of the Executive Council hearing and Darling's restraint in not revealing the grounds for John's suspension had worked to John's advantage and to the Governor's disadvantage. Those moaning about Darling's regime added John to their list of martyrs and his suspension to their growing list of gripes. Would the truth have silenced the liberals? Considering the liberal press' ability to pluck spurious facts out of thin air, it seems unlikely.

The *Sydney Monitor* adopted a surprising attitude, ignoring the reason behind John's suspension but expressing umbrage at the insult to him as a gentleman:

> Mr John Stephen Junr was dismissed from the magistracy with as little ceremony as a ticket-prisoner-constable is dismissed. Although Mr Stephen

holds one of the King's household appointments, and is certainly entitled on that account (were his family out of the question) to the title of Esquire as much as our skipper and huxter magistrates are, yet he was designated as *Mister* John Stephen Junr. We see no good occasion for such a departure from courtesy and good breeding. Men may punish their political and other foes, but gentlemen should always be gentlemen.

Some who were privy to the truth were ashamed of John's behaviour. His brother Sidney Stephen wrote to Governor Darling some months later:

> I cannot blame you if you were forever to shun every member of our family as wholly unworthy of your acquaintance after the dishonourable and ungrateful conduct of my brother towards you. The Sins of the Father will be visited upon the children: this is too generally found to be a true adage for me to hope for an entire exemption from this rule of judging people. Should it unhappily be my destiny thus to be classed with some of my family, I must then trust to conscience as my best protector.

In the aftermath of the Executive Council hearing, John found himself without a job, an income or any other visible means of support. His spendthrift habits came back to haunt him. Ironmonger Launcelot Iredale had sued John in April 1829 for £50 for goods purchased and work undertaken, and the case reached the courtroom on 17 June, the same day the constables launched their midnight ambush. The judges ruled against John, signing the final judgement on 23 July.

By then, word of John's difficulties had filtered through the community. His creditors swarmed. On 24 July James Melville sued John for £45 for goods purchased. On 27 July cabinet-maker William Holmes issued a warrant for John's arrest claiming damages of £70. On the same day William Bowen issued another warrant for John's arrest claiming damages of £40. And on the same day, John Stephen Jnr slipped out of the country.

But he did not depart empty-handed. Over the following months, the coffers of the deceased estates' trust fund proved to be deficient. The Supreme Court had authorised John as Registrar to take responsibility for the proceeds of two intestate estates. Yet upon his departure, John had left no documentation relating to these estates, the proceeds from which had a combined value of £137.

The executors approached the government. Attorney-General Baxter refused to institute legal proceedings for the recovery of private property, and recommended an approach to the Supreme Court. Receiving no satisfaction through the court, the executors demanded reimbursement from the Colonial Treasury, arguing that John had misappropriated the funds while employed by the Colonial Government. Governor Darling refused his consent.

Word that John had plundered the deceased estates' fund reached the Colonial Office in 1831, yet surprisingly John was not questioned. Nor was he chastised when an opportunity later arose in New South Wales. Evidently the authorities considered the missing £137 was not their problem.

John's pilfering proved paltry compared with that of his replacement, John Edye Manning, who learnt the lesson of his predecessor well. Although the authorities were unwilling or, as they claimed, unable to assist those who had suffered from John's depredations, they expressed their determination to prevent a recurrence. The Supreme Court forced Manning to lodge a £2000 security and ordered him to deposit the intestate money in the Savings Bank and provide a quarterly audit. Yet the Supreme Court judges failed to enforce their own rules. When Manning fell victim to the depression in the early 1840s, his debts amounted to £30000 of which £10000 was trust money that had been kept in his private account.

The behaviour of these government officials not only exposed ongoing inadequacies within the bureaucracy and the government's lack of accountability, it epitomised the inequities of the British judicial system. Whereas members of the 'criminal class' were sentenced to death for stealing goods worth £2, John Stephen Jnr purloined seventy times that amount and escaped without retribution, while Manning received little more than a rap across the knuckles for embezzling an amount that in today's terms would be worth many millions of dollars.

No wonder men like John Stephen Jnr considered themselves above the law.

On 27 July 1829, John slunk out of Sydney on board the *Eliza* bound for England. No family; few possessions. When later condemned for such a hasty and unceremonious exit, John bleated:

> With respect to my abrupt departure, I humbly observe that it was the consequence and not the cause of my suspension. The suspension preceded my departure by upwards of a month, and I consider that the unnecessary delay of even one day where my honour and reputation might have been at stake would have been construed by my harsh accuser as evidence of my guilt, and with my friends have created an impression to my prejudice. I would not have traversed so immense a distance with the mere object of re-instatement to an office, the emoluments of which barely produced a comfortable subsistence even with my other resources. But I returned to the country of my friends and relatives to convince them of my integrity by that acquittal at the Secretary of State's hands which the *ex parte* misrepresentations of a Governor demanded.

Before the *Eliza* sailed, John had first to face the Governor's wrath. 'I was subjected to the personal inspection by six constables of my cabin and trunks,' John raged, 'and I was further insulted on my embarkation by having a friend's boat's crew and myself closely examined by special order to ascertain Our Sex!'

Captain Rossi had taken his revenge.

At a time when journeys between Britain and the Antipodes usually took around four months, a surprisingly long eight months passed before John reached Britain's shores. The *Eliza* sailed initially to Mauritius, a voyage of around two months. Lying in the Indian Ocean some 1200 miles off the east coast of Africa, the sub-tropical island was considered by many to be a taste of heaven. Perhaps John was tempted to disembark by this vision of paradise, although the rumourmongers in Sydney believed Mauritius was his intended destination. Indeed Governor Darling denounced John as having abandoned his wife and children when he relocated there.

But the persecution continued after John disembarked. 'I found that a communication had been made to the Police at Mauritius,' he later complained to the British authorities, 'charging me with having harboured the female prisoner Jane New on board the ship in which I was a passenger, and which was accordingly closely searched.'

Captain Rossi had previously served as General Superintendent of the Convict Department in Mauritius. John had met his match.

John attempted to impress the worthies of Mauritius upon his arrival, strutting around in the uniform of the King's Household. It had little effect. His reputation had been traduced by this communication, John moaned, and he was consequently a proscribed character during his four months in Mauritius. He had evidently found himself unwelcome at the dinners and balls, the theatre and race meetings that the elite flocked to during the winter social season.

Realising that he had little chance of obtaining financially rewarding employment, John pondered his future. 'I was forced to remain in Mauritius because of a severe attack of fever from which I was slow to recover,' he quickly justified in a letter dashed off to England to account for his delayed return. He purchased a passage and returned to the country he had left under a shadow three-and-a-half years previously.

Part VI:
PERSECUTION

*It is the base attack of a cowardly
opponent who dares not meet an
open enquiry, but seeks by covert
means to injure the cause of his
adversary by undermining
his reputation.*

John Stephen Jnr

Chapter 34
DESPERATE AND DESTITUTE

Having been refused information by Governor Darling as to the grounds for the act of unmerited harshness which has deprived me of my livelihood, I have been compelled to return to Europe to seek that redress which only can be found at your hands.

John Stephen Jnr

When John Stephen Jnr departed Sydney's shores, Governor Darling probably felt a profound sense of relief. John was no longer his problem. He would not learn for some time that he had dismissed the man too hastily, that John would prove a particularly vindictive viper.

John had a double agenda, and he laid the groundwork for both in his letter from Mauritius to the Secretary of State:

Being detained at Mauritius, I have to entreat a short delay of your decision on my case until I am enabled personally to refute any calumny which General Darling may have adduced against me, to exculpate his own conduct. At the same time I shall submit such charges against His Excellency, supported by documents, as will prove him unworthy of the high office of ruler over so important a colony as New South Wales.

Upon his return to London late in March 1830, John immediately requested an interview with the Secretary of State, explaining: 'I am unwilling to see my cousin Mr James Stephen or any other member of my family until I am enabled to clear myself from General Darling's imputations.' Despite adverting to his relationship with the Colonial Office's permanent counsel, John was only granted an appointment with Under-Secretary Robert Hay. It was an ill omen he chose to ignore. John asked to see the documents connected with his case, and requested a copy. The Colonial Office despatched the papers to him on 27 April.

John also sought financial relief. He appealed to Under-Secretary Hay to have the other moiety of his salary as Commissioner of Crown Lands paid to him, since his substitute would be allowed only a half-salary while John remained under suspension. If his appeal succeeded, it would prove a welcome relief. Honour and justice were diminishing in importance against the threat represented by his financial concerns. He had returned to England to face debts arising from his Privy Council suit, a dishonoured bill, and travelling and settlement costs. And as each day passed, the tally grew.

Sir George Murray proved unsympathetic, refusing to authorise any salary payments until John exonerated himself from the Executive Council's charges. Thwarted by the stony-hearted Secretary of State, John could not resist the urge to play games. On 3 May he complained to Hay that the requested Executive Council documents had not arrived. Indeed, the delay had produced such an anxiety of mind, he whined, that an illness had confined him to bed for three weeks.

Perturbed, Under-Secretary Hay questioned his staff and learnt that the papers had been despatched to John's address on 28 April. 'The waiter at Joy's Hotel into whose hands they were delivered by the messenger,' Hay informed John, 'has reported that he forwarded them to you on the day after he received them.' Hay politely suggested that John make further enquiries.

John refused to back down. 'I beg leave to inform you that I have made every enquiry with respect to the papers without success. The porter at Downing Street assured me that he had delivered them to one of the waiters of this hotel, but they all deny the fact of having received them.

Would you be pleased to order the messenger at the Colonial Office to identify the man into whose hands he delivered the papers?'

Hay responded pointedly: 'Upon questioning the messenger belonging to this department, I find he has already, in your presence, identified the waiter into whose hands he delivered the packet. Under these circumstances, I do not conceive it necessary to take any further steps in the matter, and the task of recovering the papers rests entirely with yourself.'

The game was over; the authorities had called his bluff. John reported soon afterwards: 'The missing papers were forwarded to me last night, although I am as yet ignorant from whence they came.'

John's persistence with the game after Hay discerned the truth appears puerile and extremely short-sighted. He was the fabled scorpion who, after stinging the frog carrying him across the river, exclaimed, 'No, it's not logic, but I can't help it. It's my character!'

With such a character flaw, self-immolation inevitably beckoned.

Chapter 35
INNOCENCE INCARNATE

I trust that I have succeeded in removing from your
Lordship's mind the remotest impression that I was compelled
to resort to the artifice of falsehood to screen myself from the
imputations which rested against my character.

John Stephen Jnr

John's demands for support from the Colonial Office ceased while he perused the Executive Council documents and prepared his response. He began with an earnest entreaty for the Secretary of State's patient attention while he 'humbly but confidently' submitted his refutation. It was a prudent request as his reply covered many pages.

Governor Darling eventually received a copy of John's reply and responded with his own remarks. Some of the issues covered by the two men were minor gripes and snipes, briefly covered and soon forgotten. Others volleyed backwards and forwards as claims and counterclaims, developing a momentum of their own unrelated to their importance in the actual scandal.

Underlying the charges against John was one simple issue: whether Frances Dickson was truly Jane New. The Executive Council claimed to be satisfied that they were the same person. John naturally disagreed. He argued that the two certificates found in his room represented the Council's only proof and offered an explanation to cover this circumstance:

On 1st May 1829 James New requested that I return to him the affidavits left with me regarding his wife's freedom. This I refused to do without an order from the counsel who had delivered them into my custody; but I signed a certificate stating that she became free on the 27th April 1829 'as appeared from affidavits left with me'. After writing and handing him this paper, I wrote another for my servant Mrs Dickson who was then in Sydney purchasing some necessaries to take to the cottage in the country which I gave to her the same day before she left town. This certificate is dated by some mistake on the 10th of May.

About a week or ten days after, Mr James New returned me the certificate, stating that he should require it no further. Being at the time on horseback, just starting for the country, I put the certificate in my pocket. The bag (or side pocket as it was ingenuously called by the constable), in which this small piece of paper was found, was lent to me by Crisp's daughter for the purpose of holding my percussion caps when I went out shooting. On emptying my pocket when I quitted the cottage on the 17th June, I gave Crisp's daughter the bag and handed to her several articles as I took them from my pocket, which consisted of a few copper caps, this piece of paper — the nature of which I did not at that moment recollect — two bank notes to pay her father, and a tooth which I had preserved for its singularity. This bag Crisp's daughter placed in *her Trunk*, which she had removed into my room during my absence, and added to the contents a couple of dollars and other silver. The other certificate was found in Mrs Dickson's work box on the table in my room.

Governor Darling was not alone in dismissing John's explanation as being too absurd to merit any notice.

Having concluded that Frances Dickson was indeed Jane New, the Council had also accused John of communicating with her without alerting the police. John indignantly denied the claim. 'Infamous assertion! Where is the proof?' Governor Darling pointed out that the certificate of freedom must have been given to Jane after her escape from the Factory, and that if Jane New and Frances Dickson were indeed the same person therein lay the proof.

John countered that Frances Dickson was not Jane New and that he had offered to produce her, but Governor Darling had refused permission. Since John had not mentioned such an offer at the Executive Council hearing or on any other occasion in the following month, his claim must have astounded the Governor.

John's breaches of his official duties had been prominent in the Executive Council's charges against him. To the claim that he had exercised an authority he did not possess as a magistrate in granting Frances Dickson's certificate of freedom, John criticised the Executive Council for displaying their ignorance. 'Colonial Law,' he pompously advised, 'made it *imperative* upon magistrates to grant such certificates.' He appended an extract from the 1825 Act relating to the harbouring of runaway convicts to support his claim.[37] Darling countered that this law authorised a magistrate to provide a certificate for an employer seeking to hire a servant without the risk of incurring a fine. In John's case, Darling observed dryly, the law was clearly inapplicable as any such certificate would have been from John to himself.

To the Secretary of State, Sir George Murray, Darling's cogent argument would have overridden John's claim. On colonial shores, however, magistrates were indeed forced to adapt the law to suit the occasion, to sometimes offer certificates of freedom as passes of protection for those who had not been convicts.

But John had placed a noose around his own neck by attempting to justify his behaviour within the context of the law rather than by expedient colonial practice, and the authorities used it to garrotte him. They threw the law back at him to dispute his justification for preparing Jane New's certificate of freedom. Not only was there no employee wishing to be hired nor employer seeking security from a magistrate, Jane would have had to appear before John in his role as magistrate, which he vehemently denied. And, the authorities pointedly observed, the requisite enquiry into her status would also have brought to mind the public record filed in his office indicating that Jane New was not free, and the Supreme Court's order that John had himself prepared committing her to the Factory. Finally, they reminded him that only the Governor and Colonial Secretary had the right to prepare official certificates of freedom. 'It is easy to prove that Mr Stephen had no need or official right to issue such a document,' concluded Parliamentary Under-Secretary Viscount Howick after the issue eventually landed on his desk.

Nevertheless, John refused to let the matter rest:

> To the charge of signing a certificate of Jane New's freedom knowing it to be false, what, my Lord, is my answer? Why, nothing less than five affidavits all tending to prove that she had a right to that certificate. But my Lord Howick is led to observe that still the law did not authorise me to grant such a certificate. His Lordship must pardon me if I differ from him. The law allows and enjoins a Justice of the Peace to grant a certificate of freedom to enable a farmer to hire a labourer without penalty. But that, observes Lord Howick, was not the case in regard to Jane New. Probably; but, my Lord, I humbly contend that if the law gives this power to a Magistrate in one case it necessarily does in another, and that to certify the freedom of a convict in order that he may be hired, virtually implies the prerogative to certify his freedom in order that he may be legally free?

John crowed at his own cleverness, however he failed to impress the Colonial Office, receiving a testy reply:

> Your attempt to give a new meaning to the law respecting certificates of freedom is unsuccessful. The words of the law do not admit of two constructions. It would be idle to discuss further an incontrovertible fact.

Never one to accept defeat, John attacked from another direction, claiming that the public record listing Jane's transportation details was no document of authority. 'It is a false and mutilated document,' John shrilled, 'and although filed, I am certain that no credit is attached to it.'

Governor Darling dismissed John's denunciation, responding caustically that the 'public record' was an official letter from the Colonial Secretary of Tasmania to the Colonial Secretary of New South Wales.

In John's response to the Executive Council's charges, new issues surfaced and became the subject of vehement declamations on both sides, not so much because of the events they described, but as a reflection of doubts about John's veracity. Had Jane truly received head wounds after the *habeas corpus* hearing as John claimed? Sheriff Macquoid suggested otherwise, a statement tossed back at John who beseeched: 'Why would I volunteer so gratuitous a falsehood? In the absence of material testimony showing otherwise, I humbly conceive that I am entitled to your belief.' John later received confirmation from the constables, but no opportunity arose for him to prove that he had indeed been telling the truth.

And who was the Mr Stephen who ordered 'New, take care of your wife' after Jane escaped from the constable following the *habeas corpus* hearing? John reported that his brother Sidney was responsible. Sidney was aghast at the imputation. 'It was not I, and I know nothing of the transaction,' Sidney swore. 'I do not think it fair that I should have any suspicion excited against me of having assisted in that Woman's escape.' John quickly retracted his claim and Francis Stephen ultimately assumed responsibility, however the incident compounded concerns about John's honesty.

Finally, John offered the Supreme Court justices' certificate of commendation along with a letter from Judge Dowling as evidence that he had not 'improperly interfered' in Jane's case. But the certificate was signed in May 1829 and Dowling's letter in January 1829, well before any news filtered through regarding the certificate of freedom John had prepared for Jane New. Unfortunately for John, the Secretary of State noticed the dates and contents of the two testimonials and Parliamentary Under-Secretary Lord Howick castigated him.

Affronted at Howick's comments, John whined how every trivial expression he used was tortured into claims of attempted deception on his part. His intention had been to show that although the Council considered his interference resulted from improper motives, Judge Dowling held a different opinion. 'Had I desired to make it appear that Mr Dowling's letter alluded to the charge against me of having illegally harboured that woman or respecting the certificate I was accused of having improperly given, I would as a matter of course have omitted the date of the letter. It must be perfectly evident that I could not mean to say that Judge Dowling approved in January of circumstances which transpired in March following,' John sarcastically retorted. The Colonial Office treated John's complaint with the derision it deserved.

John covered all of these issues in his lengthy rebuttal to the Executive Council's charges. Sir George Murray's response arrived two weeks later: 'I do not perceive any circumstances alleged in defence of your conduct, to induce me to relieve you from your present state of suspension to which your refusal to consider yourself amenable to the examination of the Executive Council, and your subsequent abrupt departure from the Colony, have justly subjected you.'

Worse news followed: 'If therefore you have any view to re-employment under the colonial government,' Sir George advised, 'there is no alternative left to you but to return to the colony, and report yourself to the Governor as ready to submit to an examination into the facts of the case.'

The Secretary of State's decision to catapult the problem back to Governor Darling was in many ways understandable. In refusing to answer the Executive Council's questions, John had expressed his contempt for both the Governor of New South Wales and the Council. Sending him back to the same venue would force him to submit to their authority. Yet the decision also reflected a surprising leniency. Upon the available evidence, John's suspension could only roll over into a termination; sending him back to New South Wales offered him the opportunity to prepare an adequate defence. But unbeknown to the Secretary of State, his decision would inflict upon numerous members of the English and New South Wales establishments an interminable, frustrating and expensive exercise in futility.

Naturally, a return to New South Wales was not on John's list of desirable outcomes. He had already made an enemy of Governor Darling and had no hope of charming him into revising his decision. John penned another lengthy missive to the Secretary of State, remarking that Sir George's suggestion that he return to the colony to face examination was a tacit admission that the charges against him had not been proved. And then the bleating began:

> My return to the colony for the purpose of submitting to a re-examination would be inflicting upon me the pain of a dreadful suspense, and subjecting me to a proceeding not likely to result in my justification. From my knowledge of General Darling's character, I could little expect the reversion of his judgement, since such a reversion would be a self conviction of his impetuosity and injustice.

Instead John had conceived another solution. With unmitigated gall, he offered it up for consideration.

> Since the office which I lately held in New South Wales has been discontinued, and conceiving myself justly entitled to expect employment in His Majesty's service in consequence of the sacrifices I made at the suggestion of the late Lord Liverpool with that view, and relinquishing my prospects in the King's Household wherein I held appointments previously to accepting office abroad, I trust I may be allowed to solicit a situation in some other colony. This may be deemed, I should hope, an alternative to which I may look with confidence of success, as I feel that whatever other may be open would be disadvantageous to me to pursue.

As John's letters expanded in length and audacity, the replies from the Colonial Office became curt and concise. Sir George Murray could offer no further expectation of employment within the Department except upon the terms already spelled out. The Secretary of State for the Colonies was losing patience. Responsible for all of England's colonial possessions, the affairs of this one incorrigible man were taking up too much of his time.

Back and forth the letters flowed until, eventually, John realised that he had no hope of changing the Secretary of State's mind. At this point, he pulled out the cannons:

> Driven solely by the cruel necessity of my case it becomes my last duty to that Department, which has denied me justice, to give respectful notice of my intention to bring the subject under the consideration of Parliament. My reputation having been deeply injured, my means of support debarred, and my domestic happiness destroyed by a most unparalleled act of infamous oppression, I trust an ample excuse will be allowed for thus throwing myself on the House of Commons for protection and support.

Four days later he received the Secretary of State's reply: 'Sir George Murray does not conceive any further reply to be necessary.'

John sent a final letter, cocking a snook at the Colonial Office by forwarding a copy of his petition to the House of Commons. Sir George immediately wrote to Governor Darling appending a copy of the relevant correspondence and reporting John's intention. Could Darling inform him with as little delay as possible if any fresh information had surfaced and send copies of relevant material relating to John's case? Under the circumstances, Sir George explained, the government needed to be thoroughly briefed before facing questions in Parliament.

Although Sir George's letter reached Sydney late in 1830, Governor Darling took a further four months to reply, citing pressure of business as his excuse. Frustration and annoyance no doubt contributed to the delay. Darling expressed his disappointment that John's suspension had not been immediately confirmed: 'I had presumed that the Minute of Council afforded ample proof of Mr Stephen's criminality, both as a magistrate and as a servant of the Government, and would serve as a sufficient reply to any appeal he could make either to Parliament or the Public.' He urged that John's dismissal be confirmed to support the local authority in punishing vice and immorality. Nevertheless he prepared a lengthy response to John's rebuttal and attached a number of relevant documents.

Sir George Murray was not the recipient of Governor Darling's reply. He was replaced in November 1830 by Viscount Goderich, and the new Secretary of State had more important matters on his hands — learning to manage His Majesty's colonies abroad. In the big scheme of world affairs, John's problem was but a minor peccadillo. The matter was shelved until Governor Darling's response arrived in England in mid-1831.

Fortunately, John's petition had not been presented to the House of Commons in the intervening period. Unfortunately, John's initial attack had already come from the left flank: unexpected, unpredictable and with unimaginable consequences.

Chapter 36
THE RADICALS INVOLVED

*Mr Hume in his greediness for information rejects
nothing however nauseous or incredible.*
Major-General Henry C. Darling

Having failed to demolish Governor Darling's charges, John reacted characteristically. If he could not tarnish the message, he would crucify the messenger. He accordingly hitched himself to the anti-Darling bandwagon steered by famous British Radical parliamentarian, Joseph Hume.

The British political scene at the end of the Regency period loosely comprised three persuasions: the Tories and the Whigs who were largely drawn from the wealthy landed classes, and the Radicals who represented the 'people'. The Tories (conservative, staunchly Anglican, repressive) and the Whigs (more liberal, more tolerant of other religious persuasions, and more interested in social and political reform) swapped the balance of power between themselves, while the handful of Radicals (espousing representative government, trial by jury, freedom of the press, fiscal reform and a reduction of the landed classes' power) fought for concessions.

The parliamentary Radicals and the liberal press had long opposed the policy of patronage, particularly of bestowing important civil postings on military men who lacked the training and frequently the temperament to succeed in such roles. Governor Darling epitomised to Joseph Hume and his colleagues the failings of this patronage system.

Dogged and indefatigable, Hume began to hound Governor Darling and to rail against his continued tenure. He sought ammunition from Darling's enemies: the *Monitor*'s Edward Smith Hall who forwarded evidence of the Governor's supposed corruption and inhumanity, William Charles Wentworth who accused Darling of Joseph Sudds' murder, dissatisfied officials like Attorney-General Baxter's predecessor, Saxe Bannister, and later Baxter himself, and other disgruntled settlers. And Hume listened to John Stephen Jnr who was on his doorstep hissing in his ear.

Joseph Hume must have offered John a rapturous welcome when he learnt of the offerings he brought from Australia. John had disclosed in his letter from Mauritius that he carried documents proving Darling unworthy of office and had alluded to these in later appeals. But when he recognised that the Secretary of State would not overturn his suspension, John found a better use for his documents. He offered them to Joseph Hume to use in his fight against Governor Darling. It was the ammunition the Radicals desperately needed. Governor Darling's ambush began.

Hume's plans involved a number of parliamentarians including Irish radical Maurice O'Connell, who later championed John's petition to the House of Commons. O'Connell was the son of Daniel 'The Liberator' O'Connell, the first Catholic representative in British Parliament and another fly caught on the edge of John's web. Catholic emancipation had long been supported by the Radicals, and a close alliance developed after a number of Catholics were elected to Parliament. Like Hume, these Irish parliamentarians were troubled by the establishment's patronage system which influenced appointments to official positions in Ireland and contributed to the Irish problem. And in their agitation for political reform, the Irish Radicals were willing to attack the government on any subject and on every occasion. Hume called upon Maurice O'Connell for assistance in advancing John's case and the anti-Darling cause. O'Connell carried the banner for the following few years.

On 7 June 1830, the same day Sir George Murray dismissed John's claim and advised him to return to New South Wales, radical parliamentarian

John Stewart broached the subject of Governor Darling's administration and the impeachment proceedings forwarded by William Charles Wentworth. Sir George Murray expressed his unwillingness to table the charges: 'I have always been of opinion that it is extremely unfair to allow charges of this kind to go forth to the public and to be kept hanging over the head of a public officer, subject to all the comments and statements which might be made on them, perhaps for twelve months before he has the means of knowing what is even alleged against him.'

But Darling's enemies refused to listen. Four days later, Joseph Hume launched into a litany of complaints about Governor Darling and his administration. Evidence of John's vindictiveness can be seen in the charges laid against the Governor: nepotism, extravagance, mistreatment of individuals, financial and administrative mismanagement.

Throughout the summer session of 1830, Darling's enemies used Parliament and the press to claw away at his credibility, reputation and administration. Hidebound by the lack of quantitative data, his supporters were unable to refute the charges, and by the time Darling's brother responded, the ambush had irreparably damaged Governor Darling's reputation. When later refuting most of the charges, Major-General Henry Charles Darling pointed out: 'Those who have attacked him in this respect have defeated their own object by letting the public plainly see that personal malice and not public spirit has dictated their proceedings.' But by this time dispassionate facts had little chance of vanquishing the passionate tirades of Darling's enemies.

The Darling family recognised the poisonous pen behind the character assassination. When Darling's brother alluded to John's collaboration with the Radicals, John defended himself without denying the charge. 'The individual accused of a very heinous offence of imparting to a Member of Parliament complaints against the Governor, without admitting or denying the assumption to be correct, feels himself imperiously called upon in vindicating his character from the aspersions of his calumniator.' As no reference to a 'heinous crime' had actually been included in the charges, John was clearly exulting in his underhanded behaviour.

By November 1830 Sir George recognised that Governor Darling's administration represented an insurmountable problem to the British Government. Darling had proved an able administrator, conscientious, industrious, diligent and concerned about the welfare of the convicts, and Aborigines (according to the standards of the times). Nevertheless, he was abrasive, inflexible and autocratic, and his behaviour had earned numerous rebukes from the Colonial Office. More importantly, he had locked the colony in a dangerously volatile political situation from which no one could escape while he retained the governorship. While Darling's enemies had remained on colonial shores, the ferocity of their anger weakened to little more than a whimper by the time it reached Britain. However, as disgruntled officials and settlers planted themselves on British soil and proclaimed their indignation and accusations to any who would choose to listen, their voices demanded attention. When the liberal press and the parliamentary Radicals lent their ears and broadcast the complaints, the strident accusations against Governor Darling could no longer be brushed aside.

Darling's reign must end, concluded the Colonial Office.

A recent ruling allowing them to limit a Governor's administration to six years served as a useful pretext. Sir George Murray offered the governorship to the liberal, conciliatory and urbane Richard Bourke who had already successfully governed the Cape of Good Hope. But before Sir George's plans could be finalised, the Duke of Wellington's government fell and for the first time in more than two decades the Whigs took over Britain's reins. Darling expressed his pleasure that Viscount Goderich, a liberal Tory, had assumed office as Secretary of State for the Colonies. But Goderich, a man who could readily comprehend the complexities and difficulties of an issue, had no intention of keeping Darling in office. He signed the paperwork authorising Governor Darling's recall.

A wanton woman had lusted after a piece of cloth; a ruler had ultimately been deposed.

Chapter 37
A QUIET INTERLUDE

Where is the statesman, poet, artist, noble, wit, politician
or philosopher who has not paid a visit to the King's Bench's
secluded courts, taken momentary shelter from the storms of life
within its peaceful haven, and gathered there new strength to contend
against a masterful world?

Hepworth Dixon, *The London Prisons*

While the bureaucratic machinery reeled Governor Darling back to England, John Stephen Jnr faced his own crisis. He had been engulfed by the tidal wave of his financial concerns. John later explained his predicament:

On my return to England I found myself liable for a debt and costs of nearly a thousand pounds which had been accorded against me in an appeal to Privy Council after I quitted England. At the same time I discovered that a confidential servant had appropriated a large sum (about £250) to his own use instead of paying some accounts due before I started, for which I now hold his forged receipts. Further I found that I was likely to be called upon to refund £300 advanced to me by Darling as back pay having signed a Bond to return it if disallowed.

Darling evinced surprise and scepticism at John's claim regarding the bond money, as no attempt had been made to recover the bond — further evidence of the iniquities and inequities of the system. But John knew that such a claim sounded more noble than the truth: that through financial excesses, mismanagement and pigheadedness, he owed an enormous amount: six times his yearly wage as Commissioner of Crown Lands.

John had continued to plead with the Colonial Office for financial assistance throughout the months he harangued them to lift his suspension. Having forwarded his rebuttal to the Executive Council's charges, he expressed confidence that his defence would prove satisfactory and requested a 'small' advance, explaining that the distressed state of the colony had forced him to obtain private bills to pay his travelling costs and that these bills amounting to £530 had been dishonoured. John's appeal failed to move Sir George. 'Suspension from office necessarily implies suspension from its emoluments,' he retorted. 'I can hold out no hopes to you of any advance.'

After hearing that his defence against the Executive Council's charges had failed to sway the Colonial Office, John requested reimbursement for his costs in coming to England to clear his character, and for those he would incur if he followed Sir George's directions to return to New South Wales. Sir George declined authorising any such reimbursement.

From Joy's Hotel at Covent Garden where he had settled upon his return to London (one of his debtors proved to be a Robert Joy), John relocated to Dartmouth Street, Westminster, then to Great Russell Street where his mother-in-law was residing, and then to Whitwell, north of London. During these months, he attempted to reach a settlement with his seven creditors, or so he later claimed. If he had hoped to escape the law's clutches by his regular changes of address, he was unfortunate. The tidal wave finally crashed over him on 5 November 1830 when the Sheriff of Middlesex caught up with him. Four days later John was transferred to the King's Bench debtor's prison.

One of the absurdities of Britain's legal system at that time was that those unable to shake off the burden of debt were thrown into prison. In the half-century since his grandfather had proclaimed the illegality of such imprisonment, nothing had changed. Precluded from following their trade or profession debtors found it difficult to meet their financial obligations. And to make matters worse, most were expected to support themselves while in prison. Provided with a small room and safe custody, they had to procure everything else at their own expense: food, clothing, furniture, bedding, coal for heating. Only the absolutely destitute were provided with the necessities, and woe betide any caught rorting the system.

John immediately petitioned for his release and was eventually discharged on 18 May 1831. Some insolvent debtors remained in prison for the rest of their lives, so John was fortunate that his creditors were willing to reach an agreement. Yet the records reveal that John's process from petition to release took considerably longer than most. John had acquired three more creditors by this time, and some had perhaps been more reluctant than others to reach an agreement.

The length of John's imprisonment was avoided when he later described this difficult period:

> I was therefore arrested and obliged to petition for my discharge. My conduct was considered so correct that the Court directed an instant discharge which I immediately received. But I beg to add that my debts amounted to £2020 whilst my assets were valued at no less than £4694 independently of my property abroad, and that settled in the Funds for my family. And I will only add that since my release I have settled the amount of £530 cash, and that every creditor would willingly take my bond for his claim, and release all my property.

John had presumably laid claim to some of his mother-in-law's assets to facilitate his release.

While John suffered the indignities of imprisonment, the *Emma Kemp* sailed back into Sydney Harbour. Having crept out through the Heads on 5 July 1829 with Jane New concealed on board, the cutter had remained offshore throughout the intervening period. News of her arrival in Sydney on 12 November 1830 sparked the authorities' immediate interest and the Harbour Master rushed his report to the Colonial Secretary's Office with a memorandum attached:

> Inform Capt Rossi it was understood that Jane New effected her escape in this vessel, which has just arrived, and request he will examine the crew immediately — the more especially as the ship's master being still out, but about to return shortly, he is now more likely to obtain correct information.

Colonial Secretary McLeay immediately ordered Captain Rossi to investigate the matter. Only one of the eight crew members proved to have been on board when the cutter departed Sydney: seaman Thomas Franklin who reported that Jane New had indeed travelled with the cutter to New Zealand, sleeping in the captain's cabin during the journey. Captain Rossi tried to confirm Franklin's statement by finding another crew member who had served on the vessel in July 1829, but without success.

A month later Captain Rossi received word via a 'Secret' official letter that Captain John Kent, the *Emma Kemp*'s master in July 1829, had returned to Sydney. Rossi was to investigate Kent's breach of the law to determine if charges could be laid. He reported back — secretly — that no other witness could be found to corroborate Franklin's claim and that the *Emma Kemp* had already sailed with Franklin on board. Without witnesses, the Attorney-General advised that they could not proceed against Captain Kent. One of the willing participants in the Jane New scandal had escaped unscathed.

Shortly before the *Emma Kemp* arrived in Sydney, John's brother-in-law, Captain Robert Robison, sailed back to England. Governor Darling had frequently lamented that the colony would never be at peace until the liberals were rooted out, and he was no doubt delighted when this second member of the pesky Stephen family left the country. But Darling would have been wise to remember the maxim 'keep one's friends close and one's enemies closer'. As with John Stephen Jnr, Captain Robison's departure from Sydney did not weaken his anger against the Governor or his resolve.

The friction between Captain Robison and Governor Darling had commenced three years earlier in the aftermath of the Sudds and Thompson tragedy, when Robison claimed that the irons forced upon the two privates weighed thirty to forty pounds and severely restricted their ability to lie down. Yet the Executive Council had reported otherwise. If Robison's claim was correct, a cover-up at the highest level of the establishment had been perpetrated. Darling despatched Robison and his men to perform garrison duty at Newcastle. Robison complained that Darling was trying to bully him into submission and that he would send details to England. Darling requested a copy of his complaint but Robison refused so Darling instituted court-martial proceedings. Found guilty, Robison was sentenced to be cashiered. Naturally, the political overtones led many to conclude that Robison had served as a scapegoat. Robison's anger festered and he too sought vengeance.

When Governor Darling later dreamt of Captain Robert Robison and John Stephen Jnr, he probably saw images of red eyes, horns and a tail. For Darling, one would become the devil incarnate and the other the devil's henchman.

Chapter 38
A GOVERNOR REVILED

The statements against General Darling are either true or false; if
the latter I am willing to submit to every stigma which should attach
to one who dares to calumniate innocent persons, and to meet the
due reward of public scorn and universal contempt.

John Stephen Jnr

In December 1831, John Stephen Jnr and Captain Robison received an
early Christmas present. London's liberal *Morning Chronicle* fired the first
salvo in yet another campaign against Governor Darling:

> For several years past, the conduct of General Darling, the Governor of
> New South Wales, has been a subject of concern and general complaint.
> We are given to understand that his recall from Australia — an act of
> the present Ministry — was in consequence of the very serious nature
> of some of the charges that have been brought against him by gentlemen
> of the first consideration holding Government appointments. A great
> variety of papers have been transmitted to us on the subject. Were we to
> judge from the documents furnished we should say that General Darling's
> notions of justice are of a very peculiar character.

Exhilarated at the prospect of a well-publicised brawl, the angry colonists fired off a supporting round. 'Miles' — a pseudonym used by John Stephen Jnr and Captain Robison[38] — forwarded a letter to the editor attacking not only Darling's character and administration, but dropping nasty insinuations:

> The period of the celebrated Mrs Clarke — notorious for her intrigues, and the sale of patronage procured from the Duke of York — is said to have been a fortunate epoch in the life of General Darling. But here history must at present be silent. If the promotion of General Darling to his high rank be through merit, the more to his credit and honour.

Alarmed at both tone and content, Darling's family fired their own salvo. *John Bull* published a letter from William Lindsay Darling blasting Miles' assertions:

> A most false and calumnious letter has appeared in the *Morning Chronicle* anonymously signed 'Miles' in which the honour and character of my brother, Lieutenant-General Darling, is most foully and slanderously attacked. The editor appeared to rely on the official absence of Lieutenant-General Darling from this country, as securing himself and his dastardly correspondent from the consequences of this literary assassination; and that one or both of them might spit forth their venom, and poison the public ear with impunity, well knowing that the traduced could not, from the distance of half the globe, immediately contradict their base and most wicked slander.

Another brother, Major-General Henry Charles Darling, snarled at the Governor's traducers through the medium of a privately published pamphlet. He concentrated on refuting the charges raised by Joseph Hume in Parliament in 1830, using as his basis the Governor's own rebuttal prepared in New South Wales and forwarded to the Colonial Office. Governor Darling had derided the source of Hume's information, referring to the statements of 'discarded public servants' and adding: 'To serve as a clue to *his friend*'s real character, he was suspended from office after a long and painful investigation before the Council, for scandalous and highly immoral conduct.'

His identity intimated and his credibility challenged, John Stephen Jnr could no longer hide behind the mask of anonymity. He defended himself and his accusations in a malicious pamphlet published two weeks later. Jeering at the Major-General's devotion, John expressed disdain at his 'disingenuous' pamphlet. The allusion to John himself — the public servant dismissed for scandalous conduct — generated the greatest wrath:

> This assertion of the General's is utterly unfounded, a base calumny wholly unsupported by facts. The individual whom he thus dares to traduce has already suffered sufficiently from the oppression of Governor Darling without having insult added by one brother, to the injury he has experienced from the other. But the day of retribution, it is trusted, is not far distant, when the public may know how to judge of the injustice of a tyrant, supported by the acrimony of a slanderer.

Such cries of foul play from one with a forked tongue.

After publicly sniping at each other, members of the pro- and anti-Darling camps retreated to their respective corners for the following few months while General Darling (no longer eligible for the title 'Governor') and his entourage trundled back to Britain.

When Darling eventually arrived in May 1832 he found himself marooned in shark-infested waters, wounded from the constant attacks of his enemies, weakened by the repudiation of both Tories and Whigs, and worried about his future prospects. Rumours whispered that another shark had arrived from the colonies and was circling. 'Supported as Mr Wentworth will be by Messrs Stephen and Robison,' Darling wrote with dismay, 'I may at least expect to be ruined in a pecuniary point of view.' Fortunately for Darling, Wentworth had remained in New South Wales. Self-interest and political expediency drove him, and since no advantage would derive from his continued pursuit, he saw little point in chasing Darling back to Britain.

However, John Stephen Jnr and Captain Robison were eyeing Darling with particular malignancy. Since July 1830 and March 1831 respectively, both had been endeavouring to petition the House of Commons for relief from their difficulties, yet neither had succeeded. For two years Parliament had been preoccupied by the politically divisive Reform Bill which expanded the voting franchise and threatened the landed families' stranglehold on Parliament. Passed shortly after Darling's return to England, it was a triumph for the Whigs and Radicals who looked for other opportunities to quash despised Tory principles and to humble those identified as opposing change. Their eyes locked on General Darling who arrived in London on 7 June.

With the parliamentary stage cleared, and Darling tentatively seating himself, those hovering in the wings had their chance in the limelight. Admittedly, John Stephen Jnr and Captain Robison's first act was staged under the cloak of anonymity. Donning again the pseudonym 'Miles', they published a pamphlet titled *Governor Darling's Refutation of the Charges of Cruelty and Oppression of the Soldiers, Sudds and Thompson.*

'June has arrived and so has General Darling,' they exulted. 'It is therefore essential NOW that the justification of "Miles" should be heard; that the charge of *"scandalous and audacious calumny"* should be repelled by the production of "proof".' Graphically depicting the instruments of torture inflicted upon Privates Sudds and Thompson, the venomous pamphlet reviewed the evidence in a manner designed to make Darling appear culpable in Sudds' death, and the government, in failing to present all of the relevant documents to Parliament, complicit. Indeed, the pamphlet called for Darling's trial on charges of murder:

> General Picton, as Governor of Trinidad, was tried on a charge of cruelty and oppression by ordering the torture to be applied to Louisa Calderon. Governor Wall, Governor of the Island of Goree, tried for the excessive punishment of one Benjamin Armstrong, from which he died a few days after, was convicted of murder, and executed. What was held to be law in these cases, must be law now. General Darling has been publicly and officially accused of accelerating, if not occasioning, the death of

Joseph Sudds. He must therefore undergo the like ordeal of Trial by Jury otherwise General Picton was a persecuted and injured individual, and Governor Wall, a MURDERED MAN.

John shed anonymity for the next act. On 14 June 1832 he sent an imperious letter to Viscount Goderich containing details of criminal and illegal activities purportedly committed by Darling. 'An unmerited degree of support having been extended to the conduct of General Darling to the prejudice of my own accusations,' John announced bombastically, 'I deem it a duty no less to myself than the numerous sufferers from General Darling's oppressive measures at once to come forward as his avowed accuser.'

John's letter failed to elicit the flurry of interest and concern he desired. The Secretary of State responded by simply acknowledging its receipt. John forwarded more letters and more cases and boasted, 'On the general correctness of the statements I defy contradiction.' He demanded details of the Colonial Office's investigation into his charges, and closed: 'I have only to add that the persecution I have experienced at General Darling's hands arises from the fear and dislike engendered in his mind from the consciousness of my being well acquainted with so many acts of misrule and tyranny.'

As it eventuated, most of John's cases proved of dubious merit and General Darling was justified in remarking: 'It is clear that these cases have been brought forward merely with a view to swell the catalogue and in the hope of making up by numbers what is wanting in importance; vague accusations unaccompanied sometimes even by a date.' Yet some were worthy of further investigation.

The Radicals seized the spotlight on 28 June, using a petition presented by the New South Wales settlers as an opportunity to vilify Darling. Lord Howick leapt to Darling's defence, referring to the 'virulence and calumny with which the gallant officer had been assailed'. Maurice O'Connell responded that he thought Howick was pronouncing an opinion prematurely on charges which had not yet been examined. 'If one-tenth of the allegations against Governor Darling can be proved,' he blasted, 'it would be sufficient to expose him to the most severe censure.'

Lord Howick again defended Darling, declaring that the charge of murder had been investigated and that the prosecution had thrown up the case. 'I have a right, therefore, to say that General Darling has been basely calumniated,' he retorted, 'and I repeat the expression.' Another parliamentarian responded caustically that the question of murder still formed one of the charges lying before the Colonial Office, an allusion to John's recently submitted cases.

Under the circumstances, Darling must have considered timely his decision to publish a letter refuting Hume's 'atrocious observations' which had been printed in the *Sydney Monitor*. He was pleased at the *Times'* response:

> If the statement which General Darling puts forward respecting his administration be correct, never was a man more cruelly misinterpreted than he has been in this instance. An enquiry must be instituted and if that officer can prove the plain unvarnished tale which he tells in this publication, no public man will ever have passed so triumphantly as he through the ordeal of a State inquisition.

Incensed, John dashed off a letter to the *Times*:

> As one of those who have officially preferred charges against General Darling, I must be allowed to protest against the mode which has been resorted to in vindication of his conduct. However justified he may be in endeavouring to prepossess the public opinion in his favour through the medium of the press, yet to be denounced as 'calumniators' before that tribunal who may hereafter be called upon to exercise their judgement is an act of injustice towards his accusers which cannot be palliated.

John would have been happier with the *Satirist's* response:

> Is the man — we ask with astonishment — is the man over whose head hang such frightful charges, suffered to remain at liberty in England? Would this be the case with any poor man accused of a millionth part of

these crimes? And what must the people of England think of those who shall suffer this to continue for another week?

On 23 July 1832, three years and one month exactly since the Executive Council hearing that precipitated his suspension, John's moment in the parliamentary spotlight arrived. Maurice O'Connell presented John's petition to the House of Commons for consideration. During his battle with the British authorities, John had prepared two petitions: a brief version in 1830 when he first paraded his intention to appeal to the House of Commons, and a more detailed petition some time later. These contained the usual lies and distortions as well as the indignant claim that he had been declared guilty without a legal trial or even a legal accusation.

The parliamentarians had no way of knowing the truth. They could only trust that petitioners had such a reverential respect for august bodies like the Church or Parliament that they would communicate the truth, particularly in cases like John's where distance prevented claims from being thoroughly examined. In John's case, such hopes were in vain. He willingly and knowingly misled Parliament.

Lord Howick jumped to the government's defence: 'The petitioner was dismissed as unfit to serve the Crown with advantage to the public. Everyone must be aware that it is of the utmost importance that no prisoner should be aided to escape from the punishment adjudged by the law. Any deficiency of zeal in the discharge of an officer's duty amply justifies the Government in calling him to account. There were circumstances of suspicion attached to Mr Stephen regarding a woman in his house who had been previously convicted and sentenced to punishment. Yet when Mr Stephen was called to answer the charge against him he refused to do so. The Governor was therefore obliged to suspend him from office. Instead of protesting against his suspension and bringing the matter to a legal decision at New South Wales in the regular way, Mr Stephen quitted the colony and came to England where Sir George Murray was obliged to tell him that he must go back and have the case investigated by the Council in the regular manner.'

A grumble of dissatisfaction radiated from the Radicals. Like a well-rehearsed ensemble, five parliamentarians slipped onto the stage. Mr Henry Lytton Bulwer, the first to speak, had previously involved himself in John's affairs, acting as a signatory to one of his appeals to the Colonial Office. Bulwer's role required him to dismiss the relevance of John's conduct and to direct the House's attention towards the legality of his interrogation. 'Has he been examined in a legal manner? Further enquiry is absolutely necessary.'

If any parliamentarian remained uncertain about John's conduct, Joseph Hume, the next speaker, could assuage their concerns. 'Mr Stephen had been the Registrar of the Court and a Magistrate of the Colony, and what he did might be shown to have been done in his public capacity and upon full information,' Hume soothed. He added that enquiries about John's character had elicited perfectly satisfactory responses. 'If the Governor was to send police officers to search the house of such a man, was it not an insult of a very unjustifiable kind?'

As each parliamentarian spoke, the Radicals' underlying agenda became clear. They were shunting the House's attention away from John's case and towards Darling's conduct.

Mr Dixon agreed with Hume: 'Even if there were no other charges than having broken open Mr Stephen's house at midnight, that would be good enough ground for investigating General Darling's conduct. Mr Stephen had been told to go back to Sydney, but for what? The office he had held was abolished so that even if he were exonerated from every suspicion, his going back would do him no service. I have no doubt that the office was abolished as a punishment for Mr Stephen for daring to complain.'

The knife thrust was swift and deadly. Not only had Dixon questioned General Darling's conduct as an officer of the Crown, he had raised doubts about Darling's conduct as a gentleman. Mr Hunt thrust the knife further: 'This is a case of great oppression. A most rigid enquiry ought to be made into the conduct of the Governor.'

Sir Charles Forbes, the final speaker, articulated the Radicals' primary agenda: 'I must express my disapprobation of so many military Governors being appointed to the Colonies.'

Orders were given for John's petition to be printed. Maurice O'Connell announced that he would request the King to direct an investigation into John's allegations. Joseph Hume gave notice that on 2 August he would move for an enquiry into General Darling's conduct.

'I am assailed on all points,' Darling wailed after realising upon his arrival in London that he faced assaults on so many fronts. 'I am so much out of order at present,' he complained to Governor Arthur a day after parliament heard John's petition, 'having been in London the last seven weeks teased and worried to death by Messrs John Stephen, Bannister, Baxter, and Co. who have threatened all sorts of things that I am only surprised I am able to write a line.'

But Darling retained friends and ammunition of his own. He decided to launch his own attack, circulating among the parliamentarians a printed memorandum exposing John's behaviour and character. 'I shall confine myself at present to Mr Stephen's own case, presuming that if I can show that Mr Stephen was removed from the situations he held under the Colonial Government in consequence of the most flagrant dereliction of duty, his accusations will be considered undeserving of attention, being influenced alone by malignant and vindictive feelings.'

'Insidious, unjust and scandalous,' John screeched upon reading the memorandum. Demands for support followed, but the Colonial Office failed to oblige. 'This does not require any answer,' declared the minute across the corner of John's plea, 'amongst other reasons because it is impossible to make out what way the intervention of the Secretary of State is expected.'

John also offered his brother's word as evidence that the charges were founded on misrepresentations, reporting that Alfred Stephen was then in London. Predictably, the Colonial Office files include no such letter from Alfred Stephen. Any man with aspirations — and Alfred was to scale the highest heights in colonial affairs — would suffer reservations about lending his name in support of John's veracity. And Alfred, more so than most, would have known how much credence could be placed in his brother's avowals of innocence.

Stewing over the injustice, John considered his options. Governor

Darling would soon learn that threats from a family of lawyers were never empty.

No motion for an enquiry into Governor Darling's administration surfaced in the House of Commons on 2 August 1832. Indeed concerns regarding General Darling's conduct and administration reduced to a simmer and the radical's interest in John's cause fizzled.

Was John suitably chastened? His ensuing silence suggested so. In truth, the quiescent period merely represented the eye of the hurricane, the calm before the final explosion in John's campaign of retribution against General Darling. The memorandum itself detonated this last act of vengeance. John sued Darling for libel.

John lodged his Motion for Criminal Information against General Darling on 30 October. Darling's intention in delivering his memorandum to the parliamentarians was malicious, John claimed. He intended to injure John in the esteem and opinion of the public and most particularly the parliamentarians who were to judge his complaints against General Darling, to prejudice him in his cause and to throw doubts on the other charges he had preferred against Darling, to blacken and ruin his character, to draw upon him the hatred and contempt of his fellow citizens, and to cause others to believe that he had been guilty of wilful falsehood and the corrupt administration of his office.

This, of course, was exactly what Darling intended to do. But John had set the precedent.

To counter Darling's claims that he had signed Jane New's certificate of freedom knowing it to be false, John concocted a new defence based upon the uncertainties arising after Jane's *habeas corpus* hearing. The judges' ruling disallowed the relocation of serving convicts between penal settlements, a subject of particular interest to Australia's legal officers. As John's brother, Tasmanian Solicitor-General Alfred Stephen was in England at this time, his input in crafting the new defence, in providing a legal loophole that could allow John to slither free of the charges, seems a certainty.

John claimed that as Jane had passed two of her seven years' servitude in Sydney and had a further year added to her sentence, she might upon her return to Tasmania be forced to serve an additional three years. So, argued John's new defence, the letter to Dr Officer and accompanying petition were grounded upon the hardship she faced if forced to suffer these additional years' servitude.

It was a clever argument. Of course, it lacked credibility to those in the Colonial Office, having been conjured up three years after the event. But the judges on the King's Bench were not privy to three years of exhaustive correspondence.

On 2 November 1832, John's counsel, Mr J.J. Williams, appeared before the King's Bench to present his motion against General Darling. Were John and General Darling in attendance? If so, the bitterness and acrimony emanating from both sides of the courtroom would have been palpable.

Justice Parke probed: 'Is this paper not an answer to some case published by Mr Stephen which impugned General Darling's conduct?'

'I believe not,' Williams replied innocently. 'I have the affidavit of Mr Stephen denying every sentiment contained in the libel and offering every explanation. The affidavit states that the certificates of freedom referred to had been granted in open court on an application by counsel in the usual manner.'

General Darling could have clarified for Mr Williams and the court how much credence should be allowed John's affidavits.

After listening to the arguments, Justice Parke opined: 'It appears to the Court that this is not an original charge, but merely an allegation made in consequence of your charge against the Governor. Therefore we think that we ought not to interfere in this special way.' John's suit was dismissed.

Immense relief must have swept over Darling. One less source of tension; one less drain on his coffers. Exhilaration would later surface when he realised that this was John's curtain call, that the fangs of this particular viper had ejected their final dose of poison.

But John's henchman was still at large. Captain Robison had walked in John's shadow in the two years they jointly campaigned against Darling, however when John bowed out, Robison stepped into his shoes. Robison and Darling danced their own two-step in the ensuing years as each grappled for control: petitions, pamphlets, accusations, denigrations, charges of libel against Robison and his eventual imprisonment. Yet Robison failed to be subdued, and the demands for Darling's accountability over the Sudds and Thompson affair proved irrepressible. However, at the eventual hearing in 1835 Robison equivocated in answering questions about the irons used to punish the two privates, and lost. Darling was knighted although never again employed in government service.

Robison continued to bitterly rail against the treatment he had received until 1837 when he was appointed paymaster for three Irish counties and his complaints ceased.[39] The decade-long Sudds and Thompson affair and the Stephen family's involvement with General Sir Ralph Darling had at last ended.

Chapter 39
SWAN SONG

With a clear conscience of having fulfilled all my official duties with
integrity and zeal, and in no instance of having departed from a
strict rectitude of conduct in public as well as private life, I once
more venture to appeal to the consideration of Your Lordship.

John Stephen Jnr

Throughout the eighteen months following John's release from prison in May 1831, he had continued to harass the Colonial Office with appeals to have his suspension lifted. With a new government and a new ear in the Colonial Office, John had hoped that party politics could be manipulated in his favour. He would try to convince the liberal Secretary of State to ignore the judgement of his conservative predecessor regarding the actions of the conservative New South Wales Governor and agree to a re-examination of John's situation.

John's first letter contained 'a few desultory remarks with reference to the Colony of New South Wales'. In reality it comprised a twenty-page manifesto outlining John's ideas for the colony's administration. If John had intended to present an image of calm reasonableness, a magnanimous concern for the wellbeing of Britain and her colonial possessions, the portrait shattered a week later. A frantic and furious John demanded support from the Colonial Office when a communication from New South Wales tabled in Parliament exposed his embezzlement of the deceased estates' trust fund. 'I have to request Your Lordship's interference to protect me from the imputations of such calumnious assertions,' John insisted hysterically. 'The charges are of so grave a nature as to call upon Your Lordship for the severest animadversion on the conduct of the Colonial Secretary of New South Wales.' He succeeded in having some information removed, however McLeay's indictment remained on the public record. John would not forget.

By mid-August, John had returned to the subject of his suspension. The Secretary of State had declared that his complaint against Governor Darling should be referred for further enquiry, however the results of that enquiry had not been communicated to him, John advised. Of course, John failed to mention that he was supposed to return to New South Wales to face that particular enquiry. As his letter was directed to the new Secretary of State, John offered an explanation of his case — the 'what did I do wrong?' version. John had so many versions to account for his suspension — his 'casual remark' about the Governor's recall, the Governor's refusal to return him to his previous position after the new Registrar arrived, his own refusal to sign the address to the Governor — it seems surprising that he could recollect which excuse he had presented to whom.

Viscount Goderich's response was ruthless. John's impression that his complaint was being referred for further enquiry was erroneous, he replied. The grounds for his suspension were sufficiently strong, and he saw no reason for taking a different view of the case.

Rather than silencing John, this spurred him to compose another letter. But if the grounds were sufficiently strong, John argued, why was I directed to return to New South Wales so that my case might be re-examined? And if my suspension was justifiable, why did the Secretary of State hold out the prospect of further employment if I returned to the colony?

The Secretary of State realised that subtleties were wasted on John.

> By recommending you to return to the colony to undergo a re-examination, it is not to be inferred that this recommendation proceeded from any doubt in Sir George Murray's mind as to the merits of your suspension

from office. It was the only course open to you to disprove charges which
the Secretary of State could not but consider as well founded, from your
refusal to answer the questions put to you by the Colonial Authority or to
afford them that explanation of the circumstance which they had a right
to demand and which it was your duty as an officer of the Government to
have afforded.

Silence. The Colonial Office probably hoped that their message had
at last penetrated. Instead, on 19 September John began a new strategy,
forwarding a draft affidavit from James New attesting to John's innocence
in helping Jane New escape, and claiming that four other individuals in
London could assist him in refuting Governor Darling's aspersions. When
the Colonial Office evinced no interest and referred him to their previous
decision, John whined that they had misunderstood him. He had not been
intending to refute the charges, having satisfactorily done so a year earlier as
Sir George Murray had clearly admitted. But as he had witnesses available
he considered it his duty to offer the Colonial Office the opportunity
to confirm his statements, and to determine the truth regarding General
Darling's insinuations.

The Colonial Office was probably amused by the illogicality of
John's appeal. If Sir George Murray had indeed admitted that John had
satisfactorily disproved the charges, why would the Colonial Office need
to question witnesses? They did not deign to respond.

Two months later John politely reported that he had received no reply.
The sense of exasperation felt by those in the Colonial Office pervades
Under-Secretary Hay's response: 'I have been directed to repeat to you
what has been so often stated in former communications.'

Early in 1832, John attempted a different approach. He aimed an
appeal at the Secretary of State's heartstrings:

It is a distressing situation for me, my Lord, to be removed from all my
family including three infant children to the distance of 16,000 miles and
unable to procure redress against the oppressive conduct of as reckless a
tyrant as ever disgraced human nature. Two years and a half have elapsed

since I became the victim of General Darling's malignity, and the wrongs of which I complain are still unredressed. Conscious of my own upright conduct I cannot but persist in appealing to Your Lordship's justice, and I implore you to extend your consideration to my very hard fate.

The Secretary of State was not moved.

John drafted a lengthy petition to Viscount Goderich to which eleven parliamentarians added their recommendations: Joseph Hume, the Irish Liberator Daniel O'Connell, two other Irish Radicals and seven English parliamentarians. John's petition received short shrift.

Joseph Hume also approached the Colonial Office on John's behalf and received a lengthy response from Lord Howick, Parliamentary Under-Secretary. 'You seem to have been impressed with an idea that Mr Stephen's statements have been received with negligence or with prejudice. Neither, I can assure you, has existed. Never has a case been more fairly examined, nor, I am sorry to add, did I ever see one in which the result seemed to me more unequivocal.' Howick proceeded to cover the main issues relating to John's case. He mentioned John's involvement with Jane New: that his continued interest in 'that woman' was sufficiently apparent from the papers Hume possessed, that John was said to have been notoriously living with Jane for some time previous to her first escape, and that he was suspected of having harboured her after her second escape. 'It is very unpleasant to be compelled to allude to such subjects at all,' Howick added distastefully, 'but as Mr Stephen is evidently disinclined to spare himself from exposure, the painfulness of the discussion is rendered indispensable.'

Howick revealed his doubts regarding Sir George Murray's wisdom in granting John permission to face a re-examination in New South Wales:

Had Mr Stephen been able to make it appear that his conduct with respect to Jane New had been really unimpeachable, the step which he took in leaving the colony where alone the charges against him could be satisfactorily investigated would still have been most ill-advised and have rendered it difficult for the Secretary of State to have interfered on his behalf. But while the explanation he offered was (I think justly) considered by Sir George Murray to be unsatisfactory, that officer showed him, in my opinion, great indulgence in allowing him the option of returning to the colony for the purpose of submitting his conduct to an investigation upon the spot.

Howick agreed with John's observation regarding the hopelessness of establishing his case after so long an interval. 'But what does this prove?' he continued. 'It may prove that the laxity of giving Mr Stephen a choice was mistaken and useless, but it cannot prove that he ought to have been reinstated without any answer at all to the strong case against him.' A scathing remark about John's recent exploits concluded Howick's letter:

> Since the time when Sir George Murray made him this offer, it seems to me that the conduct of Mr John Stephen has been such as to make him totally unfit to be admitted into the public service, whatever may be the truth as to the original charges against him. The very incorrect representations which he has permitted himself to put forward in his defence, would in themselves prove the impropriety of employing him in a situation requiring the confidence of the Government.

The silence thereafter from the radical parliamentarians reflected their realisation that this cause was perhaps unworthy of their consideration after all.

But John's letters to the Colonial Office continued, particularly after Viscount Goderich reluctantly expressed his willingness to receive another communication from John justifying his actions. Twenty pages here; twenty-four there. Some received replies; some were ignored. Having received no reply to a letter written in November 1832, John wrote again a month later requesting an immediate response. He had been compelled to engage a passage for his family to New South Wales and the vessel was soon to depart.

With an end in sight, the Colonial Office prepared a detailed response, rebutting every claim, statement and denial John had made in his attempts to counter the charges and confuse the issue. Explaining that John's case had been frequently discussed and considered, that a limit had to be set, and that Viscount Goderich declined entering into any further correspondence on the subject, the letter concluded:

> In this present communication, there has been no wish needlessly to hurt your feelings. But you must be aware that if an individual persists in incorrect statements, not merely confined to his own exculpation but also involving serious accusations against deserving public servants, it would be an injustice to withhold, out of tenderness to his feelings, the refutation which such misstatements and aspersions demand.

John must have been affronted at the patronising tone. But recognising, finally, that he had no hope of swaying the Colonial Office, John asked if he could follow Sir George Murray's original suggestion and meet the charges before a tribunal in New South Wales. He entreated an immediate reply as his vessel was due to depart, a request the Colonial Office was undoubtedly happy to provide. Governor Bourke, they responded, would be instructed to provide John with the same opportunity to vindicate himself as was offered before he left the colony.

'I beg to differ that an opportunity to vindicate myself was offered to me whilst in the colony,' John wailed a few days later and added another twenty-two pages of explanation. His tone of calm reasonableness was slashed by the occasional spiteful diatribe against his accusers, which by this time included both the Permanent and Parliamentary Under-Secretaries to the Colonial Office. No reply was forthcoming.

Astonishingly, John had the temerity to try one more appeal:

> I had the honour a short time since to address to Viscount Goderich a request that a small advance might be made to enable me to effect my outfit and passage to NSW, to which I have not been favoured with a reply. I trust that under all the circumstances of my case there will be no objection to my receiving a loan of One Hundred Pounds conditioned that if I do not substantiate my defence before General Bourke I shall be required to refund that amount. I am sorry to be compelled to throw

myself upon the kind consideration of the Colonial Department in this matter, but I am pained to confess that my application is a case of extreme necessity, and if I could enter into particulars I feel convinced that my solicitation would meet a favourable result. As my ship sails positively by day break on Saturday next I hope I shall be excused in requesting an early answer.

Minuted across the corner of John's letter was the remark: 'His Lordship imagines that Mr Stephen would see upon reflection that there is no possible ground upon which the advance he solicits could with propriety be made to him.'

At long last John bailed out. No more attacks against General Darling. No more support for his brother-in-law, Captain Robison. No more assistance towards the colony's petition for political reform. Self-interest, as ever, had prevailed.

Part VII
RETRIBUTION

Though it may cost me a voyage
round the world, yet will I obtain
justice for myself, eventually.

John Stephen Jnr

Chapter 40
DR JEKYLL OR MR HYDE?

If I am the character General Darling represents and his proofs of
my impropriety are as strong as he asserts, surely I must be worse
than a fool to seek that complete exposure which must ensue.

John Stephen Jnr

John's decision to return to New South Wales had reportedly been finalised in August 1832, when he purchased a passage for his family on board the 405-ton *Westmoreland* which was due to sail on 15 September. His agreement with the ship's agent included the provision of a cow for his heavily pregnant wife, and he lodged a £100 downpayment and signed a £150 bill due for payment upon his arrival in Sydney. John acquired apartments for his family at Gravesend, however they were forced to wait for four months and at great expense and inconvenience until the vessel eventually sailed on 8 January 1833. The agent rejected John's offer to sacrifice £50 of his passage money if he could remove his luggage (which served as security against the bill) and obtain a passage in another vessel.

Or so John claimed in a legal suit later brought against the ship's captain. It seems a surprising claim. Why would John purchase a passage to New South Wales in August 1832 when the Secretary of State had just agreed to receive additional information in his defence, when he was awaiting some desperately needed funds from his mother-in-law's estate, and when he was

281

planning the ultimate revenge against his accuser? And could anyone classify a woman four-and-a-half months with child as 'heavily pregnant'?[40]

The delayed departure was a harbinger of the voyage to come. No provision had been made for a cow, the food was scant and of poor quality, the wines, spirits and beer were so deleterious that the surgeon forbade their consumption, the drinking water became putrid from exposure to the tropical sun, the medical supplies were consumed long before the journey's end, and the vessel leaked so badly that the crew — only six in total — had to pump it out every two hours throughout the journey. 'The lives of every person on board were placed in imminent danger and they were kept in a state of anxiety and alarm,' John fumed.

Upon their arrival in Sydney on 19 May 1833, John refused to pay the remaining £150. Court action ensued but, surprisingly, John lost. Although the assessor agreed that Captain Brigstock had failed to meet the contract's obligations, the court ruled that John's luggage served as security against the bill and not against the passage money, the type of legal hair-splitting that frustrates the lay community. John no doubt felt unjustly served. With hindsight, the Sydney community would soon realise that for once justice had indeed been served.

The news of John Stephen Jnr's return was greeted with delight by Edward Smith Hall and the liberals. All hail the conquering hero was the tone of the *Sydney Monitor*'s welcome, as the editor jubilantly embraced the opportunity to obtain inside knowledge about Britain's political situation, General Darling's affairs, and the colonists' drive for reform. He gushed:

> The Colony is indebted to Mr John Stephen Jnr far beyond anything it conceives. His whole time, the last two years, has been devoted to his own claims on the Home Government, and through them to the best interests of the Colony.

The worthies of Sydney showed their appreciation. 'SUBSCRIPTION DINNER,' announced the *Monitor* three days later, explaining that it was to honour John's indefatigable exertions on the colony's behalf. But John declined the invitation:

> My return to this country has been directed by Viscount Goderich in order that I may relieve my character from base and unfounded calumnies which a relentless foe had accumulated upon me; and I am most unwilling to enter into public society until I have exculpated myself from every dishonourable imputation.

While some saw courage and humility, others glimpsed the face of Mr Hyde. Auctioneer Thomas Bodenham was the most unsuspecting of the blameless crowd lashed by John's wrath. When John decided to shrug off the burden of having misappropriated the deceased estate funds, he sued Bodenham.

John's suit masked a strategy of astonishing deviousness. He claimed that in 1827 he had authorised Bodenham to sell some of his own goods and furniture and that the sale must have generated proceeds exceeding £300 although he had only received £62 18s 8d. 'I am unable to set forth an account of the goods, wares and merchandise so placed in Bodenham's hands, nor does he know what articles have been sold by him nor the prices sold. Bodenham refuses to deliver an account,' John complained.

Horrified to find himself attacked in such a way, Bodenham explained that although his wife had displayed John's goods she had not sold them for him nor received any commission, and that the only goods he had sold for John were those from the two deceased estates. His attached accounts revealed the true story, that the sum of £62 18s 8d comprised the net proceeds from one of the sales, and that the proceeds from the remaining sales had been largely swallowed by goods John purchased for his own use.

John's suit against Bodenham was essentially extortion, although extortion was intended only as a lucrative side benefit. If he won, he would destroy Bodenham's credibility enabling him to swathe Bodenham with the shroud of financial mismanagement and embezzlement he had himself been forced to wear. If he lost, he would have raised doubts in the minds of

Sydney's worthies. Surely, they would ask, no one could be so unprincipled as to launch such a suit without some claim to the truth.

John's plans were foiled in an unexpected manner. A day or two before the hearing, Bodenham died. A long lingering illness, claimed the newspapers. It was a tragic end for one who did little more than drift into John's shadow.

While Bodenham's death effectively extinguished John's claim, he benefitted in all ways but the pecuniary as doubts about Bodenham's veracity must inevitably have lingered. Yet John refused to leave the Bodenhams in peace. A year later he attempted to reactivate the suit by suing Bodenham's widow.

⁓⊱⊰⁓

Governor Bourke also glimpsed the face behind the mask. Soon after his return, John reported to the Governor and requested copies of documents relating to his case. He also enclosed in one of his communications a vitriolic letter addressed to the Colonial Secretary. That he should use Governor Bourke as the medium for such a communication earned him a cold rebuke from the Governor's private secretary. John apologised profusely, although it took him days to do so. And the demands continued: for a copy of Viscount Goderich's despatch regarding his hearing, for Colonial Secretary McLeay's withdrawal from the hearing, and for Goderich's instructions regarding his reinstatement to office and the magistracy. Governor Bourke did not feel himself at liberty to exclude any Council members, came the response, nor could he furnish copies of the despatch, and Viscount Goderich had not intimated that John was to be re-employed.

'Would any man court an enquiry into his conduct wherein no benefit could result to himself?' John raged. He then quoted Lord Howick's comment on the hopelessness of establishing his case after so long an interval, argued that the question of Frances Dickson's identity — the subject of the enquiry according to Viscount Goderich's despatch — was not the main charge against him, and appended a copy of his House of Commons petition which claimed that his suspension resulted from his repetition of the information about the Governor's recall. And he again protested at McLeay's involvement.

Governor Bourke responded that his case would be considered when the Executive Council was finished with the Legislative Council's business for the session. The session ended in August, the Executive Council adjourned, but John heard nothing further. By mid-September, he had devised a strategy of unsubtle coercion. He knew that any complaint to the Secretary of State for the Colonies had to pass through Governor Bourke's hands and would indirectly put him under pressure. 'It is with great regret,' he wrote to the new Secretary of State, Edward Stanley, 'that I feel myself compelled to draw your attention from more important affairs to one of a private nature . . . '

John's strategy proved successful. Pressing business and the Executive Council's need to peruse the voluminous mass of papers associated with his case had delayed proceedings, the Governor's secretary explained, and the Governor had intended to schedule a day during the following week to commence the hearing. 'However, if it is your intention that your application to Mr Secretary Stanley shall supersede the Executive Council's enquiry, I request that you will make His Excellency acquainted with your wishes.'

Naturally, that was not John's intention at all and he dashed off a response. Two weeks later he received word that his hearing would commence on 14 October. He would be informed of the course of the investigation at that time and should be prepared with any additional information he wished to submit.

Chapter 41
A TRUSTWORTHY TRIBUNAL

*I implore you to dismiss from your minds any preconceived opinions
on my case. I have been slandered in private, and a portion of the
public press has also been employed to disseminate its influential
poison on my name.*

John Stephen Jnr

Monday, 14 October 1833

The day had arrived. John's moment in the Executive Council spotlight; his
chance to vindicate himself from the charges laid against him. Did he feel
a mixture of excitement and trepidation? Most likely his emotions swung
from swaggering exultation at the strategy he had devised to vengeful wrath
at the injustices heaped upon him.

Ushered into Council chambers, John faced the panel who would decide
his future. The Council was led by His Excellency Governor Richard Bourke,
a liberal Whig and a devoted family man still desperately mourning his
recently deceased wife. Lieutenant-Colonel Kenneth Snodgrass represented
the military. A gallant and decorated military officer, he had been forced to
retire from active duty because of a head wound and had arrived in Sydney
shortly before the Jane New affair began. Had John any knowledge of
Snodgrass' bitterness and increasingly vocal complaints that serving military

officers were forbidden land grants whereas civil officers like John had benefited greatly from such indulgences? Archdeacon William Broughton represented the church. A religious and political conservative, he had fought bitterly and publicly with Governor Bourke. John must have known that Broughton's political views and moral values would not favour him. Colonial Secretary Alexander McLeay was the Governor's right-hand man and the only member who had served at the previous Executive Council hearing into John's activities. McLeay had also been the victim of John's attacks so his presence on the Council caused John great concern. Colonial Treasurer Campbell Riddell represented the civil department and was another conservative hostile to the Governor. It was an Executive Council fraught with political tension and unknown implications for John and his case.

Soon after John had taken his seat, Governor Bourke addressed the Council. 'In reference to the proceedings on 23 June 1829, I am laying before the Executive Council a despatch from the Right Honourable the Secretary of State for the Colonies. Should Mr John Stephen Jnr offer to bring forward evidence in disproof of the alleged identity of Jane New and Frances Dickson, Viscount Goderich directs that I should convene the Council and request them to receive the evidence he shall produce, taking such steps as may seem proper for bringing the matter to a definitive issue before the Council.'

Colonial Secretary McLeay interceded. 'I wish to withdraw during the discussion of Mr Stephen's case,' he requested, 'having assisted at the hearing in June 1829.'

'We will accede to your request,' the Council agreed, 'although it does not appear that you have taken any part in Mr Stephen's case except when called upon in your official capacity and as a member of this Council.'

It seems a surprising statement. Governor Bourke must have known that in John's determination to fight his suspension, he had slandered the Colonial Secretary and that Edward Smith Hall had turned slander into libel. It would take the wisdom of Solomon to provide an objective opinion under such circumstances.

McLeay withdrew and John was introduced. 'We are ready to proceed with your case,' Governor Bourke informed him.

John commenced with some questions about the procedures to be followed. 'Will I be allowed the assistance of counsel?' he appealed to the panel. 'Also, some of the witnesses I wish to call reside in distant parts of the colony as well as in Tasmania and New Zealand. Will Council subpoena them and guarantee their expenses as I have no other means of ensuring their attendance?'

The Council conferred. 'You cannot be allowed counsel as it has not been usual in any case to do so,' Governor Bourke responded. 'The Council also has no legal power to compel the attendance of witnesses and is not authorised to expend public money in the payment of their expenses.'

It was a triple blow. Although John had acquired considerable legal knowledge both by osmosis and in pursuing his own claims, he had neither the experience nor quickwittedness of a Wentworth. He would have to proceed alone, without expertise and without a full complement of witnesses.

'Might I be allowed to vindicate myself from the other charges made against me,' John continued, 'or do I have to confine myself to disproving the identity of Frances Dickson and Jane New?'

John had undoubtedly found the Secretary of State's directions startling. Most of the claims and counterclaims, responses and rebuttals, had centred around John's breach of regulations in preparing the two certificates. Indeed, John's actions upon first returning to the colony had focused around refuting these charges, and verifying his claims regarding the wounds Jane received from the constables after her *habeas corpus* hearing and the other peripheral incidents.

'You will first proceed with the latter as instructed by the Secretary of State, however opportunities will be afforded you of vindicating yourself from any other charges connected with these proceedings which you might suppose affect your character.'

It offered a glimpse of sunlight, however, John had to make his dissatisfaction known. 'I wish time to consult with my legal advisers as to whether it is advisable to proceed with the case before the Council,' he demanded.

'In compliance with your request, we will be ready to receive your response at two o'clock tomorrow.' The Council allowed him his moment of control.

John was not ready to communicate his intentions when the Council met again on 15 October. Instead, he had further demands. 'Can I be furnished with a copy of the Minute of Council relating to yesterday's proceeding and a copy of Viscount Goderich's letter of instructions?' The Council explained that they were not accustomed to furnishing copies of despatches or Minutes, however they would provide details of the Secretary of State's instructions, the material points from the previous day's Minutes, and information about the procedure they would follow. Clearly the Council members were willing to assist John within the limits of their own regulations. Already aware of his strategy of harassing those in authority by a barrage of letters, they were no doubt determined to resolve the issue by acceding to any reasonable request.

Although John prepared a statement, he failed to forward it for another three days. His explanation proved surprising. 'In consequence of a domestic calamity in my brother's family I have accidentally neglected to forward it before this day.' Was this a genuine drama or the first flutter in a new game of manipulation?

Expressing his deep regret that the Executive Council would not grant the concessions he desired, John continued: 'Under such discouraging circumstances, if the case were not of such great importance to myself, not only involving matters reflecting on my credibility and character, but seriously affecting the happiness and future prospects of a large family, I should not hesitate to decline the disingenuous proposition of the Secretary of State.'

John complained that Viscount Goderich had admitted the hopelessness after so long a time of being able to prove that Frances Dickson and Jane New were not the same person, yet this was the only charge mentioned in Viscount Goderich's despatch. 'Thus,' John protested, 'after undertaking a voyage of 18 000 miles, I must direct my defence to that which His Lordship considers almost an impossibility.' Nevertheless, he expressed confidence in the Council's impartiality and justice, and trusted that the Council members would not allow previous impressions to sway their judgement.

John laid out his strategy for the Council's edification. He would prove that Mrs Dickson resided at the Crisps' prior to Jane New's escape from the Female Factory and was the only female who occupied his apartments in Crisp's house. He would show that Jane New resided in Sydney after her escape from the Female Factory and left the colony with her husband on 10 May 1829. Therefore he could not have been harbouring Jane New on 18 June 1829. 'If your Honours are satisfied on these points, I shall be entitled to your acquittal,' he urged.

However, John's case would not rest there. He also intended to refute the charges resulting from the original Executive Council hearing, the only legitimate grounds, he claimed, upon which the Council justified his suspension: that he had defeated the ends of justice by exercising an authority he did not possess as a magistrate, and that he had abused the authority vested in him as Registrar of the Supreme Court by furnishing a certificate of freedom to Jane New when he had documents in his office proving the contrary.

'In establishing my defence, I shall be compelled to bring before your Honours upwards of 70 witnesses to speak solely to points of fact, and afterwards by permission of the Council, I should be desirous of producing evidence as to character, not only as regards my conduct as Registrar and as a magistrate, but also in relation to my integrity as a private individual, as a husband, parent and citizen.' No doubt, each Member of the Council stifled a groan at the import of John's communication, mentally shuffling through their calendars to reschedule their commitments. It would not be a speedy process.

A date was set — 29 October 1833 — and the Council notified John that it would continue to sit with as little interruption as possible until his case was closed. In the meantime, the Council called upon Attorney-General John Kinchela for advice on a matter of concern. 'Can we ask your opinion as to the propriety of taking evidence upon oath and the best mode of administering an oath as the Council does not have the legal authority to enforce it?'

Kinchela responded: 'Although the Executive Council have not the power to administer an oath or to compel witnesses to swear to the truth of the evidence they provide, yet they may if they think necessary and if the witness is willing to be sworn, have the witness swear before a magistrate of the colony. But in the event that the witness should swear falsely, he could not be indicted for perjury as the oath is a voluntary oath.'

John listened closely to the Attorney-General's opinion. It was the advice he wished to hear.

Chapter 42
A PLEA FOR EXONERATION

Would that I could convert the identity of Mrs Dickson
into that of Mrs New. I might have merited censure for an excess
of folly and palpable insanity, I might have been proclaimed
an idiot (and most justly, for incurring a risk that no one in their
senses would have dared to run), but my honour would have
been without reproach.

John Stephen Jnr

Tuesday, 29 October 1833

'May it please Your Excellency and Gentlemen of the Council, I hold in my hand a few remarks which I have deemed it necessary to make in opening my case, and which by your Honours' permission I will read,' John began, as he clutched 24 pages of notes.

True to form, John continued by castigating the judges rather than ingratiating himself. Repeating his complaints about the Council's refusal to allow him professional advice and his other requested indulgences, John remarked sarcastically: 'The case which under the *generous* consent of the Secretary of State I am permitted to elucidate breaches the first principles of evidence.' He exclaimed at the injustice and utter hopelessness of being forced to disprove the charges against himself, particularly when the rules

292

of evidence placed the onus on the accuser to prove guilt. Nonetheless, forced to prove his innocence, he would present his case.

'Gentlemen, the point which I am required to "disprove" is the identity of Frances Dickson with Jane New. Had the opportunity been allowed me when such a presumption was created, circumstance would then have permitted the most satisfactory contradiction to such a false imputation. But the Council did not intimate to me either directly or remotely that they entertained that idea.'

John explained that he first heard of the rumour from the Superintendent of Police and had immediately volunteered to produce Mrs Dickson. 'But I never could have supposed that such an Assembly as the Executive Council were anxious to have ocular demonstration of the falsity of such an insinuation,' he smirked. 'The appearance of the woman at the Council without their command would have been deemed an impertinent intrusion, and would have received the deserved reprobation of every man of common feeling and the slightest sense of decorum, and the merited censure of the Members of Council themselves.'

It was an astonishing claim and a recent one, briefly thrust at the Colonial Office in John's departing epistle, deemed a clever addition to his catalogue of justificatory stories in the intervening period, and elaborated upon at this time. And then John intimated that the charge regarding Frances Dickson and Jane New was merely an excuse. 'If the proof of my having harboured a female convict were so clear to the Executive Council as they pretended was the case, why should they have adopted any concealment? Why deny me the right of being informed the nature of my offence? Did this show a firm conviction in their minds of the breach of my duties? Gentlemen, I sought my impeachment in every quarter, but no man dared openly to become my accuser. Yet this is a "proof" of guilt which I am called upon to "disprove",' he sneered.

John admitted that to prove his claim conclusively he would need to exhibit both women before the Council. This was, of course, impossible, he hastily added. The alternative was to bring Frances Dickson before the Council and to confront her with one who knew her. 'It rests with the authorities of this Government whether such a measure shall be adopted,' he demurred.

Yet John ignored the most obvious strategy: to bring Frances Dickson before the Council and have her face a man of probity who had known Jane New — her trial judge, Justice Dowling, for example. This would bypass the need for dozens of witnesses and would prove John's case in an instant. That he chose not to offer this alternative must have been immediately apparent to the Executive Council.

John continued by elaborating upon his defence: 'In the absence of such positive evidence, my line of defence will rest upon a chain of trivial facts, the absence of one link being sufficient to destroy the whole. It is a line of defence never resorted to without a clear and incontrovertible statement of facts, dangerous therefore to approach without the consciousness of justice, and the most secure when based in truth.' John probably glanced around the Council chambers at this point to see if he had captured their attention. 'I will provide proof that Mrs Dickson could not be Mrs New. I will prove an alibi!' he announced triumphantly.

After providing a time-line for the two women's activities from March to June 1829, John continued: 'Independently of the facts relating to Frances Dickson and Jane New, some consideration will be allowed for the total improbability of any improper connection existing between myself and Mrs New. I deem it expedient to show that a very strong and mutual affection existed between that woman and her husband, that his kindness and attention towards her was unceasing, and that during their short abode in this colony they were too strongly attached to seek or consent to any separation, much less that either would have quitted the colony leaving the other behind.'

And it was preposterous, that a successful publican like James New would sacrifice everything in order to clandestinely leave the country unless it were for an important reason such as the removal of his wife from persecution. 'Caution and mystery marked his conduct,' John exclaimed. 'Although his acquaintances were aware of his intention to carry Mrs New out of the colony, yet he engaged her passage in a vessel under an assumed name, he hired private lodgings in a different part of town, he made her disguise her person in male attire, he placed her on board at daybreak of the day the ship left the port, and finally, so anxious was he to rejoin her on board that he actually forfeited a quantity of her property.

'On the other hand,' John contended, 'how far different was my conduct regarding Mrs Dickson. She was placed in a settler's house surrounded by a large family and many servants. She was taken there in broad daylight by Thomas Henry Hart, an individual between whom and myself there could have been no collusion in any breach of the law. She was sent into a neighbourhood abounding with police, and my visits to Crisp's house were as notorious as a gossiping community could make them.'

John protested that the harbouring charge was founded on a piece of paper showing Jane's name which an illiterate constable had concluded was evidence that she had occupied his apartments. They had ignored the other obvious conclusion, that the piece of paper containing Frances Dickson's name testified that she was the tenant. 'I would ask the most obtuse reasoner,' he added derisively, 'to explain a possible or even probable inducement for giving the same party two different appellations in similar documents.'

John continued beguilingly: 'I wish it were possible to offer proof that would convert the identity of Mrs Dickson into that of Mrs New, for the difficulty now imposed upon me of proving a negative would have merged into a comparatively trifling defence. It was perhaps unfortunate for me that even a distant resemblance existed between the two females. But even this similarity of person makes a very strong argument in my favour, for had I desired any concealment, I should assuredly have taken a contrary step to that of placing upon record the fact of that resemblance, and thereby tendering something like confirmation to the suspicion entertained of harbouring Mrs New.'

John stressed that he had only ever sought an open and fair enquiry and had not used private influence to achieve this end. He had not requested assistance from the Members of Parliament who signed his petition. He had abstained from communicating with his cousin, James Stephen, in case it generated a perception that he required such an intercession. He had not attempted to bias Governor Bourke, with whom he claimed a slight acquaintance. 'Having deemed it my duty to make these remarks in acquittal of any dishonest and dishonourable manoeuvre to procure a favourable consideration, I can only hope that the opposite parties have been equally upright and just, as honest and as honourable.'

The Council members had already perused the documents relating to John's case. He later intimated that at least one Council member made little effort to stifle sniggers of scorn.

'Your verdict in my favour will restore me to society and my family to happiness,' John beseeched, 'whilst it can only convict my opponent of a trivial error. On the other hand, your condemnation can neither afford gratification nor advantage to him, whilst it must consign me to degradation and misery, and my family to eternal, irretrievable ruin.'

John's appeal to their heartstrings probably met granite-like countenances. The Council members had realised that it would indeed be an exceedingly long hearing.

Chapter 43
AN IMPRESSIVE INTRODUCTION

I trust that my witnesses' characters will be found as irreproachable
as their testimonies will be unimpeachable. Having no favour to
expect at my hands nor any benefit to receive, they will come before
your Council with no other object than to speak the truth.

John Stephen Jnr

Prior to calling his witnesses, John explained how he had acquired their details: 'James New casually heard that my case was coming before Parliament, and finding out my residence in London, he transmitted me a letter offering testimony in refutation of the charges against me. I immediately addressed a letter to the Colonial Office offering James New's oral testimony, but his Lordship declined acceding to my reasonable request. I called upon James New to furnish me with details of the circumstances and to give me the names of persons who could corroborate them. From his information I acquired the testimony I shall produce.'

Yet rather than proceed by constructing a solid foundation of evidence, John called Solicitor David Poole whose only significance to the case was that he had witnessed a declaration being signed. Admittedly, the signatory was Notary Public John Raine who had attached his signature to Frances Dickson's declaration. However, Poole neither saw Frances Dickson then nor later and was unaware of the declaration's contents.

Poole did serve another useful purpose. He recognised the signatures appended to the affidavits of Amos Crisp, Thomas Henry Hart and John Raine which John intended to submit to the Council. He also attested to the signatures of Captain Rossi and John Stephen Jnr which were attached to John's contentious affidavit offering to produce Frances Dickson. And he served as a character witness, reporting that John had honourably discharged the duties of his office and had a favourable private character untouched by the breath of scandal. Nevertheless, his testimony proved a surprisingly insipid commencement to a proceeding of such magnitude in determining John's future.

John immediately faced problems, with the Council expressing concern at the nature of his evidence. He was allowed to submit affidavits and declarations, they explained, however the signatories had to appear personally or John must show satisfactory cause as to why such documents should be received in lieu of a personal appearance.

While John's first witness was forgettable, his second witness ultimately proved a liability. Thomas Caines attested to knowing the News in 1829, having bought a horse and accoutrements from James two days before he left the colony, and he offered his recollections regarding James' intended departure and the theft of his trunk. However Caines then pursued an unexpected path. He reacted angrily when his testimony appeared to contradict the statement he had signed three months previously. 'I never made a declaration of the particular time I was acquainted with Mr New. I told Mr Stephen that I did not know the year or the month that New left the colony. I never stated that the robbery of his clothes took place before the sale. I know Martin the Governor's coachman but I never made a declaration which he attested as a witness.'

John tried to recover from such revealing admissions. 'Should you have thought it very extraordinary or improper in the lad who drew up the statement for your signature inserting the actual date and year when the purchase took place, more especially if he held a certificate from the Supreme Court that the robbery took place on 8 May 1829?'

'I never saw such a thing or heard it read,' Caines retorted.

Manipulating a witness' statement? The Council could not have been impressed. It was neither a good start nor a good ending for the first day of testimony.

The hearing continued the following day. John began by submitting an extract from the *Sydney Gazette* reporting the brig *Mary's* departure for Batavia on 10 May 1829. He called four Sydney residents to supply details about the News' activities in the preceding few weeks. Chief Clerk Gurner of the Supreme Court provided a certificate documenting James Dooley's conviction on charges of receiving James New's stolen property on 8 May 1829. Maria Bruce attested to the affection between James and Jane, and James' intention around the time of the robbery to sneak her out of the colony. James Middleton, a resident in the News' household when Jane escaped from the Factory, described her return home, his knowledge of James' preparations to flee the colony on the *Mary*, his belief that Jane did indeed leave the colony with her husband on 10 May, and his later discovery that his name had been added to the *Mary's* passenger list. Eliza James Jones covered the News' tenancy in her lodging house, James' purchase of a passage on the *Mary*, his departure on the morning of the 10th, and his return to collect his own forgotten linen. None of these witnesses reported seeing the News embark on the *Mary*, merely attesting to the relationship between the couple, James' departure plans, and the couple's disappearance thereafter. Nonetheless, they were strong witnesses, their stories both credible and consistent.

With his next witness, John struck a slightly discordant note. He called Amos Crisp's friend, John Lake, who knew Frances Dickson when she was residing at the Crisps'. Lake's testimony was a vital component in John's defence. Perhaps before the hearing adjourned for the evening, John wished to juxtapose information about Frances Dickson's country sojourn against testimonies reporting the News' departure from the colony, to introduce the all-important alibi.

Lake reported that Frances arrived at the Crisps' in the summer season, visited his property two or three times a week for a period of three or four months, and read the newspapers to him during her visits. Frances' literacy was critical to the alibi John was offering, as Jane New was illiterate. 'Do you speak confidently of that fact?' John asked Lake.

'Yes. She used to read the newspapers every time she was over. I used to get her to read them to me, being no scholar myself.'

'Is it at all probable that a prisoner of the Crown could have been harboured at Crisp's house for one week without being apprehended?' John asked.

'I should think not.' Lake was adamant. 'Crisp was in the habit of breaking horses, and there was not a week passed without some of the gentlemen of the neighbourhood being there.'

'Is Crisp's house surrounded by the dwellings and farms of magistrates and constables?'

'Yes,' Lake said. 'Captain Brooks' is about a mile from it, Mr Cordeaux's nearly two miles, Captain Coghill's about five miles, and there are farms close by. There is a constable stationed within about a mile, and another at Mr Brooks', besides all the Liverpool constables and the mounted police that come round the neighbourhood once or twice a week.'

The Council followed, asking questions about the Crisp property. 'Are you well acquainted with Crisp's house?'

'I have been there some scores of times,' Lake said.

'Are you aware that there is a separate entrance to one of the apartments?'

'There is one room that you have to go totally out of the house in order to get into it. It is like a separate cottage. You enter it from the garden,' he said.

'Does it come within your knowledge that this apartment was occupied by Mrs Dickson?'

'Crisp told me that Mr John Stephen rented this room, and that the woman was there to keep the place to rights — his housekeeper, I understood.'

'How often have you been in this room?'

'I don't know that I was ever in it,' Lake confessed.

The Council jumped on his answer. 'Then a person might have been harboured there without your knowing?'

'Yes, they might have been,' Lake allowed.

Alarmed, John attempted to recover his witness' testimony. 'Had that room a glass-door coming down to the ground?' he demanded.

'Yes, both the doors that came into the garden were glass doors.'

'Did Mrs Dickson ever seem afraid or ashamed to meet the constables or others that came to Crisp's house?'

'I never saw that she did,' he said. 'I have seen her walking about in the yard, when many persons were there.'

'Do you know what is become of Mrs Dickson?'

'I do not,' John Lake admitted as his examination ended.

Lake's wife Frances later provided her own testimony. 'Do you recollect a woman named Frances Dickson who resided at Crisp's house in the year 1829?' John asked her.

'Yes.'

'Was she in the habit of constantly visiting in company with Crisp's daughter at your house?'

'Yes.'

'Was Mrs Dickson on her visits at your house in the habit of reading the newspapers to your husband?'

'Yes.'

The abruptness of Mrs Lake's responses to John's questions contrasted sharply with her replies to the Council's questions. 'How did you first make Mrs Dickson's acquaintance?' the Council asked.

'By visiting the Crisp family,' Mrs Lake explained. 'I had a little girl of Crisp's in keeping from the time the mother died.'

'At what time did you first see her at Crisp's?'

'Early in March. I could not exactly say the day,' she hesitated.

'What makes you recollect the time of her coming to Crisp's?'

'On account of going on some business to Crisp's family, on the death of his wife,' she said.

'When did his wife die?'

'She died in October 1828, and this was in March 1829,' Mrs Lake claimed. The Council Members were not to know that Elizabeth Crisp had died in October 1827, not 1828.

'Are you positive that you saw Mrs Dickson at Crisp's at that time?'

'Yes,' she said.

'Had Mrs Dickson been very intimate with you?'

'She was in the habit of coming over with the family,' Mrs Lake acknowledged. 'She used to come over two or three times a week.'

'Had Mrs Dickson upon any part of her neck a large scar like the mark of the King's Evil?'

'No, I never saw that.' Frances Lake had just denied that Mrs Dickson bore the distinctive scar emblazoning Jane's neck. The touch of the King was renowned for curing the glandular tumours known as the King's Evil, representative of a condition medically known as scrofula.

'Can you read?' the Council continued.

'Yes.'

'Does your husband read?'

'No,' she said.

'Did you ever read the newspaper to your husband?'

'Yes, I have sometimes.'

'How often have you heard Mrs Dickson read it to him?'

'Several different times,' she said.

'Did she read well?'

'Pretty well.'

'Was anyone else ever present when she was reading the newspaper, except yourself and your husband?'

'No,' Mrs Lake admitted. 'The children would be walking in the garden.'

'Did you ever see Mrs Dickson in company with anybody beside the Crisp family?'

'No.'

'Then have you any means of knowing that her name was Frances Dickson except that she told you so herself?'

'No,' she conceded.

'Did she ever tell you any part of her history?'

'No,' came the surprising response.

'Were you in the habit of seeing Crisp's family after Mrs Dickson was gone as much as before?'

'Yes.'

'Did you ever talk to them about her?'

'Yes,' she said.

'Did you ever say that you wondered what had become of her, or did they say so?'

'We have often said we should like to see her,' she agreed.

'When was the last time you saw her?'

'To the best of my recollection two years ago,' Mrs Lake said.

'Where did you see her?'

'Opposite the market in George Street.'

'Did you speak to her?'

'Yes.'

'Was she alone?'

'Yes.'

'Was there anyone in company with you?'

'No one,' she admitted. 'I was in a cart.'

'Did she tell you where she lived?'

'No; she did not,' she said firmly.

The Council expressed surprise. 'Did you consider it unfriendly that she did not tell you where she lived in Sydney and did not ask you to her house?'

'No, she had no opportunity to tell me.'

'Did you tell your husband that you saw her when you went home?'

'I don't recollect,' Mrs Lake said evasively, no doubt uncertain about the contents of her husband's testimony.

'Did you tell anybody of it?'

'I don't recollect that I did.'

John would have been satisfied with the Lakes' testimonies. They had confirmed Frances Dickson's arrival at Crisp's in March 1829, and revealed that she was literate, that she did not carry Jane's distinctive scar, and that she was still resident in the colony long after Jane New's departure. The Council however noted that no corroborating witnesses had been offered to support any of their claims.

When the hearing reconvened the following day it proved another insipid beginning. John again called the Supreme Court's chief clerk, John Gurner, who produced a certificate detailing the recent conviction of Thomas Henry

Hart, the man who had delivered Frances Dickson to the Crisps' property. Gurner's testimony was intended to justify John's failure to call Hart himself and to allow Hart's affidavit to be admitted. Perhaps John failed to realise that this testimony merely served to undermine his earlier claim that he and Hart could not have colluded in a breach of the law.

Chief Clerk Gurner also attested to having signed Amos Crisp's affidavit, yet the absence of any testimony from Crisp himself was evident. The Council took note.

John then returned to the subject of the News' departure on the *Mary* on 10 May 1829. Landing waiter Frederick Garling recognised the handwriting of tide-surveyor Thomas Oliver in the *Mary*'s list of crew and passengers. The duly submitted list included the names of the three passengers: William Bourke, James New and James Middleton. William Bourke, who had signed a statement two months previously declaring that his name had been used to effect Jane's safe embarkation, was not called before the Council, another surprising and unexplained omission.

The following four witnesses attested to the New's departure on the *Mary* in May 1829. Watermen Thomas John Parkes, James Wood and William Smith provided detailed recollections of their involvement with the News. Parkes testified that he rowed the News to the *Mary* shortly after sunrise, although stating that the vessel sailed on 18 May 1829. He explained that he had initially thought he was carrying two men.

'Had you known James New and his wife before this?' the Council asked under cross-examination.

'I had not,' he declared decisively.

'How do you know that it was Jane New that you took on board?'

'By the mate saying to them when they went on board, "Good morning, Mr New" and "Good morning, Mrs New". I was then satisfied it was a female,' Parkes said helpfully.

'Did the mate say openly, "Good morning, Mrs New"?'

'No, he shook hands with New and went aft to give orders to heave short and loose the fore-topsail.' The Council ignored the discrepancy.

'What was the object of heaving short and loosing the fore-topsail?'

'It is customary as a signal.'

'Was there anything to prevent their going to sea?'

'No,' Parkes admitted.

'Was the pilot on board?'

'Yes.'

'How long did you remain on board?'

'About half an hour or three-quarters of an hour,' he recalled.

'You say that it was ten o'clock when you reached home.'

'Between nine and ten o'clock in the morning,' he acknowledged. 'I had a strong tide to pull against.'

Yet waterman James Wood reported rowing James New alone to the *Mary* and boarding him at eleven o'clock. He also described seeing Mrs New in male disguise, her unsolicited greeting 'Goodbye Jem', and his resulting astonishment and concern. 'I wished to get away from the ship as quick as I could,' he added fervently.

The Council asked, 'Do you recollect when it was?'

'It is four years ago, last April or May.'

'Was there a Custom House officer on board at the time?'

'I cannot swear,' he said with uncertainty, 'but Mr Oliver was, I think.'

'Was the pilot on board?'

'That I cannot swear.' After hesitating, Wood then added triumphantly: 'Of course he was; Mr Watson, I think.'

'Did you know any of the crew of the *Mary*?'

'I did not — only the Captain.'

'What was the Captain's name?'

'I don't know,' Wood said.

'Was James New alone when he came to the Wharf?'

'He was,' he reported firmly.

'How many bundles had he with him?'

'Several — three or four.'

'Did one of them contain money?'

'Yes, about £20 or £30, by what I could guess.'

'Did he carry this money openly through the streets, so that you could see what it was when he came down to the Wharf?' the Council asked with surprise.

'Yes,' Wood said, 'in a silk handkerchief.'

'You say that you believe New was in debt. Did he come down to your boat like a man who was trying to run away from his creditors?'

'It appeared so to me,' Wood declared with conviction. 'I have seen it happen so before.'

'What time of day was it?'

'About ten o'clock when he came here.'

'Did you ever know a man who was running away from his creditors carry a handkerchief in his hand with £30 in it through the streets so that you could see what it was?' the Council asked sceptically.

'Not exactly,' Wood hesitated.

'Did you ever know anything like it?' they persisted.

'I don't know that I ever did,' he glumly acknowledged.

John attempted to retrieve his witnesses' testimony.

'Did you see the contents of any of the other bundles besides the one containing cash?'

'I did.' Wood jumped at his cue. 'They contained female apparel — gowns and petticoats, and such like.'

James Wood was unaware that Eliza James Jones had already identified the items as male undergarments rather than female apparel. John had evidently either forgotten or hoped no one would notice.

'Do you remember when you first mentioned to anyone having seen Jane New on board?' the Council asked.

'I did not say it to anyone until I heard she had gone away.'

'Do you remember when that was?'

'Some weeks after,' he recollected.

Waterman William Smith's testimony followed. 'Do you know James Wood the waterman?' John asked.

'I do,' he acknowledged.

'Do you remember at any time meeting him when he stated to you that he had just put James New on board?'

'Yes,' Smith said. 'I had just come from the ship and met him.'

'Did he tell you that James New's wife was on board?'

'I saw her on board myself,' he reported. 'Wood said that New and his wife were on board and had gone away together. This he told me immediately after he came back from the ship.'

John seemed not to notice the inconsistencies between the two watermen's statements.

Elizabeth Baker served as John's next witness. She had aged considerably in the previous few years and was bearing grey hair, wrinkles, and a hairy mole on her chin in addition to the missing teeth and flattened nose. Elizabeth mentioned the theft of James New's trunk and the couple's departure on board the *Mary* a few days later. And she provided additional support for the alibi.

'Could your daughter either read or write?' John asked her.

'No, she could not.'

'When she wanted to write would she employ a person to write for her?'

'Yes,' Elizabeth declared.

Elizabeth's reference to Jane's illiteracy was later confirmed by Jane's convict records. John had already presented two witnesses attesting to Frances Dickson's literacy. Apart from some minor hiccups, his case was proceeding to plan.

Chapter 44
A PERSUASIVE DEFENCE

*Those who know the nature of evidence in this community, know
the facility with which any fact can be verified, however false.*
John Stephen Jnr

As October slipped into November, John's hearing continued. It was time
to call the witnesses who would introduce the next component of his alibi,
that Jane had left New South Wales and was seen in Tasmania at a time
when Frances Dickson was residing in New South Wales. Butcher George
Glew was John's first witness on the fourth day of the hearing. 'Were you
at Launceston in Tasmania during the latter part of the month of May
1829?' John asked.

'I was,' Glew confirmed.

'Did you see Jane New at the house of a man called John Kettle on that
occasion?'

'I did in the month of May 1829.'

'Did she tell you how she came to Tasmania?'

'She did,' he declared. 'She told me that she and her husband shipped
on board the *Mary*. She was dressed in men's apparel under the name of
James Middleton. As soon as she was outside the Heads, she was put into
another vessel that was bound for Launceston.'

His alibi presented, John handed his witness over to the Council, perhaps with assurance, perhaps with trepidation. The Council asked details about Glew's trip to Launceston, when and where he saw Jane, and when she left for Launceston, before continuing: 'Did you know that Jane New broke out of the Factory?'

'I heard that she had made her escape out of the Factory,' Glew admitted, 'but I do not know how she got out.'

'Did you know she was a convict?'

'No, I did not,' he denied firmly. 'It was generally reported by the inhabitants that she was a free woman on the first of April.'

'Have you ever heard of a free woman breaking out of the Factory?'

'No, although I dare say it might be done at times. Free men break out of the gaol!' Glew retorted.

'How recently had you seen her in Sydney?'

'I think I saw her in Sydney in men's clothes about five or six weeks before I saw her at Launceston. It was on the Rocks in the dusk of the evening.'

'Did she tell you how long she had been in Launceston, or by what ship she came?'

'I did not ask her the question,' he admitted before adding decisively, 'and she did not tell me.'

'Did you enquire how she escaped or any particulars as to her coming away from Sydney?'

'I did not,' he said. 'She only stated how she came herself.'

'Are you quite certain that this was the Jane New you had known in Sydney?'

'I am certain because I knew both her and her husband very well.'

'Did she go openly in Launceston by the name Jane New?'

'I heard Mr Kettle call her by that name several times,' he acknowledged, 'as did several other people who used to go there eating and drinking.'

'Did she act like a person who was a prisoner at large and wishing to conceal themselves?'

'She did not.'

'What did she wear?'

'Female apparel,' Glew disclosed.

Yet Jane had disguised herself in Sydney and had used the same camouflage to slip out of New South Wales. Why would she discard such an effective method of concealment in Tasmania where she was well-known and where Sydney newspapers regularly arrived with lists of absconded prisoners? The Executive Council continued to gnaw at the subject of her lack of concealment. 'Did you know that the police magistrate in Launceston, Mr Mulgrave, was a very strict and vigilant magistrate, particularly with respect to prisoners?'

'He is a very severe man, I believe,' Glew admitted.

'Did it never strike you to be a very dangerous thing for Jane New to be living in Launceston with so strict a man at hand?'

Glew tried to slither away from the question. 'It is a very wilderness place, and people were not so particular at that time.'

'What do you mean by "a wilderness place"?'

'There were no buildings and most of the people were prisoners,' he hedged. 'There were very few inhabitants.'

The Council refused to allow him to escape with such a response, forcing him to agree that Launceston had a civil commandant and soldiers as well as a government house, large church, gaol, court house and regular streets. Attempting to reclaim some credibility, Glew obstinately countered that these might be classified as regular streets but they comprised 'dirt up to your knees'.

Launceston lodging-housekeeper John Kettle confirmed that George Glew visited Launceston during Jane's tenancy in his lodging house. When John Stephen Jnr questioned him about Jane's arrival, he repeated the story of her transfer to the *Mary*, adding that she had shipped in the name of Middleton in men's clothes. The Council asked if he knew any details of Jane's arrival in Launceston. He did not.

'Can you tell from other information which vessel might have carried her?'

'I cannot,' Kettle admitted.

'In what month did she come to your house?'

'In May 1829, the latter end of May.'

'About what day of the month did she come?'

'It was about the 25th or 26th.'

'Was George Glew ever at your house lodging when Jane New was there?'

'He was not lodging,' he explained, 'but he used to call two or three times a day.'

'Do you know what ship he went down to Launceston in?'

'One of the Launceston traders.'

'Can you recollect the name?'

'I rather think he said he came up with Captain Hassall in the *Hetty*,' Kettle recalled, 'but I will not be positive.'

'Did he tell you that?'

'Glew told me. I rather think that was the vessel — but it is so long since,' he added dismissively.

'Though you don't exactly remember, do you think it likely that a person like Glew coming down from Sydney would tell you by what ship he came?'

'Certainly,' Kettle said, 'very few vessels came to Launceston in those days.'

The trap had been set. The Council then suggested that Kettle should have known Jane's ship of arrival.

Kettle equivocated: 'I never asked Mrs New by what vessel she came.'

The Council tried again. 'Was it much more likely, when so few persons came, that you should know what ship she came by?'

Kettle evaded the question by repeating his previous response.

The Council changed direction. 'Did you know Jane New before she left Tasmania?'

'Yes, in Hobart Town. Her husband kept a public house.'

'Then you knew her features very well?'

'Yes,' he said.

'Did you ever observe anything particular about her face or neck?'

'Nothing particular,' he replied warily.

'How did Jane New first come to your lodging house?'

'She came by herself. She knocked at the door and asked for lodgings. I knew her as soon as I saw her, and she knew me,' he added helpfully.

'How was she dressed at that time?'

'In female apparel.'

'Did she always wear female apparel while she remained with you?'

'While she remained at Launceston she did,' he reported.

'Did she wear low gowns, or particularly high in the neck?'

'She wore them as other females do.'

'So you could see her neck?'

Kettle was astute enough to recognise the Council's attempt to trap him again. He responded evasively: 'She generally had a handkerchief or shawl over her shoulders. It was cold weather.'

'Did you know that she was considered a prisoner in Tasmania?'

'Yes, I knew she was a prisoner there,' he admitted cautiously.

'Did you know the laws with respect to harbouring prisoners?'

'Yes.'

'Were you not afraid you might be brought into trouble by keeping her in your house?'

'No. She told me she had become free some months before she left Sydney.'

'Are you sure she said some months?'

'She said a month, or two months, or something in that way,' he replied dismissively.

Hovering in the air between them, unspoken, was the question: 'Did you ask to see her certificate of freedom?' As they all knew, emancipated convicts carried certificates of freedom to protect themselves and anyone lodging or employing them. A simple request to see such a certificate would have exposed Jane's illegal status.

The Council aired their suspicions. 'If she were free, did you not think it strange that she should come away in disguise?'

'Yes. I asked her several times what was the reason of it, but she never told me any particular reason,' he explained ingenuously.

'How long did she remain at your house?'

'I believe she was there four nights.'

'Can you remember the day that she left?'

'No, I cannot.'

'Where did she go when she left your house?'

'She told me she was going to Hobart Town,' he said.

'Did you see her set out?'

'I did not.'

'How did she go?'

'I could not say,' he shrugged. 'There was a caravan running at the time backwards and forwards between Launceston and Hobart Town.'

John's next alibi witness, James Dow, testified to Jane's appearance in Hobart early in June 1829. Dow reported that his friends Mills and Dickson had pointed out Jane as 'the notorious Jane New' and that she had made no attempt at secrecy during her period in Hobart.

'How are you certain that her name was Jane New?' cross-examined the Council.

'I remained in company with her for some hours and heard her addressed by the name of Jane New,' he disclosed.

'Have you any means whatever of knowing that it really was Jane New?'

'Afterwards I mentioned the circumstance to others,' he said, 'and they told me that she was the same individual who had been an assigned servant to Dr Officer of New Norfolk and that she and her husband had kept a public house in Hobart Town.'

'Did she appear to use any secrecy or to keep herself particularly retired and private at the time of your seeing her?'

'No.'

'Can you positively swear that it was in the early part of June 1829 that you saw Jane New in Hobart?'

'From certain private family circumstances, I can fix the date to being previous to the 14th of that month,' he said.

'What are the private circumstances that fixed the date in your mind?'

'I cannot mention them,' he declared firmly. 'They are family circumstances.'

'Did she tell you how she got to Hobart?'

'She told me that she had crossed the country from Launceston in male attire, and showed me a suit of clothes which she said she had worn in coming across,' he added helpfully.

'When did she say that she came across?'

'I cannot charge my memory with her having told me at the time,' he admitted. 'I think she said a few days before.'

'Did she state why she put on male attire to come across the island?'

'No.'

'Had you not the curiosity to ask why she put on men's clothes?' the Council queried.

'No. From the manner in which she spoke, I thought it had been done for her own amusement,' Dow responded artlessly.

'Had she men's clothes on at the time she showed them to you?'

'No,' he said.

'Did she inform you how she came to Launceston?'

'Yes, she said that she came shortly before from Sydney,' he reported.

'Did she give the name of the ship on which she arrived?'

'No. She mentioned the captain's name, but I do not recollect it.'

'Would you know it if you heard it?'

'No. I could not charge my memory with it,' he added resolutely.

John would have been content with his 'Tasmanian' witnesses. Apart from the revelation of Jane's lack of concealment, which the Council could not expect them to explain, their testimonies were sound.

To complete his story of a Tasmanian alibi, John called his brother, Sidney Stephen. 'Do you recollect receiving this letter purporting to be from Jane New and dated Hobart Town, 1st June 1829?' John asked, handing the relevant letter to his witness.

'I recollect receiving a letter to this effect respecting her clothes at the Factory. This letter was found about a month ago amongst the papers in my office relative to Jane's case, and I have every reason to believe it is the same letter I received. I do not believe that I acted upon it, or took any notice of it.'

The Council asked: 'Did you at the time of receiving this letter, entertain the least doubt that it came from Jane New at Hobart Town?'

'I can hardly recollect whether I had or had not,' hedged the barrister. 'I think it possible I had some doubts, without however having any facts to fix them in my memory so as to recollect whether I really had any.'

'Does this explain why this letter, which you would appear to have received within ten days of the search at Crisp's, was not produced at the time in proof of Jane New being in Hobart Town?'

'In the first place I am not aware that I received that letter before the period of the proceedings of the Executive Council,' the barrister cavilled. 'Nor can I state, if I had received it, what may have prevented me from communicating it, whether it was from disregard of the letter, thinking it of no importance.'

'How came the letter to be found after the lapse of four years?'

'Knowing that these proceedings were to take place before the Executive Council, I searched among the papers in my office for all the papers relative to Jane New, and showed them to my brother, Mr John Stephen, who fixed upon that letter as the only one of importance to him.'

'Did he fix upon it as of importance in showing that Jane New could hardly have been at Crisp's at the time of the search?'

'Yes,' he admitted. 'Decidedly he did.'

'Do you think that it would have conveyed the same impression to any other person if shown to them in 1829?'

'To some people it would,' and I can conceive that others would be differently affected,' Sidney replied shrewdly.

Sidney's sardonic response ended John's day on a less than satisfactory note. The Council ordered a three-day break in order to meet their own obligations, commencing again on Monday 5 November.

Matron Ann Gordon of the Female Factory served as John's first witness in the second week of testimony. She confirmed that the clothes described in Jane's letter to Sidney Stephen matched those deposited at the Factory, and reported that details of the inmates' deposited possessions were not readily accessible. Matron Gordon's testimony was an essential component of John's alibi, providing the conclusive evidence that Jane New must have been responsible for the letter sent from Hobart to Sidney Stephen.

And then John called Notary Public John Raine. The atmosphere in the chamber probably intensified. Apart from his brother, Raine was the first gentleman John had called to testify regarding Jane New and Frances Dickson.

'Did you take the declaration of Frances Dickson on 6 July 1829 which I now produce?' John asked.

'I took it from the female who presented herself on the day in accordance with the request of Mr John Stephen,' Raine acknowledged importantly.

'From having seen Jane New frequently you are able positively to swear that Frances Dickson was not Jane New?'

'Certainly,' Raine announced. 'The female who presented herself was a little taller and paler than Jane New, but there was a very strong personal resemblance between them.' (Raine's evasive responses in failing to identify hi visitor as 'Frances Dickson' were undoubtedly apparent to the Executive Council.) 'But I know from another circumstance that this woman could not have been Jane New.'

'Have you any objection to state the circumstances which confirmed you in that knowledge?'

'I have no objection to state the circumstances and facts, but I have an objection to state the names of the parties,' he declared. 'The impression on my mind is that she had left some weeks or months before, around the time that I saw her at the house of a merchant in George Street whose name I do not wish to mention.'

The Council expressed their annoyance at Raine's refusal to name the merchant. As they had no power to compel a witness to answer, they ordered John to discontinue his line of questioning. John tackled it from a different direction.

'Why do you decline to give the name of the merchant at whose house you saw Jane New?'

'At that time Mrs New's case excited great interest and it was generally believed she was a free woman. I know the assistance he rendered her was under the impression that she was free, and not with the intention of infringing the regulations of the port.'

'Then if his name were now given, do you think he would be liable to the consequences of the infringement of the law, which subjects him to two years imprisonment and a fine of £500?'

'It is under that impression that I decline to state his name,' Raine admitted.

The Council cross-examined him. 'Admitting that Crisp's house was searched and that someone ran away from the alarm, may not that individual and the one who appeared before you, very possibly have been different persons?'

'I should think not from the sincere manner in which the woman made the declaration.'

'Is it possible that Jane New may have been at Amos Crisp's on 17 June 1829, but that a different person denominated Frances Dickson appeared before you on 6 July?'

'I should certainly say not,' Raine stated pompously, 'for I feel convinced that it was prior to the woman Frances Dickson calling upon me that I saw Jane New at the house I mentioned. I cannot speak with exact certainty as to the time, it being upwards of four years ago.'

'Do you think that proves that Jane New could not have been at Amos Crisp's on 17 June?'

'I should think it does, unless she returned to this colony.'

'Was anyone else present when Frances Dickson made this declaration?'

'I believe Mr Poole was but I am not certain,' he vacillated, 'or whether he only witnessed my signature.' In fact, David Poole had already testified that he had not seen Frances Dickson when he witnessed Raine's signature.

'Did she subscribe her name to the declaration?' the Council asked curiously.

'It is not usual for them to do so,' he explained. 'She did not. I entered it in my Journal as I am bound to do by my oath as a Notary Public. It was carefully read over to her and assented to.'

John had further questions for his witness. 'Have you ever seen Mrs Dickson since my departure from the colony?'

'I have several times. I think the last time I saw her was about twelve months ago when I met her on Brickfield Hill,' he recollected. 'I told her that Mr Stephen was coming out. I asked her what she was doing. She said she was married, and enquired the time I expected Mr Stephen to arrive.'

'Do you know where Mrs Dickson is at present?' John asked in conclusion.

'I do not.'

John Raine was a member of the Council members' social milieu, a man they would meet again. What must they have been thinking?

Raine's surprising testimony was followed by wardsman Bernard Fitzpatrick's strange testimony regarding the warrant issued for James New's arrest shortly before he left the colony in May 1829. Testifying to having acted both irregularly and irresponsibly, Fitzpatrick achieved little more than to impeach himself and by association, John Stephen Jnr. He was a perplexing choice for one of the final witnesses in defence of John's behaviour and in essence his honour and integrity.

Chapter 45
AN OFFICER AND A GENTLEMAN

*I have made it a rule not to condemn Mr Stephen until I had been
put in possession of the whole circumstances connected with those
reports, believing him to be incapable of conduct that was attributed
to him by those public rumours.*

Edward Smith Hall

Having presented his 'alibi' through the testimonies of a considerable number
of witnesses — although the numbers fell far short of the 70 witnesses he
had proposed to call — John continued his case by flooding the Council
with character testimony. He asked numerous witnesses their opinion of his
official achievements and of his personal qualities. The distinguished Sir John
Jamison was John's first witness. A physician, landowner and constitutional
reformer, Sir John moved in the Stephens' social circle. He remarked: 'When
Mr Stephen was last in the colony, I was rather intimately acquainted with
him. He has occasionally been several days with me at Regentville. I have
been entertained by him frequently in Sydney, and frequently met him in
Society. During that time, I never observed anything in him derogatory to
the character of a gentleman or a man of honour. In fact I considered him
then rather a polished member of our Society.'

'Has anything occurred since to induce you to alter that opinion?' John
enquired.

Sir John Jamison possibly indicated with a frown or a glare that this topic should not be pursued. John quickly withdrew the question.

John called another twenty character witnesses from among the worthies of Sydney. Many were drawn from the legal profession, his family background and position as Registrar leading to a closer involvement with these Sydney residents. Some testified only to his professional character; others only to his private character. Some inadvertently testified to neither. Solicitor James Norton explained that he had been unable to judge John's character as a government officer but considered him a gentleman.

'Do you mean to affirm,' asked the Council, 'that in speaking of Mr Stephen as a private individual you had perfect confidence in him as a man of probity and that you considered him incapable of falsehood or deception?'

Norton quickly backtracked. 'I must in answering that question state that I had not the honour of being personally acquainted with Mr Stephen, but no circumstances have come within my own personal observation to induce me to entertain a contrary opinion.'

Some of the witnesses described John's character as 'perfectly correct' and 'highly respectable'. One was suspected of financially induced bias. Solicitor Edward Keith praised John as efficient in his official roles and as a gentleman in his private life. 'Are you not counsel for Mr Stephen in this matter?' the Council hinted.

'I am not. He has consulted me as a friend and I have provided my opinions gratuitously,' Keith bristled.

Some used weaker expressions of praise such as 'unexceptional' and 'nothing to his discredit'. Some were decidedly unenthusiastic. Solicitor-General John Plunkett admitted to a slight acquaintanceship with John in England. 'Do you think that in the Society in which we met,' John asked, 'I should have been received if my character had not been that of a man of integrity and honour?'

'We never met in Society but once, which was at the breakfast table of Mr O'Connell and if Mr O'Connell thought that Mr Stephen was not a man of character and honour I suppose he would not have been associated with him.'

Some admitted to having seen little of John since his return to the colony. After Deputy Commissary-General James Laidley described John as a gentleman-like man in all their transactions, the Council asked if he had recently seen much of John.

'No, I have not,' admitted Laidley.

'Does your reason arise from reports that have been circulated prejudicial to me, and not from any knowledge on your own part?' John queried.

'Certainly the reports with respect to Mr Stephen's conduct relating to the case of Jane New induced me to abstain from renewing his acquaintance until those reports are done away with,' he responded distantly.

Others refused to judge John's character upon the basis of rumours. Crown Solicitor William Moore announced: 'I have always entertained a very high opinion of Mr John Stephen both as a public officer and as a gentleman.' When asked by the Council if he knew anything to John's disadvantage, he mentioned having heard reports that John had secreted a prisoner named Jane New.

'Did that report change your opinion of him?' asked the Council.

'No, it did not,' Moore professed. 'I knew nothing of the transaction except from report, and I am not able to form any opinion as to the truth of it.'

'Do you think that an unsubstantiated report should operate in any honourable mind to the prejudice of an individual?' asked John.

'I think it should not operate to his prejudice,' agreed Moore.

'Supposing the reports to be confirmed,' asked the Council, 'would that induce you to alter your opinion?'

'I don't recollect at the present time to what extent those reports went, but as far as I do recollect, if I were satisfied as to their truth they would operate in my mind to his prejudice,' he admitted.

And on they rolled: solicitors George Allen, Charles Chambers, and Frederick Unwin, barristers John Mackaness and William Kerr, Assistant Police Magistrate Charles Windeyer, Principal Postmaster James Raymond, Surveyor-General Major Thomas Mitchell, Surgeon William Bland, soapmaker John Mackay and ironmonger Launcelot Iredale. John also called the colonial equivalent of a parliamentarian: conservative

Legislative Council member Alexander Berry, who observed, 'Previous to some occurrences the general impression of Mr Stephen's character was extremely favourable.'

John even summoned members of the judiciary, although he was thwarted in his attempts to have the Chief Justice's testimony introduced as Forbes was unable to attend in person. Justice James Dowling reported that John was always respectful to the judges and had discharged his duties with diligence and ability. Of his personal character, however, Dowling claimed to know 'little'. 'I have met him repeatedly at Government House when I had the honour of being invited on public occasions during the Government of General Darling and he appeared to me in every sense of the word to have the manners of a Gentleman. I have also seen Mr Stephen at the private tables of the officers of the Government, where his carriage was of the like description. I believe I have also partaken of Mr Stephen's hospitality once or twice at his own residence, and felt that I was in the society of a Gentleman.' Considering Dowling's effusive words to John some months prior to the Jane New scandal — 'with unaffected esteem and regard, I am, my dear sir, very faithfully yours' — it is clear that Dowling was also distancing himself.

The media followed. Predictably, Edward Smith Hall offered the most enthusiastic praise, although adding: 'I should beg to explain that Mr Stephen's character has been very seriously impugned the last three or four years by various reports. But owing to the peculiar state of the colony in point of politics, the characters of other gentlemen of equal worth have also been impugned more or less.'

Finally, John asked if the Council would hear the testimony of William Charles Wentworth who had previously protested against the Council's power to hear evidence upon oath and who refused to be sworn. The Council declined.

Having finished parading his character witnesses, John reported that he had further witnesses to examine but they could not be in attendance for some time. The hearing adjourned until 19 November.

Despite John's array of character witnesses, one group proved noteworthy by their omission. John had called no men of the cloth. At a time when church and state were closely intertwined and when an official appeal often required a chaplain's support, such an omission was revelatory. It would have been particularly noted by Council member, Archbishop Broughton.

Chapter 46
DAMNED AND DENIGRATED

*I must claim from Your Excellency as Head of the Council
some protection from the jeers and contemptuous conduct I have
experienced from one of the Members, not only towards my
witnesses, but personally towards myself.*

John Stephen Jnr

What had John been intending to do in the interlude? Procure more witnesses or prepare his summary of the evidence? Instead he discovered that a magistrate was gathering information to discredit his witnesses' evidence.

When the hearing resumed on 19 November, John complained indignantly: 'If my case is to be decided by evidence publicly adduced before Council, I shall be contented with the result; but if on the other hand I am to be subjected to the secret machinations of enemies, justice cannot be satisfied unless those parties receive the reprobation of your Honours for such unfair, ungenerous attempts to prejudice my case.'

Evidence would only be received at the hearing, the Council agreed, and John would be at liberty to cross-examine any witnesses they called. When John indicated that he would rest his case for the time being, the Council adjourned the hearing, explaining that they would keep him abreast of their intentions.

On 20 November, the Council convened without John's presence to discuss his case. As he had provided no grounds for the non-appearance of Amos Crisp and Frances Dickson, they resolved to inform him that Crisp's affidavit and Dickson's declaration would be omitted from his evidence. The Council also discussed the information they would require to substantiate or refute John's claims, and noted the names of witnesses they wished to examine.

Governor Bourke then laid before the Council the affidavit of seaman Thomas Franklin who reported having sailed from Sydney to New Zealand on the *Emma Kemp* on 5 July 1829 with Jane New on board. The Council agreed to forward a copy to John.

John's face was undoubtedly a picture of consternation when he read the enclosure. In itself, Franklin's affidavit did not incriminate him. But it shot a hole in the defence he was assiduously building, that Jane New had departed the colony on 10 May 1829. John's determination to push that particular story had turned a blank into a bullet.

The hearing re-convened on 27 November, when the Council commenced their own case. They called Amos Crisp's neighbour, Mary Seymour, as their first witness. Did John hear the death knell tolling this time?

Mary Seymour provided details about Mrs Dickson's arrival at the Crisps' in the winter sowing season — not the summer season as John's witnesses had claimed — and recounted the story of Frances' revelation that she was Jane New, and of her escape from the constables. It was a damning testimony. John adopted his usual approach for dealing with incontrovertible evidence — sully the messenger and hope to destroy all credibility.

'Where is your husband?' John demanded.

'He is at the Cowpastures now.'

'Then you are not living with him?'

'At present I am not,' she admitted

'Are you living with any other person?' John accused.

The Council interceded, ordering John to desist with this line of questioning. John attacked from a new angle. 'Do you think that a person wishing to conceal themselves would have run the risk of detection by walking publicly about at Crisp's farm and constantly passing the very door of the district constable?' he asked derisively.

'I know that she did pass the door of the constable,' Mary Seymour retorted. 'I heard him say so, but he did not know who she was. He asked me one day who she was.'

John's strategy was to convince the Council that Mrs Seymour's testimony lacked plausibility because a runaway would never take such a risk. Perhaps the Council members considered this a reasonable argument, having little personal knowledge of Jane. Yet they must have conjured up mental portraits of the woman at the centre of the scandal, adding brushstroke after brushstroke as they perused each document and absorbed each testimony. And as the administrators of a penal settlement, they had perhaps unwittingly identified some common characteristics among the criminal populace including the thrill-seeking nature of many shoplifters. The Council members could probably readily picture Jane strutting past and cooing to a constable.

Having attacked the story's credibility, John focused on Mrs Seymour's honesty. He fired question after question about the details of her testimony and her failure to report Jane's presence to the authorities. He asked who had procured her testimony and how she would profit from attending the hearing. He asked if she had confided in a certain William Ryan that she knew nothing about Jane New until long after the constables' search and that she had been told to say Frances Dickson was Jane New. Mrs Seymour indignantly denied the charge. The Council must have considered it significant that John failed to call William Ryan to rebut Mrs Seymour's denial.

The Council returned to the witness, asking Mrs Seymour whether she understood the consequences of taking a false oath.

'Yes, I know the nature of it,' she acknowledged earnestly. 'In the first place I could not expect forgiveness for it, and in the next place I heard my daughter reading in the newspaper of a woman who did take a false oath, and the punishment which she was going to receive. I would be very sorry to come forward to take a false oath to subject myself to the same punishment.'

'From the instruction you have received, should you fear to take a false oath even if there were no punishment in this world?'

'Yes. I should expect I would receive punishment in the next world,' she admitted.

The Council continued by asking if Jane New had revealed any information about her crime, about the silk or satin stolen from the French lady.

'Yes,' Mrs Seymour disclosed. 'She would have told me more, but a son of mine came in at the time.'

'Did you gather from her that she had any concern in it?'

'She was just going to tell me something about a basket when my son came in.'

'Was it your impression that she had been in some way or other concerned in this robbery of silk and satin?' prodded the Council.

'Yes, I used to think so afterwards,' she agreed.

Infuriated by Mrs Seymour's response, John asked witheringly: 'Do you mean the Council to believe that any woman would be so simple as to confess to you, a perfect stranger, not only that she was an escaped convict, but also that she had been guilty of a robbery?'

'What I have stated is the truth!' Mrs Seymour retorted angrily. 'In short, Mr Stephen, you told me that she was and that you would get her out of the way of the constables. You also said you wished you had been there when the constables entered your room.'

'And so I made you my confidante?' he sneered. 'Entrusted you with the secret?'

'You told me that. The next day you told me that you knew her in England before she came to this colony.'

'Was that all I said?' John taunted her.

'I believe it was. I did not take much notice. I did not think that I should have been here upon the subject.'

Bested by an illiterate woman. John's fury must have radiated through the Council chambers.

Constables Frederick Meredith and John Skinner added gloss to the picture painted by Mary Seymour by describing the search at Crisp's, the discovery of the two certificates, and their conclusion that Crisp's female tenant had only just eluded them. Principal Superintendent of Police, Captain Francis Rossi followed.

In John's triumvirate of loathed administrators, Captain Rossi vied with Colonial Secretary McLeay for second place. Rossi had ordered the constables to search John's residence, refused to hand over the certificates of freedom found among John's possessions, transmitted the certificates to the Governor precipitating the Executive Council hearing that led to John's suspension, denied reading John's affidavit offering to produce Frances Dickson, and forwarded information to Mauritius leading to John's inauspicious arrival and unwelcoming reception. Waves of anger and resentment must have emanated from John as Rossi crossed the floor.

The Council's primary interest lay in Rossi's involvement in the *Emma Kemp* investigation and in obtaining Thomas Franklin's affidavit. After covering these topics, they questioned Rossi about the events of 19 June 1829 when John appeared in court, demanded the certificates of freedom, and asked Rossi to sign his affidavit. Their questions answered, the Council members poised themselves in anticipation. Would John call Rossi to task about the affidavit, about his repeated denials that he had read John's offer to produce Frances Dickson and his refusal to forward John's affidavit to the Governor? The perfect moment hovered, and passed, never to return. John completely ignored the subject of his own affidavit.

Instead, John returned to the topic of Thomas Franklin's affidavit, which rebutted his claim that Jane had left Sydney on 10 May. 'Should you believe a statement made by a man who appears by his own affidavit to be both illiterate and a drunkard, if such a statement were not supported by other testimony?' he asked Captain Rossi belligerently.

'The man was perfectly sober when he came before me, and I therefore do not see why I should not believe him,' Rossi responded dismissively.

'Were you aware that this man Franklin had been discharged by his Captain for propagating the report of Jane New having escaped in that vessel with a view to take revenge on the Captain for such a proceeding?' John demanded. It was a curious and almost self-incriminating question, suggesting that Franklin had spread the report to take revenge on the captain for having conspired in her escape. Rossi merely replied that he knew nothing about it and the questions moved on.

'Were any steps taken in consequence of this affidavit?'

'None that I am aware of.'

'Of what use could such an affidavit have been in the absence of the party accused?' John challenged.

'I cannot tell,' Rossi shrugged uncaringly.

'Do you not conscientiously believe that Thomas Franklin's affidavit was taken more with a view to justify the proceedings to which I have been subjected, than to take measures against the captain who was absent from the colony and not likely to return to it?'

Rossi brushed off the question. John, of course, was not privy to Governor Darling's failed attempt to indict Captain Kent for assisting in Jane's escape. Incensed by her escape, Darling would happily have vented some of his anger by convicting any guilty party.

John continued to use Rossi's cross-examination to justify his repeated claims that justice had been swept aside in the authorities' determination to incriminate him. Rossi countered or slipped away from each charge. Against such an important witness, John's examination was surprisingly vapid. John had met his match in Captain Rossi who treated him with unconcealed disdain.

Francis Mitchell, the owner of the *Emma Kemp*, drained the lifeblood from John's defence. Mitchell described hearing from the *Emma Kemp*'s master that he had indeed ferried Jane New to New Zealand in July 1829 after she embarked near the Heads dressed in male clothing. He provided the support for Franklin's affidavit that John did not wish to hear. Naturally, John tried to undermine its value. 'How often since the month of July 1829 has Captain Kent visited Sydney?' he demanded of Mitchell.

'About eight or ten times,' Mitchell disclosed.

'If there had been any accusation against him for assisting a convict to escape were there not plenty of opportunities of bringing him in to answer the charge?'

'Yes,' he admitted.

But the Council knew otherwise.

One after another, the Executive Council's remaining witnesses vaunted their testimonies. Pilot John Gray, who had seen no passengers on the *Mary* or any passenger transhipment, made a few concessions. 'Was it impossible that boats could have passed between the ships outside of the Heads?' asked the Council.

'They could have joined after I left the ship,' Gray admitted.

'After standing on their different courses?'

'If they had a mind to do so.'

In his cross-examination, John queried Gray's assertion that he would have recognised Jane although he contrived to pose the question indirectly. 'Could a person have been on board so disguised that although you had previous knowledge of them they might have passed you without observation?'

'They might — being in disguise,' Gray allowed.

Happy with Gray's answer, John referred to the *Mary*'s passenger list, although again choosing to phrase his question indirectly.

'If the tide-surveyor furnished a list of the crew and passengers which sailed from the harbour, would you place confidence in his certificate?'

'Certainly,' Gray acknowledged. 'The tide-surveyor when he musters the ship's company and passengers generally delivers it up with the clearance to the captain.'

'But if he furnished a document under his own hand and signature as a list of the crew and passengers, would you hesitate to believe that his statement was correct?'

'Certainly not,' vouchsafed the pilot.

The Council quickly undermined the value of Gray's responses to John's hypothetical questions by homing in on the specifics. 'Did you see the tide-surveyor muster the Mary's crew and passengers on the day she sailed?'

'Yes.'

'Were there any passengers present?'

'I don't recollect seeing any,' Gray admitted.

'Did you see the crew?'

'I did,' came the simple response.

Captain Samuel Ashmore, who commanded the *Guide* when it sailed for Torres Strait on 10 May 1829 in convoy with the *Mary*, reported that he neither saw nor heard of any passengers on board the *Mary* or a passenger transhipment. However he also made some concessions when cross-examined by John.

'In speaking of passengers, do you allude to cabin or steerage?' John asked.

'Cabin passengers,' Ashmore said.

'Might there have been steerage passengers without your knowledge?'

'There might certainly,' he admitted.

The Council directed questions to Ashmore about the passenger transhipment. 'Shortly after passing the Heads, did you see any boat leave the *Mary* to put a passenger on board any other vessel?'

'No,' he responded bluntly.

'Do you think such a circumstance could have occurred at any short distance from the Heads without your perceiving it or without your knowledge?'

'I think it might,' he acknowledged.

John's ears pricked up at this admission.

'Was it possible that after the *Mary* left the Heads a passenger should be transhipped from her on to a vessel whose course was to the southward?' the Council continued.

'At the moment I hardly recollect the strength of the wind at the time. If it were a light breeze I think it would be possible for a boat to go from one vessel to the other.'

Aware that a favourable testimony would support his claim that Jane departed on the *Mary*, John questioned Ashmore about the possible passenger transfer. 'You say that the *Mary* followed your ship. Were you so closely occupied in watching her movements as to be able to say positively that no transhipment of a passenger could have been effected?'

'I certainly was not employed watching her constantly,' Ashmore admitted.

'Then such a transhipment might have taken place without your observation?'

'I think it is within the scope of possibility,' he conceded.

Cocky at these admissions, John continued questioning Ashmore rather than leaving well alone. Ashmore had been unable to recollect seeing the Tasmania-bound schooners. John asked: 'If one schooner was half a mile ahead and another schooner astern of the *Mary*, and you say you did not see either, might not so small an object as a boat have passed between the ships without your noticing it?'

John's persistence annoyed Captain Ashmore. 'I say I do not recollect seeing either of them, or any other vessel but the *Cumberland*.'

'Then might not your memory be equally fallacious with regard to a boat?'

Antagonising Captain Ashmore proved a foolish decision. 'I think that if any boat had been passing, the mates or some person would have noticed or mentioned it as a strange thing after leaving here,' he retorted.

The significance of Ashmore's statement was obvious to those in the Council chambers. Even if the *Guide*'s crew had not noticed a passenger transfer, the *Mary*'s crew would undoubtedly have mentioned this strange incident during their port of call at Sir Charles Hardy's Island before they ventured into Torres Strait. Indeed they would have crowed at their cleverness in duping the authorities. And word would have filtered back to Sydney, to join the other gossip upon which such an isolated community thrived.

Perhaps the location of the boats made them invisible to each other, John countered. 'When a vessel has cleared the Heads and is standing upon an East-North-East course, might a vessel tacking under the North shore or lying to be invisible although she might be only a very short distance away?'

'No I should think not, unless she was a considerable way out.'

'What distance?'

'Six or seven miles.'

It was the mortal blow. Two ships undertaking a passenger transfer would not stand six or seven miles apart in the open ocean and force a small boat to row such a long distance.

⚜

John's most compelling evidence documenting the News' embarkation on the *Mary* was the tide-surveyor's list of passengers. It came under scrutiny when the Controller of Customs, Burman Langa, testified. Langa reported having searched for departing passenger lists, however only one such list for 1829 had survived.

'Can you state the probable cause of your not being able to find the lists?' asked the Council.

'The lists of passengers were written on slips of paper, instead of being written on the ship's content, which appears to have been the practice adopted in the Custom House previous to my arrival in the colony. Some of those slips of paper may have been destroyed as waste paper.'

'But in point of fact you cannot furnish an authentic official list of passengers that left the colony in May 1829?' the Council persisted.

'I cannot.'

After examining the list Langa agreed that the handwriting was that of tide-surveyor, Thomas Oliver, however he had doubts about the list's authenticity.

'Is that a paper which should officially be in the tide-surveyor's charge?' the Council asked.

'I never knew the tide-surveyor to have any such list,' Langa admitted.

'Is it part of his duty to keep such lists in his possession?'

'No,' came the bald response.

'At the time he took that list ought he to have delivered it into one of the officers of the Customs?'

'I don't know how he could have come by such a list as this,' Langa reported, 'except if it was to compile it for himself or for some other purpose.'

'Then there are no means of establishing that list which you hold in your hand as a genuine document,' Council probed.

'Only if we were so lucky as to find the list of the *Mary*'s passengers and found that it corresponded with this list.'

Having questioned the validity of the document, the Executive Council directed their attention to the document-maker. 'Do you know Mr Oliver, the tide-surveyor?'

'I do,' Langa acknowledged.

'What has his state of health latterly been?'

'He has been suffering under the effects of delirium tremens.'

'Is he still unwell?'

'He is unwell, but I believe he is better,' he reported.

To undermine the validity of the *Mary*'s passenger list was disastrous. John Stephen Jnr quickly attempted to recover lost ground. 'Do you believe that Mr Oliver could be capable of manufacturing such a document under any circumstances?'

'No,' admitted Langa.

Pleased with the response, John continued, 'Then do you believe it to be a genuine and correct copy from some record which he may have found in the Custom House?'

John had pushed too far. 'I cannot speak of its correctness,' Langa admonished. 'I think he would be very likely to make it incorrect from his mode of life.'

'Was he of sound mind at the time the ship left the colony in May 1829?' John countered.

'Yes, but he was a very hard drinker,' Langa added pointedly.

'Letting aside all extraneous considerations as to the irregularity of preparing such a document, do you believe it to be a bona fide statement?'

'I have no reason to doubt the truth of it, because it is in his handwriting, and I believe him to be incapable of manufacturing the list,' Langa kindly concluded.

Despite Langa's generous conclusion, he had soundly hammered the nails into John's coffin.

John was never to learn that the Council had one more witness willing to testify. Thomas Henry Hart, who was suffering the horrors of servitude in Norfolk Island, had written to Colonial Secretary McLeay on 11 October 1833:

In consequence of a private communication, I have the honour to state that from the period of Jane New's escape from the Factory at the instance of Mr John Stephen, up to her clandestine departure from the colony by the joint assistance of Captain Robison and Mr Stephen, I can and am willing to render every information (save self-crimination) should it be deemed necessary and expedient with the assurance of present secrecy.

The Council decided against Hart's assistance. The testimony of any convict, serving or emancipated, was tainted by their status, all the more so when the convict was under sentence of colonial transportation. The authorities were also aware that Norfolk Island inmates resorted to desperate measures — sometimes murder — to get themselves off the island. What was a little matter of perjury in comparison?

Chapter 47
A RENEWED DEFENCE

Having thus, I dare to say, victoriously once more answered the
charges against me, I rest my case.
John Stephen Jnr

Despite initially rejecting Amos Crisp's affidavit, the Council reconsidered their position a few days into their own case. They 'advised' John that Amos Crisp and his daughter should be requested to personally appear at the hearing. The Council's revised decision followed their receipt of a letter from Executive Council member, Campbell Riddell. Amos Crisp had reportedly talked to a mutual acquaintance about John Stephen Jnr keeping Jane New at his property, and would provide details if brought to Sydney. 'Should not Crisp be had up?' Riddell urged. 'I think we have now the key to Mr Stephen's not calling him.'

John took the Council's advice and brought Amos Crisp to the hearing. Before calling him, however, he introduced Constable John Burrows to rebut the Council's witnesses. Burrows resided only a mile from Crisp. He described Crisp's numerous visitors, including constables who occasionally searched the property, and he mentioned seeing Crisp's female visitor pass his property on a few occasions. John asked if he knew Mrs Seymour and what she had said to him about this visitor.

'After the search at Crisp's property, Mrs Seymour told me she saw a woman there,' Burrows disclosed, 'but they called her Mrs Dickson. When the constables came to search Crisp's house, Mrs Dickson escaped up to her house, and as the constables came to the front door, she told me Mrs Dickson went out at the back, and that she understood that her name was Jane New.'

'When did she tell you that she first suspected Mrs Dickson's name to be Jane New?'

'Not until a few days after the disturbance was over.'

The Council were confused by Burrows' response, uncertain whether he meant that Mrs Seymour first suspected the truth regarding Frances Dickson's identity a few days after her escape or whether she first told Burrows of her suspicions at that time. They asked for clarification. 'It was after the search she told me — that's all,' he initially confirmed, and then after John asked for further clarification: 'She told me she did not suspect her to be Jane New until after the constables made the search.' The Council later reported that in their minds this equivocation undermined his testimony.

'Do you know anything of Mrs Seymour's character?' John enquired.

'Nothing but hearsay,' he conceded before elaborating: 'She bears a very bad character of being a loose woman.'

Unhappy with this slur on their important witness, the Council challenged: 'Do you hear anything of Mrs Seymour much worse than you hear of hundreds of others in the colony?'

'No,' he admitted.

'Have you ever had the slightest reason to believe that she would knowingly make a false oath?'

'I cannot say that she would,' he acknowledged.

Although Burrows was in essence a credible witness, the Council recognised the unlikelihood that Mrs Seymour would reveal to the local constable her long-term knowledge of a runaway convict residing next door.

Amos Crisp's testimony followed. Other than Frances Dickson herself, Crisp and his daughter were the witnesses of particular interest to the Council as they had spent the most time with John's tenant. But on which side of the fence would Amos Crisp's testimony fall?

John began by using Crisp's testimony to discredit the Council's primary witness. 'Did you ever employ Mrs Seymour to wash for your family?' he asked Crisp.

'No, I never did and am certain my daughter never did,' Crisp denied firmly. 'My daughter always washed her own things and everything belonging to the house. She never had occasion to hire anyone.'

'Did she wash at all for Mrs Dickson?'

'Never,' he declared emphatically. 'At the time Mrs Dickson was at my place she used to wash her own clothes and to assist my daughter in washing the children's.'

'Do you think Mrs Seymour was a woman of that character that she would make use of the words "damned fools"?'

'Yes, I have often heard her make use of worse words,' he said.

'Was she or was she not in fact the sort of woman addicted to swearing?'

'I very often heard her make use of ill language to her husband when she had taken a glass.'

Having traduced Mrs Seymour's character by intimating that she was a coarse-tongued tippling liar, John returned to the subject of Crisp's tenant.

'Did Mrs Dickson ever appear fearful of showing herself to strangers?'

'Why it could not appear like it,' Crisp responded with surprise. 'She was always outside of the house. I have known her to sit down to table with four or five people, strangers.'

'Was your house very much frequented?'

'Yes it was,' he affirmed. 'There was scarcely a day that there were not four or five people. I had horses breaking in for different people round about the neighbourhood and more than that I had two entire horses [stallions] at the time in my stable. I had mares running there from different people in Sydney who used to come up to see them. They were sent there for the services of the horse.'

'Was your house so concealed that it could not be seen until you came close to it?'

'Why it could not be seen a great way,' he admitted, 'but it was not so concealed that you might not see it in one or two directions half a mile.'

'Did Mrs Lake ever advise you to send away Mrs Dickson for fear of your getting into trouble?'

'No, she never did,' he objected. 'Mrs Lake was always too partial to Mrs Dickson.'

'Have you had any conversation with any person upon the subject of the woman who lived in your house within the last three or four weeks?'

'I have had no conversation particularly with any person about her, except Mr Macalister who came to my house last Saturday week and took me to the Plains with him on Sunday morning, and wrote out a deposition of what I knew of the case.'

'Who is Mr Macalister?'

'He is a Magistrate there, and likewise Superintendent of the Mounted Police, I believe.'

The Council began their cross-examination. 'Whom do you believe the person you call Mrs Dickson to be?'

'I believe her to be Mrs Dickson,' he acknowledged warily.

'Do you believe that name to have been fictitious and assumed while she lived in your house?'

'I have no reason to believe it.' The caginess of Crisp's responses was immediately apparent.

'Did you swear a deposition before Mr Macalister on 24 November 1833?'

'Yes.'

'Did you state in that deposition that you had every reason to believe that the name of Dickson was fictitious?'

'Since she left my house, from the way people have been talking I considered it to be fictitious, but never while she was living at my house,' Crisp equivocated.

'Have you not just sworn that you still believe that woman to be Mrs Dickson?'

'I have no other reason to believe so, but people talking,' Crisp repeated obstinately.

'But the question is, have you not just now sworn that you still believe that person to be Mrs Dickson?'

'Yes,' he agreed.

'Then is what you swore before Mr Macalister or what you have just now sworn here the truth?'

'What I have now sworn is the truth. I think you will find that I have not sworn that I supposed her to be any person but Mrs Dickson,' he remonstrated.

'Did you ever swear that you believed the real name of the woman was Jane New?'

'No . . .' Crisp hesitated. 'I did not. I said I supposed from what I had heard people say, and the description that had been given of her, that she very much resembled Jane New. The reason that caused me to think so was her eloping from the place.'

'But did you ever swear,' the Council asked exasperatedly, 'that for those reasons or for any other you had every reason to believe that the real name of the woman was Jane New?'

'I never had any reason to believe it except from what people talked of after she was gone,' Crisp stated defiantly.

'But the question is: did you on that account ever swear that you believed the real name of the woman was Jane New?'

'I believe Mr Macalister asked me that question.' Crisp continued to wriggle away from the question.

'Did you swear to that fact?'

'I did not,' he denied forcefully.

Indeed he had, as the Council members well knew, having perused his recent affidavit and his testimony at the previous Executive Council hearing. 'Have you conversed with any person whatever upon this subject since you made the deposition before Mr Macalister?'

'Yes.'

'State with whom.'

'Several people who were talking of it on the road, and Mr Stephen,' he recollected. 'I met him.'

'Where did you meet him?'

'In Liverpool. He told me that I should have to go down to Sydney and that I should have to come before the Council about the woman who lived at my house, Mrs Dickson.'

'Was anyone with Mr Stephen when he met you at Liverpool?'

'Yes, there was a gentleman in the gig with him,' Crisp recalled. 'I think his name was Raine.'

'Did this conversation pass while they continued in the gig?'

'Yes,' he admitted.

'Why, then, did you say that you had no conversation with anyone but Mr Macalister upon this subject?'

'I considered I was being asked whether I had been before anyone about it,' he retorted obstinately.

'Do you understand what "conversing" with any person is?' the Council asked caustically.

'I do, but mistook the word,' he shrugged.

'What did you suppose the word to be?' the sardonic tone seeped through the question.

'I thought I had been asked whether I had been before any other person but Mr Macalister,' he responded defiantly.

'Was not the question read over to you before you answered it?'

'Yes,' Crisp admitted.

'Do you think that to tell one part of the truth and to keep back another part is agreeable to the oath you have taken?'

'I have told the truth as far as lays in my power,' Crisp blustered.

'When you were before the Council formerly, what occasioned you to say that it was five weeks ago to the best of your recollection since Mrs Dickson had come to your house?'

'Why I cannot say, I am sure, what the reason was,' Crisp exclaimed.

'How came you afterwards to swear that she had been there more than three months?'

'Referring to my accounts at home, I found that she had been there a deal longer than I expected,' Crisp explained.

'What circumstance made you find out when she came?'

'I cannot say exactly what it was, I am sure,' he admitted.

John Stephen Jnr returned to his witness, trying to regain some credibility. 'You have stated in your deposition that the woman came to your house under the name of Mrs Dickson which you had every reason to believe was fictitious, and that her real name was Jane New. Did you mean to say that you drew the inference solely from the current rumour or from circumstances within your own knowledge?'

'It was only the talk of other people that caused me to think so since she left. I never had any reason to suspect it was any other person but Mrs Dickson, myself,' he responded earnestly.

'The impression which the report had created in the public mind was that it was Jane New, and you might have had your doubts at the time of making this deposition before Mr Macalister, yet since your return to Sydney have you not met a person who knew both Mrs Dickson and Mrs New and who assured you that Mrs Dickson was not Jane New?'

'Yes, I have,' Amos Crisp said with relief.

'Who is that person?'

'Mr Solomon.'

As John triumphantly readied himself to call this new witness, the Council had one last question for Amos Crisp.

'Do you still hold a ticket-of-leave?' they asked darkly.

'Yes,' came the innocent response.

Lewis Solomon was a last-minute godsend for John Stephen Jnr. Crisp had met Solomon that very morning in George Street. During their conversation, Crisp asked if Solomon had visited his Lower Minto property in 1829 and could recollect seeing a female visitor, and if he had known Jane New and could distinguish between the two women. 'Certainly,' Solomon exclaimed, 'my boy was residing with you at the time, attending school with your children. I dined on several occasions and it was not Jane New that I dined with. I was introduced to her by the name of Dickson. I was there upon one occasion when Mrs Dickson asked me to take charge of a letter for her to Sydney.'

The Council had their doubts about such a propitious witness. 'Is the statement you made to Amos Crisp true?'

'It is,' he announced beguilingly.

John continued to question Solomon. 'Can you fix the time when this occurred by any circumstance?'

And, most conveniently, Solomon could. 'I can fix the time on one occasion that I went to Mr Crisp's and saw Mrs Dickson there. I had gone to fetch my boy home to a little merry making at my house on St Patrick's Day in the month of March 1829. My little boy went to live at Crisp's at the latter end of 1828.'

The Council asked: 'Was Mrs Dickson in appearance very like Jane New?'

'No, she was a much plainer woman. She was more taller than her and had a more ruddy complexion. She was redder in the face, Jane New was pale,' he revealed.

'You say that a letter was given to you. By whom was it given?'

'It was given to me from the hands of the female whom I saw write it — Mrs Dickson,' he reported with a flourish.

Solomon's testimony neatly covered all the issues. John was undoubtedly crowing. Had he noticed Solomon's error? Official records described Jane with a ruddy complexion, while other witnesses indicated that Mrs Dickson had a paler complexion. Lewis Solomon had reversed their descriptions.

After Solomon's testimony, the Council conferred for a moment and reached a decision. 'Unless you wish to produce Crisp's daughter or any other witness,' they informed John, 'the proceedings in the case will be adjourned until an answer is received to the questions sent to Tasmania.'

'I decline calling any further witnesses at present,' John responded, and was left to ponder his fate.

Chapter 48
THE TRUTH EXPOSED

Ridiculous as this enquiry may appear, I have been compelled to
submit to its folly and injustice.

John Stephen Jnr

Over the following four months, responses floated in from Tasmania. These
included a communication from Captain Young, master of the Launceston-
bound *Resolution* on 10 May 1829 and a man whose veracity (according
to the Tasmanian authorities) could be relied upon: he remembered Jane
New from Sydney and was willing to swear that she had not sailed on
board the *Resolution* nor did he fall in with any vessel bound for Batavia or
receive any passengers on board. An affidavit from the late supercargo on
the Launceston-bound *Henry* reported similarly.

From Launceston itself came lists from the Custom House detailing the
passengers who had arrived on the *Henry*, the absence of passengers on the
Resolution, and the revelation that not only had George Glew's *Hetty* arrived
in Launceston a week after he and John Kettle had reportedly farewelled
Jane, but Glew was not even listed as a passenger. Police Magistrate
Lyttleton reported being unable to find any trace of Jane New and from
her notoriety believed that her arrival could not have escaped the police's
attention. John Pascoe Fawkner, owner of Launceston's Cornwall Hotel
and editor of the *Launceston Advertiser* from 1828 to 1830 remarked that he

could also find no account of Jane New in Launceston but had heard of her escape to Batavia with Mr Stephen.

And on to Hobart. The Principal Superintendent of Convicts reported that he had heard nothing of Jane's return and thought it unlikely that she had done so unless clandestinely as he knew her personally (he was well acquainted with the Officer family). Dr Officer himself stated that he had not heard of Jane' return to Tasmania. Joseph Dickson who had reportedly spent time with Jane in Hobart in June 1829 declared that he had never heard of Jane New, had not visited Hobart between 1827 and 1830, and had received word late in 1827 that his purported companion Mills was dead.

John's coffin was in the grave and the sods were falling thick and fast.

On 8 April 1834, John wrote to the Governor asking when his hearing would resume. He wished to proceed with his case, he informed Bourke, in order to transmit the evidence to his parliamentary supporters or to return to England at an early period.

The break had proved longer than intended, Bourke responded, because of delays in receiving evidence from Tasmania but the hearing would resume again the following Saturday. When the Executive Council reconvened on 12 April, only three members were present: Governor Bourke, Lieutenant-Colonel Snodgrass and Colonial Treasurer Riddell. McLeay's withdrawal continued and Archdeacon Broughton was also absent; he travelled to England in 1834 to promote the interests of the Anglican church in Australia.

The Council welcomed John into the chambers and the hearing commenced. A letter from Tasmanian Colonial Secretary Burnett was read along with the attached affidavits. And then the Council directed their attention to John.

'The Council considers your case now closed,' Governor Bourke informed him, 'except so far as you might desire to address the Council in summing up or commenting upon the evidence.'

John's shock was evident. 'But I wish to produce further evidence disproving the identity of Frances Dickson and Jane New,' he blustered.

'The Council considers that the fullest opportunity has already been afforded you to bring forward all evidence that you thought necessary to establish your case. You cannot now be allowed to recommence an examination in chief as it would be impossible to foresee the length of the investigation. We recommend that the case should now be brought to a close except, as before stated, should you desire to avail yourself of your expressed intention of summing up the evidence.'

'Under these circumstances,' John protested, 'I request time to consider whether or not I should sum up.' He received a two-day adjournment.

John had prepared another epistle by the time the hearing continued on Monday 14 April, another longwinded diatribe railing against the whole proceeding. He had been required to meet a supposititious charge by proving its non-existence; he should be allowed to refute the new evidence particularly after the Council had delayed the hearing for four months in order to procure it; he had been promised the opportunity to contradict the testimony produced by the Council's witnesses. 'This is my undoubted right!' John raged, adding that according to the Secretary of State's despatch it was the Executive Council's duty to receive his evidence. 'I declare my perfect ability to refute the suborned evidence of the one witness which is the sole support of my opponents' cause, and in so doing establish that Frances Dickson was not Jane New. Should your Honours reconsider and permit me to proceed with my case, I shall lose no time in bringing it to a speedy conclusion. If on the other hand you are determined to adhere to your decision that I must sum up the case, I must decline to accede to that decision.'

The Council called John's bluff. 'As you have expressed your intention not to sum up the evidence, the Council deems the investigation to be closed. We will proceed to consider the evidence entered on the Minutes and will communicate the decision to you.'

'Since Your Excellency and Council have come to this decision,' John pontificated, 'I beg to inform you that it was my intention to have produced Frances Dickson herself before the Council.'

'Do you wish to have this communication entered on the Minutes?' the Governor asked dryly.

'I have no objection whatever,' John agreed snidely.

Despite refusing the right to sum up, John eventually did so. Another epistle written over the following month summarised John's intentions in questioning his witnesses and contained extracts from the relevant testimonies.

In order to meet the enquiry's demands, John explained, he had found himself in a difficult position. 'From the circumstances attending Mrs Dickson's residence at Crisp's Farm,' John explained coyly, 'even if the possibility had existed of producing her before the Executive Council, I could not suppose that such a tribunal of honour could have ever permitted me to take a step so fraught with consequences of domestic inquietude.'

For the first time in five years, and despite his previous vehement denials to the contrary, John had actually acknowledged the illicit nature of his relationship with the woman occupying his room at Amos Crisp's. So simple an admission; so profound the implications.

Labouring under this difficulty, John continued, he had realised that his most effective strategy would be to show that while Mrs Dickson was at Crisp's, Jane New was either in the Factory, concealed in Sydney or in Tasmania. His witnesses had clearly established the first two parts of the alibi, John contended, and while the Council had taken great pains to invalidate Jane New's voyage to Tasmania, they had offered no 'presumptive proof'. He admitted that two of his witnesses had mentioned some 'immaterial points' which had been denied in written documents, however no evidence of the documents' authenticity had been offered. (In an aside, John grumbled that while the Council submitted documentary testimony, he had not been allowed the same opportunity even when it involved a statement from the Chief Justice himself!) All it proved, John insisted, was that the captain of one schooner did not see the embarkation of Jane New on another schooner and that Jane New was not so imprudent as to make a public embarkation when endeavouring to privately leave the colony.

John's ability to dismiss the truth must have astonished even the Council.

Yet independently of the alibi, John argued, Mrs Dickson's literacy and Jane New's illiteracy showed beyond all doubt that the two women were not the same. And when he offered to produce Frances Dickson and invalidate the only testimony that supported the allegation, the Council refused to receive her testimony. 'Can this be just,' John protested, 'or in accordance with the order from the Secretary of State?'

Finally, John complained, he had been kept in a state of suspense for five years, had incurred losses and expenses to a ruinous extent, had been refused the aid of counsel, and had been allowed no means of enforcing or inducing the attendance of witnesses while the whole power of the Colonial Secretary's Office had been employed against him. 'When Your Honours reflect upon the extreme frivolity of the original imputation, I trust that a sense of honour and justice, if not of compassion and kindness, will induce you to rescind that stern decision which will continue me perhaps for years to come in a state of mental anxiety and intolerable annoyance. You cannot do justice without hearing the witnesses I may produce to rebut the testimony (irregular as it is) which you have received.'

John's letter also included statements from two more individuals declaring that the woman at Crisp's was not Jane New. The Council reconvened, considered John's letter, examined the statements, saw no reason to rescind their former decision, and agreed to forward his letter with the other evidence to the Secretary of State. They would soon, they informed John, communicate their decision.

Chapter 49
WITH A WHIMPER

It is fortunate that weakness is generally the companion of
wickedness; the operation of the passions in these cases can neutralise
the effect of a mischievous or vicious mind.
General Ralph Darling

Executive Council, 20 June 1834

Did John experience a sense of déjà vu as he entered the Executive Council's offices? The same building, the same season, almost the same day as his first hearing five years previously. But different faces. Was he expecting to be invited into the chambers to face the Council, to be regaled with a detailed report?

The Council had indeed prepared a lengthy report covering the hearing and their own conclusions. It was immediately apparent, the report began, that the Council laboured under a difficulty. While John appeared as a defendant ready to refute any charges laid against him, they had no party standing before them as an accuser nor had any Council member attended the previous Executive Council hearing. Accordingly, they decided to use the Minutes of that previous hearing as the document containing the charges. John's published pamphlet containing his House of Commons petition and the correspondence relating to his suspension would assist in their considerations.

From the Minutes of the previous hearing, the Council continued, the case against John could be simplified to two charges. First, that he had abused the authority vested in him as Registrar of the Supreme Court by giving a certificate of freedom to Jane New, and second, that he had concealed Jane New under the assumed name of Frances Dickson after her escape from confinement. The second charge only was the subject of the current investigation, the Council admitted. Nevertheless, if the first charge was true, it lent such strong support to the truth of the second charge that the Council decided to refer first to the evidence and explanation provided in John's pamphlet.

John had placed his own head on the cutting block. Why, with such insouciance, had he handed the Council such a self-incriminating document? The fabled scorpion had spoken the truth.

In summing up the evidence, the Council concluded that in preparing Jane New's certificate of freedom, John had not met the requirements of the 1825 Act protecting employers against unwittingly harbouring runaway convicts. If John, acting as a Justice of the Peace, had enquired into the facts of Jane's case, had satisfied himself as to her freedom, and had given her husband a certificate of freedom on 1 May as he alleged the law required, why a few days later did he send the letter to Dr Officer and also sign the warrant for James New's arrest? The official document revealing Jane's convict status was lodged in his own office and the affidavits upon which he reportedly based her certificate of freedom could not be considered more valid than that document. The Council could reach only one conclusion. 'It appears that the Council of 1829 had good ground for declaring that Mr Stephen had abused his authority as Registrar of the Supreme Court, and exercised an authority he did not possess as a magistrate.'

The Council had just demolished John's chance of re-employment.

And what conceivable reason could anyone other than Jane New have for requiring two such different certificates of freedom, the Council enquired? Yet there was every reason for Jane New to have such a requirement: a certificate attesting to Mrs Dickson's freedom as Jane was living in Crisp's house under that name; and one attesting to Jane New's freedom in case she was recognised.

Crisp's and his daughter's conduct and false statements when their house was searched also indicated their desire to conceal the presence of their female lodger, the Council continued. If Mrs Dickson was really the person stated in her declaration, she had no reason to flee from the constables in the middle of the night and never return, not even for her possessions. Her certificate of freedom protected her. Yet the witnesses' evidence incontestably proved that John's servant was afraid of the constables, particularly Constable Skinner who knew Jane New well. No explanation was provided as to why his presence would have induced Mrs Dickson to run away, the Council observed, although it would undoubtedly have had that effect upon Jane New.

The Council then directed their attention to John's behaviour. While John had no reason for showing a marked interest in Mrs Dickson, he had taken an interest in Jane's case on several occasions. John's explanation for having Jane's certificate of freedom in his possession — that he had been on horseback and stuffed it into a 'pocket' Crisp's daughter had lent him — was anything but satisfactory as was his comment that Frances Dickson's certificate should have been dated 1 May not 10 May. 'It is not the usual course of forgetfulness for the memory of dates to be in advance of the truth several days,' the Council dryly observed, 'and it appears almost incredible that so great a mistake could be made by any person not wholly illiterate or living in seclusion and more especially by an official person who, as Registrar of the Supreme Court, had occasion to affix dates to documents almost every day.'

The Council contended that Mrs Dickson's certificate was prepared around the day she arrived at Crisp's. 'If she had been taken to Crisp's on or about 9 March 1829 why was not such a certificate, a requisite for protection, given at that time? That was the time when Crisp would require it for his satisfaction and security.' They considered it significant that Crisp had reported to the Council in June 1829 that Mrs Dickson arrived five weeks earlier with a certificate signed by Magistrate John Stephen Jnr stating that she was free. This evidence clearly repudiated that of the witnesses John brought to the current hearing. 'It seems therefore most reasonable to suppose that the certificate of freedom for Mrs Dickson was given on 10 May, when Jane New was at large, and not on 9 March when Jane New was in confinement at Parramatta,' the Council concluded.

Regarding Jane New's departure from Sydney on 10 May 1829, the Council had grave concerns. They were surprised at the apparent indiscretions revealed by John's witnesses. 'Waterman Thomas John Parkes says that although the tide-surveyor and pilot were on board the *Mary*, yet the mate called Jane New openly by her name — an imprudence which it is difficult to imagine a person would commit who could not be ignorant of her condition, nor of the heavy penalty imposed by law for carrying off a convict.' The Council also felt uneasy about waterman James Wood's reference to the contents of the bundles carried by James New on his second journey out to the *Mary*. Although lodging-housekeeper Mrs Jones claimed that James had returned for clothes of his own, Wood described women's apparel and £20 or £30 in currency. The Council added pointedly that the money was an article unlikely to have been forgotten.

James New's openness about his plans to escape with his wife on board the *Mary* also generated suspicion. 'It is quite consistent with his purpose that he should seek to mislead others as to his intentions,' the Council remarked, 'whilst on the contrary if he did really intend to carry off a person whose escape the police would endeavour to prevent, it is not consistent that he should openly express his intention to so many persons whose assistance was not required.' And although the tide-surveyor's list was the strongest evidence supporting the News' embarkation on the *Mary*, the Council considered it impeached by pilot John Gray's evidence and rendered suspicious by Oliver's drunken habits. Accordingly, they found it impossible to place the least reliance on the story of Jane's embarkation on the *Mary*, or her arrival in Launceston late in May 1829, or her relocation to Hobart a few days later.

The Council had just thrown out John's alibi.

And what proof was there, the Council continued, that the person calling herself Frances Dickson who appeared before the Notary Public on 6 July 1829 was Crisp's tenant? If she was the same person, why wasn't Amos Crisp brought before the Notary Public to swear to her identity, or John himself? And if John's affidavit was intended to suggest that he had sworn to the fact that Mrs Dickson was not Jane New, why didn't he make a direct statement? 'He chose to use equivocal expressions capable of evasion,' concluded the Council, 'rather than plain and intelligible words admitting of no mistake upon a subject within his perfect knowledge.'

Moreover, John's actions were inconsistent with his intimation that Mrs Dickson was not Jane New, the Council denounced. He knew on 19 June 1829 that strong suspicions existed that the women were identical. His affidavit, evidently made with the aim of repudiating such suspicions, expressed his willingness to produce Mrs Dickson and showed that it was within his power. Yet he chose not to do so. In a similar manner on 14 April 1834, when assured that no further evidence would be accepted by the Council, he again disclosed his intention of producing Mrs Dickson. 'If he had the power, why not produce her at the former time, and thus put an end at once to the case by establishing his innocence of the charge of having harboured Jane New. The scruples of delicacy,' the Council remarked pointedly, 'to which he alludes in his opening address had, it seems, been got over, as he declares he *meant* to produce her.'

As for disproving the identity of Mrs Dickson and Jane New, the Council observed that the two men who claimed to have known both women provided contradictory responses. John Raine reported that the women were very similar in appearance while Lewis Solomon claimed that they were not. And against their evidence that Mrs Dickson was not Jane New, the Council offered Mrs Seymour's evidence that she was. Although John Stephen Jnr attempted to diminish the value of Mrs Seymour's statements through Constable John Burrows' testimony, the Council added, Burrows did not provide any consistent evidence regarding the time of Mrs Seymour's discovery that the woman at Crisp's was Jane New. And although Solomon testified that Mrs Dickson was at Crisp's in March 1829, his testimony was undermined by the evidence showing that Mrs Dickson did not arrive at Crisp's until around 10 May 1829.

'It may be observed here,' the Council continued, 'that the meeting between Crisp and Solomon on the very morning they both came before

Council and the nature of the examination which then took place is of a very improbable kind. Crisp's contradictions were most glaring but as he risked the loss of his ticket-of-leave if it appeared that he had knowingly been an accessory to harbouring a prisoner, he was under the strongest influence to deny the fact of Jane New having been harboured at his place. The Council, therefore, considers the evidence of Lewis Solomon liable to the greatest suspicion, and rendered still more doubtful by its connexion with that of Crisp on the subject of their alleged meeting on the morning of their examination. It is unfit to be relied on and wholly incapable of overthrowing the weight of the testimony establishing the identity of Frances Dickson and Jane New.'

After accounting for and dismissing the remaining components of the evidence, the Council reached their final conclusion. 'From the foregoing examination, the Council are led to confirm the conclusion at which they arrived after considering the case presented in Mr Stephen's pamphlet. In the opinion of the Council there are the strongest grounds for concluding that Jane New was the person whom Mr Stephen placed at Crisp's house under the assumed name of Frances Dickson.'

The eight-month investigation had ended.

But John was not invited into Council chambers to hear the report read. He had no opportunity to judge the expressions on their faces, to hear their arguments, to question them, to remonstrate with them, to supply a new defence. Instead the clerk proffered a one-page letter:

In obedience to the commands of the Secretary of State, the Executive Council received and considered the evidence produced by Mr Stephen in disproof of the alleged identity between Jane New and Frances Dickson, and having taken such steps as seemed to them proper for bringing the matter to a definitive issue, they are of opinion that the alleged identity has not been disproved.

John had just spent five years railing against the difficulty of disproving what had not been proved. With this latest judgement he would face the impossible: disproving what had not been disproved. Or was it proving what had not been disproved? It was like catching mist: the concept floated away — unable to be pursued, grappled, vanquished.

The Council had triumphed. John had finally been cast adrift, and the Jane New scandal had limped to a close.

EPILOGUE

*Mr Stephen was always considered an apt hand at sailing close to the
wind in his intromissions with the truth; but certes his merits have
never before been fairly understood because, perhaps, there was never an
occasion when so many were in a position to appreciate them properly.*

Port Phillip Patriot

Was there an inevitability to the Jane New affair? No doubt its roots lay in a
social-welfare system that failed to succour the poor and destitute and a judicial
system that considered poverty-induced criminal behaviour as a cancer that
must be hacked out rather than cured. A distant government, an autocratic
governor, and a colony fighting for a new identity: all were contributing
factors. And of course fate: had the butterfly flapped its wings a moment
earlier or a moment later, the repercussions might have been different.

Yet in essence, the Jane New scandal was simply the age-old tale of
an amoral gentleman lusting after a scheming wench, a scandal with
particularly profound legal, political and historical consequences.

Was Jane a siren? In truth, no, although she did leave a trail of
disconsolate hearts and damaged careers behind her. A political pawn?
Indeed, although she benefited more than those who attempted to

manipulate her circumstances to their advantage. A beguiling opportunist who lusted after a better life? Undoubtedly.

Glimpses of Jane can be seen in the years following the scandal. Evidence that she had slipped out of the colony first surfaced in October 1829 when the ship *Surry* returned from New Zealand. Someone on board brought news that Jane had sailed from Sydney in the *Emma Kemp* and was 'living with a man named Butler, a son-in-law to the late Chief Constable Dunn of Sydney'. Only a few years older than Jane, Samuel Butler was the son of Anglican missionary Reverend John Gare Butler who in 1819 settled with his family at Samuel Marsden's mission in the Bay of Islands, New Zealand. Samuel Butler had also served as a missionary there until a 'wicked, malicious and unfounded report' sent to the Church Missionary Society in London led to his dismissal. He had settled in Sydney in 1823, married Thomas Dunn's daughter Ann, fathered a couple of children and returned to New Zealand in 1827 apparently as a trader.

Lucyanne, the property where Jane was reportedly residing (most likely named after Butler's deceased infant daughter) lay near Thomas Raine's establishment in Hokianga in the Bay of Islands. Raine, a merchant and trader and one of the signatories to Jane's petitions, had served as the *Surry*'s master from 1814 to 1827. He was also the brother of Notary Public John Raine, who had taken Frances Dickson's declaration on 6 July 1829, the day after the *Emma Kemp* left Sydney. Thomas Raine was almost certainly the merchant John Raine mentioned in his testimony to the Executive Council as having assisted in Jane's escape, the man whose identity he would not reveal for fear of incrimination. Both brothers were undoubtedly complicit in assisting Jane to sneak out of the country.

According to the *Surry*'s report, Jane claimed to be a widow named Mrs Jones and would soon leave New Zealand in the whaler *Toward Castle* bound for England via the whaling fields. The authorities took note. A memorandum reported: 'As the whaler will doubtless be employed on her passage, notice per *Harmony* would reach England before that vessel arrives or the expiration of Mrs New's sentence.' The *Harmony* sailed for London on 23 October 1829, no doubt carrying a letter to the British authorities advising them to watch for the *Toward Castle*'s arrival and apprehend the runaway.

Was the New Zealand report correct? A few months later Governor Darling's brother-in-law, William Dumaresq, forwarded a letter from Female Factory clerk Joseph Turner telling a curious story. A convict named Jane Jefferson had been assigned to Turner's wife three weeks previously. Jefferson was a Lancashire transportee and reported that she knew Jane New and her mother in England, was transported to Tasmania with Jane on the *Henry*, and was later brought to New South Wales by a Hunter River settler. She had perhaps been boasting of her connection with the notorious Jane New and in the ensuing conversation, according to Turner's letter, revealed the following information:

> Jane New together with her husband and father-in-law and Mrs New's own mother are all residing in no fixed place on the Banks of Hunter River. The father-in-law is named Richard Baker and according to what Jefferson says plies a boat on the Hunter. Jane New and the family often move their place of abode by means of the boat belonging to her father-in-law and Mrs New is often dressed in men's clothing. The object of this party is to secrete Mrs New until she actually becomes free.

When pressed by the Turners, Jane Jefferson refused to divulge any further information and expressed regret at having said so much. She left the Turners' employ a short time later, Joseph Turner explained, having been thwarted in her desire to visit some old acquaintances, and was presently lodged in the Factory's first class. Turner warned that she would be reluctant to assist the authorities. She was an elderly person, he added (although other returns suggest that she was only 40 years of age), and very artful. Indeed, her Tasmanian conduct record exposes her unsuitability for assigned service, noting numerous punishments for abusing her master, being absent without leave, excessive insolence and singing obscene songs.

The background information provided by Joseph Turner and Jane Jefferson tallied closely with documentary evidence indicating that neither was lying. Had Jane New not left New South Wales, had she surreptitiously returned, or was the story part of Jane Jefferson's attempt to claim her moment in the limelight?

The colonial authorities made no attempt to investigate the story, evidently believing that Jane was long gone. Indeed, references to her continued residence in New Zealand drifted back to Sydney over the following few years. If the report of her intended departure on the *Toward Castle* had been circulated with the intention to mislead, it was successful. The *Emma Kemp*'s seaman, Thomas Franklin, mentioned seeing Jane in New Zealand after her disembarkation from the cutter. Late in 1830, when Captain Rossi took his affidavit, he reported: 'She landed at Hokianga and I believe she still remains there. I saw her about five months ago there. She has a house and a number of New Zealand women are there.' Was Jane running an accommodation house, a shelter or a bordello?

New Zealand was then in the grip of the horrific 'musket wars', the inter-tribal warfare that had raged since the early 1800s. The Maori traded food, tattooed heads, flax and women — often slaves forced into prostitution — in return for muskets. In choosing New Zealand as her sanctuary, Jane had risked exchanging bad for worse.

John Raine also knew of Jane's post-scandal whereabouts, reporting early in November 1833: 'I have seen persons who informed me that they had seen and conversed with her. I heard that when she left here she went to a place called Hokianga in New Zealand. It was there that Mr Gordon Davis Browne saw her, also Mr Drew and a Mr Russel who was my brother's clerk. Mr Browne has an establishment there.'

The last known reference to Jane is found in the *Australian* late in November 1833:

> The celebrated Jane New about whom so much has been said and written in this colony, sailed about three weeks since from the Bay of Islands, New Zealand, to Wahoo (about 2000 miles to the northward). The fear of the British resident, under whose nose she has resided for many months, it is supposed, was the occasion of her migration.[41]

Wahoo in the Sandwich Islands — that is, Oahu in Hawaii — was one of the ports of call on the major shipping routes. From there, Jane could have travelled anywhere. She was only 28 years of age and childless. Did she waltz to America on the coattails of another wealthy patron? If so, scandal no doubt muddied her train.

When the *Australian*'s report of Jane's departure from New Zealand reached the Tasmanian settlement, another life was possibly touched and damaged. Was James New's wife aware that her husband was a bigamist?

When James New disappeared from Sydney in May 1829, he made his way back to England. James might have carried Jane's miniature with him and her memory imprinted on his heart, but he was a more practical fellow. On 23 May 1831 at St Mary Magdalene in Bermondsey, London, he married fellow Mitcham-born resident Maria Elizabeth Whitfield. James described himself, conveniently, as a widower.

Whether James renounced Jane because he believed her to be dead or because he knew their relationship was over can only be speculated upon. Having done so, his decision to contact John Stephen Jnr a few months later seems surprising. John reported that James had heard of his petition to Parliament and had offered to refute the charges against him. But John had cuckolded him. Why would James take up cudgels in defence of the man who had seduced his wife and destroyed his marriage?

Perhaps a mutual blackmailing session had occurred.

When James contacted John in September 1831 he was allegedly on board the *John Woodall* bound for Tasmania. Colonial records confirm the vessel's arrival in Tasmania in February 1832 with James as a passenger. As expeditions to the colony were expensive, James perhaps called upon John for financial 'assistance'.

Ever the opportunist, John presumably saw a chance for personal gain. He asked James to make a statement repudiating his involvement in Jane's escapes, and attached James' statement to a letter he rushed off to the Colonial Office. James was undoubtedly one of the Tasmanian witnesses John hoped to call if the Executive Council would consent to pay the expenses. Courtesy of their refusal, James probably remained oblivious of the ongoing dramas associated with the scandal after his departure from England.

James New spent the remainder of his life in Tasmania. If he and his wife did hear about Jane's departure from New Zealand, it had little effect on their marriage. The couple had four children born in Tasmania between 1833 and 1840, and settled in Bagdad in the Brighton district north of Hobart where James returned to pubkeeping. He died there on 27 July 1865 and his second wife ten years later.

Criminality, adultery, and eventually bigamy. Such behaviour stained the News with the indelible ink of notoriety and provided the local community with a source of delectable gossip, yet the News were not responsible for the scandal that carried Jane's name. 'Scandal', wrote the cynical Oscar Wilde, 'is gossip made tedious by morality'. Colonial society had no expectations of moral behaviour from convicts like the News. The responsibility for turning gossip into scandal must ultimately lie with John Stephen Jnr. No doubt he would have leapt at the 'siren' defence if he could have used it to advantage, as he grasped every other possible defence in his attempts to disclaim responsibility for his own actions. But John's behaviour before and after his involvement with Jane New reveals that this particular fall from grace was not an isolated incident. John managed to stumble from one scandal to another throughout his adult years, the Jane New affair merely a particularly noteworthy and historically significant episode.

In the aftermath of the Executive Council hearing, its secrecy combined with time's passage meant that the character denigration John had bitterly railed against had diminished in importance. So he had taken a convict mistress and had helped her escape from New South Wales. To the colony's administrators, it was grounds enough to punish him, and he had indeed suffered through five years in the twilight until the Council's ruling abolished all hope of a new government appointment. To those steeped in religious traditions or with a strong moralistic bent, it was grounds enough to shun him, although Christian spirit dictated forgiveness if he expressed contrition for the errors of his ways. To the remainder, particularly those who had also lusted after Jane's charms, it was merely the icing on top of a particularly delicious cake.

Yet although the Jane New affair ended with the Executive Council's final condemnation, John's moment in the colonial limelight had in many ways only just begun.

John's activities in support of colonial reform redounded to his benefit in the aftermath of the scandal. When the Australian Patriotic Association formed in 1835 to lobby for representative government, the members voted Sir John Jamison as President and John Stephen as Secretary.[42] The colonists must have ignored the gossip that reached Sydney whispering of John's incarceration in the King's Bench prison as an insolvent debtor, discounted the rumours of his embezzlement of the deceased estates trust fund, and overlooked the dark clouds of creditors amassing on the horizon. Perhaps their votes were a demonstration of their willingness to allow John a second chance, in this land of second chances. If so, it was a decision they would soon regret.

The Patriotic Association was mainly composed of wealthy men and its regulations obliged members to subscribe funds towards an agency in London founded to support their political endeavours. In October 1835, John was responsible for forwarding a Treasury Bill for £500 to parliamentarian Henry Bulwer in London. In December 1836 word reached Sydney that the Treasury Bill had never arrived.

'Negligence or cupidity?' asked the shocked residents of Sydney. But John was unavailable to answer. A year earlier, as a cascade of civil suits descended upon him, John had slipped out of the country. Again.

After a short stay in England, John arrived in Hobart in January 1837 on board the *Fairlie*, which also carried the new Governor, Sir John Franklin. A few weeks later, the Sydney newspapers reached the southern settlement and broadcast the news of the missing funds. The Tasmanian newspapers expressed astonishment at their Sydney brethren's conclusion that the funds were irretrievably lost and called upon John for an explanation. They were soon charmed into believing him innocent of any wrongdoing:

> Assuredly it would have been much more becoming to have ascertained
> the fate of the bills before venturing to put forth ungenerous insinuations.

That the Association should make the non-receipt of these bills groundwork for imputing to their Secretary that which no man in his senses would have committed, and which no one with an unprejudiced mind would attribute to him, appears to us most extraordinary.

Three years later, attitudes had changed. 'On 30 October 1839 John Stephen, formerly Secretary of the Patriotic Association but late of Hobart Town, procured himself to be declared insolvent,' advertised Tasmania's *Colonial Times*, 'but previous to his examination absconded from the colony after improperly receiving money due to his estate.'

Casting around for a new home, John turned his attention to the recently established settlement of Melbourne on the southern coast of Australia. A new community; a new challenge. By 1841, John was assistant editor to the *Port Phillip Gazette*. By January 1843 he was a councillor in the recently founded and politically divisive Melbourne Town Council. With John's family background and his charm, looks, intelligence and apparent sincerity, he had the perfect profile for a politician. Had he discarded the mantle of his unfortunate past and found his niche?

But this particular tiger had not changed his stripes. And William Kerr, editor of the opposition *Port Phillip Patriot* and a Council alderman belonging to the rival political faction, had his measure. Kerr thrived on exposing folly through his newspaper. And he delighted in picking on John Stephen.

Kerr admitted that John was well qualified to take his place on the Council. Yet he hesitated to echo the *Times* report (in an article bearing all the hallmarks, Kerr claimed, of John's own pen) that John was 'a gentleman whose services to the colonial public are more remarkable than those of any other man of his age and standing in the community'. John's services certainly had been remarkable, Kerr agreed, but had they elevated the community's moral tone? 'We rather think his principle services have entitled him to such an epitaph as was concocted by our countryman, Burns, for a similar worthy who roamed in Mauchline (although for "Mauchline" read Melbourne, Sydney or Hobart Town, as you will):

Lament him, Mauchline husbands a'
He often did assist ye;
For had ye staid hail weeks awa,
Your wives wad ne'er hae miss'd ye.'

Over the following year, everything from snide digs to blatant attacks on John's character, behaviour and morals graced the pages of the *Port Phillip Patriot*: claims that he was elected by a drunken mob who in return for his grog were vociferous in their support, and reports that the said rabble then proceeded to intimidate those intending to vote for the opposition and, after the election, the female members of Alderman Kerr's household. Evidence that at least one of John's votes came from a poor ignorant Irishman who was induced to impersonate a voter. Serious charges that John had no right to a place on the Council because of his failure to fulfil the residential requirement, his insufficiency of funds and his unsatisfied insolvency. Suggestions of mendacity in his defence against the charges. Revelations that he defamed another Council member in his attempt to divert attention from his own problems.

A different orchestra; the same old tune.

And on to the personal. Frequent allusions to John's current inamorata, actress Miss Warman, and the inevitable lawyer's version of pistols at dawn:

John Stephen v. Adam Murray The lovers of sport would not lose their time by attending the Police Office this morning as these gentlemen intend exhibiting their forensic abilities for the amusement of the public. It appears that Mr Stephen took something that had been published by Mr Murray in high dudgeon, and therefore called at the *Times* office and politely intimated his opinion that Mr Murray deserved horsewhipping. Mr Murray, not to be outdone in courtesy, wrote to Mr Stephen requesting him to make his mind easy for if anyone in the province deserved a horsewhipping it was himself. Mr Stephen became still angrier when Mr Murray alluded to a lady, who, we are informed, is much respected by both gentlemen, but more especially by Mr Stephen. Who can wonder, then, that, with all those juvenescent and tender aspirations which notoriously distinguish him, the worthy and much respected Mr Stephen should, in the warmth of his 'too generous youth' have allowed his indignation to overcome his prudence, to have demanded — what? — pistols and coffee! Oh, bless you, no! a summons was all he wanted. Obviously this is a very manly course on the part of Mr Stephen, for he is young and inexperienced while Mr Murray is, it cannot be denied, verging towards the 'sear and yellow leaf' and of much experience in the ways of the world. Mr Stephen will naturally therefore labour under some disadvantage, but being an excessively 'nice man for a small tea-party' it is to be hoped that he will this day clearly show that he does not deserve a horsewhipping.

But at the appointed hour, John failed to present himself. John was ill, explained Miss Warman's father as he scuttled into the police office. Yet three hours later John graced a Licensed Victuallers Society meeting, Kerr gleefully reported, exhibiting no trace of his serious indisposition.

And then came the climax of Kerr's campaign: conclusive evidence of John's involvement with his previous inamorata, housekeeper Mary Anne Rogers alias Mrs Gardiner, in the form of an 'interesting cherub' baptised John Alfred Sydney Stephen. Under the headline Bastardy, the *Port Phillip Patriot* revealed all.

Of course, John sued Kerr for libel. But difficulties arose in using the bastardy article as the basis for his suit as he had admitted paternity of the child. So he latched onto some of Kerr's other outrageous declarations: that John's latest revelations meant that the rival *Port Phillip Herald*'s editor should 'look to his laurels for he is no longer without a rival near the throne in the art of gasconading, or as it is vulgarly known — lying.' Kerr had also also written: 'So much for Mr Stephen's veracity! Poor man, his Melbourne career is obviously drawing to a close; he has made a more decided hit here than anywhere else he has been. But we fear that his exit hence must ultimately be as hurried as it was from London, Sydney and Hobart Town.'

The suit proved little more than a farce. John employed a barrister but pushed him aside and took over the case. He called witnesses who hamstrung themselves by admitting under cross-examination that if the falsehoods attributed to John were indeed falsehoods and the behaviour indeed debauched, then the libels could not be libels. Alderman Kerr called witnesses to prove the truth of his statements, one of whom demurred at being called to give evidence and slunk out of the courtroom when the court's attention was directed elsewhere. And when another began to point out one by one the falsehoods in John's statements, John jumped up and shouted that he would not suffer such evidence to be taken. A 'long altercation' ensued with John ranting that evidence of the libels' truth was inadmissible while Kerr bellowed that he had the right to rebut John's testimony. No wonder the *Port Phillip Patriot* regularly exhorted its readers to attend John's court cases.

As it turned out, John chose not to bolt from Melbourne as Alderman Kerr predicted. His 'youthful and innocent face' evidently covered an impenetrable hide. That John remained in residence despite Kerr's campaign of exposure indicates that financial considerations rather than revelations of scandalous behaviour precipitated his previous hasty departures. Having joined Melbourne's legal fraternity as a solicitor, John proved more able at managing his financial affairs and had no need to seek another haven. He eventually died from heart disease in Melbourne on 30 October 1854 at the age of 56.

Although John managed to brush off the evidence of his illicit and immoral activities, the amiable Amos Crisp soon found the colony too hazardous for his own wellbeing. Despite his imprisonment following the constables' discovery of Jane New's certificate of freedom, and his first-hand reminder of the horrors of double irons and solitary confinement, Crisp remained an opportunist. A few months later, he rustled a thirsty drover's most valuable cattle after an innkeeper friend seduced the drover inside with the offer of refreshments. The two escaped a colonial conviction by a hair's breadth.

Tussles with the law continued for the following few years, leading Crisp to abandon his residence in Minto and decamp to the relatively lawless 'New Country' on the outskirts of settlement. But he rustled livestock once too often and in 1836 found himself in Sydney Gaol facing trial. This time there would be no escaping the consequences. The evidence was compelling; the witnesses convincing. Nor could he defend himself by claiming a good reputation: the authorities described him as a notoriously bad character with whom no honest man would deal.

Crisp, however, was a student of chicanery and had quickly grasped the lessons of the Jane New scandal. He donned the female attire his daughter brought to the gaol, slipped out under the eyes of the guards, sauntered down to the dock where he could acquire a passage on an ocean-going vessel, and . . .

But that's another story.

ENDNOTES

1   Prologue, p. 1: Although the 1828 Census records Sydney's population as 10 815, this statistic omitted members of the military and their families, the Aborigines living within or on the periphery of settlement, those accidently omitted, and a considerable number of Sydneysiders whose Household Returns appear to have been lost. Sir Roger Therry listed Sydney's population at that time as 15 000, although it possibly was as low as 13 500.

2   Chapter 1, p. 5: Maria, daughter of Isaac Wilkinson of Headingly (the baptism register provides no details of maternity), was baptised on 13 October 1805 at Headingly parish. The child's father was probably mason and widower Isaac Wilkinson who married Elizabeth Cormack (probably an error for Cromack) on 23 April 1804 at St Peter's Church of England, Leeds. Although Jane later described herself as a Presbyterian, the nonconformists had to marry within the established church at that time. As the aforementioned was the only marriage recorded for an Isaac Wilkinson in the Leeds area between 1779 and at least 1812, and as no other baptism for a child named Maria Wilkinson has been found in church registers for the Leeds district covering the early 1800s, this couple were probably Jane's parents and this child Jane herself. Jane claimed to be thirteen when first incarcerated, which tallies neatly with this baptism date.

3   Chapter 1, p. 11: Although Jane's sentence was to be 'remanded', that is, returned to the Salford gaol, she later mentioned having spent twelve months in Liverpool Gaol which, if true, must have followed this conviction. The records for Liverpool Gaol have not survived so her statement cannot be confirmed.

4   Chapter 2, p. 12: This wonderfully evocative judgement was bestowed upon a convict transported from Britain to North America where the transportees were more at the mercy of fate (as they filled the role of indentured servants) rather than the law.

5   Chapter 3, p. 17: When Elizabeth Wilkinson was mustered upon her arrival in New South Wales, she mentioned that she had a daughter arriving on the *Henry*. Given the time constraints and the distance, this is not the type of information she would have known unless the Lancashire and Cheshire convicts were forwarded together to London or had met during the journey.

6 Chapter 3, p. 21: Robson in *The Convict Settlers of Australia* reveals that 30 per cent of females transported to Tasmania had sentences longer than seven years as compared with 21 per cent of their New South Wales counterparts. They were also more likely to be former offenders.

7 Chapter 5, p. 26: James was baptised on 31 March 1800 at St Peter and St Paul Church of England in Mitcham, County Surrey. His parents remained in Mitcham parish. His father was buried on 6 May 1860 aged 90 years and his mother on 4 November 1863 aged 96 years, both at Mitcham. [Parish Registers: Church of St Peter & St Paul, Mitcham, transcribed by East Surrey Family History Society. Fiche M58 Entries 407 & 723]

8 Chapter 6, p. 32: While some sources suggest that James New was a publican in Hobart, the Hotels Index at the Hobart Archives Office records that George William Robinson was granted the licence for the Spread Eagle in September 1824 and in October 1827. He probably also held it in the intervening period.

9 Chapter 6, p. 32: No reference to James' return has been found in either New South Wales or Tasmanian records.

10 Chapter 6, p. 36: A native of London, James Palmer was convicted at the Middlesex Sessions in January 1821, six months after James New sailed from England. Transported to Tasmania on the *Countess of Harcourt* later in 1821, he was under sentence of retransportation to Port Macquarie in April 1823 when offloaded in Sydney and absorbed into government employ.

11 Chapter 7, p. 38: The Rens arrived in Sydney on the *Phillip Dundas* on 30 January 1827, having sailed from Batavia on 30 November 1826. Many transcribed and published documents incorrectly record Madame Rens' surname as Reus or even Rous. Madame Rens was listed as 'Coymanos Vidonia Rens' in the published 1828 Census, and described herself as a milliner. Her daughter Jeanette was sometimes listed as 'Jane'.

12 Chapter 7, p. 41: Hannah Antroby/Antrobus was born around 1807 in Manchester and was a housemaid and nursemaid according to her own report when convicted of shoplifting on 18 July 1825. She sailed from London in September 1826 on the *Grenada*, arriving in Sydney in January 1827, and married Richard Ralph on 5 November 1827 at St Philips, Sydney. Hannah and Jane New possibly first met at the Salford gaol shortly before Jane's release in July 1822.

13 Chapter 8, p. 47: James Stephen's knighthood occurred long after the period of the Jane New scandal, so he has been referred to as James Stephen throughout.

14 Chapter 8, p. 48: Justice John Stephen (c1771-1833) and his wife Mary Anne Pasmore (?-1863) had the following offspring: Sidney (born c1796-1857), John (born c1798-1854), George Milner (1800-1810), Alfred (1802-1894), Francis (1804-1837), Sibella (1806; married Captain Robert Robison), Mary (c1808-1809), Mary Anne (c1810-1869), George Milner (c1812-1894) and Clara (c1813-1862).

15 Chapter 9, p. 51: Francis returned to New South Wales on board the *Lang* which arrived in Sydney on 29 August 1827.

16 Chapter 9, p. 53: Sidney Stephen and his family arrived in Sydney on board the *Albion* on 27 January 1828, having sailed from London via Hobart.

17 Chapter 10, p. 57: John Stephen Jnr and Mary Matthews Hamilton's first marriage — on 24 June 1820 at St Pancras Church, London — was mentioned in the *Times'* marriage notices, although no entry is included in the St Pancras marriage registers. Mary's lack of

legal guardian was evidently recognised before the the the register was filled in. The couple remarried on 27 January 1821 at the same church. Six children are known to have been born to their marriage: Hamilton Farish (1822), Percival Sydney Francis (1823), Frederica Mary (c1826), Claudia (c1828), Virginius Alfred William Carlyle (1833) and Fitzroy Charles Dalhousie (1834). Hamilton Farish Stephen was born on 24 Aug 1822 and baptised on 5 Nov 1822 while Percival Sydney Francis was born on 29 Nov 1823 and baptised on 17 Dec 1823; both baptism ceremonies were performed at St Pancras Old Church, London. Virginius Alfred William Carlyle Stephen was born 6 January 1833 (probably at Gravesend) and baptised on 4 July 1833 while Fitzroy Charles Dalhousie Stephen was born on 7 October 1834 at Birchgrove, Sydney, and baptised on 3 November 1834; both ceremonies were performed at St James, Sydney.

18 Chapter 10, p. 59:   A bill of exchange is similar to a cheque.

19 Chapter 10, p. 61: A later notice regarding insolvent debtors listed the Cape of Good Hope as one of John's residences. As the list omitted Mauritius — where John spent some time — the reference to the Cape of Good Hope could have been an error.

20 Chapter 10, p. 61: Shipping arrival records in Tasmania and NSW list four children arriving with John's family although other sources suggest that the couple had only three children at this time. Perhaps one of the children belonged to a relative.

21 Chapter 13, p. 85: The questions asked by the counsel for the prosecution and defence during examination and cross-examination as well as those asked by the 'court' (presumably the judge) and jury were not transcribed into Dowling's Notebook, only the responses. Their omission could possibly lead to a misinterpretation of the significance of some of the responses.

22 Chapter 14, p. 93: Madame Rens made no reference to the nature of Jane New's basket, however her daughter Jeanette described it as a covered basket. Sidney Stephen raised the unlikelihood of the fabric being glimpsed from a covered basket. This of course presupposes the accuracy of Jeanette's testimony regarding the robbery, which Sidney himself indicated must have been a fabrication as he provided affidavits to show that Jeanette was not present during the robbery. [SRNSW ref: 2/3470 p. 203]

23 Chapter 14, p. 97:   Occam's Razor is referred to in Keith Laidler's *The Divine Deception*, Headline Book Publishing, London, 2000, p. 279. This is a more useful adaptation of the exact translation 'plurality should not be posited without necessity'.

24 Chapter 15, p. 103: The signatories were: John Stephen Jnr, George Bunn, John S. Jackson, Thomas Macvitie, Don Macleod, A.B. Spark, Ellis Scott, John [?], Alexander Berry, Edward Aspinall, Thomas Raine, George T. Savage, W.H. Moore, W. Balcombe.

25 Chapter 15, p. 103: This letter was noted as having disappeared by December 1830. [ML ref: A1267[-16] pp. 89–91; CY Reel 895]

26 Chapter 16, p. 107: Chief Justice Forbes wrote on 7 February 1828: 'The Judges having taken the case of Jane New into their consideration, with reference to their Letters to your Excellency under date the 1st of April and 7th of July [1828] respectively, are of the opinion that such case does fall within the rule of law laid down by the Judges in the cases of Joseph Lee and others, who were tried and received sentence under Statutes which had been repealed and were not in force at the time of the offences committed, and consequently that the conviction of Jane New is not valid.' [SRNSW ref: 4/1516 pp. 91–2; Reel 2436]

27 Chapter 16, p. 112: Reports variously record Jane's transfer as 20 or 21 February 1829, however the earlier date seems more likely.

28 Chapter 18, p. 123: The relevant legislation was Section 9 of 9 George IV, c83.

29 Chapter 20, p. 136: Samuel Cleme was around 54 years of age at this time, a time-expired convict who had arrived some 25 years earlier on the *Glatton* with a fourteen-year sentence. [1828 Census — Entry No.C1419]

30 Chapter 20, p. 137: Thomas Evans had arrived free per *Dromedary* in 1820 and was a 56-year-old householder in Phillip Street. [1828 Census — Entry E0607]

31 Chapter 20, p. 138: The Sydney Gaol Entrance Book records that Jane was retaken on 27 March, that is, the Friday, and sent to the Parramatta Female Factory on the 28th [SRNSW ref: 4/6431 1829 Mch 03 — Jane New] while other sources record that she was taken on the 28th.

32 Chapter 20, p. 138: Ellen Hatton was convicted in Lancashire in July 1822, arrived in New South Wales on the *Mary* in 1823, and married wealthy Scottish ex-convict baker and publican Andrew Frazier, who was forty years her senior. Ellen's drinking and bad behaviour soon drove her husband to distraction and ultimately to an early death, a story briefly covered in Grace Karskens' *The Rocks*.

33 Chapter 21, p. 143: William Balcombe was buried on 23 March 1829.

34 Chapter 25, p. 170: In addition to John Stephen Jnr, the signatories included George Bunn, Thomas Raine, John S. Jackson, William Henry Moore, George Thomas Savage, John Thomas Campbell JP, Edward Joseph Keith, Thomas Maeirtic JP, J.S. Harrison, David Maziere, Thomas Horton James, G.R. Nicholls, William Bean JP, Charles Dodwell Moore, Edward Riley, J.R. Lawson and David Poole.

35 Chapter 28, p. 189: For a detailed biography of Amos Crisp, see Carol J. Baxter's *Nash: First Fleeters & Founding Families*, Chapter 21, and E.W. Northwood's *Defend the Fold: Cartwright Family History 1625–1983*.

36 Chapter 29, p. 201: The date of departure for the *Emma Kemp* is variously recorded as 5 or 6 July 1829. Harbour Master John Nicholson was asked to read his entry from the Shipping Report which was dated 6 July 1829 and noted that the *Emma Kemp* had sailed the previous day.

37 Chapter 35, p. 244: This Act (5 George IV, no. 3) was 'An Act to prevent the harbouring of runaway convicts and the encouraging of convicts' tippling and gambling, taken from the Act of Council no. 3 dated 19 January 1825'.

38 Chapter 38, p. 261: While Brian Fletcher in *Ralph Darling: A Governor Maligned* suggested that 'Miles' reflected a consortium of contributors, 'Miles' himself in *Governor Darling's refutation of the charges of cruelty . . .* indicated that the author was a single person. His use of the singular ('writer', 'correspondent') combined with John Stephen Jnr's response to the earlier attacks on 'Miles' by publishing his own pamphlet, indicates that John was the driving force although Captain Robison undoubtedly had some input.

39 Chapter 38, p. 271: For the full story of Captain Robison and the Sudds and Thompson affair see Brian Fletcher, *Ralph Darling: A Governor Maligned*.

40 Chapter 40, p. 282: John and Mary Stephen's son was born on 6 January 1833, two days before the *Westmoreland* departed from Gravesend. [SRNSW ref: vol. 17 no. 273; Reel 5004]

41 Epilogue, p. 359: James Busby was appointed British resident in the Bay of Islands in 1833.

42 Epilogue, p. 362: The appellation 'junior' had disappeared after his father's death late in 1833.

SOURCES

Abbreviations

BL — British Library, London, England

CRO — Cheshire Record Office, Chester, Cheshire

JSY — Jersey Archives, Channel Islands

LMA — London Metropolitan Archives, London, England

LRO — Lancashire Record Office, Preston, Lancashire, England

ML — Mitchell Library, Sydney, NSW, Australia

RBDM-VIC — Registry of Births, Deaths & Marriages, Victoria, Australia

SLTX/AO — State Library of Tasmania — Archives Office, Hobart, Tasmania, Australia

SRNSW — State Records of New South Wales, Kingswood, NSW, Australia

TNA — The National Archives, Kew, Surrey, England

I   Temptation

Epigraph: Chief Justice Dowling, 16 Feb 1839, quoted in Sturma, *Vice in a Vicious Society*, pp. 1–2

1 The siren awakes

Epigraph: Alfred Stephen to James Macarthur, c1857–58, Macarthur Papers [ML ref: A2924, vol. 28, p. 132] quoted in Sturma, *Vice in a Vicious Society*, p. 2

Colonial Secretary Correspondence File — Jane New [SRNSW ref: 4/2023 File 29/2007]
–   Description: Prisoner Jane Henrie alias Wilkinson alias New (no letter number)
–   Particulars for Jane Henrie als &c. taken from Muster for Ship *Henry* 1825 (Enclosure with no. 29/3634)
–   Copy of the Record of the Conviction of Jane Henrie alias Maria Wilkinson, convicted 27 Apl 1824 (no letter number)

Governor's Despatches — Case of John Stephen Jnr [ML ref: A1267⁻¹⁶; CY Reel 895]
–   Testimonies: John Kettle, 6 Nov 1833 pp. 354–62; Frances Lake, 6 Nov 1833, pp. 343–54; Elizabeth Baker, 31 Oct 1833, pp. 304–7

Criminal & Transportation Records
–   Indictment: Elizabeth Wilkinson, Maria Wilkinson, Josephine Townley, Epiphany 1819 [LRO ref: QJI I 1819 January Session Part 5]; Bills of Costs of Prosecution [LRO ref: QSP/2774/245]; Quarter Session Order Book [LRO ref: QSO/2/188 vol. 69]
–   Calendar of Prisoners in New Bailey Prison, Salford, Manchester on 19 Jan 1819 [LRO ref: QSB 1/1819 — January Part 4 nos 36–38]
–   Bills of Costs of Prosecution: Maria Wilkinson & Ann Ogden, Michaelmas 1820 [LRO ref: QSP/2774/206 & 245]; Quarter Session Order Book [LRO ref: QSO/2/189 vol. 70]; Indictment [LRO ref: QJI I 1820 October Session Part 3 nos 70 and 71]
–   Calendar of Prisoners in New Bailey Prison, Salford, Manchester on 23 Oct 1820 [LRO ref: QSB 1/1820 — October Session Part 4 nos 70 and 71]
–   Indictment Rolls — Elizabeth Wilkinson & Elizabeth Hotchin, Epiphany 1821 [LRO ref: QJI I 1821 January Session Part 8 and 9]
–   Bills of Costs of Prosecution: Maria Wilkinson & Ann Bates, Midsummer 1821 [LRO ref: QSP/2786/107]; Quarter Session Order Book, July Session 1821 [LRO ref: QSO/2/190 vol. 71]; Indictment [LRO ref: QJI I 1821 July Session Part 5]
–   Calendar of Prisoners in New Bailey Prison, Salford, Manchester on 22 Jly 1822 — Hannah Antrobus [LRO ref: QSB 1/1822 — Jly Session Part 3 no. 136]
–   *Grenada* 1825: Elizabeth Wilkinson [SRNSW ref: 4/4009A p. 134; Fiche 654]

Newspapers
–   *Sydney Gazette*, 14 Apl 1829 p. 3e
–   *Wheeler's Manchester Chronicle*, 30 Jan 1819 p. 4e

Miscellaneous
–   Parish Registers: Chapelry of Headingly, Yorkshire — Baptism: Maria Wilkinson 13 Oct 1805 [LDS ref: Reel 599301 Item 2]

Internet Sites
– Joseph Nadin [www.spartacus.schoolnet.co.uk/PRnadin.htm]

Publications
– Hindle, *Salford's prison*

2 Riches or ruin?
Epigraph: Bentham, *The Rationale of Punishment*, 1830, Book 5, Chapter 2 quoted in Kercher, *Perish or Prosper*, p. 528

Colonial Secretary Correspondence File — Jane New [SRNSW ref: 4/2023 File 29/2007]
– Description: Prisoner Jane Henrie alias Wilkinson alias New (no letter number)
– Particulars for Jane Henrie als &c. taken from Muster for Ship *Henry* 1825 (Enclosure with no. 29/3634)
– Copy of the Record of the Conviction of Jane Henrie alias Maria Wilkinson, convicted 27 Apr 1827 (no letter number)

Criminal & Transportation Records
– Cheshire Quarter Sessions — File: Easter 1824 — Jane Henrie [CRO ref: QJF 252/2]; Session Book [CRO ref: QJB 4/3 p. 143] & [CRO ref: QJB 5/1 p. 388]
– Indictment: Elizabeth Wilkinson, Midsummer 1823 [LRO ref: QJI 1823 Jly Sessions Parts 1–3]
– Convict Indent — *Grenada* 1825: Elizabeth Wilkinson [SRNSW ref: 4/4009A p. 134; Fiche 654]

Published volumes
– Simpson, *Chester Castle*

3 The wild ones
Epigraph: Breton, *Excursions in NSW*

Colonial Secretary Correspondence File — Jane New [SRNSW ref: 4/2023 File 29/2007]
– Description: Prisoner Jane Henrie alias Wilkinson alias New (no letter number)
– Particulars for Jane Henrie als &c. taken from Muster for Ship *Henry* 1825 (Enclosure with no. 29/3634)
– Copy of the Record of the Conviction of Jane Henrie alias Maria Wilkinson, convicted 27 Apl 1824 (no letter number)

Criminal & Transportation Records
– *Grenada* 1825: Elizabeth Wilkinson [SRNSW ref: 4/4009A p. 134; Fiche 654]
– Orders for transportation: Jane New [CRO ref: QAB 5/2/55–177; Reel 96/4]
– Transportation Register: *Grenada* & *Henry*, 1824 [TNA/ML ref: HO 11/5; ML Reel 89]

– Surgeon Superintendent's Journal: *Henry* 1824–5 [TNA/ML ref: ADM 101/33; Reel 3197]
– Musters and Papers — *Henry* 1825: Jane Henrie alias Maria Wilkinson [SRNSW ref: 2/8262 p. 167; Reel 2422]

Newspapers
– *Hobart Town Gazette*, 11 Feb 1825 p. 2a

Published volumes
– Bateson, *The Convict Ships*, pp. 346–7, 381–4
– Cunningham, *Two Years in New South Wales*, vol. II, p. 273
– *Encyclopaedia Britannica*, 1969, vol. 4, pp. 828–9 ('Cape Verde Islands')
– Guy, *Van Diemen's Land Settler*, pp. 5–6
– Prinsep, *Voyage from Calcutta to VDL*, pp. 50–1 etc.
– Robson, *The Convict Settlers of Australia*, pp. 130, 212, 277
– Sweeney, *Transported in Place of Death*, p. 42

4 A prison without bars

Epigraph: Charlotte Bronte, *Jane Eyre*

Colonial Secretary Correspondence File — Jane New [SRNSW ref: 4/2023 File 29/2007]
– Officer to Arthur, 1 Jun 1829 (no letter number)

Newspapers
– *Hobart Mercury*, 9 Jly 1879 p. 2 c.3 and 10 Jly 1879 p. 2 c.6 (Obituary of Sir Robert Officer)
– *Hobart Town Gazette* 25 Oct 1823 (Marriage of Robert Officer)

Miscellaneous
– Letter: Colonel Sorell, 1 Jun 1824 [SLTX/AO ref: CSO 1/114/2828 p. 32]
– Births: Robert Officer — 14 March 1825; & Eliza Officer — 7 May 1826 [TASBDM ref: RGD 32/1 nos 1815 & 2212; Reel 117]
– Marriage: James New & Maria Wilkinson alias Jane Henry [TASBDM ref: Rgd 32/1 — 1826 Marriages solemnised in the Parish of New Norfolk; Reel 168]

Published volumes
– *ADB*, vol. 2 (1788–1850), pp. 297–8 (Sir Robert Officer)
– Guy, *Van Diemen's Land Settler*, p. 8
– McKenzie, *Scandal in the Colonies*, p. 137
– Prinsep, *Voyage from Calcutta to VDL*, p. 52
– Robson, *The Convict Settlers of Australia*, p. 130
– Stone & Tyson, *Old Hobart Town and Environs*, pp. 72–3
– Sweeney, *Transported in Place of Death*, p. 137
– Tasmanian Pioneers Index to Births, Deaths and Marriages — Officer children

5 A match made in heaven

Epigraph: George Barrington, *The History of New South Wales*, 1801 — actually written by Henry Carter as quoted in Clune, *Rascals, Ruffians and Rebels*

Criminal & Transportation Records

- Old Bailey Session Papers 1819–21: Trial of James New, 5 May 1820 [ML ref: Year: 1820 p. 348; Reel FM4/7170]
- Newgate Calendar: James New [TNA ref: HO 77/27 Apr Session 1820 no. 172]
- Hulk Registers — *Retribution* [TNA/ML ref: 9/6 & 9/7 p. 92; Reel 4880]
- Musters and Papers — *Maria* 1820: James New [SRNSW ref: 2/8268 p. 345; Reel 2424]
- Conduct Record: James New per *Maria* 1820 [SLTX/AO ref: CON 31/29; Reel Z2552]
- Male Convicts 1818–21: Convicts per *Maria* 1820 — no. 261 James New [TNA/ML ref: HO 10/43; Reel 77]
- Tasmania: List of Male Convicts 1822–3 [TNA/ML ref: HO 10/44; Reel 77]; & 1823 [TNA/ML ref: HO 10/45; Reel 77]

Newspapers

- *Colonial Times*, 1 May 1829 p. 3b (Obituary of James Neill Snr)
- *Hobart Town Gazette*, 2 Dec 1820, p. 2a & 2b (notes that the *Maria* sailed on 10 Aug 1820, probably the date it left the Downs)
- *Sydney Gazette*, 18 Aug 1825 quoted in Crowley, *A Documentary History of Australia*, vol. I, p. 293

Miscellaneous

- Parish Registers: Church of St Peter & St Paul, Mitcham, transcribed by East Surrey Family History Society. Baptism: James New on 31 March 1800 [Fiche M48 Entry 2197]
- Tasmanian Correspondence File: Neill family [SLTX/AO ref: Neill family]

Published volumes

- Bateson, *The Convict Ships*, pp. 356–7, 383
- Black, *Black's Guide to Surrey* — Mitcham
- Branch, *The English Prison Hulks*, pp. 33, 98
- Crowley, *A Documentary History of Australia*, vol. I, p. 293
- Guy, *Van Diemen's Land Settler*, p. 16
- *HRA* III/4, p. 850 (New Norfolk area)
- Mayhew & Binny, *The Criminal Prisons of London*, pp. 607–8
- Montague, *Mitcham*, pp. 14–19
- Stone & Tyson, *Old Hobart Town and Environs*, p. 72
- Sweeney, *Transported in Place of Death*, p. 59
- Wise, *The Italian Boy*, p. 186

6 A besotted husband

Epigraph: Peter Pindar, *Epistle to Mrs Clarke* in Venetia Murray, *High Society*, p. 156

Criminal & Transportation Records

- Old Bailey Session Paper — Second session 1819: Richard Baker et al [ML ref: FM4/7169 p. 125]
- Convict Indents — *Grenada* 1819: Richard Baker [SRNSW ref: 4/4006 p. 416; Fiche 642]
- Convict Indents — *Grenada* 1825: Elizabeth Wilkinson [SRNSW ref: 4/4009A p. 134; Fiche 654]
- Justice Dowling's Notebooks — vol. 14: *Rex vs Jane New* [SRNSW ref: 2/3197 pp. 87–90]
- Justice Dowling's Notebooks — vol. 26: *Rex vs James Dooling* [SRNSW ref: 2/3209 pp. 159+]
- Certificate of freedom: Elizabeth Wilkinson [SRNSW ref: 4/4302 no. 30/0585; Reel 986]

Governor's Despatches — Case of John Stephen Jnr [ML ref: A1267[-16]; CY Reel 895]

- Testimonies: John Kettle, 6 Nov 1833, pp. 354–62; James Dow, 7 Nov 1833, pp. 375–80; James Middleton, 30 Oct 1833, pp. 263–70; Eliza James Jones, 30 Oct 1833, pp. 270–77; John Gray, 28 Nov 1833, pp. 458–62; Bernard Fitzpatrick, 6 Nov 1833, pp. 362–7
- Mrs New to Sydney Stephen, 1 Jun 1829, p. 226

Colonial Secretary Correspondence File — Jane New [SRNSW ref: 4/2023 File 29/2007]

- Petition: James New, 24 Sep 1827 (unnumbered)
- Memoranda attached to Petition: James New, 24 Sep 1827 (unnumbered)
- Memorandum: Crew/Passenger List to sail per Medway, 25 Sep 1827 (unnumbered)
- Burnett to McLeay, 26 Sep 1827 (Enclosure with no. 30/255)
- Description: Prisoner Jane Henrie alias Wilkinson alias New (unnumbered)
- Particulars for Jane Henrie als &c. taken from Muster for Ship *Henry* 1825 (Enclosure with no. 29/3634)
- Turner to Dumaresq, 22 Jan 1830 (unnumbered)

Colonial Secretary Records

- Richard Baker [SRNSW ref: 4/3501 p. 4; Reel 6007]
- Richard Baker [SRNSW ref: 2/8283 p. 113; Reel 6028]
- Petition of James New, 14 Jan 1828 [SRNSW ref: 4/1963 No.28/556]

Shipping Records

- *Albion* 18 May 1827 [SRNSW ref: 4/5198]
- *Medway* 2 Oct 1827 [SRNSW ref: 4/5198]

Newspapers

- *Hobart Town Gazette*, 12 May 1827 p. 5a
- *Sydney Monitor*, 9 Mch 1829 p. 1524 c3–4

Correspondence

- McLeay to Magistrates, 14 Mch 1826 [SRNSW ref: 4/3518] quoted in Fletcher, *Ralph Darling*, p. 125
- McLeay to Hely — 4 Oct 1827 [SRNSW ref: 4/3665 p.504; Reel 1041]

- Jane New to James New, 3 Apl 1829 in *HRA* I/15, p. 48
- Broughton to Darling, 19 Jun 1830 in *HRA* I/15, pp. 725–8

Miscellaneous
- Tasmanian Correspondence File — Jane New: Letter: S.G. Gunthorpe, Acting State Librarian to Prof. E Morris Miller
- Extract from the Minutes of the Executive Council, Minute no. 24, 23 Jun 1829 in *HRA* I/15, pp. 28–41
- University of Tasmania, 7 Mch 1951 [SLTX/AO ref: Jane New File]
- Parish Registers: St Mary's RC Registers — Marriage: Richard Baker & Elizabeth Wilkinson [ML ref: SAG Reel 0006 p.25]
- Hotels Index — Card Catalogue [SLTX/AO]
- Civil Jurisdiction: Process Book — *Morris vs New* [SRNSW ref: 5/4526 1828 Second series no. 151]. Process papers [SRNSW ref: 9/2268 no. 151]

Published volumes
- Bateson, *The Convict Ships*, pp. 346 & 358
- Baxter, *General Muster List of NSW 1823/4/5*, entry 11078
- Fletcher, *Ralph Darling*, p.125
- Karskens, *The Rocks*, pp. 38–41, 91, 222–5
- Nicholson, *Shipping Arrivals*, pp. 21, 25
- Sainty & Johnson, *Census of NSW, November 1828*, Entries B0143–4
- Smith, *A Cargo of Women*, p. 53
- Therry, *Reminiscences*, pp. 34–42

7 A criminal intent
Epigraph: Quoted in D.V. Canter & M. Ioannou's 'Criminals' Emotional Experience During Crime', in *International Journal of Forensic Psychology*, vol. 1, no. 2, September 2004, pp. 71–81

Colonial Secretary Correspondence File — Jane New [SRNSW ref: 4/2023 File 29/2007]
- Rens to McLeay, Sep 1828 (unnumbered) — translated by Susan Holberton

Governor's Despatches — Case of John Stephen Jnr [ML ref: A1267⁻¹⁶; CY Reel 895]
- Testimonies: James Middleton, 30 Oct 1833, pp. 263–79; Thomas Caines, 29 Oct 1833, pp. 255–9
- Rens to McLeay, Jan 1829 (no. 29/651) — translated by Susan Holberton

Criminal & Transportation Records
- Calendar of Prisoners in New Bailey Prison, Salford, Manchester on 22 Jly 1822 — Hannah Antrobus [LRO ref: QSB 1/1822 — Jly Session Part 3 no. 136]
- Convict Indent — *Grenada* 1827: Hannah Antrobry [SRNSW ref: 4/4012 p.1; Fiche 663].
- Justice Dowling's Notebooks — vol. 14: *Rex vs Jane New* [SRNSW ref: 2/3197 pp. 73–95]
- Persons tried before NSW Supreme Court — Case of Jane New: Information — 3 Jan 1829 [SRNSW ref: SCT 29 Box 29/6 no. 70]

Newspapers
- *Australian*, 20 Aug 1828 p.3e
- *Sydney Monitor*, 16 Aug 1828 p.1293 c2; 23 Mch 1829, p.1537 c.3

Miscellaneous
- Marriage: Hannah Antrobus & Richard Ralph [SRNSW ref: vol. 11 no. 94; Reel 5003]

Published volumes
- Bateson, *The Convict Ships*, pp. 346–7
- Sainty & Johnson, *Census of NSW, November 1828*, Entry no. R0509

II   Pretension

Epigraph: William Charles Wentworth quoted in the *Argus*, 10 Aug 1850, p. 2d

8 The Stephen ménage
Epigraph: James Stephen in *ADB*, vol. 2, pp. 474–6

Newspapers
- *Australian*, 30 Dec 1824 p.2 c.1–2

Miscellaneous
- St Kitts almanac owned by John Stephen snr's wife Mary Anne (née Pasmore) lodged with the Stephen Papers [ML ref: MSS 777/2 Pt 1]
- Letter: Elizabeth Milner (née Stephen) to Mary Stephen (née Pasmore), 27 Jly 1810 quoted in Bedford, *Think of Stephen*, p. 5
- Death Certificate: John Stephen 1854 [RBDM-VIC ref: 1854/5584]

Published volumes
- *ADB*, vol. 2, pp. 474–8 (Sir James Stephen & John Stephen Snr)
- Arrowsmith, *Charterhouse Register*, p. 355
- Bedford, *Think of Stephen*, pp. 4, 252, 256–62 (reference to 'younger children' from Sir Alfred Stephen's reminiscences)
- Chancellor & Eeles, *Celebrated Carthusians*, p.15
- *DNB*, vol. LIV, pp. 161–4 (James Stephen)
- Dyde, *St Kitts*, p. 34
- Liston, *Campbelltown*, pp. 39–40
- Mowle, *A Genealogical History*, 1978, p. 331
- Sainty & Johnson, *Census of NSW, November 1828*, Entry nos: S2395–2406 (Stephen family)
- Therry, *Reminiscences*, pp. 337–8
- Wilkins, *Great English Schools*, p. 215

9 Brothers-in-arms
Epigraph: Darling to Hay, 19 Jan 1828 in *HRA* I/13, pp. 727–9

Correspondence

- Brisbane to Bathurst, 3 Nov 1824 & 24 Oct 1825 in *HRA* I/11, pp. 407, 892 & 961 Note 235
- Hay to Darling, 26 Sep 1826 in *HRA* I/12, p. 587
- Darling to James Stephen, 16 Dec 1827 in *HRA* I/13, pp. 650–2
- Wentworth to Darling, 19 Dec 1827 in *HRA* I/13, pp. 729–30
- Francis Stephen to Colonel Lindsay, 29 Dec 1827 in *HRA* I/13, p. 729
- Darling to Forbes, 1 Jan 1828; Forbes to Darling, 5 Jan 1828 in *HRA* I/13, pp. 732–3
- Darling to Hay, 19 Jan 1828 in *HRA* I/13, pp. 727–9
- Murray to Darling, 30 Aug 1828 in *HRA* I/14, p. 363
- Francis Stephen to Forbes 3 Feb 1829 in *HRA* I/14, p. 667
- Forbes to Darling, 10 Feb 1829 in *HRA* I/14, p.665
- John Stephen Jnr to Officer, 5 May 1829 in *HRA* I/15, pp. 33–4
- Arthur to Montagu & Stephen, 30 Apr 1829 in *HRA* III/8, pp. 399–403
- Sydney Stephen to McLeay, 26 Feb 1831 in *HRA* I/16, p.253–4
- Darling to Goderich, 20 Jly 1831 [ML ref: A1209 pp. 473–4; Reel CY 542]

Newspapers

- *Argus*, 10 Aug 1850 p. 2d (The Stephen Deluge)
- *Hobart Town Gazette*, 4 Aug 1827 p. 5
- *Sydney Gazette*, 3 Aug 1827 p. 2b

Miscellaneous

- Petition of Francis Stephen, December 1828 [SRNSW ref: 9/5190 Francis Stephen]
- Dowling's Select Cases, vol. 2 — In re Francis Stephen [SRNSW ref: 2/3462 pp. 119+]
- Lincoln's Inn Records [Society of Genealogists, London]
- Colonial Secretary — Returns of the Colony 1828: Sydney Stephen [SRNSW ref: 2/867 p. 84]

Internet Sites

In re Stephen (1829) NSWSC 2 (1 January 1829) [www.austlii.edu.au/special/NSWSupC/1829/2.html]

- *An Encyclopaedia of New Zealand*, 1966 [www.teara.govt.nz/1966/S/StephenSidney/en.htm]

Published volumes

- *ADB*, vol. 1 pp. 282–6 (Ralph Darling); vol. 2, p. 476 (John Stephen); & vol. 6, pp. 180–7 (Sir Alfred Stephen)
- Bedford, *Think of Stephen*
- Currey, *Sir Francis Forbes*, p. 313
- Fletcher, *Ralph Darling*, p. 263
- Nicholson, *Shipping Arrivals 1826 to 1840*, p. 28
- Sainty & Johnson, *Census of New South Wales, November 1828*, Entries S2395–S2400
- Scholefield, *A Dictionary of New Zealand Biography*, p. 328 (Sidney Stephen)

10 The black sheep

Epigraph: Darling to Hay, 10 Jan 1828 in *HRA* I/13, p. 693

Correspondence
- Darling to Goderich, 26 Oct 1827 in *HRA* I/13, p. 563
- Darling to Hay, 10 Jan 1828 in *HRA* I/13, p. 693
- Darling to Forbes, 14 Feb 1828 in *HRA* I/13, p. 805
- Forbes to Darling, 15 Feb 1828 in *HRA* I/13, pp. 806, 811
- Darling to Hay, 15 Feb 1828 in *HRA* I/13, p. 784
- Darling to Hay, 16 Feb 1828 in *HRA* I/13, pp. 787–8
- Forbes to Huskisson, 16 & 26 Feb 1828 in *HRA* I/13, pp. 817–21 (includes Darling's remarks)
- Darling to Forbes, 18 Feb 1828 in *HRA* I/13, p. 808
- Forbes to Huskisson, 26 Feb 1828 in *HRA* I/13, pp. 828–9 (includes Darling's remarks)
- J. Stephen Jnr to Murray, 15 Jun 1830 in *HRA* I/15, pp. 697–8
- Darling to Goderich, 27 Apr 1831 in *HRA* I/16, pp. 247–8

Newspapers
- *The Times*, 30 Jan 1821 p. 3 (Marriage John Stephen & Mary Matthews Hamilton)
- *Gentleman's Magazine*, 1821, p. 181 (ibid.)
- *Hobart Town Gazette*, 24 Feb 1827, p. 2a & 31 Mch 1827 p. 4
- *Port Phillip Patriot*, 2 Feb 1843 p. 2 (Quo Warranto Case)

Miscellaneous
- Earl of Courtown to Home Office, 19 Jan 1823 & 29 May 1824 [TNA ref: HO 44/13 no. 5; and HO 44/14 no. 72]
- Privy Council Registration Book 1824–5: *Stephen vs Poingdestre* [TNA ref: PC 2/206 p. 276]
- Privy Council Minute Book: *Stephen vs Poingdestre* [TNA ref: PC 4/17 pp. 43, 71, 206, 218, 222, 229]
- *Poigndestre vs Stephen* in the Royal Court of the Island of Jersey, 25 Oct 1824 and 4 Dec 1824 [JSY ref: D/7/F1/154 pp. 221–2 & 317–8]
- Will: Josiah Tattnall 1813 [TNA ref: PROB 11/1545]
- Will: John Hamilton 1817 [TNA ref: PROB 11/1588]
- Registers of St Pancras Old Church, London: Marriage: Stephen & Hamilton, 27 Jan 1821 [LMA ref: X030/027 No.566]; & Baptisms: Hamilton Farish Stephen, 5 Nov 1822 & Percival Sydney Francis Stephen, 17 Dec 1823
- Vicar-General Marriage Licence Allegations: Stephen & Hamilton, 1821 [Society of Genealogists, London]
- Shipping Arrivals: *Admiral Cockburn* 2 Apr 1827 [SRNSW ref: 4/5198]
- Returns of the Colony 1828: John Stephen [SRNSW ref: 2/867 p. 76]
- NSW Governor's Despatches — Memorandum: On the case of Mr John Stephen Jnr from General Darling, 31 Jly 1831 [ML ref: A2146 pp. 140–2; Reel CY 1011]
- Autobiographical information: John Stephen Jnr, 3 Aug 1832 [TNA/ML ref: CO 201/230 f.416–27; Reel 188]. Includes General Ralph Darling's appended remarks.

– Memorial: John Stephen Jnr, March 1832 [ML ref: A2146 pp. 334–8; Reel CY 1011]
– The King on the prosecution of John Stephen Jnr Esq against Lieutenant-General Darling: Brief Affidavits on Motion for Criminal Information [TNA/ML ref: CO201/230 f.451–61; Reel 188]

Internet sites
– Honourable Corps of Gentlemen at Arms in *Wikipedia* [www.en.wikipedia.org/wiki/Honourable_Corps_of_Gentlemen-at-Arms]
– Silver Stick in *Wikipedia* [www.en.wikipedia.org/wiki/Silver_Stick]
– Military Establishment: Gentlemen Pensioners (Gentlemen at Arms) 1660–1837, p. 4 [www.luc.edu/depts/history/bucholz/DCO/Database-Files/Chamber7.list.pdf]

Published volumes
– *American National Biography*, vol. 9, pp. 922–3
– Bedford, *Think of Stephen*, pp. 252, 278
– Blanco, *The American Revolution*, vol. 1, p. 730
– Currey, *The First Three Chief Justices of the Supreme Court of NSW*, p. 7
– Currey, *Sir Francis Forbes*, pp. 320, 322
– *Dictionary of National Biography*, vol. 22, pp. 378–80 (Charles Grant); vol. 54, pp. 163–4 (James Stephen)
– Powell, *Dictionary of North Carolina Biography*, vol. 3, pp. 16–17
– Purcell, *Who was Who in the American Revolution*, p. 210
– Sainty & Johnson, *Census of New South Wales, November 1828*, Entry S2401
– Thiselton, *Regia Insignia*, pp. 225, 253–61

11 An unwilling adversary

Epigraph: William Shakespeare, *Julius Caesar*

Governor's Despatches — Case of John Stephen Jnr [ML ref: A1267⁻¹⁶; CY Reel 895]
– Testimony of John Raine, 5 Nov 1833, pp. 331–42

Correspondence
– Forbes to Wilmot-Horton quoted in Fletcher, *Ralph Darling*, p. 74
– Bathurst to Horton, 6 Jan 1825 quoted in Fletcher, *Ralph Darling*, p. 74

Published volumes
– *ADB*, vol. 1, pp. 282–6 (Ralph Darling); vol. 2, p. 586 (W.C. Wentworth)
– Berry, *By Royal Appointment*
– Currey, *Sir Francis Forbes*, p. 172
– Fletcher, *Ralph Darling*
– Forbes, *Sydney Society in Crown Colony Days*, p.66
– Hogue, *Governor Darling, the Press and the Collar* in *JRAHS*, vol. 2, p. 309
– Walker, *The Newspaper Press in NSW*, pp. 8–10

III   Infatuation

Epigraph: *HRA* III/8, p. 900, note 409

12 A masterful manipulator
Epigraph: Quoted in Thomas Swan, *The Da Vinci Deception*, Newmarket, New York, 1998

Colonial Secretary Correspondence File — Jane New [SRNSW ref: 4/2023 File 29/2007]
- Rens to Morison [Morisset], 16 Aug 1828 (unnumbered)
- Rens to McLeay, Sep 1828 (unnumbered) — translated by Susan Holberton
- Morrisset to McLeay, 6 Sep 1828 (no. 28/7074)
- Baxter to McLeay, 9 Sep 1828 (no. 28/7201)
- McLeay to Hely, 22 Sep 1828 (no. 28/50)
- Memorandum, unsigned, undated &c. (unnumbered)
- Rens to McLeay, Jan 1829 (no. 29/651) — translated by Susan Holberton
- Baxter to McLeay, 13 Jan 1829 (no. 29/361)
- Morisset to McLeay, 13 Jan 1829 (no. 29/435)
- Morisset to McLeay, 13 Jan 1829 (no. 29/582)

Correspondence
- McLeay to Baxter, 10 Jan 1829 [SRNSW ref: 4/3737 p. 106 no. 29/5; Reel 624]
- McLeay to Hely, 10 Jan 1829 [SRNSW ref: 4/3827 p. 89 no. 29/1; Reel 2807]
- John Stephen Jnr to Officer, 5 May 1829 in *HRA* I/15, pp. 33–4
- Darling to Murray, 29 Jun 1829 in *HRA* I/15, pp. 28–33

Newspapers
- *The Tasmanian*, 12 Sep 1828 p. 2a

Miscellaneous
- Bench of Magistrates — Jane New 23 Aug 1828 [SRNSW ref: X821 p.59 no. 6; Reel 660]
- Sydney Gaol — Entrance Books 1825–28 [SRNSW ref: 4/6430 1828 Aug 23 — Jane New]
- Justice Dowling's Notebooks — vol. 14: *Rex vs Jane New* [SRNSW ref: 2/3197 pp. 73–95]
- Shipping Arrivals: *Sydney Packet* — 21 Sep 1828 [SRNSW ref: 4/5199] and [SRNSW ref: 4/4823]
- Persons tried before the Supreme Court — Case of Jane New: Subpoena — Dec 1828; Information, 3 Jan 1829 [SRNSW ref: SCT29 Box 29/6 no. 70]
- Memorandum: John Stephen Jnr, 3 Jan 1829 [SLTX/AO ref: CSO 1/185/4448, pp. 335–6; Reel Z1795]
- Cutting from *The Sun*, 5 Mar 1912, in Newspaper Cuttings, vol. 25 [ML ref: Q991/N pp. 147–8]

Published volumes
- *ADB*, vol. 1, pp. 74–5 (Alexander MacDuff Baxter) & vol. 2, pp. 260–61 (James Thomas Morisset)

–   Crowley, *A Documentary History of Australia* Vol I, pp. 375–6

13 The trial
Epigraph: A Norfolk Island convict quoted in Therry, *Reminiscences*, p. 43

Colonial Secretary Correspondence File — Jane New [SRNSW ref: 4/2023 File 29/2007]
–   Petition: Jane New, 7 Jan 1829 (unnumbered)
–   Baxter to McLeay, 13 Jan 1829 (no. 29/361)

Correspondence
–   Darling to Hay, 10 Jan 1828 *HRA* I/13, p.693
–   Sidney Stephen to Dowling, 14 Jan 1829 [SRNSW ref: 2/3470 pp. 193–5]
–   Sidney Stephen to Dowling, 3 Feb 1829 [SRNSW ref: 2/3470 pp. 196–205]
–   John Stephen Jnr to Officer, 5 May 1829 in *HRA* I/15, pp. 33–4

Miscellaneous
–   Justice Dowling's Notebooks — vol. 14: *Rex vs Jane New* [SRNSW ref: 2/3197 pp. 73–95]
–   Persons tried before Supreme Court in NSW — Case of Jane New: Subpoena — Dec 1828 [SRNSW ref: SCT29 Box 29/6 no. 70]
–   Affidavit of William Henry Kerr, 10 Jan 1829 [SLTX/AO ref: CSO 1/185/4448, p. 307; Reel Z1795]

Published volumes
–   Bennett, *A History of Solicitors in NSW*, pp. 33–6
–   Karskens, *The Rocks*, p.47
–   Sainty & Johnson, *Census of NSW, November 1828*, Francis Girard — Entry no. G0505

14 Guilty or innocent?
Epigraph: John Stephen Jnr to Officer, 5 May 1829 in *HRA* I/15, pp. 33–4

Colonial Secretary Correspondence File — Jane New [SRNSW ref: 4/2023 File 29/2007]
–   Sidney Stephen to McLeay, 26 Feb 1831 (unnumbered)

Petition to Governor Arthur re Jane New [SLTX/AO ref: CSO 1/185/4448; Reel Z1795]
–   Affidavits Emma Thompkins, [?] Jan 1829 & 12 Jan 1829, pp. 310–11 and 312–13; William Henry Kerr, 10 Jan 1829, p. 307; John Serocold Jackson, 10 Jan 1829, p. 309; John Stephen Jnr, 7 Jan 1829, pp. 324–6 and 9 Jan 1829, p. 308; George Bunn, [?] Jan 1829, p. 314; Henry James, 9 Jan 1829, p. 315; James New, 9 Jan 1829, p. 316; 17 Jan 1829 (and attached Subpoena to Kelly, 23 Sep 1828, pp. 321–3); Ellen Gravestocks, 9 Jan 1829, p. 317; Maria Mackay, 9 Jan 1829, p. 318; Maria Ryley, 9 Jan 1829, p. 319; Thomas Macvitie, 10 Jan 1829, p. 320

Correspondence
- Hely to McLeay, 3 Nov 1827 [SRNSW ref: 4/1953 no. 27/10341]
- Sidney Stephen to Dowling, 14 Jan 1829 [SRNSW ref: 2/3470 pp. 193–5]
- Sidney Stephen to Dowling, 3 Feb 1829 [SRNSW ref: 2/3470 pp. 196–205]
- John Stephen Jnr to James New, 15 Apl 1829, pp. 333–4
- John Stephen Jnr to Officer, 5 May 1829 in *HRA* I/15, pp. 33–4

Newspapers
- *Australian*, 8 Aug 1827 p.3 c.2; 24 Oct 1828 p. 3 c.4
- *Sydney Gazette*, 24 Oct 1828 p. 2 c. d-e

Miscellaneous
- Justice Dowling's Notebooks — vol. 14: *Rex vs Jane New* [SRNSW ref: 2/3197 pp. 73–96]

15 The value of a life
Epigraph: Adapted from Bennett, *Lives of the Australian Justices: Sir James Dowling*, p. 49

Colonial Secretary Correspondence File — Jane New [SRNSW ref: 4/2023 File 29/2007]
- Petition: Jane New, 7 Jan 1829 (unnumbered)
- Baxter to McLeay, 13 Jan 1829 (no. 29/361)
- Dowling to McLeay, 24 Dec 1830 (unnumbered)

Governor's Despatches — Case of John Stephen Jnr [ML ref: A1267⁻¹⁶; CY Reel 895]
- Extract from Minute no. 25, 29 Oct 1833, pp. 89–91

Correspondence
- McLeay to Hely, 10 Jan 1829 [SRNSW ref: 4/3827 p. 89 no. 29/1; Reel 2807]
- McLeay to Baxter, 10 Jan 1829 [SRNSW ref: 4/3737 p. 106 no. 29/5; Reel 624]
- Dowling to John Stephen Jnr, 13 Jan 1829 in HRA I/15, pp. 689–90
- John Stephen Jnr to Officer, 5 May 1829 in *HRA* I/15, pp. 33–4

Newspapers
- *Sydney Gazette*, 8 Jan 1829 p.2e
- *Australian*, 9 Jan 1829 p.3a
- *Sydney Monitor*, 12 Jan 1829 p.1461 c.1

Miscellaneous
- Judgement in *The King vs Jane New* [SRNSW ref: 2/3470 p. 186]
- Prisoners tried before the Supreme Court, Jan 1829 [ML ref: A1206 p. 545; Reel CY 539]
- Persons tried before Supreme Court — Case of Jane New: Information — 3 Jan 1829; Statement by Jane New, 6 Jan 1829 [SRNSW ref: SCT 29 Box 29/6 no. 70]
- Memorandum: John Stephen Jnr, 3 Jan 1829 [SLTX/AO ref: CSO 1/185/4448, pp. 335–6; Reel Z1795]

Published volumes
- *ADB*, vol I, p.317
- Bennett, *Lives of the Australian Justices: Sir James Dowling*, pp. 41, 49–50
- Kercher, *Perish or Prosper*, p.528

16 A second opinion
Epigraph: Darling to Huskisson, 1 Mch 1828, quoted in Fletcher, *Ralph Darling*, p. 261

Colonial Secretary Correspondence File — Jane New [SRNSW ref: 4/2023 File 29/2007]
- Dumaresq to McLeay, 21 Feb 1829 (no. 29/1430)
- McLeay to Female Factory Committee, 25 Feb 1829 (no. 29/83)
- Memorandum, unsigned, undated &c. (unnumbered)
- Sidney Stephen to McLeay, 26 Feb 1831 (unnumbered)

Governor's Despatches — Case of John Stephen Jnr [ML ref: A1267[-16]; CY Reel 895]
- Matron Gordon's extracts in reference to Jane New per *Henry*, p. 330
- Statement of Jane New, 21 Mch 1829, pp. 57–8

Correspondence
- Darling to Bathurst, 17 Mch 1827 in *HRA* I/12, pp. 166–8 quoted in Fletcher, *Ralph Darling*, p. 106
- Forbes to Wilmot Horton, 7 Mch 1828 in Catton Papers, vol. 52, Derbyshire Public Library, England, quoted in Fletcher, *Ralph Darling*, p. 83
- Sidney Stephen to Dowling, 14 Jan 1829 [SRNSW ref: 2/3470 pp. 193–5]
- Dowling to John Stephen Jnr, 15 Jan 1829 [SRNSW ref: 2/3470 p. 196]
- Sidney Stephen to Dowling, 3 Feb 1829 [SRNSW ref: 2/3470 pp. 196–205]
- Dowling to Forbes, 4 Feb 1829 [SRNSW ref: 2/3470 p. 205]
- Dowling to Darling, 4 Feb 1829 [SRNSW ref: 2/3470 p. 205]
- Forbes to Darling, 7 Feb 1829 [SRNSW ref: 4/1516 pp. 91–3; Reel 2436]
- Darling to Dowling, 11 Feb 1829 [SRNSW ref: 2/3470 p. 209]
- McLeay to Macquoid, 19 Feb 1829 [SRNSW ref: 4/3896 p. 85 no. 29/26; Reel 1062]
- Darling to Murray, 20 May 1829 in *HRA* I/14, pp. 762–3

Newspapers
- *Australian*, 6 Feb 1829 p. 2e
- *Monitor*, 30 Mch 1827
- *Sydney Gazette*, 24 Feb 1829 p. 2e; 26 Feb 1829 p. 2e; 12 Mch 1829 p. 3e

Miscellaneous
- Minutes of the Executive Council — 8 Jan 1829 [SRNSW ref: 4/1516 p. 84; Reel 2436]
- Minutes of the Executive Council — 7 Feb 1829 [SRNSW ref: 4/1516 pp. 91–2; Reel 2436]
- Justice Dowling's Notebook — vol. 14: *Rex vs Jane New* [SRNSW ref: 2/3197 pp. 73–96]

- Justice Dowling's Notebook — vol. 14 [SRNSW ref: 2/3197 p. 112]
- Chief Justice's Letterbook 1824–35 [SRNSW ref: 4/6651 pp. 209–10]
- 'Missing' NSW Governor's Despatches [ML ref: A1267⁻ᴵᴵ p. 610; Reel CY 902 (Pt2)]
- Case of Jane New: Affidavit of James New — 7 Mch 1829 & Statement of Ann Gordon, probably dated 14 Mch 1829 [SRNSW ref: SCT 29 Box 29/6 no. 70]
- Sydney Gaol — Entrance Book 1829–31 [SRNSW ref: 4/6431 1829 Jan 06 — Jane New]

Published volumes
- *ADB*, vol. I, pp. 317–20 (Sir James Dowling)
- Burn, *The Bushrangers*
- Cumes, *Their Chastity was not too Rigid*, pp. 93, 94
- Currey, *Sir Francis Forbes*, pp. 292–3, 314
- Fletcher, *Ralph Darling*, pp. 106, 115–8, 261
- Forbes, *Sydney Society in Crown Colony Days*, pp. 126–7
- Harris *Settlers & Convicts* quoted in Fletcher, *Ralph Darling*, p. 115
- *HRA* I/14, pp. 763–4, p. 943 note 218; *HRA* I/15, pp. 687–8 (Affidavit of Jane New, 21 Mch 1829); *HRA* III/8, p. 900 note 409
- O'Brien, *The Foundation of Australia*, Chapter 2
- Salt, *These Outcast Women*, pp. 43–4, 52, 69–70, 72–4, 76–8, 85, 99, 104–5
- Shaw, *Convicts and the Colonies*, pp. 131–2
- Smith, *A Cargo of Women*, pp. 53, 55
- Sweeney, *Transported in Place of Death*, p.138.

17 An illegal imprisonment

Epigraph: Chief Justice Forbes in Ex parte Jane New, 21 March 1829 in *HRA* I/14, pp. 765–71

Colonial Secretary Correspondence File — Jane New [SRNSW ref: 4/2023 File 29/2007]
- Forbes to Gordon, 9 Mch 1829 (Enclosure with no. 29/2007)
- Gordon to McLeay, 13 Mch 1829 (no. 29/2007)
- Innes to McLeay, 16 Mch 1829 (no. 29/2089); & 18 Mch 1829 (no. 29/2182)

Correspondence
- McLeay to Innes, 17 Mch 1829 [SRNSW ref: 4/3827 p.191 no. 29/140; Reel 2807]
- Sidney Stephen to McLeay, 26 Feb 1831 [SRNSW ref: 4/2023 File 29/2007 (unnumbered)]

Newspapers
- *Australian*, 10 Mch 1829 p. 2b-c
- *Sydney Gazette*, 10 Mch 1829 p. 2f; 28 Mch 1829 p. 3c
- *Sydney Monitor*, 9 Mch 1829 p. 1524 c3–4

Miscellaneous
- Case of Jane New: Affidavit of James New, 2 March 1829, filed 7 Mch 1829 [SRNSW ref: SCT 29 Box 29/6 no. 70]

- Dowling's Select Cases, vol. 2: In re Jane New, 6 March 1829 [SRNSW ref: 2/3462 pp. 145–50]
- Chief Justice Forbes in Ex parte Jane New, 21 March 1829 in *HRA* I/14, pp. 765–71

Published volumes
- *ADB*, vol. 2 (1788–1850), p. 585 (William Charles Wentworth)
- Kercher, *Perish or Prosper*, p. 573

18 The *habeas corpus* hearing
Epigraph: *Australian*, 20 Mch 1829 p. 2c-d

Correspondence
- McLeay to Macquoid, 19 Feb 1829 [SRNSW ref: 4/3896 p.85 no. 29/26; Reel 1062]
- McLeay to Hely, 16 Mch 1829 [SRNSW ref: 4/2023 File 29/2007 no. 29/183]

Newspapers
- *Australian*, 20 March 1829
- *Sydney Gazette*, 26 Mch 1829, 17, 19, 21, 24

Miscellaneous
- In re Jane New (1829) [http://www.law.mq.edu.au/scnsw/Cases1829–30/html/in_re_jane_new_1829.html]
- Justice Dowling's Notebook no. 15: In re Jane New [SRNSW ref: 2/3198 pp. 93+]
- Case of Jane New: Affidavits of James New & Alexander McLeay — 18 Mch 1829 [SRNSW ref: SCT 29 Box 29/6 no. 70]

Published volumes
- Bennett, *Sir James Dowling*, p. 26 (Murray to Darling, 31 Jly 1828)
- Currey, *Sir Francis Forbes*, p. 244–50 & 254 (*Australian* 3 August 1827)
- *HRA* I/15 pp. 670–1; III/8 p. 900 note 409
- Kercher, *Perish or Prosper*

19 The Decision
Epigraph: *Sydney Gazette*, 26 March 1829

Correspondence
- Murray to Darling, 31 Jly 1828 quoted in Bennett, *Sir James Dowling*, p. 26
- Darling to Supreme Court Judges, 4 Apl 1829 in *HRA* I/14, pp. 764–5
- Darling to Murray, 20 May 1829 in *HRA* I/14, pp. 762–3
- Arthur to Twiss, 2 Jun 1829 in *HRA* III/8, pp. 393–7
- Montagu and Stephen to Arthur, 4 Aug 1829 in *HRA* III/8, pp. 486–9
- Alfred Stephen to Arthur, 15 Aug 1829 in *HRA* III/8, p. 496
- Murray to Darling, 30 Jan 1830 in *HRA* I/15, pp.346–8

Miscellaneous
– *Rex v Wardell* (no. 3) p. 2 [www.law.mq.edu.au/scnsw/Cases1827–28/html/r_v_wardell _no_3_1827.htm]
– Mr Twiss' Paper in *HRA* I/15, pp. 348–53

Newspapers
– *Sydney Gazette*, 24 Mch 1829 p. 2a; 26 Mch 1829 p. 2; 28 Mch 1829 p. 2
– *Sydney Monitor*, 23 Mch 1829 p. 1537 c.3–4; 31 Mch 1829 p. 1545 c.2
– *Australian*, 24 Mch 1829 p. 2c; 27 Mch 1829 p. 2a; 25 May 1827

Published volumes
– *ADB*, vol. I pp. 500–1 (Edward Smith Hall)
– Bennett, *Sir James Dowling*, pp. 26, 32–4, 37
– Currey, *Sir Francis Forbes*, pp. 208–9, 343, 345
– Currey, *The First Three Chief Justices of NSW*, pp. 7–8
– Forbes, *Sydney Society in Crown Colony Days*, vol. I, pp. 80–3
– Kercher, *Perish or Prosper*, pp. 572 & 578–9
– Walker, *The Newspaper Press*, pp. 3–8, 12–13, 15, 16ff

IV   Gratification

Epigraph: Darling to Murray, 29 Jun 1829 in *HRA* I/15, p. 30

20 A confounded constable

Epigraph: *Australian*, 24 Mch 1829, p. 3d

Colonial Secretary Correspondence File — Jane New [SRNSW ref: 4/2023 File 29/2007]
– John Stephen Jnr to McLeay, 21 Mch 1829 (no. 29/2242)
– Macquoid to McLeay, 28 Mch 1829 (no. 29/2790)

Governor's Despatches — Case of John Stephen Jnr [ML ref: A1267⁻¹⁶; CY Reel 895]
– Statement of James New, 14 Apl 1829, p. 206
– Prout to John Stephen Jnr, 29 May 1833 & Statement of Constables, &c, pp. 176–8
– Testimonies: Ann Gordon, 5 Nov 1833, pp. 323–9; Sidney Stephen, 1 Nov 1833, pp. 316–22
– Copy of Charges preferred by Lt-General Darling agst John Stephen Jnr Esq, with added remarks by John Stephen Jnr, pp. 14–27

Correspondence
– Dowling to Darling, 4 Feb 1829 [SRNSW ref: 2/3470 p. 205]
– McLeay to Macquoid, 28 Mch 1829 [SRNSW ref: 4/3896 p. 108 no. 29/67; Reel 1062]
– Macquoid to McLeay, 28 Mch 1829 in *HRA* I/15, p. 43
– John Stephen Jnr to Officer, 5 May 1829 in *HRA* I/15, pp. 33–4
– Darling to Murray, 29 Jun 1829 in *HRA* I/15, pp. 28–33

Newspapers
- *Australian*, 24 Mch 1829 p. 3d; 31 Mch 1829 p. 3b; 8 Apl 1829
- *Sydney Gazette*, 24 Mch 1829 p. 2d; 31 Mch 1829 p. 2d

Miscellaneous
- Statements: J. Kelly, S. Cleme & Under-Sheriff Prout, 28 Mch 1829 in *HRA* I/15, pp. 44–5
- Minutes of Proceedings of the Committee for the management of the Female Factory, 6 Apl 1829 in *HRA* I/15, p. 47
- Affidavit by J. Stephen Jnr, 9 Apl 1829 in *HRA* I/15, p. 48
- Investigation: Gifts offered to Factory Matrons, Apl 1830 [SRNSW ref: 4/2071 File 30/2968]
- Reply of John Stephen Jnr to charges preferred by General Darling, 17 May 1830 in *HRA* I/15, pp. 679–85

21 Accusations unleashed

Epigraph: *Governor Darling's Refutation of the charges of cruelty and oppression of the soldiers Sudds and Thompson at Sydney NSW, Nov 26th 1826, by 'Miles'* [ML ref: DSM 991/D p. 9]

Colonial Secretary Correspondence File — Jane New [SRNSW ref: 4/2023 File 29/2007]
- Sampson to McLeay, 21 Mch 1829 (unnumbered)
- Macquoid to McLeay, 21 Mch 1829 (unnumbered)
- Macquoid to John Stephen Jnr, 21 Mch 1829 (unnumbered)
- John Stephen Jnr to Macquoid, 21 Mch 1829 (unnumbered)
- John Stephen Jnr to McLeay, 26 Mch 1829 (unnumbered)

Governor's Despatches — Case of John Stephen Jnr [ML ref: A1267^{-16}; CY Reel 895]
- Statement of James New, 14 Apl 1829, pp. 206–7

Correspondence
- McLeay to Macquoid, 27 Mch 1829 [SRNSW ref: 4/3896 p.107 no. 29/64; Reel 1062]
- Macquoid to McLeay, 28 Mch 1829 in *HRA* I/15, p. 43
- John Stephen Jnr to Dr Anderson, 13 Apl 1829 in *HRA* I/15, pp. 695–6
- Dr Anderson to John Stephen Jnr, 17 Apl 1829 in *HRA* I/15, p. 696
- John Stephen Jnr to Under-Secretary Hay, 7 Jun 1830 in *HRA* I/15, p. 695

Miscellaneous
- Statements: J. Kelly & S. Cleme, 28 Mch 1829 in *HRA* I/15, p.44
- Minutes of Proceedings of the Committee for the Management of the Female Factory, 6 Apl 1829 in *HRA* I/15, p.47
- Registers of Baptisms, Marriages & Burials — Burial: William Balcombe [SRNSW ref: vol. 11 no. 1094; Reel 5003]
- Affidavit by John Stephen Jnr, 9 Apl 1829 in *HRA* I/15, p. 48
- Executive Council: Minute No. 24, 23 Jun 1829 in *HRA* I/15 pp. 39–40
- Reply of John Stephen Jnr to charges preferred by General Darling, 17 May 1830 in *HRA* I/15, pp. 679–85

Published volumes
– Currey, *Sir Francis Forbes*, pp. 320–3
– Fletcher, *Ralph Darling*, p. 56

22 Manipulations and machinations
Epigraph: Darling to Murray, 29 Jun 1829 in *HRA* I/15, pp. 28–33

Colonial Secretary Correspondence File — Jane New [SRNSW ref: 4/2023 File 29/2007]
– Petition: James New, 24 Sep 1827 (unnumbered)

Governor's Despatches — Case of John Stephen Jnr [ML ref: A1267⁻¹⁶; CY Reel 895]
– Statement by Sidney Stephen, 8 Aug 1833, p. 227
– Extract from Minute No. 15, 7 Jun 1834, pp. 105–43

Correspondence
– Burnett to McLeay, 26 Sep 1827 [SRNSW ref: SCT 29 Box 29/6 no. 70]
– Forbes to Darling, 24 Jun 1829 in *HRA* I/15, p. 35

Miscellaneous
– Remarks by Governor Darling on Mr John Stephen's Answer to the Five Charges which he deduces from the Proceedings of Council in *HRA* I/16 pp. 249–53
– Affidavits: Jane New, 21 Mch 1829; James Horton, William Bell Carlyle & James New, 26 Mch 1829; Frederick Finlay, 29 Jun 1829 in *HRA* I/15, pp. 687–9
– Affidavit: James New, 28 Mch 1829; unsigned, undated petition to the Supreme Court judges [SLTX/AO ref: CSO 1/185/4448, pp. 329, 327–8; Reel Z1795]

23 A whirlpool of intrigue
Epigraph: Remarks by John Stephen Jnr, undated [ML ref: A1267⁻¹⁶ pp. 218–19; CY Reel 895]

Colonial Secretary Correspondence File — Jane New [SRNSW ref: 4/2023 File 29/2007]
– McLeay to John Stephen Jnr, 4 Apr 1829 (Enclosure with no. 29/2857)
– John Stephen Jnr to McLeay, 10 Apr 1829 (no. 29/2857)
– William Carter to McLeay, 16 Apr 1829 (Enclosure with no. 29/2857]

Governor's Despatches — Case of John Stephen Jnr [ML ref: A1267⁻¹⁶; CY Reel 895]
– Remarks by John Stephen Jnr, undated, pp. 218–19

Correspondence
– Murray to Darling, 14 Dec 1829 in *HRA* I/15, pp. 282–3
– Darling to Murray, 10 Jun 1830 in *HRA* I/15, p. 549
– Darling to Murray, 18 Aug 1830 in *HRA* I/15, pp. 712–13
– Darling to Goderich, 27 Apr 1831 in *HRA* I/16, pp. 247–8

24 Desperation
Epigraph: Dickinson, Emily, 'I never hear the word "Escape"'

Colonial Secretary Correspondence File — Jane New [SRNSW ref: 4/2023 File 29/2007]
– Statements: James Pegg & Robert Gordon 8 Apr 1829 (Enclosures with no. 29/2812)
– Hearing: Richard Baker, 8 Apr 1829 (Enclosure with no. 29/2812)
– Innes to McLeay, 8 Apr 1829 (no. 29/2812)
– 'In the matter of Richard Baker & James New,' Attorney-General's Office, 11 Apr 1829 (no. 29/2877)
– Memorandum: Correspondence in Case of Jane New between 8 Sep 1828 & 25 Jun 1829 (unnumbered)

Governor's Despatches — Case of John Stephen Jnr [ML ref: A1267-16; CY Reel 895]
– Testimonies: James Middleton, 30 Oct 1833, pp. 263–70; Ann Gordon, 5 Nov 1833, p. 325

Correspondence
– Jane New to James New, 3 Apr 1829 in *HRA* I/15, p. 48
– McLeay to Baxter, 10 Apr 1829 [SRNSW ref: 4/3737 p. 170 no. 29/38; Reel 624]

Newspapers
– *Sydney Gazette*, 9 Apr 1829 pp. 2d; 14, 21 & 28 Apr 1829 (notices of abscondment)

Miscellaneous
– Minutes of Proceedings of the Committee for the Management of the Female Factory, 6 Apl 1829 in *HRA* I/15, pp. 45–8
– Investigation: Gifts offered to Factory Matrons, Apr 1830 [SRNSW ref: 4/2071 File 30/2968]

Published volumes
– Salt, *These Outcast Women*, pp. 59, 86

25 A temporary haven
Epigraph: *Sydney Gazette*, 14 Apl 1829, p.3e

Colonial Secretary Correspondence File — Jane New [SRNSW ref: 4/2023 File 29/2007]
– Petition: James New to Governor Arthur, Apr-May 1829 (unnumbered)
– Officer to Arthur, 1 Jun 1829 (unnumbered)]
– Burnett to Officer, 5 Jun 1829 (unnumbered)
– Arthur to Darling, 20 Jun 1829 (unnumbered)

Governor's Despatches — Case of John Stephen Jnr [ML ref: A1267-16; CY Reel 895]
– Testimonies: James Middleton, 30 Oct 1833, pp. 263–70; Eliza James Jones, 30 Oct 1833, pp. 270–7; Thomas Caines, 29 Oct 1833, pp. 255–9
– Statement of John Jobbins, 5 Aug 1833, pp. 222–3
– Documents, statements & testimonies, pp. 220–511

Correspondence
- John Stephen Jnr to Officer, 5 May 1829 in *HRA* I/15, pp. 33–4
- Darling to Murray, 29 Jun 1829 in *HRA* I/15, pp. 28–33
- Affidavit of Robert Officer, 4 May 1833 [SLTX/AO ref: CSO 1/185/4448 pp. 341–2; Reel Z1795]

Newspapers
- *Sydney Gazette*, 14 Apl 1829 p. 3e
- *Tasmanian & Asiatic Review*, 24 Apr 1829 p. 115c

Miscellaneous
- Justice Dowling's Notebook — vol. 26: *The King vs James Dooley* [SRNSW ref: 2/3209 pp. 159–66]
- Sydney Gaol Records [SRNSW ref: 4/6431 'D' 4 Sep 1829 — Dooley, James; Reel 851]

26 A surprising tale
Epigraph: Lewis Carroll, *Alice's Adventures in Wonderland*

Governor's Despatches — Case of John Stephen Jnr [ML ref: A1267[-16]; CY Reel 895]
- Statement & Testimony of Bernard Fitzpatrick, 8 Aug & 6 Nov 1833, pp. 227, 362–72; Testimony of Charles Windeyer, 8 Nov 1833, pp. 391–6

27 Tasmania bound
Epigraph: Sir Walter Scott, *Marmion*

Colonial Secretary Correspondence File — Jane New [SRNSW ref: 4/2023 File 29/2007]
- Lyttleton to Burnett, undated — Enclosure with Burnett to McLeay, 21 Dec 1833 (unnumbered)

Governor's Despatches — Case of John Stephen Jnr [ML ref: A1267[-16]; CY Reel 895]
- Testimonies: Eliza James Jones, 30 Oct 1833, pp. 270–7; Thomas Caines, 29 Oct 1833, pp. 255–9; Elizabeth Baker, 31 Oct 1833, pp. 304–7; Thomas John Parkes, 31 Oct 1833, pp. 298–301; James Wood, 31 Oct 1833, pp. 287–95; William Smith, 31 Oct 1833, pp. 296–7; James Middleton, 30 Oct 1833, pp. 263–70; John Kettle, 6 Nov 1833, pp. 354–62; George Glew, 1 Nov 1833, pp. 307–15; James Dow, 7 Nov 1833, pp. 375–80; Sidney Stephen, 1 Nov 1833, pp. 316–22; Daniel Egan, 3 Dec 1833, pp. 479–85; John Gray, 28 Nov 1833, pp. 458–62; Samuel Ashmore, 29 Nov 1833, pp. 473–8; Burman Langa, 28 Nov 1833, pp. 463–7
- List of the Crew and Passengers of the Ship *Mary* (Luccock, Master) bound for Batavia, pp. 286–7
- Mrs New to Sidney Stephen, 1 Jun 1829, p. 226
- Statement of William Burke, 16 Aug 1833, p. 223
- Affidavit of Hugh McLean, 16 Jan 1834, pp. 513–14
- Statement of Joseph Dixon, 27 Jan 1834, pp. 514–15
- Extract from Minute no. 18, 7 Jun 1834 , pp. 129–30 & 134

Published volumes
– Nicholson, *Shipping Arrivals & Departures: Tasmania 1803–1833*, pp. 156–7

28 A new sanctuary
Epigraph: *Tasmanian & Asiatic Review*, 31 July 1829 p. 229 c.3

Governor's Despaches — Case of John Stephen Jnr [ML ref: A1267^{-16}; CY Reel 895]
– Testimonies: Amos Crisp, 4 Dec 1833, pp. 493–505; John Burrows, 3 Dec 1833, pp. 485–9; Mary Seymour, 29 Oct 1833, pp. 405–29; John Lake, 30 Oct 1833, pp. 277–84; Frances Lake, 6 Nov 1833, pp. 343–54; Amos Crisp, 4 Dec 1833, pp. 493–505
– Statement: John Stephen Jnr, 29 Oct 1833, pp. 241–52
– Extract from the Minutes of the Executive Council, Minute no. 24, 23 Jun 1829, pp. 54–5 & 208–9
– Extract from Minute no. 15, 7 Jun 1834, pp. 105–43

Newspapers
– *Sydney Gazette*, 10 Nov 1821 p. 3c (Lachlan & Waterloo Flour Company theft); 29 Sep 1825 p. 4c; 23 May 1827 p. 3f
– *Sydney Monitor*, 15 Dec 1828 pp. 1429, 1432

Miscellaneous
– Convict Indent — *Ocean* 1816: Amos Crisp [SRNSW ref: 4/4005 p. 141; Fiche 636]
– Admiralty Records — A List of Convicts' Names &c on board the *Lord Melville* about to proceed to NSW: Free Women & Children [TNA ref: ADM 108/27]
– Ticket-of-Leave Butts — Amos Crisp 1830 [SRNSW ref: 4/4077 no. 30/821; Reel 914]
– Land & Stock Muster 1818 — Liverpool district: Amos Crisp [SRNSW ref: 4/1226; Reel 1256]; also 1819 & 1821 [SRNSW ref: 4/1228 + 4/1229; Reel 1256]
– List of Carts licensed in Sydney in Bigge Appendix [ML ref: A2146 pp. 271+; CY POS 1011] which immediately preceded an almost identically structured 'List of Bakers'
– Affidavit of John Stephen Jnr, 19 Jun 1829 in *HRA* I/15, p. 686
– Testimony of Amos Crisp, 23 Jun 1829 in *HRA* I/15, pp. 38–9
– Executive Council: Minute no. 24, 23 Jun 1829 in *HRA* I/15, p. 35
– Affidavits: Amos Crisp, 9 Jly 1829; and Thomas Henry Hart, 9 Jly 1829 in *HRA* I/15, pp. 690–91

Internet site
– The Proceedings of the Old Bailey — Amos Crisp [www.oldbaileyonline.org/html-units/1810s/t18141026–14.html]

Published volumes
– Baxter, *General Muster List 1823/4/5*. Entries 17479–86; Also 15404, 16530, 21347, 29000, 35037, 38459, 46227, 46399 & 37916

29 By a whisker
Epigraph: *Statement read to the Executive Council by John Stephen Jnr, 29 Oct 1833* [ML ref: A1267–16 pp. 241–52; CY Reel 895]

Colonial Secretary Correspondence File — Jane New [SRNSW ref: 4/2023 File 29/2007]
–   Report of arrival of *Emma Kemp*, 12 Nov 1830 (unnumbered)

Governor's Despatches — Case of John Stephen Jnr [ML ref: A1267⁻¹⁶; CY Reel 895]
–   Testimonies: Francis Rossi, 27 Nov 1833, pp. 433–9; John Skinner, 29 Nov 1833, pp. 468–72; Frederick Meredith, 28 Nov 1833, pp. 446–56; Mary Seymour, 29 Nov 1833, pp. 405–29; Francis Mitchell, 28 Nov 1833, pp. 439–46; John Nicholson, 28 Nov 1833, pp. 462–3
–   Affidavit of Thomas Franklin, 25 Nov 1830, pp. 403–4

Correspondence
–   Statements: John Skinner & Frederick Meredith, 18 Jun 1829 in *HRA* I/15, pp. 41–3
–   Rossi to Macleay, 19 Jun 1829 in *HRA* I/15, p.41
–   Executive Council: Minute no. 24, 23 Jun 1829 in *HRA* I/15, p. 35
–   Darling to Murray, 29 Jun 1829 in *HRA*, I/15, p. 30
–   Darling to Goderich, 27 Apr 1831 in *HRA* I/16, pp. 247–8

Newspapers
–   *Australian*, 22 & 29 Jun 1827 & 17 Mch 1829 &c quoted by Irving, Kinstler & Dupain, *Fine Houses of Sydney*, pp. 16–27

V   Indignation

Epigraph: John Stephen Jnr to Stanley, Sep 1833 [ML ref: A1267⁻¹⁶ pp. 157–60; CY Reel 895]

30 Smoke and mirrors

Epigraph: John Stephen Jnr to Goderich, 19 Dec 1832 [TNA/ML ref: CO 201/230 f.469–79; Reel 188]

Colonial Secretary Correspondence File — Jane New [SRNSW ref: 4/2023 File 29/2007]
–   Memorandum: Correspondence in Case of Jane New between 8 Sep 1828 & 25 Jun 1829 [SRNSW ref: 4/2023 File 29/2007 (unnumbered)]
–   Rossi to McLeay, 30 Jun 1829 (unnumbered)
–   Rossi to McLeay, 14 Feb 1831 (no. 31/1171)

Governor's Despatches — Case of John Stephen Jnr [ML ref: A1267⁻¹⁶; CY Reel 895]
–   Testimonies: John Skinner, 29 Nov 1833, pp. 468–72; Frederick Meredith, 28 Nov 1833, pp. 446–56; Amos Crisp, 4 Dec 1833, pp. 493–505; Francis Rossi, 28 Nov 1833, pp. 433–9; John Gurner, 31 Oct 1833, pp. 284–5
–   John Stephen Jnr's comments, undated, p. 209
–   John Stephen Jnr's remarks against letter from Rossi to McLeay, 19 Jun 1829, pp. 27–8

Correspondence
–   Huskisson to Darling, 21 May 1828 in *HRA* I/14, p. 193
–   Murray to Darling, 11 Nov 1828 in *HRA* I/14, p. 447

- McLeay to John Stephen Jnr, 29 May 1829 [SRNSW ref: 4/3737 p. 220 no. 29/96; Reel 624]
- McLeay to John Stephen Jnr, 5 Jun 1829 [SRNSW ref: 4/3737 p. 223 no. 29/98; Reel 624]
- Moore & Kinghorne to Rossi, 18 Jun 1829 in *HRA* I/15, p. 41
- Rossi to McLeay, 19 Jun 1829 in *HRA* I/15, p. 41
- Darling to Murray, 18 Aug 1830 in *HRA* I/15, pp. 712–13
- McLeay to Rossi, 11 Feb 1831 [SRNSW ref: 4/3829 pp. 408–9 no. 31/116; Reel 2807]
- Howick to Hume, 8 Aug 1832 [TNA/ML ref: CO 202/28 f.203–11; Reel 221]
- John Stephen Jnr to Goderich, 12 Nov 1832 [TNA/ML ref: CO201/230 ff.437–47; Reel 188]
- Hay to John Stephen Jnr, 11 Dec 1832 [TNA/ML ref: CO202/29 ff.50–58; Reel 221]
- John Stephen Jnr to Goderich, 19 Dec 1832 [TNA/ML ref: CO 201/230 f.469–79; Reel 188]

Miscellaneous
- Shipping Arrivals — *Melville*, 6 May 1829 [SRNSW ref: 4/5000]
- Registers of Governor's Minutes Received: 1826–1829 [SRNSW ref: 4/1073 no. 49; Reel 2725]
- Certificates of Judges and Attorney-General, 25 May 1829 in *HRA* I/15, p. 689
- Statements: John Skinner & Frederick Meredith, 18 Jun 1829 in *HRA* I/15, pp. 41–3
- Affidavit of John Stephen Jnr, 19 Jun 1829 in *HRA* I/15, p. 686
- Testimony: Amos Crisp, 23 Jun 1829 in *HRA* I/15, pp. 38–9
- Affidavit: Amos Crisp, 9 Jly 1829 in *HRA* I/15, pp. 690–91
- Phoenix Hulk Entrance Book [4/6281 p. 94 no. 2294]
- Phoenix Hulk Occurrence book [SRNSW ref: 4/6278 Tues 23 Jun 1829]
- Reply of John Stephen Jnr to charges preferred by General Darling, 17 May 1830 in *HRA* I/15, pp. 679–85
- Darling's remarks appended to Autobiographical information: John Stephen Jnr, 3 Aug 1832 [TNA/ML ref: CO 201/230 f.416–27; Reel 188]
- Supreme Court Criminal Jurisdiction no. 8 — Nov. 1829: Amos Crisp [SRNSW ref: T29B Case 29/320]

Published volumes
- Sainty & Johnson, *Census of NSW, November 1828*. Seymour family: Entry nos. S0433–41

31 The Executive Council hearing

Epigraph: Reply of John Stephen Jnr to charges preferred by General Darling, 17 May 1830 in *HRA* I/15, pp. 679–85

Colonial Secretary Correspondence File — Jane New [SRNSW ref: 4/2023 File 29/2007]
- Correspondence in Case of Jane New between 8 Sep 1828 & 25 Jun 1829 (unnumbered)
- John Stephen Jnr to McLeay, 22 Jun 1829 (unnumbered)

Governor's Despatches — Case of John Stephen Jnr [ML ref: A1267⁻¹⁶; CY Reel 895]
– Testimony of Mary Seymour, 29 Nov 1833, pp. 405–29; Frederick Meredith, 28 Nov 1833, pp. 446–56; John Skinner, 29 Nov 1833, pp. 468–72
– Extract from Minute no. 15, 7 Jun 1834, pp. 105–43

Correspondence
– Executive Council: Minute no. 24, 23 Jun 1829 in *HRA* I/15, pp. 35–6
– Forbes to Darling, 24 Jun 1829 in *HRA* I/15, p. 35
– Darling to Murray, 29 Jun 1829 in *HRA* I/15, pp. 30–32
– Reply of J. Stephen Jnr to charges preferred by General Darling, 17 May 1830 in *HRA* I/15, pp. 679–85
– Autobiographical information: John Stephen Jnr, 3 Aug 1832 [TNA/ML ref: CO 201/230 f.416–27; Reel 188]

Miscellaneous
– Statements: John Skinner & Frederick Meredith, 18 Jun 1829 in *HRA* I/15, pp. 41–3
– Elizabeth Crisp to John Stephen Jnr, 21 Jun 1829 in *HRA* I/15, p. 687
– Testimonies: John Stephen Jnr, 23 Jun 1829; and Amos Crisp, 23 Jun 1829 in *HRA* I/15, pp. 36–9
– Reply of J. Stephen Jnr to charges preferred by General Darling, 17 May 1830 in *HRA* I/15, pp. 679–85
– Executive Council: Minute no. 24, 23 Jun 1829 in *HRA* I/15, pp. 39–40
– Phoenix Hulk discharge book — Amos Crisp [SRNSW ref: 4/6285 p.81 no. 2026]

32 The repercussions
Epigraph: Darling to Goderich, 27 Apr 1831 in *HRA* I/16, pp. 247–8

Colonial Secretary Correspondence File — Jane New [SRNSW ref: 4/2023 File 29/2007]
– Burnett to McLeay, 20 Apr 1829 (no. 29/3634) & 3 Aug 1829 (no. 29/6582)
– Arthur to Darling, 20 Jun 1829 (unnumbered)
– Affidavit: Alexander McLeay, 29 Jun 1829 (Enclosure with no. 30/255)
– Charges: To Francis Nicholas Rossi & to George Jilks from W.C. Wentworth, 17 Jly 1829 (Enclosures with no. 29/5750)
– Baxter & Sampson to McLeay, 25 Jly 1829 (no. 29/5911)
– Memorandum: Henry Emmett, 28 Jly 1829 (unnumbered)
– Rossi to McLeay, 14 Feb 1831 (no. 31/1171)

Governor's Despatches — Case of John Stephen Jnr [ML ref: A1267⁻¹⁶; CY Reel 895]
– John Stephen Jnr to Murray, 4 Jly 1829, pp. 7–8
– Testimony: John Raine, 5 Nov 1833, pp. 331–43
– Copy of Charges preferred by Lt-General Darling agst John Stephen Jnr Esq, as furnished by order of Sir George Murray, with added remarks by John Stephen Jnr, pp. 14–27

Correspondence
– McLeay to Burnett, 6 Mch 1829 & 29 Mch 1829 [SRNSW ref: 4/3522 pp. 401, 422 no. 29/8; Reel 898]

– Darling to Forbes, 24 Jun 1829; Darling to Forbes, 25 Jun 1829; Forbes to Darling, 26 Jun 1829 [SRNSW ref: 4/6651 pp. 237–40]
– Forbes to Darling, 24 Jun 1829 in *HRA* I/15, p. 35
– McLeay to John Stephen Jnr, 26 Jun 1829 in *HRA* I/15, pp. 692–3
– Darling to Murray, 29 Jun 1829 in *HRA* I/15, pp. 28–33
– John Stephen Jnr to G. Darling, 2 Jly 1829 in *HRA* I/15, pp. 48–9
– McLeay to John Stephen Jnr, 4 Jly 1829 in *HRA* I/15, p. 693
– McLeay to Baxter & Sampson, 23 Jly 1829 [SRNSW ref: 4/3737 p. 270 no. 29/90; Reel 624]
– Darling to Goderich, 27 Apr 1831 in *HRA* I/16, pp. 247–8

Newspapers
– *Australian*, 3 Jly 1829 p. 2d-e
– *Sydney Gazette*, 15 Sep 1829 p. 2 c1–2; 27 Jun 1829, p. 1; 26, 29 & 31 Dec 1829
– *Sydney Monitor*, 4 July 1829 p. 2 c. 4

Miscellaneous
– Case of Jane New: Letter from John Burnett — 26 Sep 1827; Information — 3 Jan 1829 [SRNSW ref: SCT 29 Box 29/6 no. 70]
– Minutes of the Executive Council no. 2, 25 Jun 1829 [SRNSW ref: 4/1516 p.171]
– Dowling's Select Cases, vol. 2 — In re Jane New [SRNSW ref: 2/3462 pp. 204–8]
– Decisions of the Superior Courts of NSW 1788–1899 published by the Division of Law at Macquarie University: *R v Hall* no. 8 [www.law.mq.edu.au/scnsw/Cases1829–30/html/r_v_hall_no_8_1829.htm]
– Remarks by Governor Darling on Mr John Stephen's Answer to the Five Charges which he deduces from the Proceedings of Council in *HRA* I/16, pp. 249–53
– Affidavits: John Raine, 6 & 9 Jly 1829; Frederick Finlay, 29 Jun 1829 in *HRA* I/15, pp. 688–92
– Dowling's Select Cases, vol. 2 [SRNSW ref: 2/3462 p.121]
– Case of John Raine, Edward Lee and Richard Kemp [SRNSW ref: SCT28 B no. 28/223 no. 62]
– Testimony: Amos Crisp, 23 Jun 1829 in *HRA* I/15, pp. 38–9
– Affidavits: Amos Crisp & Thomas Henry Hart, 9 Jly 1829 in *HRA* I/15, pp. 690–92

Published volumes
– Bennett, *Sir James Dowling*, p. 67
– Darling, *Statement of Lieut-Gen R. Darling in reference to the petition of Mr John Stephen jnr to The House of Commons*, p. 18
– *Oxford Dictionary of National Biography*, vol. 52, pp. 435–9 (James Stephen)

33 Malefactor or martyr?

Epigraph: *Tasmanian & Asiatic Review*, 31 July 1829, p. 229 c.3

Colonial Secretary Correspondence File — Jane New [SRNSW ref: 4/2023 File 29/2007]
– Sydney Stephen to Darling, 6 Dec 1829 (unnumbered)

Governor's Despatches — Case of John Stephen Jnr [ML ref: A1267⁻¹⁶; CY Reel 895]
- John Stephen Jnr to Murray, 12 Dec 1829, pp. 8–9
- Testimony of John Raine, 5 Nov 1833, pp. 331–42

Correspondence
- Baxter to John Stephen Jnr, 25 Jly 1829 in *HRA* I/15, p. 689
- McLeay to Baxter, 31 Dec 1829 [SRNSW ref: 4/3737 p. 428 no. 29/226; Reel 624]
- Darling to Hay, 13 Jan 1830 in *HRA* I/15, pp. 333–4
- Baxter to McLeay, 15 Jan 1830 [SRNSW ref: 4/2197.1 File 33/3736 no. 30/371]
- Hay to J. Stephen Jnr, 7 Jun 1830 in *HRA* I/15, pp. 694–5
- J. Stephen Jnr to Murray, 15 Jun 1830 in *HRA* I/15, pp. 697–8
- Darling to Goderich, 27 Apr 1831 in *HRA* I/16, pp. 247–8
- McLeay to Chambers, 4 Oct 1831 [SRNSW ref: 4/3740 p. 89 no. 31/219 & p. 175 no. 31/257; Reel 626]
- McLeay to Manning, 6 Feb 1832 [SRNSW ref: 4/3740 p. 288 no. 32/37; Reel 626]

Newspapers
- *Tasmanian & Asiatic Review*, 31 July 1829 p. 229 c.3
- *Sydney Monitor*, 27 Jun 1829 p. 1649 c.4; 4 July 1829 p. 3 c. 4

Miscellaneous
- Civil Jurisdiction Process Book: Kemp vs Stephen & Stephen [SRNSW ref: 5/4526 1828 no.165]. Process papers [SRNSW ref: 9/2268 1828 4th Term, no. 165]
- Civil Jurisdiction Process Book: *Iredale vs Stephen* [SRNSW ref: 5/4527 1829 no. 115]. Judgement book [SRNSW ref: 9/923 p.37 no. 136]. Judgement Roll [SRNSW ref: 9/5263 no. 136]
- Civil Jurisdiction Process Book: *Melville vs Stephen* [SRNSW ref: 5/4527 1829 no. 568]. Judgement book [SRNSW ref: 9/923 p.55 no. 52]. Judgement Roll [SRNSW ref: 9/5270 no. 52]
- Civil Jurisdiction Process Book: *Holmes vs Stephen* [SRNSW ref: 5/4527 1829 no. 617]. Process Papers [SRNSW ref: 9/2271 no. 617]
- Civil Jurisdiction Process Book: *Bowen vs Stephen* [SRNSW ref: 5/4527 1829 no. 620]. Process Papers [SRNSW ref: 9/2271 no. 620]
- Colonial Secretary Correspondence File re John Stephen Jnr [SRNSW ref: 4/2197.1 File 33/3736]
- Reply of John Stephen Jnr to charges preferred by General Darling, 17 May 1830 in *HRA* I/15, pp. 679–85
- Autobiographical information: John Stephen Jnr, 3 Aug 1832 [TNA/ML ref: CO 201/230 f.416–27; Reel 188], Nicholson, p. 42

Published volumes
- *ADB*, vol. II, pp. 202–3 (John Edye Manning); p. 399 (Francis N. Rossi)
- Blaikie, *Great Australian Scandals*, pp. 39–43
- Fletcher, *Ralph Darling*, pp. 30, 247–8 & 272–4
- Sainty & Johnson *Census of NSW, November 1828*. Entries no: K0459 (Richard Kemp); J1018 (Launcelot Iredale)

– *Votes and Proceedings of the Legislative Council* 1832, pp. 15, 56

VI   Persecution

Epigraph: John Stephen Jnr, 6 Aug 1832 [TNA/ML ref: CO201/230 f.428; Reel 188]

34 Desperate and destitute

Epigraph: John Stephen Jnr to Murray, 12 Dec 1829 [ML ref: A1267⁻¹⁶ pp. 8–9; CY Reel 895]

Governor's Despatches — Case of John Stephen Jnr [ML ref: A1267⁻¹⁶; CY Reel 895]
– John Stephen Jnr to Murray, 12 Dec 1829, pp. 8–9; 27 Mch 1830, p. 9
– John Stephen Jnr to Hay, 3 May 1830, pp. 11–12; 7 May 1830, p. 13
– Hay to John Stephen Jnr, 3 May 1830, p. 12; 7 May 1830, p. 13

Correspondence
– John Stephen Jnr to Hay, received 29 Mch 1830 [TNA/ML ref: CO 201/215 p.636; Reel 177]
– Hay to John Stephen Jnr, 3 Apr 1830 & 27 Apr 1830 in *HRA* I/15, pp. 678–9
– John Stephen Jnr to Hay, 24 Apr 1830 in *HRA* I/15, pp. 678–9
– Hay to John Stephen Jnr, 30 Apr 1830 in *HRA* I/15, p. 679
– John Stephen Jnr to Hay, 4 May 1830 [TNA/ML ref: CO 201/215 p. 642; Reel 177]

Miscellaneous
– Reply of John Stephen Jnr to charges preferred by General Darling, 17 May 1830 in *HRA* I/15, pp. 679–85
– Autobiographical information: John Stephen Jnr, 3 Aug 1832 [TNA/ML ref: CO 201/230 f.416–27; Reel 188]

Internet site
– Tierney, *Orson Welles: Ten Years After His Death*, [www.kinema.uwaterloo.ca/tiern952.htm]

35 Innocence incarnate

Epigraph: John Stephen Jnr to Goderich, 12 Nov 1832 [TNA/ML ref: CO201/230 ff.437–47; Reel 188]

Colonial Secretary Correspondence File — Jane New [SRNSW ref: 4/2023 File 29/2007]
– Sidney Stephen to Darling, 6 Dec 1829 (unnumbered)
– McLeay to Manning, 21 Dec 1830 (no. 30/255)
– Manning to McLeay, 21 Dec 1830 (Enclosure with no. 30/255)
– Hely to McLeay, 21 Dec 1830 (no. 30/9648)
– Affidavit: Thomas Ryan, 21 Dec 1830 (unnumbered)
– Macquoid to McLeay, 22 Dec 1830 (unnumbered)
– Rossi to McLeay, 14 Feb 1831 (no. 31/1171)

Governor's Despatches — Case of John Stephen Jnr [ML ref: A1267^{-16}; CY Reel 895]

- Copy of Charges preferred by Lt-General Darling agst John Stephen Jnr Esq, as furnished by order of Sir George Murray, with added remarks by John Stephen Jnr, pp. 14–27
- John Stephen Jnr to Murray, 12 Dec 1829, pp. 8–9
- Hay to John Stephen Jnr, 16 Jly 1830, p. 83
- John Stephen Jnr to Hay, 22 Jly 1830, pp. 83–4
- John Stephen Jnr to Francis Stephen, 30 May 1833, pp. 202–3
- Francis Stephen to John Stephen Jnr, 1 Jun 1833, pp. 203–4
- Sydney Stephen to John Stephen Jnr, 14 Jun 1833, p. 202
- Statement of Constable Cleme, undated, p. 204
- Statement of Constables, undated, p. 205
- Various letters & statements, May-June 1833, pp. 186–93
- John Stephen Jnr to Prout, 27 May 1833, Prout's reply, 29 May 1833, Statements of Constables, pp. 176–8
- Extract from Minute no. 15, 7 Jun 1834, pp. 105–43

Correspondence

- Dowling to John Stephen Jnr, 13 Jan 1829 in *HRA* I/15, pp. 689–90
- John Stephen Jnr to Hay, 20 May 1830 in *HRA* I/15, p. 694
- Hay to John Stephen Jnr, 27 May & 7 Jun 1830 in *HRA* I/15, pp. 694–5
- John Stephen Jnr to Hay, 7 Jun 1830 in *HRA* I/15, p. 695
- Hay to John Stephen Jnr, 9 Jun 1830, pp. 75–6
- John Stephen Jnr to Murray, 15 Jun 1830 in *HRA* I/15, pp. 697–8
- Hay to John Stephen Jnr, 28 Jun 1830 in *HRA* I/15, p. 698
- John Stephen Jnr to Hay, 1 July 1830 in *HRA* I/15, p. 698
- Hay to John Stephen Jnr, 3 Jly & 26 Jly 1830 in *HRA* I/15, pp. 698 & 701
- John Stephen Jnr to Hay, 12 Aug 1830 [TNA/ML ref: CO 201/215 p. 687; Reel 177]
- Murray to Darling, 12 Aug 1830 in *HRA* I/15, p. 678
- Darling to Goderich, 27 Apr 1831 in *HRA* I/16, pp. 247–8
- McLeay to Hely, 21 Dec 1830 [SRNSW ref: 4/3670 p. 81; Reel 2649]
- Sidney Stephen to McLeay, 26 Feb 1831 in *HRA* I/16, p. 253–4
- Howick to Hume, 8 Aug 1832 [TNA/ML ref: CO202/28 f.203–11; Reel 221]
- John Stephen Jnr to Goderich, 12 Nov 1832 [TNA/ML ref: CO201/230 ff.437–47; Reel 188]
- Hay to John Stephen Jnr, 11 Dec 1832 [TNA/ML ref: CO202/29 ff.50–58; Reel 221]
- John Stephen Jnr to Goderich, 19 Dec 1832 [TNA/ML ref: CO 201/230 f.469–79; Reel 188]

Miscellaneous

- Statement by S. Cleme, 28 Mch 1829 in *HRA* I/15, p. 44
- Certificates of Judges and Attorney-General, 25 May 1829 in *HRA* I/15, p. 689
- Reply of John Stephen Jnr to charges preferred by General Darling, 17 May 1830 in *HRA* I/15, pp. 679–85

– Remarks by Governor Darling on Mr John Stephen's Answer to the Five Charges in *HRA* I/16, pp. 249–53

36 The Radicals involved

Epigraph: Darling, Henry C. *Statement of the Refutation of Accusations made by Mr Hume MP* [ML ref: PAM 83/149 p. 8]

Governor's Despatches — Case of John Stephen Jnr [ML ref: A1267⁻¹⁶; CY Reel 895]
– John Stephen Jnr to Murray, 12 Dec 1829, pp. 8–9

Correspondence
– John Stephen Jnr to Hay, 6 July 1830 in *HRA* I/15, pp. 699–700

Published volumes
– Darling, *Statement of the Refutation of Accusations made by Mr Hume MP and others against Lt-Gen Darling*, p. 8
– Fletcher, *Ralph Darling*, pp. 288–305
– Hansard's *Parliamentary Debates*, vol. 22 p. 1314; vol. 25 pp. 27, 286–7, 435–50, 1110–14 & 1125–30; 1830–31, vol. II p. 88–90
– Stephen, *Reply to Major-General Darling's 'Statement in Refutation of Accusations made by Mr Hume MP'*

37 A quiet interlude

Epigraph: Dixon, *The London Prisons*, p. 102

Colonial Secretary Correspondence File — Jane New [SRNSW ref: 4/2023 File 29/2007]
– Memorandum: regarding arrival of *Emma Kemp*, 12 Nov 1830 (unnumbered)
– Rossi to McLeay, 25 Nov 1830 (unnumbered)
– John Nicholson to McLeay, 26 Nov 1830 & 'Tuesday' (probably 1 Dec 1830) (unnumbered)
– Affidavit: George Thom, 29 Nov 1830 (unnumbered)
– Harrington to Rossi, 30 Dec 1830 (unnumbered)
– Innes to Harrington, 'Thursday morning' (unnumbered)

Governor's Despatches — Case of John Stephen Jnr [ML ref: A1267⁻¹⁶; CY Reel 895]
– Hay to John Stephen Jnr, 16 Jly 1830, p. 83
– Affidavit of Thomas Franklin, 25 Nov 1830, pp. 403–4
– Testimony: Francis Rossi, 27 Nov 1833, pp. 433–9

Correspondence
– John Stephen Jnr to Hay, 20 May 1830 in *HRA* I/15, p. 694
– Hay to John Stephen Jnr, 27 May 1830 in *HRA* I/15, p. 694
– John Stephen Jnr to Hay, 1 & 6 July 1830 in *HRA* I/15, pp. 698–700
– McLeay to Rossi, 13 Nov 1830 [SRNSW ref: 4/3829 pp. 209–10 no. 30/805; Reel 2807]

Newspapers
- *United Kingdom Gazette*, 28 Apr 1831 p. 4 c.2

Miscellaneous
- King's Bench Commitment Book [TNA ref: PRIS 4/41 p. 127 no. 986]
- Discharges from King's Bench 1831 [TNA ref: PRIS 7/50 John Stephen]
- List of discharged prisoners [TNA ref: PRIS 10/139 — 18 May 1831]
- Petitions of Prisoners 1830 [TNA ref: B 8/6 no. 29337]
- King's Bench Daily Schedule [TNA ref: PRIS 10/35 — 18, 19 Feb ; 18 May 1831]
- Autobiographical information: John Stephen Jnr, 3 Aug 1832 [TNA/ML ref: CO 201/230 f.416–27; Reel 188]

Published volumes
- Dixon, *The London Prisons*, p. 102
- Fletcher, *Ralph Darling*, pp. 267–70
- Nicholson, *Shipping Arrivals 1826 to 1840*, p. 57

38 A Governor reviled
Epigraph: John Stephen Jnr to Viscount Goderich, 14 Jun 1832 [ML ref: A2146 pp. 344–5; Reel CY 1011]

Governor's Despatches — Case of John Stephen Jnr [ML ref: A1267^{-16}; CY Reel 895]
- John Stephen Jnr to Murray, 12 Dec 1829, pp. 8–9

Correspondence
- J. Stephen Jnr to Hay, 6 July 1830 in *HRA* I/15, pp. 699–700
- Darling to Eliza Darling, 9 Jun 1832 quoted in Fletcher, *Ralph Darling*, p. 303
- John Stephen Jnr to Goderich, 14 & 27 Jun 1832 and 19 Jly 1832 [ML ref: A2146 pp. 344–5, 367–8 & 383–3; Reel CY 1011]
- Darling to Arthur, 24 Jly 1832 [ML ref: A2167 p. 7; Reel FM4/3670]
- John Stephen Jnr, 6 Aug 1832 [TNA/ML ref: CO201/230 p. 428; Reel 188]
- John Stephen Jnr to Goderich, 7 Aug 1832 [ML ref: A2146 pp. 386–7; Reel CY 1011]
- Hay to John Stephen Jnr, 11 Dec 1832 [TNA/ML ref: CO202/29 ff.50–58; Reel 221]

Newspapers
- *John Bull*, 19 Dec 1831 p. 406 c.3
- *Morning Chronicle*, 8 Dec 1831 p. 2 c.5; 9 Dec 1831 p. 3 c.5; 14 Dec 1831 p. 3 c.5, 28 Dec 1831 p. 3 c.4
- *The Satirist*, 8 Jun 1832 p. 4 c.2–3
- *The Times*, 5 Jly 1832 p. 4; 9 Jly 1832 p. 6; 24 Jly 1832 p. 2 c.3; 3 Nov 1832 p. 6

Miscellaneous
- Remarks by Lt-Genl R. Darling on certain Statements and Observations reported in the

'Mirror of Parliament' and the *Times* newspaper to have been made by Mr Hume, MP in *HRA* I/15, pp. 851–63

- Memorandum: On the case of Mr John Stephen Jnr from General Darling, 31 Jly 1831 [sb 1832] [ML ref: A2146 pp. 140–42; Reel CY 1011]. Although the date 1831 was printed in this memorandum, the printer later testified that the date 1831 was printed in error and should have been 1832.
- The King in the Prosecution of John Stephen Jnr agst Lt-Gnl Darling, 30 Oct 1832 [TNA/ML ref: CO 201/230 f.451–61; Reel 188]

Published volumes
- Darling, *Letter Addressed by Lieut-Gen Darling late Governor of NSW to Joseph Hume Esq MP*
- Darling, *Statement of the Refutation of Accusations made by Mr Hume MP and others against Lt-Gen Darling*
- Darling, *Statement of Lieut-Gen R. Darling, Late Governor of New South Wales in reference to the petition of Mr John Stephen Jnr*
- Fletcher, *Ralph Darling*, pp. 298–305
- Hansard's *Parliamentary Debates*, Series 3 (1832), vol. 10, pp. 32–3; vol. 13, pp. 1089, 1109–13; vol. 14, pp. 638–40
- 'Miles', *Governor Darling's Refutation of the charges of cruelty and oppression of the soldiers Sudds and Thompson*, pp. 3, 4, 30, 32
- Stephen, *Reply to Major-General Darling's 'Statement in Refutation of Accusations made by Mr Hume MP'*

39 Swan song
Epigraph: John Stephen Jnr to Howick, 29 Aug 1831 [TNA/ML ref: CO201/224 f.496–7; Reel 183]

Governor's Despatches — Case of John Stephen Jnr [ML ref: A1267^{-16}; CY Reel 895]
- Hay to John Stephen Jnr, 17 Dec 1832, p. 163

Correspondence
- Baxter to McLeay, 15 Jan 1831 [SRNSW ref: 4/2197.1 File 33/3736 no. 30/371]
- John Stephen Jnr to Goderich, 20 Jly 1831 [TNA/ML ref: CO201/224 f.470–80; Reel 183]
- John Stephen Jnr to Howick, 28 Jly 1831 [TNA/ML ref: CO201/224 f.480–1; Reel 183]; & 2 Aug 1831 [TNA/ML ref: CO201/224 f.482–5; Reel 183]
- John Stephen Jnr to Goderich, 12 Aug 1831 [TNA/ML ref: CO201/224 f.487–8; Reel 183]
- Howick to John Stephen Jnr, 17 Aug 1831 [TNA/ML ref: CO 202/23 f.213; Reel 220]
- John Stephen Jnr to Howick, 20 Aug 1831 [TNA/ML ref: CO201/224 f.489–90; Reel 183]
- Howick to John Stephen Jnr, 26 Aug 1831 [TNA/ML ref: CO 202/28 f.1; Reel 221]
- John Stephen Jnr to Howick, 29 Aug 1831 [TNA/ML ref: CO201/224 f.496–7; Reel 183]; & 23 Nov 1831 [TNA/ML ref: CO201/224 f.495–6; Reel 183]

- Hay to John Stephen Jnr, 30 Nov 1831 [TNA/ML ref: CO202/28 f.64–5; Reel 221]
- John Stephen Jnr to Goderich, 17 Dec 1831 [TNA/ML ref: CO201/224 f.497–9; Reel 183]; & 20 Jan 1832 [ML ref: A2146 p. 333; Reel CY 1011]
- Hay to John Stephen Jnr, 26 Jan 1832 [TNA/ML ref: CO 202/28 f.89; Reel 221]; 30 Mch 1832 [TNA/ML ref: CO202/28 f.128; Reel 221]
- John Stephen Jnr to Goderich, 31 Mch 1832 [ML ref: A2146 p. 339; Reel CY 1011]
- Hay to John Stephen Jnr, 5 Apr 1832 [TNA/ML ref: CO202/28 f.132; Reel 221]
- John Stephen Jnr to Hay, 13 Apr 1832, 4 May 1832 [ML ref: A2146 pp. 340–43; Reel CY 1011]
- Hume to Howick, 4 Aug 1832 [TNA/ML ref: CO 201/230 f.413–4; Reel 188]
- Howick to Hume, 8 Aug 1832 [TNA/ML ref: CO 202/28 f.203–11; Reel 221]
- John Stephen Jnr to Goderich, 12 Nov 1832 [TNA/ML ref: CO201/230 ff.437–47; Reel 188]
- John Stephen Jnr to Hay, 3 & 30 Oct 1832 [ML ref: A2146 pp. 389 & 390; Reel CY 1011].
- Hay to John Stephen Jnr, 11 & 31 Oct 1832 [TNA/ML ref: CO 202/29 ff.25 & 38; Reel 221]
- John Stephen Jnr to Goderich, 12 Nov 1832 & 1 Dec 1832 [TNA/ML ref: CO201/230 ff.437–47 & 463–8; Reel 188]
- Hay to John Stephen Jnr, 11 Dec 1832 [TNA/ML ref: CO202/29 ff.50–58; Reel 221]
- John Stephen Jnr to Goderich, 19 Dec 1832 [TNA/ML ref: CO 201/230 f.469–79; Reel 188]
- John Stephen Jnr to Hay, 27 Dec 1832 [ML ref: A2146 pp. 395–6; Reel CY 1011]
- Hay to John Stephen Jnr, 29 Dec 1832 [TNA/ML ref: CO 202/29 f.70; Reel 221]

Miscellaneous
- Petition: To the Right Hon. the Viscount Goderich, His Majesty's Principal Sec. of State, Colonial Dept &c The Humble Memorial of John Stephen Jnr Esq late Sydney, NSW, but now of no. 19 Manchester Buildings Westminster, 1832 [ML ref: A2146 pp. 334–8; Reel CY 1011]

Published volumes
- *HRA* I/15, pp. 837–63 and *HRA* I/16, pp. 2–3 (Dennis McHue's case)

VII   Retribution

Epigraph: John Stephen Jnr to Goderich, 19 Dec 1832 [TNA/ML ref: CO 201/230 f.469–79; Reel 188]

40 Dr Jekyll or Mr Hyde?

Epigraph: John Stephen Jnr to Goderich, 7 Aug 1832 [ML ref: A2146 pp. 386–7; Reel CY 1011]

Governor's Despatches — Case of John Stephen Jnr [ML ref: A1267[-16]; CY Reel 895]
- John Stephen Jnr to Bourke, 1 Jun 1833, pp. 146–7

- R Bourke Jnr to John Stephen Jnr, 3 Jun 1833, p. 147
- R Bourke Jnr to John Stephen Jnr, 22 Jun 1833, pp. 147–8
- John Stephen Jnr to R Bourke Jnr, 25 Jun 1833, pp. 148–9
- R Bourke Jnr to John Stephen Jnr, 28 Jun 1833, pp. 149–50
- John Stephen Jnr to R Bourke Jnr, 4 Jly 1833, pp. 150–1
- R Bourke Jnr to John Stephen Jnr, 6 Jly 1833, pp. 151–2
- John Stephen Jnr to R Bourke Jnr, 10 Jly 1833, pp. 152–6
- R Bourke Jnr to John Stephen Jnr, 15 Jly 1833, p. 157
- John Stephen Jnr to Stanley, Sep 1833 plus enclosures, pp. 157–70

Correspondence
- John Stephen Jnr to Goderich, 19 Dec 1832 [TNA/ML ref: CO 201/230 f.469–79; Reel 188]
- John Stephen Jnr to Howick, 2 Aug 1831 [TNA/ML ref: CO201/224 f.482–5; Reel 183]
- Colonial Secretary Correspondence File [SRNSW ref: 4/2197.1 File 33/3736]
- Hay to Bourke, 6 Feb 1833 in *HRA* I/17, p. 30
- John Stephen Jnr to Wentworth, 29 May 1833 published in *Sydney Monitor*, 1 June 1833

Newspapers
- *Sydney Gazette*, 4 Jun 1833 p. 2d-e
- *Sydney Morning Herald*, 3 Jun 1833 p. 2c
- *Sydney Monitor*, 2 Feb 1833 p. 2d; 22 May 1833 p. 2a; 25 May 1833 p. 3c; 1 June 1833
- Obituary: Thomas Bodenham in *Australian*, 23 May 1834; *Sydney Morning Herald*, 24 May 1834 p. 3a; *Sydney Gazette* 22 May 1834 p. 3e

Miscellaneous
- Court of Equity Jurisdiction: *John Stephen vs William Bottomley* & *John Brigstock*, 30 May 1833 [SRNSW ref: 7/3427 no. 71]
- *Stephen vs Bodenham*: Bill filed 5 Aug 1833; Motion for an attachment for want of answer, granted 26 Oct 1833; Answer of Defendant filed 7 Nov 1833; Bill of Reviver filed 9 May 1835 [SRNSW ref: 7/3427 no. 70]
- Shipping Arrivals: *Westmoreland* 19 May 1833 [SRNSW ref: 4/5204] — John, his wife and two children are recorded on the passenger list.

Internet sites
- Stephen vs Brigstock [www.law.mq.edu.au/scnsw/Cases1833–34/html/Stephen_v_brigstock_1833.htm] & [www.law.mq.edu.au/scnsw/Cases1835 36/html/Stephen_v_brigstock_1835.htm]

41 A trustworthy tribunal

Epigraph: John Stephen Jnr to the Executive Council, 16 Oct 1829 [ML ref: A1267⁻¹⁶ pp. 235–6; CY Reel 895]

Governor's Despatches — Case of John Stephen Jnr [ML ref: A1267⁻¹⁶; CY Reel 895]
- Deas Thomson to John Stephen Jnr, 15 Oct 1833, pp. 234–5

- John Stephen Jnr to the Executive Council, 16 Oct 1833, pp. 235–6
- Extract from Minute no. 22, 14 Oct 1833; Minute no. 23, 15 Oct 1833; & Minute no. 25 , 29 Oct 1833, pp. 86–91

Published volumes
- *ADB*, vol. 1, pp. 128–33 (Sir Richard Bourke); pp. 158–64 (William Grant Broughton)
- *ADB*, vol. 2, pp. 177–80 (Alexander McLeay); pp. 377–9 (Charles Drummond Riddell); pp. 454–5 (Kenneth Snodgrass); King, *Richard Bourke*, pp. 154–5

42 A plea for exoneration
Epigraph: Statement read to the Executive Council by John Stephen Jnr, 29 Oct 1833 [ML ref: A1267⁻¹⁶ pp. 241–52; CY Reel 895]

Governor's Despatches — Case of John Stephen Jnr [ML ref: A1267⁻¹⁶; CY Reel 895]
- Statement read to the Executive Council by John Stephen Jnr, 29 Oct 1833, pp. 241–52

Correspondence
- John Stephen Jnr to Goderich, 19 Dec 1832 [TNA/ML ref: CO 201/230 f.469–79; Reel 188]

43 An impressive introduction
Epigraph: Statement read to the Executive Council by John Stephen Jnr, 29 Oct 1833 [ML ref: A1267⁻¹⁶ pp. 241–52; CY Reel 895]

Governor's Despatches — Case of John Stephen Jnr [ML ref: A1267⁻¹⁶; CY Reel 895]
- Affidavit of John Stephen Jnr, 19 Jun 1829, pp. 254–5
- Statement read to the Executive Council by John Stephen Jnr, 29 Oct 1833, pp. 241–52
- Testimonies: David Poole, 29 Oct 1833, pp. 253–4; Thomas Caines, 29 Oct 1833, pp. 255–9; Maria Bruce, James Middleton & Eliza James Jones, 30 Oct 1833, pp. 260–77; John Lake, 30 Oct 1833, pp. 277–84; Frances Lake, 6 Nov 1833, pp. 343–54; John Gurner, 31 Oct 1833, pp. 284–5; Thomas John Parkes, 31 Oct 1833, pp. 298–301; James Wood, 31 Oct 1833, pp. 287–95; William Smith, 31 Oct 1833, pp. 296–7; Elizabeth Baker, 31 Oct 1833, pp. 304–7
- Statements: Thomas Caines, James Middleton, William & Maria Bruce, and John Gurner, 7/8 Aug 1833, pp. 222–5; William Burke, 16 Aug 1833, p. 223; Thomas Ryan, 5 Nov 1833, pp. 430–2
- Extract from Minute no. 25, 29 Oct 1833, pp. 89–91; Minute no. 26, 30 Oct 1833, p.91; Minute no. 27, 31 Oct 1833, p.92

Miscellaneous
- Certificate of freedom: Elizabeth Wilkinson [SRNSW ref: 4/4302 no. 30/0585; Reel 986]

Internet sites
- Chamber's Book of Days — 9 January (the King's Evil) [www.thebookofdays.com/months/jan/9.htm]. Examined August 2005

44 A persuasive defence

Epigraph: J. Stephen to Robert Officer, 5 May 1829 in *HRA* I/15, pp. 33–4

Governor's Despatches — Case of John Stephen Jnr [ML ref: A1267⁻¹⁶; CY Reel 895]
– Testimonies: George Glew, I Nov 1833, pp. 307–15; John Kettle, 6 Nov 1833, pp. 354–62; James Dow, 7 Nov 1833, pp. 375–80; Sidney Stephen, I Nov 1833, pp. 316–22; Ann Gordon, 5 Nov 1833, p. 324; John Raine, 5 Nov 1833, pp. 331–42
– Statement & Testimony of Bernard Fitzpatrick, 8 Aug & 6 Nov 1833, pp. 227 & 362–72
– Extract from Minutes: no. 28, I Nov 1833, p.92; no. 29, 5 Nov 1833, pp. 92–3

45 An officer and a gentleman

Epigraph: Testimony of Edward Smith Hall, 7 Nov 1833 [ML ref: A1267⁻¹⁶ pp. 384–5; CY Reel 895]

Governor's Despatches — Case of John Stephen Jnr [ML ref: A1267⁻¹⁶; CY Reel 895]
– Testimonies: Edward Smith Hall, 7 Nov 1833, pp. 384–5; Sir John Jamieson, I Nov 1833, pp. 315–16; James Laidley, 7 Nov 1833, pp. 372–4; George Allen, 7 Nov 1833, p.374; Charles Henry Chambers, 7 Nov 1833, pp. 382–3; James Norton, 7 Nov 1833, pp. 380–1; Edward Joseph Keith, 7 Nov 1833, pp. 381–2; John Mackaness, 8 Nov 1833, p. 398; William Bland, 7 Nov 1833, p. 383; John Mackay, 7 Nov 1833, p. 385; Frederic Wright Unwin, 8 Nov 1833, pp. 400–1; Charles Windeyer, 8 Nov 1833, pp. 391–6; William Henry Kerr, 8 Nov 1833, pp. 390–1; James Raymond, 8 Nov 1833, pp. 396–7; Thomas Livingstone Mitchell, 8 Nov 1833, p. 401; Launcelot Iredale, 8 Nov 1833, p. 400; William Henry Moore, 7 Nov 1833, pp. 386–7; John Hubert Plunkett, 8 Nov 1833, pp. 387–9; Justice James Dowling, 8 Nov 1833, pp. 389–90; Alexander Berry, 8 Nov 1833, p. 399; Edward Smith Hall, 7 Nov 1833, pp. 384–5
– Extract from Minutes: no. 32, 8 Nov 1833; no. 34, 19 Nov 1833, pp. 94–7
– Enclosure XXX to Minute no. 32/1833, pp. 402–3

Published volumes
– *ADB*, vol. I, pp. 92–5 (Alexander Berry); vol. 2, pp. 10–12 (Sir John Jamison)

46 Damned and denigrated

Epigraph: Letter: John Stephen Jnr — Minute no.14/34, 14 May 1834, [ML ref: A1267⁻¹⁶ pp. 518–23; CY Reel 895]

Colonial Secretary Correspondence File — Jane New [SRNSW ref: 4/2023 File 29/2007]
– Hart to McLeay, 11 Oct 1833 (unnumbered)

Governor's Despatches — Case of John Stephen Jnr [ML ref: A1267⁻¹⁶; CY Reel 895]
– Enclosure XXX to Minute no. 32/1833, pp. 402–3
– Extract from Minutes no. 34–36, 19, 20, 27 Nov 1833, pp. 96–9
– Deas Thomson to John Stephen Jnr, 20 Nov 1833, pp. 404–5
– Testimonies: Mary Seymour, 29 Nov 1833, pp. 405–29; Francis Nicholas Rossi, 28 Nov 1833, pp. 433–9; Francis Mitchell, 28 Nov 1833, pp. 439–46; Frederick Meredith,

28 Nov 1833, pp. 446–56; John Skinner, 29 Nov 1833, pp. 468–72; John Gray, 28 Nov 1833, pp. 458–62; Burman Langa, 28 Nov 1833, pp. 463–7; Samuel Ashmore, 29 Nov 1833, pp. 473–8; Daniel Egan, 3 Dec 1833, pp. 479–85

— Statement of John Gurner & Copy of the Certificate of Conviction of Thomas Henry Hart, 31 Oct 1833, pp. 284–5

— Letter: John Stephen Jnr — Minute no. 14/34, 14 May 1834, pp. 518–23

Published volumes
— McKenzie, *Scandal in the Colonies*, pp. 111–17

47 A renewed defence

Epigraph: John Stephen Jnr to Goderich, 12 Nov 1832 [TNA/ML ref: CO201/230 ff.437–47; Reel 188]

Governor's Despatches — Case of John Stephen Jnr [ML ref: A1267^{-16}; CY Reel 895]
— Letter: C.D. Riddel, 11 Nov 1833 (unnumbered)
— Deposition of Amos Crisp, 24 Nov 1833, p. 506
— Extract from Minutes no. 38–40, 29 Nov 1833, 3 & 4 Dec 1833 pp. 100–101
— Testimonies: John Burrows, 3 Dec 1833, pp. 485–9; Amos Crisp, 4 Dec 1833, pp. 493–505; Lewis Solomon, 4 Dec 1833, pp. 507–9

48 The truth exposed

Epigraph: Letter: John Stephen Jnr — Minute no. 14/34, 14 May 1834 [ML ref: A1267^{-16} pp. 518–23; CY Reel 895]

Governor's Despatches — Case of John Stephen Jnr [ML ref: A1267^{-16}; CY Reel 895]
— Affidavit of Hugh McLean, 16 Jan 1834, pp. 513–14; Hanbury Clements, 6 May 1834, p. 537
— Statement of Joseph Dixon, 27 Jan 1834, pp. 514–15
— John Stephen Jnr to Governor Bourke, 8 Apr 1834; Deas Thomson to John Stephen Jnr, 10 Apr 1834, pp. 511–12
— Extracts from Minutes no. 8–10, 9, 12 & 14 Apr 1834, pp. 101–5; & no. 15, 7 Jun 1834, pp. 105–43
— Letter: John Stephen Jnr — Minute no. 10/34, 14 Apr 1834, pp. 515–18
— Klensendorlffe to John Stephen Jnr, 5 Jan 1834, pp. 538–9

Correspondence
— Henry Arthur & Theodore Bartley to Burnett, 9 Dec 1833 [SLTX/AO ref: CSO 1/185/4448 pp. 126–7; Reel Z1795]
— Officer to [?], 9 Dec 1833 [SLTX/AO ref: CSO 1/185/4448 p.129; Reel Z1795]
— Lyttleton to Burnett, 18 Dec 1833 [SLTX/AO ref: CSO 1/185/4448 pp. 133–5; Reel Z1795]
— Spode to Burnett, 18 Dec 1833 [SLTX/AO ref: CSO 1/185/4448 p. 131; Reel Z1795]
— Fawkner to Lyttleton, 19 Dec 1833 [SLTX/AO ref: CSO 1/185/4448 p. 136; Reel Z1795]

Published volumes
- *ADB*, vol. I, p.160 [William Grant Broughton]

49 With a whimper
Epigraph: Darling to Bathurst, 15 March 1820, quoted in Fletcher, *Ralph Darling: A Governor Maligned*, p. 35

Governor's Despatches — Case of John Stephen Jnr [ML ref: A1267⁻¹⁶; CY Reel 895]
- Extract from Minute no. 15–16, 7 & 20 Jun 1834, pp. 105–43

Epilogue
Epigraph: *Port Phillip Patriot*, 22 Feb 184 p. 2

Colonial Secretary Correspondence File — Jane New [SRNSW ref: 4/2023 File 29/2007]
- Memorandum [1]: re Jane New (unsigned), 21 Oct 1829 (unnumbered)

Governor's Despatches — Case of John Stephen Jnr [ML ref: A1267⁻¹⁶; CY Reel 895]
- Affidavit of Thomas Franklin, 25 Nov 1830, pp. 403–4
- Extract of letter from James New to John Stephen Jnr, 18 Sep 1831, p. 220
- James New's statement, 19 Sep 1831, p. 220
- Statement read to the Executive Council by John Stephen Jnr, 29 Oct 1833, pp. 241–52
- Testimony of John Raine, 5 Nov 1833, pp. 331–42 [CY Reel 895]

Correspondence
- Turner to Dumaresq, 22 Jan 1830 [SRNSW ref: 4/2023 File 29/2007 no. (unnumbered)]
- Darling to Murray, 18 Aug 1830 in *HRA* I/15, pp. 712–13
- Darling to Viscount Goderich, 27 Apr 1831 in *HRA* I/16, pp. 247–8
- John Stephen Jnr to Howick, 19 Sep 1831 [TNA/ML ref: CO201/224 f.491–3; Reel 183]
- Howick to John Stephen Jnr, 27 Sep 1831 [TNA/ML ref: CO 202/28 f.10; Reel 221]

Newspapers
- *Australian*, 22 Nov 1833 p. 3c (Jane New); 27 Feb 1837 p. 3b; 2 Jly 1840 p. 1b
- *Bent's News*, 14 Jan 1837 p. 4d; 11 Feb 1837 p. 4d; 18 Feb 1837 p. 2b
- *Colonial Times*, 7 Jan 1840 p. 3d
- *Port Phillip Patriot*, 2 Jan 1843 p. 2a–c; 5 Jan 1843 p. 2g; 9 Jan 1843 p. 3; 12 Jan 1843 p. 2; 2 Feb 1843 p. 2; 11 Sep 1843 p. 2; 22 Feb 1844 p. 2; 4 Mch 1844 p. 2d; 25 Mch 1844 p. 2e; 28 Mch 1844 p. 2
- *Sydney Gazette*, 24 Dec 1833 p. 3d (Justice John Stephen); 28 Feb 1837 p. 3d (Francis Stephen); 22 Dec 1836 (re funds to Bulwer)
- *Sydney Monitor*, 30 Jan 1837 p. 2a
- *Sydney Morning Herald*, 8 Apr 1844 p. 2b

Miscellaneous

- Supreme Court — Civil Jurisdiction: Index to Judgement Books 1834+ [SRNSW ref: 9/911]
- Death Certificate: John Stephen 1854 [RBDM-VIC ref: 1854/5584]
- Birth Certificates — New children [TASBDM ref: 33/26 nos.185–8; Reel 127]
- Death Certificate — James New [TASBDM ref: 35/34 no. 31; Reel 157]
- Death Certificate — Maria Elizabeth New [TASBDM ref: 35/44 no. 397; Reel 160]
- General Card Index — James New [SLTX/AO]
- Marriage: James New, 23 May 1831, St Mary Magdalene, Bermondsey [LDS ref: Reel 0254556]. (Confirmation that this James New was Jane's husband comes from the fact that James and Maria returned to Tasmania and had a large family, and that personal information for this man tallies with that of Jane's husband.)
- Statement of James New, 19 Sep 1831 [TNA/ML ref: CO201/224 f.491–3; Reel 183]
- Tasmanian Colonial Collection 1803–1903: John Woodall, 17 Feb 1832 [AOTAS ref: Reel 15–4 CUS 30/1 p.74 Film SLTX/AO/EP/447]
- Manuscript Card Index, Mitchell Library, Sydney: references to Madame Rens
- Conduct File — Jane Jefferson [SLTX/AO ref: CON 40/4; Reel Z2589]

Internet sites

- *An Encyclopaedia of New Zealand 1966* — John Gare Butler [www.teara.govt.nz/1966/B/ButlerJohnGare/ButlerJohnGare/en] Examined Jan 2006.

Published volumes

- *ADB*, vol. II, pp. 359–60 (John & Thomas Raine)
- Bohan, New Zealand: The Story so far, pp. 18–24
- Crowley, *A Documentary History of Australia, vol. 1*, p. 480
- Fletcher, *Ralph Darling*, Chapters 15 & 16
- Kerr's *Melbourne Almanac and Port Phillip Directory*, 1841
- McIntyre & Cathro, *Thomas Dunn*, pp. 38–9, 93
- Mein Smith, *A Concise History of New Zealand*, pp. 34–42
- Mowle, L.M. (ed.) *A Genealogical History of the Pioneer Families of Australia*, 1978, pp. 331–4
- Northwood, *Defend the Fold*, pp. 53–4
- Sainty & Johnson, *Census of New South Wales, November 1828*, J0226 (Jane Jefferson), K0442 (W.D. Kelman), T1285 (Joseph Turner), S2401 (John Stephen Jnr).

BIBLIOGRAPHY

Printed Books, Journals, Manuscripts and Internet sites

American National Biography, American Council of Learned Societies, 1991.

Arrowsmith, R.L., *Charterhouse Register 1769–1872*, Phillimore, Chichester, 1974.

Australian Council of National Trusts, *Historic Buildings of Australia: 1*, Cassell, Australia, 1977.

Australian Dictionary of Biography [ADB]: Volumes 1 and 2, Melbourne University Press, Melbourne, 1966 & 1967.

Bateson, Charles, *The Convict Ships: 1787–1868*, Library of Australian History, Sydney, 1983.

Baxter, Carol J. (ed.), *General Muster List of New South Wales 1823, 1824 & 1825*, Australian Biographical & Genealogical Record, Sydney, 1999.

——, *Nash: First Fleeters & Founding Families*, (privately published), Sydney, 2004.

Beales, Derek, *From Castlereagh to Gladstone*, Nelson, London, 1969.

Bedford, Ruth M., *Think of Stephen*, Angus & Robertson, Sydney, 1954.

Bennett, J.M., *A History of Solicitors in NSW*, Legal Books, Sydney, 1984.

——, *Lives of the Australian Justices: Sir James Dowling, Second Chief Justice of NSW 1837–1844*, Federation Press, Sydney, 2001.

Benoit, Marie, *Let's Visit Mauritius*, Macmillan, London, 1987.

Berry, Paul, *By Royal Appointment: A biography of Mary Ann Clarke, Mistress of the Duke of York*, Femina, London, 1970.

Black, A. & C., *Black's Guide to the History, Antiquities and Topography of the County of Surrey*, Edinburgh, 1864.

Blaikie, George, *Great Australian Scandals*, Rigby, Australia, 1979.

Blanco, R.L. (ed.), *The American Revolution 1775–1783: An Encyclopaedia*, Garland Publishing Co., New York & London, 1993.

Bohan, Edmund, *New Zealand, The Story so Far: A Short History*, HarperCollins, Auckland, 1997.

Breton, W.H., *Excursions in NSW, Western Australia & VDL during the years 1830, 1831, 1832, & 1833*, Richard Bentley, London, 1834.

Burn, David, *The Bushrangers* (written 1829), Heinemann Educational Australia, Melbourne, 1971.

Canter, D.V. & Ioannou, M., 'Criminals' Emotional Experience During Crime' in *International Journal of Forensic Psychology*, vol. 1, no. 2, September 2004, pp. 71–81.

Chancellor, F.B. & Eeles, H.S., *Celebrated Carthusians*, Philip Allan, London, 1936.

Clune, Frank, *Rascals, Ruffians and Rebels of Early Australia*, Angus & Robertson, Sydney, 1987.

Crosby, Alan, *A History of Cheshire*, Phillimore, Chichester, 1996.

Crowley, Frank, *A Documentary History of Australia, vol. 1: Colonial Australia 1788–1840*, Thomas Nelson, Melbourne, 1980.

Cumes, J.W.C., *Their Chastity Was Not Too Rigid: leisure times in early Australia*, Melbourne, Longman Cheshire, 1979.

Cunliffe, B et. al., *The Penguin Illustrated History of Britain and Ireland: From earliest times to the present day*, Penguin, London, 2001.

Cunningham, Peter, *Two Years in New South Wales: a series of letters comprising sketches of the actual state of society in that colony . . .* , Libraries Board of South Australia, Adelaide, 1966 (originally published in 1827).

Currey, C.H., *The First Three Chief Justices of the Supreme Court of New South Wales*, Sydney, 1933.

——, *Sir Francis Forbes: The First Chief Justice of the Supreme Court of NSW*, Angus & Robertson, Sydney, 1968.

Darling, Henry C., *Statement of the Refutation of Accusations made by Mr Hume MP and others against Lieutenant-General Darling, Governor of NSW by Henry C. Darling, Major-General, London*, J McGowan, London, 27 December 1831 [ML ref: PAM 83/149].

Darling, Ralph, *Letter Addressed by Lieutenant-General Darling late Governor of NSW to Joseph Hume Esq MP, London*, printed by J. McGowan, Great Windmill St, Haymarket, 1832 [signed Ralph Darling, Govt House, 20 Oct 1831] [ML ref: 991/D].

——, *Statement of Lieutenant-General R. Darling, Late Governor of New South Wales in reference to the petition of Mr John Stephen Jnr to The House of Commons, and other matters brought forward by him*, J. McGowan, London, 1833 [ML ref: 991/S].

Davies, C. Stella, *A History of Macclesfield*, E.J. Morton, Dudsbury, Manchester & Macclesfield, 1976.

Decisions of Superior Courts of New South Wales 1788–1899, published by the Division of Law, Macquarie University <www.law.mq.edu.au> [examined January 2006].

Dickens, Charles, *Sketches by Boz*, Scene 25 in *A Web of English History*, <www.historyhome.co.uk> [examined June 2005].

Dictionary of National Biography, Smith, Elder, London, 1885–1900.

Dixon, H., *The London Prisons*, Garland Publishing Co., New York & London, 1985 (originally published 1850).

Dyde, Brian, *St Kitts: Cradle of the Caribbean*, Macmillan, London, 1989.

Earnshaw, Beverley, *The Larrikins of Lavender Bay: The Story of the Phoenix Hulk*, North Shore Historical Society, Sydney, 1996.

Encyclopaedia Britannica (1966), Cape Verdes Islands, Cheshire, Leeds, Manchester, St Kitts.

Female Occupations C19th Victorian Social History <www.fashion-era.com/Victorian_occupations_wojtczak.htm> [examined June 2005].

Fletcher, Brian H., *Ralph Darling, A Governor Maligned*, Oxford University Press, Melbourne, 1984.

Flynn, Michael, *The Second Fleet: Britain's Grim Convict Armada of 1790*, Library of Australian History, Sydney, 1993.

Forbes, Lady Amelia S., *Sydney Society in Crown Colony Days*, 1914 [ML ref: Q991/F].

Forbes, George, *Under the Broad Arrow: Australia's Most Remarkable Criminal — The Pathetic History of Jane New and the Monstrous Record of Her Evil Genius, John Fitch*, 'Truth' Popular Press Print, Sydney, 1913 [NLA ref: NLp 365.9944 FOR].

Fraser, Rebecca, *A People's History of Britain*, Pimlico, London, 2003.

'Gorgeous Jane charmed her way to a freedom', in *Sunday Telegraph*, 16 May 1986.

Goudy, Ginny, 'Existential Criminal' <www.mdx.ac.uk/www/study/xgoudy.htm>.

Guy, Samuel, *Van Diemen's Land Settler: the Letter of Samuel Guy, Van Diemen's Land, 1823*, St Mark's Press, Sydney, 1991 [SLTX ref: 994.602/Guy].

Hansard's *Parliamentary Debates*, 1830–32.

Hindle, Robert, *Salford's Prison: an account of the New Bailey prison in 1836*, Salford Local History Society, 1978.

Historical Records of Australia [HRA], Series I: vols 13–17; Series III: vol. 4; Series IV: vol. I.

Hogue, J.A., *Governor Darling, the Press and the Collar*, in *JRAHS*, vol. 2, pp. 308–22.

Huch, R. & Ziegler, P.R., *Joseph Hume: The People's MP*, American Philosophical Society, Philadelphia, 1985.

Irving, R., Kinstler, J. & Dupain, M., *Fine Houses of Sydney*, Methuen, Australia, 1982.

Johnson, William Branch, *The English Prison Hulks*, Christopher Johnson, London, 1957.

Karskens, Grace, *The Rocks: Life in Early Sydney*, Melbourne University Press, Melbourne, 1997.

Kercher, Bruce, 'Perish or Prosper: The Law and Convict Transportation in the British Empire, 1700–1850', in *Law and History Review*, Fall 2003, pp. 527–84.

Kerr's *Melbourne Almanac and Port Phillip Directory*, Melbourne, 1841.

King, Hazel, *Richard Bourke*, Oxford University Press, London, 1971.

Lewis, Samuel, *A Topographical Dictionary of England*, London, 1845.

Liston, Carol, *Campbelltown: The Bicentennial History*, Allen & Unwin, Sydney, 1988.

Mayhew, H. & Binny, J., *The Criminal Prisons of London and Scenes of Prison Life*, Charles Griffin & Co., London, 1862.

McIntyre, Perry & Cathro, Adele, *Thomas Dunn: Convict and Chief Constable and his descendants*, Sydney, 2000.

McKenzie, Kirsten, *Scandal in the Colonies*, Melbourne University Press, Melbourne, 2004.

Mealey, Linda, 'The Sociobiology of Sociopathy: An Integrated Evolutionary Model', *Behavioural & Brain Sciences* 18 (3), pp. 523–99, <www.bbsonline.org/Preprints/Old Archive/bbs.mealey.html>.

Mein Smith, Philippa, *A Concise History of New Zealand*, Cambridge, Melbourne, 2005.

'Miles', *Governor Darling's Refutation of the charges of cruelty and oppression of the soldiers Sudds and Thompson at Sydney NSW*, 26 Nov 1826, London, 1832 [ML ref: DSM 991/D].

Montague, E.N., *Mitcham: a brief history*, Merton Historical Society, Morden, 1987.

Mowle, L.M. (ed.), *A Genealogical History of the Pioneer Families of Australia*, 1978.

Murray, Venetia, *High Society: A social history of the Regency period, 1788–1830*, Viking, London, 1998.

Nicholas, Stephen, *Convict Workers: Reinterpreting Australia's past*, Cambridge University Press, Sydney, 1988.

Nicholson, I.H., *Shipping Arrivals & Departures: Tasmania 1803–1833*, Roebuck, Canberra, 1983.

Northwood, E.W., *Defend the Fold: Cartwright Family History 1625–1983*, (privately published), Carlton NSW, 1984.

O'Brien, Eris, *The Foundation of Australia (1786–1800): A study of English criminal practice and penal colonisation in the eighteenth century*, London, Sheed & Ward, 1937.

Oxford Dictionary of National Biography: From the Earliest Times to the Year 2000, Oxford University Press, 2004.

Pool, Daniel, *What Jane Austen Ate and Charles Dickens Knew: From fox hunting to whist — the facts of daily life in nineteenth Century England*, Simon & Schuster, New York, 1993.

Powell, W.S., *Dictionary of North Carolina Biography*, University of North Carolina Press, Chapel Hill & London, 1988.

Prinsep, A., *The Journal of a Voyage from Calcutta to Van Diemen's Land comprising a description of that colony during six months' residence*, Smith, Elder & Co., London, 1833.

Purcell, L.E., *Who was Who in the American Revolution*, Facts on File, New York, 1993.

Rees, Sian, *The Floating Brothel*, Hodder, Sydney, 2001.

Robson, L.L., *The Convict Settlers of Australia*, Melbourne University Press, Melbourne, 1965.

Roderick, Colin, *The Lady and the Lawyer*, Angus & Robertson, Sydney, 1955.

Romance Ever After, <www.romanceeverafter.com/19th_century_class_system.htm>.

Sainty, M.R. & Johnson, K.A. (eds.), *Census of New South Wales, November 1828*, Library of Australian History, Sydney, 1985.

Salt, Annette, *These Outcast Women: the Parramatta Female Factory 1821–1848*, Hale & Iremonger, Sydney, 1984.

Scholefield, G.H. (ed.), *A Dictionary of New Zealand Biography*, Department of Internal Affairs, Wellington NZ, 1940.

Shaw, A.G.L., *Convicts & the Colonies: A Study of Penal Transportation from Great Britain and Ireland to Australia and other parts of the British Empire*, Faber & Faber, London, 1966.

Simpson, Frank, *Chester Castle*, Griffith, Chester, 1925 [BL ref: X709/24647].

Smith, Babette, *A Cargo of Women: Susannah Watson and the Convicts of the Princess Royal*, New South Wales University Press, Sydney, 1988.

Stephen, John, *Reply to Major-General Darling's 'Statement in Refutation of Accusations made by Mr Hume MP and others against Lieutenant-General Darling, Governor of New South Wales'*, 1832 [ML ref: 991/S].

Stone, C.R. & Tyson, P., *Old Hobart Town and Environs, 1802–1855*, Pioneer Design Studio, Lilydale, Victoria, 1978.

Sturma, M., *Vice in a Vicious Society: Crime and Convicts in Mid-Nineteenth Century New South Wales*, University of Queensland Press, St Lucia, 1983.

Strong, Roy, *The Story of Britain: A people's history*, Pimlico, London, 1998.

Sweeney, Christopher, *Transported in Place of Death: Convicts in Australia*, Macmillan, Melbourne, 1981.

Therry, Sir Roger, *Reminiscences of Thirty Years' Residence in New South Wales & Victoria*, London, Sampson Low & Son, 1863; facsimile Royal Australian Historical Society, Sydney University Press, 1974.

Thiselton, W.M., *Regia Insignia or An Account of the King's Honourable Band of Gentlemen Pensioners or Gentlemen at Arms*, Sherwood, Neely & Sons, London, 1819.

Tierney, Kevin, *Orson Welles: Ten Years After His Death: A Reflection on his work*, <www.kinema. uwaterloo.co/tiern952.htm>.

Votes and Proceedings of the New South Wales Legislative Council.

Walker, R.B., *The Newspaper Press in NSW 1803–1920*, Sydney University Press, Sydney, 1976.

Waugh, Max, *Forgotten Hero: Richard Bourke*, Australian Scholarly Publishing, Melbourne, 2005.

Weidenhofer, Margaret, *The Convict Years: Transportation and the penal system 1788–1868*, Landsdowne Press, Melbourne, 1973.

Wilkins, H.T., *Great English Schools*, Noel Douglas, London, 1925.

Wise, Sarah, *The Italian Boy*, Pimlico, London, 2004.

Zivanovic, Bojana, 'Psycho-Social Issues: Amorality and Criminal Behaviour', [<www.see-ran.org>].

INDEX